The Sepoys and the

To my parents

The Sepoys and the Company

Tradition and Transition in Northern India
1770–1830

Seema Alavi

OXFORD
UNIVERSITY PRESS

OXFORD

UNIVERSITY PRESS

YMCA Library Building, Jai Singh Road, New Delhi 110001

Oxford University Press is a department of the University of Oxford. It
furthers the University's objective of excellence in research, scholarship, and
education by publishing worldwide in

Oxford New York

Auckland Cape Town Dar es Salaam Hong Kong Karachi
Kuala Lumpur Madrid Melbourne Mexico City Nairobi
New Delhi Shanghai Taipei Toronto

With offices in

Argentina Austria Brazil Chile Czech Republic France Greece
Guatemala Hungary Italy Japan Poland Portugal Singapore
South Korea Switzerland Thailand Turkey Ukraine Vietnam

Oxford is a registered trade mark of Oxford University Press
in the UK and in certain other countries

Published in India
by Oxford University Press, New Delhi

© Oxford University Press1995

The moral rights of the author have been asserted
Database right Oxford University Press (maker)

First published 1995
Oxford India Paperbacks 1998
Second impression 2006

ISBN-13: 978-0-19-564595-8
ISBN-10: 0-19-564595-2

Printed in India at Pauls Press, New Delhi 110 020
Published by Oxford University Press
YMCA Library Building, Jai Singh Road, New Delhi 110 001

Preface

This book is a revised version of the PhD dissertation I submitted to the University of Cambridge, England, in 1991. My interest in the Mughal tradition and its transition in the late eighteenth century emanated from the rigorous course work that I completed as part of my MA and M Phil programme at the Centre for Historical Studies, Jawaharlal Nehru University, New Delhi.

This book owes its origin to the constant encouragement that I have received from my teachers: Professor Muzaffar Alam, who introduced me to the pleasures of historical research, and Professor C. A. Bayly, who supervised my thesis with his characteristic patience, good humour and generosity. It has been a delight completing this work with their unflinching support.

I have also benefited from the comments of Dr Dilip Menon, Dr G. Arunima, Dr Ravi Vasudevan, Dr Radhika Singha, Dr Kathy Prior and Dr Ajay Skaria. Professor Harbans Mukhia, Dr Anand Yang and Dr H. Strachan offered interesting insights. I had several lively discussions with Mr Gautam Bhadra.

I would like to thank the Aga Khan Foundation, Geneva, which awarded me an International Student Fellowship in 1987 to do research at the University of Cambridge. I am grateful to the staff of the India Office Library, London; the British Museum; the National Army Museum, Chelsea; the Cambridge University Library, and the Centre for South Asian Studies, Cambridge; the National Archives of India, New Delhi; the Uttar Pradesh State Archives, Lucknow; the Allahabad Regional Archives, Allahabad;

Dehra Dun Regional Archives, Dehra Dun; Varanasi Regional Archives, Varanasi; Bihar State Archives, Patna; and the West Bengal State Archives, Calcutta.

I must express my special gratitude to the British Library (India Office Library) for kindly permitting me to publish plates 1, 3, 4, 6 and 9; and to my publishers for helping me shape my thesis into a book.

My Cambridge colleagues and friends provided a stimulating and pleasant work environment. In particular I would like to thank Anu, Dilip, Radhika, Ravi, Kathy, Swarna, Sylvia, Taiyong, Ajay, Nonica and Nandini for their loving care and support. Simon Dunkley, Elke Nachtigal, Colm O'Higgin, Athena Plakitsi, and Meena Bhargava have been very close friends who have shared the travails and pleasures of my research work.

I owe a debt of gratitude to my late uncle, Shahid Khwaja, who inculcated in me a love for history through his own sensitive appreciation of Lucknow and its people. It is sad that he did not live to see the completion of this work.

To my parents, Roshan and Shariq Alavi, I do not have words to express my gratitude. Only they know how much I owe to them.

S. A.

Contents

Illustrations

Glossary

amil	subordinate revenue official; often applied (incorrectly) to a farmer of revenue (*mustajir*).
angarkha	long tunic or coat worn both by Hindus and Muslims; the former tie it on the left, the latter on the right breast.
arzi	petition or representation.
ashraf	person of rank, Muslim gentleman.
barkandaz	matchlock man, but commonly applied to a native of Hindustan, armed with a sword and shield, who acts as a doorkeeper, watchman, guard or escort.
bigha	measure of land varying in extent in different parts of India.
bhaiyachara	village land or certain rights and privileges held in common property either entirely or in part, as in the perfect or imperfect pattidari tenure, by a number of families forming a brotherhood, originally perhaps descended from a common ancestor.
chakledar	superintendent; proprietor; rentier.
chaprasi	messenger or courier wearing a chapras, most usually a public servant.
chappar	thatched roof; shed; any temporary thatched structure, set up for the celebration of a marriage, or for giving water to travellers; a mat, screen, etc.
chaudhuri	headman of village, caste, market, etc.
chauki	police or customs post; guard, watch, or the post where they are placed.
chela	servant, slave, pupil, disciple; especially one brought up by a religious mendicant to become a member of his order.

dafadar	commandant of body of horse; head of party of police; police officer.
diwani	of or relating to a diwani (civil as opposed to criminal substance); the office, jurisdiction, emoluments, etc. of a diwan. The right to receive the collections of Bengal, Bihar and Orissa conferred on the East India Company by the titular Mughal.
Dars-i-Nizamiya	curriculum followed in Firangi Mahal.
faujdar	officer of the Mughal Government invested with the charge of the police, and jurisdiction in all criminal matters criminal judge, magistrate, chief of body of troops.
faujdari	office of magistrate or head of police or criminal judge.
gunj	small fixed market, emporium for grain.
ghatwali	land granted either rent-free or at a low rate of assessment to public ferrymen, or to officers guarding passes in the hills.
ghat	landing place, steps on the bank of a river, wharf where customs are commonly levied; pass through the mountains.
havaldar	native officer of the Indian army, subordinate to the subahdar.
hundi	mercantile note of credit.
izzat	honour, credit, reputation, character.
jagir	assignment of land revenues.
jaidad	place, employment; assets, funds, resources, an estate, property; the means or capabilities of any district in respect of revenue; an assignment of the revenue of a tract of land for the maintenance of an establishment, or of troops, granted for life but very commonly with permitted succession to the next of kin, sometimes with a rent reserved.
jamadar	native subaltern officer.
jamabundi	settlement of the amount of revenue assessed upon an estate, a village; village or district rent roll; registry of village holdings.
jama	amount, aggregate, total in general, but applied especially to the debit or receipt side of an account, and to the rental of an estate; also to the total amount of rent or revenue payable by a cultivator or zamindar including all cesses as well as land tax. It is more

	especially applied to the revenue assessed upon the land alone.
jotadar	farmer or cultivator.
khelat	dress of honour; any article of costume presented by the ruling or superior authority to an inferior as a mark of distinction.
khidmatgar	servant, especially one serving at table; a personal attendant.
kotwali	office of kotwal or anything relating to it; an impost formerly levied on the plea of providing for his salary; a variety of town duties.
kushti	wrestling.
lashkar-i-dua	army of the devout.
madad-i-mash	grant for charitable or religious purposes.
malikana	pertaining or relating to the Malik or proprietor as his right or due; applied especially in revenue language, to an allowance assigned to a zamindar or to a proprietory cultivator, who from some cause, as failure in paying his revenue, or declining to accede to the rate at which his lands are assessed, is set aside from the management of the government collector. In such cases a sum not less than five per cent, and not exceeding ten per cent on the net amount realized by the Government was finally assigned to the dispossessed landholder.
mansabdar	person with an official Mughal rank derived from personal status and military responsibility.
manjis	title borne by headmen among Rajmahal mountaineers.
milkiat	land held in absolute right, free of rent.
muharrir	clerk, writer, scribe.
mukhtiyar	agent, representative, attorney.
najib	noble, either by birth or conduct; but the term was applied to a body of irregular infantry under the native government. Some corps were retained chiefly as a kind of militia under the British government for a time, but the designation appears to have become obsolete.
pakka	ripe, mature; cooked, dressed.
parda	veil, screen, curtain, especially one which excludes the women of a family froin the gaze of men.
patta	deed from the government district officer, held by the pradhan, setting forth his liabilities, duties, dues, etc.

pandit	learned Brahman, one who makes some branch of Sanskrit learning his special study and teaches it.
pargana	subordinate unit in revenue administration.
piada	infantryman.
pugree	turban.
purabia	easterner.
purohit	family priest; one who conducts the domestic ceremonies of a tribe, a household or family.
qanungo	district revenue official who received landed property and oversaw the working of the village accountant or patwari.
qasbah	country town; seat of subordinate revenue administration and Muslim gentry.
risaldar	native officer commanding a troop of irregular horse.
sanad	grant; a diploma; a charter; a patent; a document conveying to an individual emoluments, titles, privileges, offices, or the rights to revenue from land etc., under the seal of the ruling authority. The Mughal government had different forms of sanads according to the nature of the grant.
sardar	chief, headman; commander; head of a set of palankin bearers.
sarkar	extensive division of country under the Mughal government; a sub-division of a subah, containing many parganas; a district, a province.
sawar	trooper.
sazawal	native collector of revenue; an officer especially appointed to take charge of and collect the revenue of an estate from the management of which the owner or farmer has been removed. Land steward; a bailiff, an agent appointed by a landowner to compel payment of rent by tenants or leaseholders.
sudr or sadr	eminence, superiority, chief, supreme, the highest or foremost of anything; the chief seat of government, the presidency, as opposed to the provinces or mufassil. But also commonly applied to denote establishment or individual employed in the judicial and revenue administration of the state.
subah	province; one of the larger subdivisions of the Mughal dominions, such as Awadh, Bengal, Bihar.
sipahi	soldier, sepoy.
subahdari	office of viceroy or governor.

subahdar   governor of a province, viceroy under the Mughal government; a native officer in the Company's army holding a rank equivalent to that of captain under the European officers.

thanah   police station, military post; village or station assigned to the Company's invalid sipahis.

tuppah   small tract or division of country, smaller than a pargana, but comprising one or more villages. A division for the revenue of which only one engagement is entered into with the government.

vakil   representative or ambassador; court pleader.

zamindar   landholder.

zillah   side, part; a division of a district under the British administration; a province, a tract of country constituting the jurisdiction of a commissioner or circuit judge and the extent of a chief collectorate.

Abbreviations

Adjtt. Gen.	Adjutant General
ARA	Allahabad Regional Archives
BBC BB	Bengal Board of Commissioners Bihar and Benares
BBR LI	Bengal Board of Revenue Lower Provinces
BC	Boards Collection
BC BB	Board of Commissioners Bihar and Benares
BCJ	Bengal Criminal Judicial
BCJ LP	Bengal Criminal Judicial Lower Provinces
BCJ WP	Bengal Criminal Judicial Western Provinces
BM	British Museum
BMC	Bengal Military Consultations
BRC	Bengal Revenue Consultations
BRBC CCP	Bengal Revenue Board of Commissioners and Conquered Provinces
BRFW	Board of Revenue Fort William
BRIP	Board of Revenue Invalid Proceedings
BRMP	Board of Revenue Miscellaneous Proceedings
BRR	Bhagalpur Revenue Records
BPS	Bengal Political Consultation
BRWP	Board of Revenue Western Provinces
BSA	Bihar State Archives
BSC	Bengal Secret Consultations
BSMC	Bengal Secret Military Consultations
Consult.	Consultation
DDPMR	Dehra Dun Pre Mutiny Records
DDRA	Dehra Dun Regional Archives
Deptt.	Department

FW	Fort William
GCRR PM	Gorakhpur Commissionary Revenue Records Pre Mutiny
GO	General Orders
GOGG	General Order of Governor General
GOCC	General Order of Commander-in-Chief
IESHR	*Indian Economic and Social History Review*
IOL	India Office Library
JASB	*Journal of Asiatic Society of Bengal*
Lt. Gov.	Lieutenant Governor
L	Letter
MAS	*Modern Asian Studies*
MCR	Muzaffarpur Collectorate Records
MDR	Muzaffarpur District Records
NAI	National Archives of India
No.	Number
NWP	North Western Provinces
PFD P	Proceedings of Foreign Department Political
PFD S	Proceedings of Foreign Department Secret
PFD-SP	Proceedings of Foreign Department Secret Political
Pol.	Political
Procds	Proceedings
Rev.	Revenue
RPB	Residents Proceedings Benares
SCPMR	Saharanpur Collectorate Pre-Mutiny Records
SDR	Shahabad District Records
Sec.	Secret
UPSA	Uttar Pradesh State Archives
WBSA	West Bengal State Archives

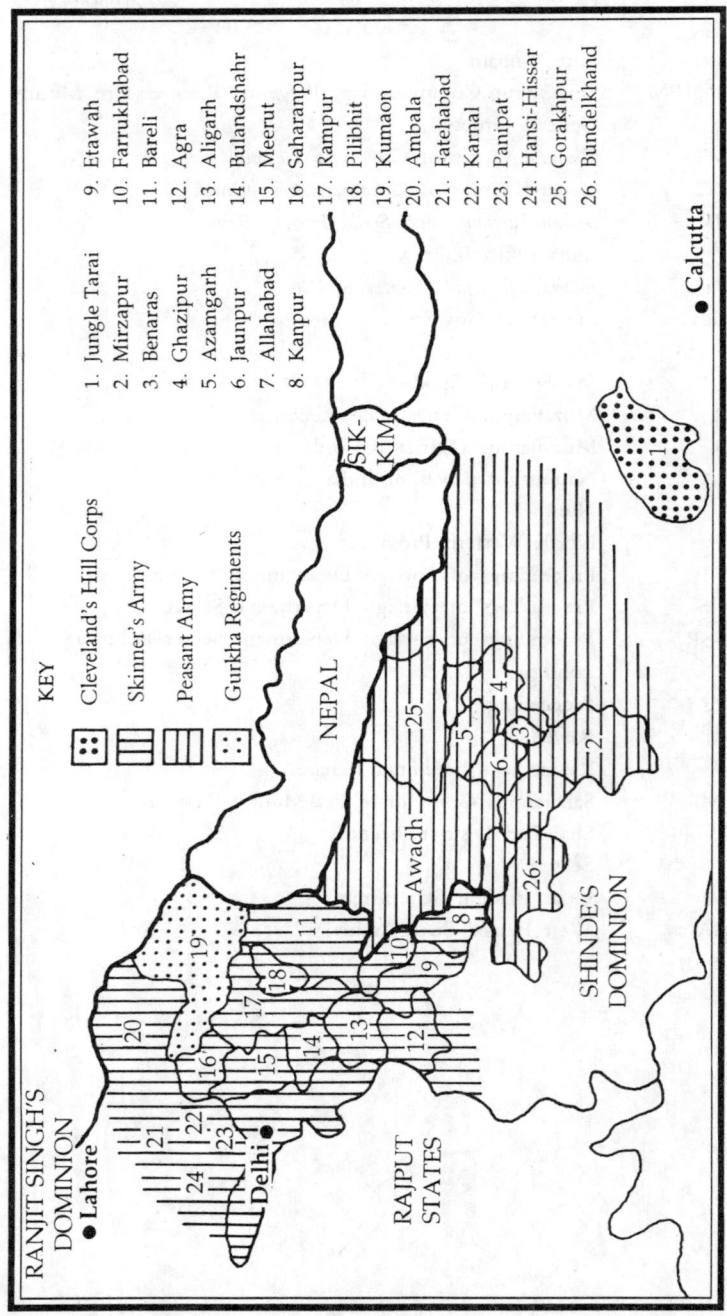

Map 1. Location of military experiments, Northern India, c. 1820.

KEY

Cleveland's Hill Corps	
Skinner's Army	
Peasant Army	
Gurkha Regiments	

1. Jungle Tarai
2. Mirzapur
3. Benaras
4. Ghazipur
5. Azamgarh
6. Jaunpur
7. Allahabad
8. Kanpur
9. Etawah
10. Farrukhabad
11. Bareli
12. Agra
13. Aligarh
14. Bulandshahr
15. Meerut
16. Saharanpur
17. Rampur
18. Pilibhit
19. Kumaon
20. Ambala
21. Fatehabad
22. Karnal
23. Panipat
24. Hansi-Hissar
25. Gorakhpur
26. Bundelkhand

RANJIT SINGH'S DOMINION

• Lahore

• Delhi

RAJPUT STATES

SHINDE'S DOMINION

NEPAL

SIK-KIM

Awadh

• Calcutta

Introduction

This work studies the formation of the Indian regiments of the East India Company's Bengal Army in the period between 1770 and 1830 in an attempt to make a contribution to the study of the process of state formation and the nature of early colonial rule in north India. It analyses the military culture of north India as it evolved to keep pace with the political expansion of the East India Company, thereby making a break from the 'guts and glory' popular narrative of campaigns and regimental histories that generally constitute the military history of the subcontinent.[1] The study goes beyond the army organizational command and structure[2] to show that the boundary between army and society was much more blurred than it came to be in the later nineteenth century.

In this study the term 'military culture' is used in an all-encompassing sense to denote the context in which the army operated as a military organization embracing the complexities of the Indian *sipahi's* lifestyle, religion, family, dress, deportment, and dietary habits. As the Company struggled to consolidate its rule in north India it exhibited a keen interest in these matters because the deportment of the sipahi constituted one of the few ideological bridges between the Company and Indian society, and formed a major source of legitimacy for it. Indeed, the

---

[1] J. B. Norris, *The First Afghan War, 1838–42* (Cambridge, 1967); H. T. Lambrick, *Sir Charles Napier and Sind* (Oxford, 1952); and John Pemble, *The Invasion of Nepal: John Company at War* (Oxford, 1971).

[2] See John Pemble, 'Resources and techniques in the Second Maratha War', *Historical Journal*, XIX (1976), pp. 374–404.

maintenance of Indian regiments of high-status sipahis provided the British with a framework within which they were able to construct a cultural idiom through and by which, British authority was to be represented in India.[3]

Historians have generally explained the consolidation of Company power in terms of the superior fiscal base which it came to acquire in north India. Bayly argues that in the eighteenth century the 'commercialization of royal power' began under the Mughals, extended to meet the needs of military organization and growing bureaucratization of the numerous small polities that succeeded the Mughals. He argues that in this period Indian merchant capital was redeployed in the search for greater control over labour productivity through control over revenue collections of all sorts; and the unified merchant class met in the new *qasbahs* and the small permanent markets (*ganjs*) attached to them. It was here that the infrastructure for European trade in, and ultimate dominion over, India was constructed.[4] The efficiency and wide scale on which the Company could exercise and extend the precolonial practice of 'military fiscalism'[5] has provided another explanation for the dominant position it came to occupy, more specifically, in south India.[6] Yang highlights the role of the Indian élite in facilitating the Company's revenue collection and thereby

[3] B. S. Cohn, 'Representing authority in Victorian India' in B.S. Cohn (ed.), *An Anthropologist among the Historians and Other Essays* (Delhi, 1987), pp. 632–82. I differ here from Cohn who argues that in the first half of the 19th century the British, finding it difficult to construct a cultural idiom within which their political authority could be defined, continued to use the Mughal idiom of the Darbar to represent their power and authority to the nobles and the Indian élite. He shows that even though the Mughal ritual was retained, its meaning was changed. In Mughal times the ritual marked the incorporation of the subjects into the Mughal polity. The British converted it into a kind of economic exchange in which the relationship between British official and the Indian subject became contractual. British rule continued to base itself on this contractual relationship throughout the 19th century.

[4] C. A. Bayly, *Rulers, Townsmen and Bazaars: North Indian Society in the Age of British Expansion, 1770–1870* (Cambridge, 1983).

[5] The collection of revenue by a centrally-controlled body of officials who collect revenue from a broad base of payers for the purpose of maintaining a centrally controlled and hegemonic military system.

[6] B. Stein, 'State formation and economy reconsidered', part I, *MAS*, vol. 19, part 3 (July 1985), pp. 387–413.

contributing to its political dominance and stability in the Saran district of Bihar. He constructs a model of 'limited Raj' to explain the arrangements that the British effected with local controllers to ensure a free flow of revenue. He analyses the dynamics of this 'limited Raj' by explaining its functioning at the lowest level where the power of the colonial state tapered off and the landholders' system of control took over. Yang argues that these two control systems collectively sustained British rule in the region.[7] More recently, the Company's superior power in north Indian politics has been explained in terms of its 'exclusive right to violence'. R. Mukherjee, analysing the 1857 mutiny, argues that 'British rule in India, as an autocracy, had meticulously constructed a monopoly of violence. The revolt of 1857 shattered that monopoly by matching an official, alien violence by the indigenous violence of the colonized.'[8] I suggest that the Company's political dominance in north India was based on its superior military power. This military superiority was not so much in terms of the advantages it enjoyed because of possessing a more advanced organization and command of technology or fighting skills,[9] but it rested more on the fact that in the first eighty years of Company rule its army had become the major guarantee of social and political stability, especially in the more outlying tracts of the Ganges valley, Jungle Tarai and the Ceded and Conquered Provinces bordering Nepal. Here, the Company's military institutions drew upon and shaped the dynamics of civilian society and provided the earliest framework through which the Company came into close contact with the Indian people. It was this incorporation within civilian

[7] Anand A. Yang, *The Limited Raj: Agrarian Relations in Colonial India, Saran District, 1793–1920* (London, 1989), p. 6.

[8] R. Mukherjee, ' "Satan let loose upon earth": the Kanpur massacres in India in the revolt of 1857', *Past and Present*, No. 128 (August, 1990), pp. 92–117.

[9] P. J. Marshall, 'Western arms in maritime Asia in the early phases of expansion', *MAS*, vol. 14, part 1 (February 1980), pp. 13–28. Marshall shows that the initiative for introducing new weapons and tactics had usually come from Europe, the professional standards of European soldiers were probably higher than those of their Asian contemporaries, and the European states and trading Companies could plan and organize the use of force with a tenacity of purpose rarely matched on the Indian side. But these advantages had been to a large extent nullified by distance. The European challenge had not been on such a scale that Asians could not adapt to or meet it.

4/ The Sepoys and the Company

society rather than an overt use of violence which assured Company rule. The variety of backgrounds from which the Company was forced to recruit its sipahis required the Company to generate knowledge of 'Indian customs and religious practices'. The knowledge so acquired, forming one of the earliest recorded British perceptions of Indians based on information collected from ordinary sipahis, became central to the British understanding of Indian society and shaped the Company's governance of most parts of north India.

At the most basic level the importance of the army for the Company and its deeper implications for military power is clearly demonstrated by the historical sources themselves. The vast number of Bengal Military Consultations and the written proceedings of the Bengal Military Department, and the even larger number of official military records of the Company army testify to the importance which the Company attached to its army.[10] Moreover, the innumerable references to the Company army in the voluminous Board of Revenue consultations as well as in the written proceedings of the Company's Secret, Foreign, Political and Public departments indicate the vital role the army played in the economic, social and political aspects of Company rule in India.

Indeed, the recruitment of the East India Company's army was central to the development of the Company's political sovereignty. In the final analysis, the objective of this (drive for sovereignty) was to erode the military and political power of all Indian powers and to gradually circumscribe their authority. The Company aimed to establish a monopoly of power throughout north India and eventually to break out of the paradigms of legitimacy and authority provided by the eighteenth-century north Indian states. Chapter 1 shows that in the initial years of its rule the Company attempted to achieve this objective by organizing

[10] IOLR catalogue, Bengal I and II. The rich source material held in the archives in India and Britain is just the tip of the iceberg. The Company's military bureaucracy generated detailed regimental records, muster rolls, and character rolls of its soldiers. Separate military offices were established, at the district level, to maintain detailed records of the sipahis' families. These records appear to have been destroyed, and I was not able to trace them in India.

peasant regiments recruited directly from the zamindaris of Bihar, the Benaras Raj and the Awadh state. The Company's recruitment from these territories gradually drew them into its military and fiscal orbit. The Company settled both its retired and its wounded soldiers on the fringes of these Indian states thereby making further inroads into their economies and political authority.

However, the Company's objective of monopolizing military force by recruiting a standing army of peasant soldiers was not entirely new. The Indian states of Awadh and Benaras had been experimenting with it since 1764, well before the Company began to recruit from their territory, but what was different was the method and procedure of recruiting a peasant army. Here, the tendency of the Company to centralize all power and political authority in its own hands came into conflict with the political views of many of its early luminaries, like Warren Hastings, who expounded the policy of preserving Indian traditions and institutions. The resolution of these tensions in north India resulted in the creation of an army of specifically high-caste Hindu soldiers whose status was protected by the military authority itself. The Bhumihar Brahmins of Bihar, who had always been denied high status by the rural high castes because they had taken to agriculture, took advantage of this military protection to improve their social status in society. For this reason the Company army became very popular in the eastern Awadh and Bihar Bhumihar zamindaris.

Yet this resolution of tensions was only temporarily successful. Chapter 2 shows that by the early nineteenth century, the Company's recruiting in north India generated severe political and social problems for it. Private individuals used the pay and pension benefits provided by the Company as well as its rhetoric of preserving the religious status of recruits, to enlist men for their private armies. Their activities became a major cause of concern to the Company officials. But the more significant consequence of recruitment in the region was the reinvention of a high-caste identity in the army. By providing a forum for sorting out the social tensions hinging around the ritual purity of the rural high caste, the army formalized these tensions and made them more rigid. But for this military recruitment the evolution of high-caste status in rural north India would have progressed differently. By the 1820s, the high-caste authority structure, which the Company had hitherto encouraged within the regiments, had come to pose a significant threat to its further political evolution. It thus negated the very objective for which the Company had opted for a directly recruited high-status peasant army.[11]

The contradictory nature of Company rule became even more apparent as its territory expanded to the frontier of the Bengal province, the Jungle Tarai, in 1772 and eventually extended further westward into the Ceded and Conquered Provinces in 1802. In these regions pragmatic difficulties in implementing its policy forced the Company to make concessions to local custom and compromise further with indigenous structures of power and authority so as to recruit its much needed military force. Chapter 4 shows that in the Jungle Tarai the Company came to rely on local notables for its supply of hill recruits. The hill regiments raised in the region were posted only within the Jungle Tarai and performed the vital social function of 'taming' the hitherto turbulent hills. Moreover, the support of local notables paved the way for creating a suitable administrative infrastructure to govern the hills. Similarly, chapters 5 and 6 show that in the freshly acquired Ceded and Conquered territory the Company stabilized its rule by working through Eurasian officers, like James Skinner, who had hitherto served in the armies of the Indian states of the region. Here, the Company contained the political and social problems generated by the mounted armies of the local bands of Rohillas, Afghans, and Mewatis by using the expertise of Eurasian officers to recruit these mounted warriors into its cavalry regiments. These officers reinvented the military tradition of the Indian states of Rohilkhand and Shinde as they incorporated Western modes of drill and discipline into their military practice.

Once again, as chapter 7 shows, in 1815, the Company began

[11] By the 1820s the sipahis of the Bengal Army had come to pose a major threat to Company rule. They were incensed because the Company's military and political transition had disturbed the power relations within which they had enjoyed financial security, and a high social status. Their resentment was most obvious during the mutiny–rebellion of 1857. Historians contributing to the subaltern school of Indian historiography perhaps need to take note of these foci of protest against Company rule.

to invent its own model of a Gurkha soldier in order to meet both the Nepali challenge and its own needs of policing the hills. The 'Company Gurkha' was shaped out of the Kumaonis, Garhwalis, and Sirmouri hillmen who flocked to its service because of Gurkha rule over their lands. This invented Gurkha tradition welded together Nepali military practice and the European drill and parade. An additional novel feature was the Company's use of Mughal imagery and military ethic. The Gurkha continued to meet the Company's requirements in the region until the mid-nineteenth century. In all these ways, political and social stability in the Company's newly-acquired territory was obtained at the cost of power devolving either to local notables or to Eurasians who had hitherto been regarded as mavericks by the Company. These conflicting imperatives were best reflected in the variety of military traditions that it was forced to maintain in different regions of north India in order to sustain its rule (map 1).

The East India Company's goals were dictated not merely by the ambition of securing a lucrative trading monopoly; inevitably they were drawn into providing the military machine whereby they could enforce such a monopoly, which equally inevitably led to the need to provide the finance for such an infrastructure.[12] Stokes emphasized the political gains that accrued to private interests in the Company, which thrust the political frontier well beyond the actual economic one.[13] P. J. Marshall emphasized that the success of British merchants trading in Awadh furthered the political crumbling of a state already weakened by the series of political obligations it had been forced into by the Company. According to him, 'in the Ganges valley, at least, both the political and the economic frontiers of British India appear to have been mobile. In Oudh, British merchants were able to take advantage of a state already weakened by a connection with the East India

[12] R. Mukherjee, 'Trade and empire in Awadh, 1765–1804', *Past and Present*, No. 94 (February, 1982), pp. 85–102. See also Radhika Singha, 'The despotism of law: British criminal justice and public authority in North India, 1772–1837', PhD thesis, Cambridge University, 1990.

[13] E. Stokes, 'British expansion in India in the 18th century: social revolution or social stagnation', *Past and Present*, No. 58 (February 1973), p. 143; C. A. Bayly, *Imperial Meridien: the British Empire and the World, 1780–1830* (London, 1989), p. 10.

Company going back to the battle of Buxar. They may have helped to weaken Oudh further, but the amputation of territory in 1801 seems to have had little to do with them.'[14] More recently it has been argued that the Company's concept of the rule of law was 'another facet of the expansionary momentum which drew Indian states into the fiscal and military orbit of the Company.'[15] I suggest that the process of recruiting and maintaining a Company army, and the Company's efforts to project its benevolence by providing long-term pensionary benefits to both its old-age pensioners as well as young wounded soldiers, provided an equally strong drive in the westward expansion of the Company up the Ganges valley. As chapter 3 shows, the settlement based upon the so-called Invalid Thanah contributed significantly to the process of urbanization and the creation of a money economy in hitherto peripheral areas.

This study shows that the careful balancing between the army, polity, and society which had stabilized Company rule in most parts of north India and thereby camouflaged the basic contradictions inherent in Company rule, began to be disturbed by the late 1820s. There were two main reasons for this: first, in this decade of financial strain the Company began reducing its military strength because it had defeated its major political rivals and there was less need for a big military establishment. Such retrenchment gained momentum because by this period the Company had developed a relatively advanced administrative infrastructure to sustain itself, and the army was no longer needed to contain the social and political tensions in the Company territory. But more importantly, the Company soon realized that its diverse military traditions, which were based on the sharing of its power and authority with local notables and high-caste sipahis, showed signs of rebounding to its disadvantage. The increasing instances of desertions and mutiny in its élite regiments, most of which were related to the infringements of the sipahi's high-caste status, alarmed the Company. At the same time it was no less concerned

[14] P. J. Marshall, 'British economic and political expansion: The case of Oudh', *MAS*, vol. 9, No. 4 (October 1975), p. 482.

[15] Singha, 'The despotism of law', p. 5.

at the threat posed to its rule by the local notables it had hitherto encouraged to recruit its hill regiments in the western frontier of Bengal—the Jungle Tarai.

These alarming developments in the social politics of the Company army brought to the surface the tensions between the Company's desired objectives and the practical mode of functioning it had evolved in north India. By the 1830s, the politically mature Company state appeared to be resolutely determined to finally resolve these contradictions. In this decade the Company's reformers homogenized the diverse traditions that had constituted the Bengal Army and the peasant army tradition began to be extended as a uniform military culture all over north India. Chapter 3 shows that in this era of fiscal reforms the Company spent large amounts of money to establish new military institutions and modify the existing ones so as to maintain a more rigorous control over the peasant sipahi and his family. The Company officers maintained detailed records of the sipahis' families and defined what they regarded as the 'legal' heirs of the sipahis. Moreover, they intervened in disputes related to inheritance, which disturbed the soldiers' families. In all these ways the soldier's family and village were drawn into the military ambit of the Company. In the short term this made it possible for Company officials to exercise greater control over its increasingly turbulent peasant regiments, but in the long run the military reforms of the 1830s created widespread discontent in the Company army, which eventually culminated in the mutiny-rebellion of 1857.

The administrative divisions of Gangetic north India underwent a series of changes between *c.* 1770 and 1830. The erstwhile Mughal provinces of Bihar–Bengal remained the core of the Bengal Presidency throughout our period. After 1782, the semi-independent Benaras Raj was, at least for administrative purposes, incorporated into the East India Company's Bihar–Bengal administrative unit. In 1774–5, the semi-independent state of Awadh expanded to include considerable parts of the erstwhile Indian state of Rohilkhand and the Allahabad–Kara region, called the Doab. These areas had been part of the former Mughal provinces of

Delhi and Allahabad. In 1802, Awadh ceded to the East India Company its territorial acquisitions in the Rohilkhand region including its lands in Gorakhpur, bordering the Nepal Tarai. The following year the Company further extended its territorial orbit by conquering some lands from the Maratha leader Shinde. The lands which had been acquired from Awadh, as well as those which had been conquered from Shinde, were placed under one administrative unit and called the Ceded and Conquered Provinces.

Chapter 1

North Indian Military Traditions and the Company

The evidence cited in this chapter and the argument postulated differs from the recent work on Indian military culture by Dirk Kolff.[1] Basing his argument on Abul Fazl's *Ain-i-Akbari*, folk songs, and the travelogues of the sixteenth and seventeenth century, Kolff shows the existence of a tradition of 'armed peasants' in the Bhojpur region from the time of the Emperor Sher Shah (1540–5). He uses the term 'military labour market' to designate the large pool of semi-trained men of rural origin who always appear to be available for service in north India. Kolff argues that from the mid-sixteenth century the Mughal Emperors began to create specialized peasant armies by separating *naukari* (military service) from the agricultural responsibilities of the recruits. But he goes on to show that despite the Mughal state's efforts to create peasant soldiers the distinction between soldier and peasant remained blurred even in the heyday of the Empire. In the eighteenth century, he argues, the East India Company took the logic of the peasant army tradition to its culmination by the recruitment of specialized peasant armies from the region. Kolff is of the view that the success of the East India Company 'demilitarized' north Indian society and dried the 'military labour market'. He does not explain the actual process of this 'demilitarization' but

[1] Dirk Kolff, *Naukar, Rajput and Sepoy: the Ethnohistory of the Military Labour Market in Hindustan, 1450–1850* (Cambridge, 1990).

goes on to argue that it became particularly acute after the Pindari campaign of 1818. The 'military labour market' in this part of India was given a final burial after the mutiny of 1857.[2]

Kolff's argument about a long-standing 'peasant army tradition' in Hindustan poses certain difficulties. In the first place the optimism of Abul Fazl about the success of the Mughal state in drawing large numbers of foot soldiers from its *subas* at short notice has to be seen in the light of a court historian's attempt to glorify the efficiency of state institutions and the popularity of Akbar's rule. Besides, the 'armed peasant' needs to be differentiated from the professionally trained peasant soldiers which this study argues was a novelty of the eighteenth-century Indian states. Given the insecurity of life and property in the Mughal villages, particularly those on the fringes of the Mughal subas, it was inevitable that the peasant would be armed for his own defence. But this was not enough to shape him into a peasant soldier. The Mughal state had a predominantly cavalry-based army and, given the nature of warfare in the seventeenth century, the state did not feel the need for a professionally trained peasant army. Moreover, the separation of the peasant soldiers from civilian society was difficult for a state which did not have a tradition of military exclusivity. Kolff himself shows that the infantrymen recruited by the state were numerically small and in most of the cases were armed levies supplied by the zamindars.[3]

Kolff does not distinguish between an armed peasant and a peasant soldier because he does not trace the evolution of the armed peasant tradition from the heyday of the Mughal Empire to the period of the eighteenth-century states of Awadh and Benaras. These states adopted sophisticated techniques to recruit peasants directly from the countryside. These peasant recruits were separated from civilian society so as to be shaped into professional peasant soldiers. It was the involvement of the Indian states in the recruitment of peasant soldiers that vastly expanded the 'military labour market'. Indeed, the existence of different foreign and indigenous employers made the market complex. Very often the militarization

[2] Ibid., pp. 3, 7, 30–3, 38.
[3] Ibid., pp. 24–5, 169.

of the regional states resulted in the mushrooming of a sub-military tradition. Here, local individuals, independent of the military structure of the ruling house, created a military niche for themselves. The 'military labour market' obtained a further fillip once the East India Company started recruiting from it. The Company adopted a method of recruitment based on the rhetoric of high-caste status and the appeal of well-paid service abroad. In the early nineteenth century this became the general language used by individuals as well as different recruiting agents to build their political and military power in the region. This intensified the dynamism of the 'market' and made it more volatile.

THE MUGHAL MILITARY SYSTEM: URBAN-BASED 'GENTLEMEN TROOPERS'

The cavalry was the mainstay of the central imperial army of the Mughals.[4] This was a branch in which the Mughal state could effectively display its superiority for the Mughals not only had access to the best horses from Afghanistan, Iran and Arabia but had also perfected the fighting skills of cavalry warfare. Moreover, in India the horse had been a symbol of valour, status, and power ever since the Vedic period. Its recognition as a symbol of social status by both the conquerors and the vanquished made it an ideal idiom in which to express power relations.

The Mughal cavalry may be called the preserve of the 'gentleman trooper'. The term 'gentleman trooper' is used here to emphasize the predominance of the Indian and foreign élites in the Mughal cavalry. For the Mughal cavalry served as a meeting ground not only for the Indian and Mughal élite but also for the Mughal and the Turkish, Afghan, Iranian and Turanian chiefs in India. It was organized as a patronage system with the Mughal Emperor as its chief patron. The Emperor had direct relations only with the military commandants and at the local level the army thrived on a system of support based on clan and kinship ties. Every

---

[4] Ibid., pp. 24–5. Mughal Emperors like Akbar had as many as 12,000 matchlockmen who were foot soldiers. But the number of regular infantry in the standing army of the Emperor did not show any increase in the period. It remained localized in the provinces and was not included in the front line of any major military campaign.

suba or province had a cantonment where the *mansabdar* stationed his troops and trained them in the art of cavalry warfare. He provided them with a maintenance allowance for their horses or with a horse itself if they did not possess one. The military training and discipline of the recruits laid emphasis only on physical fitness and did not intrude into the domains of their personal or domestic life. Military exercise was offensive in nature and concentrated on the physical impairment or destruction of the enemy. One form of basic training for both *sawars* and *paidal* was *shamshir zani* or sword exercise.[5] *Teer andazi* or archery was another very popular exercise practised by both the paidal and troopers. Sharif Muhammad Mubarak Shah, the author of *Adabul Harab*, described the beneficial effects these exercises had in regulating the soldier's body functions: 'the body gets softened, the joints get loose, flesh becomes hard, eyesight improves, hand and feet become straight and strong and the man becomes brave.'[6] The army never created an alternate regulatory institution to exercise and discipline the sipahi. Even when the sipahi was sick he was granted sick leave and sent home.[7] In this sense it differed fundamentally from the Company army which as we shall show deployed a whole range of disciplining institutions from the regiment to the military hospital.

Though many of the cavalrymen were from a rural background the central and predominant feature of the Mughal cavalry was its urban social base. The military élite, in direct contact with the state, were either themselves of an urban social background or else tried to emulate the lifestyle and etiquette of the court. They resided in the towns and qasbahs along with their family and military establishment. These residences were generally in

[5] The sword was the symbol of Mughal valour, and was an essential part of every sipahi's kit. The major focus of Mughal military skill was efficient use of the sword, both by foot soldiers, as well as the cavalry. The Mughal military commanders believed that sword exercises kept the soldier physically fit and active.

[6] Syed Sabahuddin Abdul Rahman, *Hindustan ke ahde waste ka fauji nizam* (Azamgarh, 2nd ed., 1981), pp. 25–6. *Kushti* (wrestling) was another very popular Mughal military exercise.

[7] Ibid., p. 399. One month's sick leave was allowed to him on half salary, when the sipahi was allowed to visit his family, and continued to receive all his other allowances.

the neighbourhood of their military jagirs, but they could also often be quite distant from their jagir. Their urban consumption pattern and taste for luxuries revealed the large extent to which the mansabdari institution channeled the revenue of the countryside to support this life style.[8] The more rigorous training of archers by well-trained professionals, and the sale and purchase of horses increased the contact of troopers with the outside world of traders and merchants.[9] To a large extent this urban influence determined the trooper's tastes and the direction of his investments.[10]

Further, the military lifestyle provided opportunities for interaction between the trooper and the urban middle classes. These were the *ashraf* or the *shurafa* class of society who were closely linked to the Mughal court through racial, religious or clan ties. The trooper, also linked to the Mughal court culture, shared an urban outlook with the ashraf. This created an empathy between the trooper and the ashraf class. The Mughal state seems to have encouraged this close contact between the troopers and the urban literati, for the Mughal armies included *qazis*, *muftis*, teachers, learned men, poets, jesters, reporters and the like. The commanders enjoyed listening to recitations of heroic poems composed by eminent poets who glorified the adventurous deeds of their masters.[11]

One of the classic examples of this kind of affinity between trooper and literate ashraf groups was the social background of some of the members of Firangi Mahal, one of the centres of Sunni Islamic learning in Lucknow. Two sons of Mulla Qutubuddin,

[8] S. Moosvi, *The Economy of the Mughal Empire, c. 1595* (Delhi, 1987) p. 299. She has shown that 18.6% of a mansabdar's personal income went to the service sector, and 18.5% was spent on direct consumption of the rural produce. Of the entire amount paid as personal salary to a mansabdar 63.26% was spent, in various ways, to maintain the craft sector. On the basis of these figures she argues that the urban economy of the Mughal Empire was largely supported by investments made by mansabdars.

[9] H. K. Naqvi, *Mughal Hindustan* (Karachi, 1972), pp. 27, 50–1. All sales of horses were carried out in specially constructed livestock markets, called *nakhhas*, by open auction. Official and unofficial markets in livestock were located in Delhi, Agra, Lahore and other centres. These markets were frequented by cavalrymen.

[10] Moosvi, *The Economy of the Mughal Empire*, p. 299.

[11] M. Y. Kokań, *Arabic and Persian in Carnatic, 1710–1960* (Madras, 1974), p. 6.

the founder of Firangi Mahal, had taken part in Aurangzeb's campaigns to the Deccan. On their return to Delhi they were rewarded with land in the Bahraich district of Awadh and a big house in Lucknow which had belonged to a French adventurer (probably a horse dealer) who had named it Firangi Mahal. With royal patronage Qutubuddin engaged himself in fulfilling his and his class' self-perceived responsibility of guarding the intellectual heritage of the Faith.[12]

There were many such instances of close contact between soldiers of the imperial army and the ashraf and literati of Mughal society. Indeed many military servicemen of the Mughal Empire were also the leading prose writers and poets of their time. For instance, Nawab Ghulam Ali Khan, the *qiladar* of Kotla in the reign of Aurangzeb, was also a great Persian poet and author of *Lama't-at-Tahireen*. Love for poetry ran in his family and his son Nawab Baqir Ali Khan was also a great poet.[13] Jaswant Rai Munshi, another soldier of Aurangzeb's army, composed one of the finest poems in praise of the Nawab Saadatullah Khan of Hyderabad when he visited him in 1706. Later in the decade he took up military employment in the Hyderabad state and accompanied the Nawab in many of his campaigns. He composed long poems which glorified the adventurous deeds of the Nawab. His masterpiece is the *Sayeednamah* which is regarded as one of the most important histories of the Nawab of Hyderabad.[14]

The ashraf families of Mughal society respected the military profession and their sons were trained in military skills like archery and wrestling. Interestingly, their literary interests were also encouraged and some of the best literary figures of the Mughal

---

[12] Maulana Abdul Inayatullah, *Tazkira-i-Ulema-i-Firangi Mahal* (Lucknow, AH 1349), pp. 9–12. The contributions towards Islamic learning by the descendants of Qutubuddin were remarkable. Firangi Mahal attracted scholars from all parts of India, Arabia and China. Initially, there was no *madrasa* in Firangi Mahal; members of the family simply taught students who came to them in search of knowledge, in their homes. But later the descendants of Qutubuddin travelled widely as teachers. They propagated a new curriculum called the *Dars-i-Nizamiya*, which was based on Græco–Arab rational sciences and had incorporated traditional Islamic theology.

[13] Kokan, *Arabic and Persian in Carnatic*, p. 12.

[14] Ibid., pp. 19–22.

period were also expert archers and swordsmen. For instance, Syed Shah Abdul Lateef Zawqi (AH 1151–94), who later became well known as the poet, author, and mystic of Vellore, was an expert archer and wrestler as well. These were skills he had picked up alongside learning Persian and Arabic from his father and his teacher Hafiz Muhammad Hussain.[15] Similarly, Mirza Ali Bakht Azfari (AH 1174–1235), the poet and author of Delhi who settled in Madras, studied Arabic, Persian, Turkish and medicine while perfecting his skills in archery.[16]

THE MILITARY STRUCTURE OF THE AWADH NAWABI

The importance of the 'gentleman trooper' who had close contacts with the urban and rural professional groups of the qasbahs continued into the period which followed imperial decline. Many qasbahs and towns of Awadh including Faizabad—the Nawabi's most beautiful and historically most significant town—owed their origin to the investment and consolidation of the 'gentleman trooper' class. For instance, Burhan-ul-Mulk, a Mughal mansabdar who later became the first Nawab of Awadh, pitched his tent two *kos* from the populated area when he reached Awadh to assume charge of the Imperial Naib. After a few days a thatched bungalow was constructed and it was enclosed by a huge boundary wall of mud. Within this compound his *piadas*, *sawars* and *topkhana* were accommodated. When Burhan-ul-Mulk died and Safdar Jung became the new ruler of Awadh this *abadi* was designated Faizabad. In Safdar Jang's reign this embryonic urban site expanded and many risaldars continued to contribute to its development. For instance, Ismail Khan, a Mughal risaldar, helped in building up a small township there. Many courtiers and high as well as low-ranking risaldars built their houses at the site. Along with the risaldars the service gentry class also invested its income in this city. Sons of Diwan Atma Ram and some shop owners built many new markets and *havelis*, and laid the foundations of many public gardens.[17]

---

[15] Ibid., p. 130.

[16] Ibid., p. 146.

[17] Najmul Ghani, *Tarikh-i-Awadh* (4 vol., Lucknow, 1919), I, pp. 36–7; also see Abdul

Apart from the influence and role of the big urban-based mansabdar families from Afghanistan, such as the Qandaharis,[18] a large proportion of the qasbah and shurafa population also looked with respect on the military profession. It was not a matter of surprise then that the qasbah population of Lucknow and Kakori swelled the ranks of Burhan-ul-Mulk's army. Muzaffar Alam has shown that the Sheikhzadas of Lucknow who were supported and encouraged by the Sayyids initially resisted the *subahdari* in Awadh.[19] But once their power had been crushed these town and qasbah populations flocked into the Awadh army in large numbers.[20] Ghulam Nabi Azad Bilgrami, in his description of the defence of Awadh against the Afghans in 1751, shows that military employment provided the livelihood of large sections of the urban population belonging to respectable ashraf families. He wrote:

In the defence of Awadh against inroads scores of noble born (*shurafa-o-nujaba*) of the province specially the Sayyids and Sheikhs of Bilgram laid down their lives.[21]

Halim Sharar, *Guzishta mashriqi tamaddum ka akhri namunah*, tr. and ed. E. S. Harcourt and Fakhir Hussain as *Lucknow: The Last Phase of an Oriental Culture* (New Delhi, 1993), p. 30.

[18] Ghani, *Tarikh-i-Awadh*, I, p. 37. Yusuf Qandahari was a very important mansabdar in the Mughal army. Successive generations of his family continued to serve the Awadh nawabs.

[19] M. Alam, *Crisis of Empire in Mughal North India, Awadh and Punjab: 1707– 48* (Delhi, 1986), p. 8.

[20] Saiyid Ibn Hasan Bilgrami, *Burhan-i-Awadh* (MS Maulana Azad Library, Aligarh), p. 36. In 1730, Burhan-ul-Mulk sent Mir Muhammad Salah Khan and Sayyid Munawwar Ali Tirmizi of Bilgram, to the *qasbahs* around Lucknow to recruit men for his army. Over 200 *sawars* and 1,000 *piadas* joined the provincial armed forces. They were placed under the leadership of one Mir Syed Muhammad Roshan. Mir Nur-ul-Hasan Khan and Mir Azim-ud-din Khan, with a large contingent of their kinsmen, soon joined this force. In 1732 a large number of Sheikhzadas from the contingent of Sarbuland Khan joined the army of Burhan-ul-Mulk. In the following years Burhan-ul-Mulk's reliance on the Sheikhzadas of Bilgram, and, for that matter, on all Sheikhzadas of Awadh appears to have grown stronger; see also *Qudratullah Jan-i-Jahan Nama* (2, Rampur MS), p. 61, cited in Alam, *Crisis of Empire*, p. 8.

[21] Cited in Alam, *Crisis of Empire*, pp. 234– 6. He shows that in 1739 a large number of local townspeople formed a substantial part of the army of Burhan-ul-Mulk. In the battle of Karnal, over 100 people from Bilgram alone died fighting for him. In 1751 when the Bangash Afghans occupied Lucknow, Sheikh Muzzu-ud-din organized an army of Sheikhzadas and forced the Afghans to vacate the town. Around Lucknow,

However, in the reign of Shuja-ud-daula, there occurred a very significant change in the composition and organization of the army. From 1764, Shuja started organizing a peasant army. In 1757, Clive had raised his famous Lal Paltan as a small body of infantry troops drilled in the European manner. It is possible that Shuja had this precedent in mind when he began to build his own infantry force. But the more immediate cause of this shift was the dismal performance of the Awadh cavalry force at the battle of Buxar in 1764, and Shuja's political problems with the 'gentlemen troopers'. Its more deep-rooted cause appears to have been related to the political and social role which the military was to play in the Nawabi.

The minority Shia ruling house in Lucknow owed its existence to the goodwill of Delhi and lacked the charisma of the Mughal Emperor. This made the control of a predominantly Sunni Muslim and Hindu populace all the more difficult for the Nawabs. By modifying and diversifying his army Shuja was able to use it to create a more advantageous balance of Mughal, European, and local networks within the state. Of course, after 1765 the army continued to reach out to the highest reference point of Mughal sovereignty by accommodating those Mughal gentlemen troopers who had migrated to Awadh following imperial decline and had influential contacts with the Delhi court. However, some of the more suspect Mughal families[22] were dispensed with, following the advice of Nawab Imad-ul-Mulk and Ahmad Khan Bangash of Farrukhabad. After the battle of Buxar when Shuja met Imad-ul-Mulk and Ahmad Khan Bangash in Bareli, they gave him the following advice:

If he now recovered the government of the province, not to trust the

---

in the qasbahs of Awadh, the Sheikhzadas fought to defend Nawabi rule against the Afghan invaders.

[22] Muhammad Faiz Baksh, *Tarikh-i-Farahbaksh*, tr. William Hoey as *Memoirs of Delhi and Faizabad* (2 vols., Allahabad, 1889), II, p. 4. Faiz Baksh, the historian of Faizabad, reported that Shuja was disappointed at the treachery of his Mughal cavalrymen in the battle of Buxar. Many of these Mughal troopers sided with the Company army, and some of them, like Raja Beni Bahadur, who commanded 10,000 troopers, remained neutral.

Mughals, but to make use of his own dependants and eunuchs and to make Faizabad his capital.[23]

Immediately after this meeting, when Shuja returned to Faizabad in 1765, he began to recruit his new cavalry and infantry units and started organizing his artillery. He also built the city of Faizabad on a grander scale and was reported to have razed the houses of the Mughals.[24] Shuja now began to recruit groups of professional warriors outside the Mughal military system. One such group was the warrior ascetics called the Gosains, who sold their services to the highest bidder.[25] Another such ethnic group incorporated in Shuja's army was that of the Mewatis. These men, from Mewat, had so far remained on the margins of the Mughal military system. But in Shuja's military force they were well represented and were often used to crush the power of the Mughal cavalrymen.[26] Finally, the Nawabi benefited from the services of European adventurers. Shuja adopted their skills and techniques to drill and discipline his peasant recruits.[27]

But most important was the practice of striking new political

[23] Ibid., p. 4.

[24] Ibid., p. 5.

[25] L. Nos. 613–16, Lieutenant G. Harper to Council, (?) Oct. 1768, FPD, Select Committee Proceedings 1768, NAI. Umraogir, the powerful Gosain leader in the Nawab's army, had 100 horsemen. He derived a substantial salary from a jagir he had in the Doab region. His brother, Himmat Bahadur, was in the service of the Mughal Emperor and had his jagir in the Banda region of Bundelkhand. He too maintained a large number of troops and had expanded his jagir west of the Jamuna, close to the borders of Jhansi; also see L. No. 234, I. Baillie to Grame Mercer, 6 June 1804, BPS, Consult., 21 June 1804, P/BEN/SEC/141, IOL. In 1804, Baillie reported that Himmat Bahadur possessed about 2,500 cavalry, battalions of infantry of about 1,500 men, and levies of matchlockmen. He parcelled out his jagirs to his brother Anupgir also.

[26] Faiz Baksh, *Tarikh-i-Farahbaksh*, II, p. 159. Maurez Khan was a Mewati who entered the service of Shuja's commandant Ali Beg Khan Jarji when he was only 18. Ali Beg being satisfied with his good service, ordered him to recruit his fellow Mewatis. He brought together 400 Mewatis, and was invested with the rank of a subaltern. In the 1770s his contingent was sent to crush the mutiny in the Mughal cavalry regiment of Shuja's army.

[27] Ibid., p. 8. Twenty-two Frenchmen such as Monsieur Sonson and Monsieur Pedrose were employed in Shuja's army, training foot regiments, establishing cannon foundries, and manufacturing implements of war in Shuja's arsenal; see also Rosie Llewellyn Jones, *A Fatal Friendship: The Nawabs, the British and the City of Lucknow* (Delhi, 1985), pp. 17–40.

alliances with the local Rajput peasants and zamindars over whom the Nawabi had established its domination. Some of these, as Mughal mansabdars, had strengthened their positions in rural society. The state apparatus began to draw peasant recruits from the Awadh zamindaris into the army. In 1767, Richard Smith, the Commander-in-Chief of the Company's forces in Awadh, in a letter to Henry Verelst, President and Governor at Fort Williams, referred to this change in Shuja's policy. He wrote:

He [Shuja] told me that now he knows the value of infantry. They were but little expense and were the only troops to be depended on in times of service. That he was therefore determined to dismiss part of his cavalry, for he could always raise as many as he pleased at a month's notice. But that the forming of infantry was a work of much time and infinite labour.[28]

There were two administrative institutions which formed the foci of all military mobilization and organization. These were the office of the *faujdar* and the *amil*. By 1722, the institution of the faujdar had come under the jurisdiction of the Governor of Awadh.[29] In Shuja's Awadh the faujdar's role extended to the military sphere also. He became one of the most important recruiting agents at the pargana and district level. Orders were sent to all faujdars to send a certain number of armed men from every pargana for military service.[30] The recruits were mainly Hindus from the Rajput zamindaris of Awadh. Once enlisted, each recruit was enrolled and the names of the village and the pargana where his family resided were recorded. These sipahis were paid regularly and Shuja maintained personal contact with them. Problems of military insubordination were solved through

[28] Richard Smith, Commander-in-Chief, to Henry Verelst, President and Governor Fort William and Gentlemen of the Select Committee, 6 Feb. 1767, BSC, Consult. FW, 23 Feb. 1768, P/A/8, IOL.

[29] Alam, *Crisis of Empire*, p. 210. Alam argues that by 1722 the institution of the faujdar had come to represent the Governor rather than the imperial agent in a district of the province. In this period the faujdar seems to have had control over the finance of his faujdari. In some parganas he even possessed qanungo and chaudhury rights. Further, the institution of the faujdar at the sarkar level, was merged with the new institution of *nizamat* and *niyabat*.

[30] Colonel R. Smith to the Gentlemen of the Select Committee, 3 Nov. 1767, BSC, Consult FW 17 Nov. 1767, P/A/7, IOL.

the novel institution of court martial.[31] By 1768 Shuja had 70,000 such sipahis arranged in seventy or eighty paltans which were in turn grouped into divisions called Telingas and Jhelingas.[32] Each paltan was commanded by military commanders who were not necessarily of the same region, religion or clan as the recruits. In fact most of the commandants of the Telinga and Jhelinga recruits, from east and south Awadh, were Afghan, Qandahari and European mercenaries.[33] None of these officers had the power of recruitment, dismissal or punishment as all such powers of control and discipline rested with Shuja.

The other administrative institution increasingly drawn into the recruitment of the army was the office of the *amil*. Muzaffar Alam has shown that the jagir administration of Burhan-ul-Mulk changed the nature of this office from one representing imperial presence at the district level to one safeguarding the subahdar's interests.[34] In Shuja's reign the rights and powers of the amil coalesced with those of the military commandant and in many areas the two offices completely fused. The military estates of Shuja's amils served as a 'nursery' of recruits for his peasant army. In fact the increasing militarization of the Nawabi, which generated

[31] H. Verelst, President and Governor, Fort William, to Select Committee, 6 Feb. 1767, BSC, Consult. FW 23 Feb. 1768, P/A/8, IOL. He was diligent in the detection of fraud and rigid in punishing offenders. One of his commandants was locked in the Chunargarh fort for two months, because he had dismissed a sipahi and entertained another without the permission of the Nawab. Another Commandant was confined to the same fort for some malpractices related to the distribution of salary to sipahis.

[32] R. Barnett, *North India between Empires: Awadh, the Mughals and the British, 1720–1801* (Berkeley, 1980), p. 135. He notes that the term Telinga was taken from the army of Haider Ali and Tipu Sultan. In these infantry regiments recruits from the Telinga region of south India were named Telingas; also see Ghani, *Tarikh-i-Awadh*, II, pp. 157–62.

[33] Ghani, *Tarikh-i-Awadh*, II, pp. 157–62. One of the commandants was Mahbub Ali Khan who had 500 sawars and 4 paltans. Some sources say he had 900 piadas armed with small arms. Akbar Ali Khan, who had 500 sawars and one paltan, and Latafat Ali Khan, who had 500 sawars and four paltans of 7,000 armed piadas, were some other important military commandants of Shuja.

[34] Alam, *Crisis of Empire*, p. 210. Burhan-ul-Mulk got the amils under his control and endeavoured to check the irregularities committed by agents of the jagirdars. The Nawab imposed a levy on the jagir. This was in lieu of the responsibility he had undertaken for the regular payment of the revenue to the jagirdar. These steps enabled him to build up his power and personal treasury.

new avenues of investment and employment, also provided revenue
farmers and amils like Almas Ali Khan the opportunity to carve
out their own independent military estates. On Almas Ali Khan's
jagir, trade, artisanal and agricultural investment was carried on
by the ruler independent of the Nawab.[35] Almas used the power
and income from his estate to recruit his own army. By 1807,
in his sprawling estate of Miangunge, Jagdishpur, Sandila, and
Haidergarh he commanded cavalry and irregular infantry, both
a thousand strong, and five battalions with sixteen guns which
belonged to the Awadh state. He had of his own 820 cavalry,
7,345 infantry and eleven pieces of cannon, making altogether
a force of 1,820 cavalry, 8,345 infantry and eighty-seven guns.
At Miangunge alone he had one battalion of 1,000 recruits, 100
irregular infantry, 200 horse and fifty-two guns with their equipment.[36] In 1807, Almas asserted his independence and refused
to pay revenue to the Nawab of Awadh. It was only when threatened
by the superior force of the Company's army that he consented
to give up his artillery to the Nawab and agreed not to oppose
the collection of revenue from his lands.[37]

The peasant army of Awadh recruited in this manner was different
from the warrior corporations of Gosains which did not confine
recruitment to peasant sipahis. Besides this, Shuja's peasant army
possessed special arms and emulated European drill and discipline.
However, there was no dependence on European arms and armaments. For instance, there was an entire artisanal establishment
attached to the Awadh army and Shuja had a personally managed
artillery park which had twenty-nine pieces of cannon mounted
on field carriages with screws.[38] The cannon, few of them exceeding
a six-pounder, were cast by a native of Bengal in the Nawab's
service. In the manner of the Europeans Shuja attempted to cast

[35] Bayly, *Rulers, Townsmen and Bazaars*, p. 99.

[36] L. No. 4, Abstract of vazir's reply to queries by Colonel John Collins, 7 April 1807,
BPS, Consult. 30 April 1807, P/BEN/SEC/201, IOL.

[37] I. Collins, Resident at Lucknow, to N. B. Edmonstone, Sec. to Govt., BPS, Consult.
19 June 1807, No. 2, P/BEN/SEC/201, IOL.

[38] Richard Smith, Commander-in-Chief, to Henry Verelst, President and Governor
Fort William, and to Gentlemen of the Select Committee, 6 Feb. 1769, BSC, Consult.
23 Feb. 1768, P/A/8, IOL.

some light pieces also. The artificer's yard, superintended by a French officer, engaged many artificers in the construction of carriages and tumbrils. Along with these big yards there also existed a foundry and places where Shuja made small arms. These were located adjacent to Shuja's palace so as to enable him to personally supervise them without any inconvenience. About 500 artificers were employed here and the sipahi's firelocks were made after the English model. In these foundries about 150–200 firelocks were made very month, and of the matchlocks with bayonets it was said, 'there was no saying how many he made.'[39] Besides Faizabad, these were manufactured in several other places as well. Shuja spared no labour or expense in the manufacture of hocquets, pikes, and swords which were made in every city or town.[40] He personally supervised his expanded military network in a manner very similar to the Mughal Emperor Akbar, and was known to spend two to three hours every morning overseeing his foundry and gunsmiths.[41] After these morning chores he supervised the drill and parade of his troops. The drills, which took place every day except Sunday which was kept as a holiday in the manner of the British regiments, were also conducted by European officers. Here, the emphasis was laid not only on physical fitness but on the creation of a corporate sense of identity and co-ordination centered around the regiment.[42]

PEASANT TROOPS AND GENTLEMEN TROOPERS

The change in the military system induced political tensions in the Nawabi. There was a gulf between the urban-based gentry class (shurafa) which had dominated the Mughal and then the pre-Buxar Nawabi army, and the country recruits. The najib, as the former were called, remained an important and considerably

[39] Ibid.

[40] Ibid.

[41] Richard Smith, Commander-in-Chief, to Henry Verelst, President and Governor Fort William and to Gentlemen of the Select Committee, 3 Nov. 1767, BSC, Consult. 23 Feb. 1768, P/A/8, IOL.

[42] Ibid.; also see Ghani, *Tarikh-i-Awadh*, I, p. 58.

larger section of the Nawab's army.[43] They prided themselves on their noble descent and urban background. Ghani mentions in his *Tarikh-i-Awadh* that the najibs, who were also referred to as *mian sahib* (a term of respect used for the ashraf), used abusive language against the peasant regiments of the Nawab's army. Referring to the popular stereotypes of the najibs among the Awadh populace he writes that 'it was said that a work for which 1000 Telingas were required could be performed by 100 najibs.' [44] The peasant troopers disliked the najibs. Shuja was also weary of the najibs' arrogance, and by the late 1760s, he was in a position to use his peasant army to curtail the power of these cavalrymen.

In the days which followed Shuja's treaty of 1775 and the commencement of Asaf-ud-daula's reign, the actual fighting force of Awadh was reduced considerably and the peasant trooper base of the Nawabi, still in its formative stage, bore the brunt of the reductions. For the Company's so-called 'reforms' were aimed at weakening this vital base of the Nawabi. For their part the peasant troopers were either taken into the Company's army or in the case of some of their more important leaders they were referred to as the Telinga Rajas. Faiz Baksh, a court chronicler of Asaf-ud-daula, lamented the unwelcome presence of these country soldiers in the Nawab's court:

Naked rustics, whose fathers and brothers were with their own hands guiding the plough, rode about as Asaf-ud-daula's orderlies . . . they rode around in disorderly fashion, on state horses with grand caparisons . . . Bhawani Singh, Moti Singh, Hulas Singh, Nawaz Singh, Maiku Singh . . . . such was the change within 2 months.[45]

Faiz Baksh actually lamented over what he saw but what he

---

[43] Ghani, *Tarikh-i-Awadh*, I, pp. 78–88. There were about 70,000 paltans of najibs in Shuja's army and their Commander-in-Chief was called Sipah Salar. Of these about 4,000–5,000 were Mughals on a salary of Rs 15 a month. The most famous was the Baisi Paltan. This was a group of 22 paltans under a commandant, Meer Ahmad, who was popularly known as Baisi Wala. Six of these paltans had about 4,000–5,000 Mughals from Delhi.

[44] Ghani, *Tarikh-i-Awadh*, II, p. 160.

[45] Faiz Baksh. *Tarikh-i-Farahbaksh*, p. 21.

observed was actually an effect of the change in the political role of the army which Shuja had initiated. Nevertheless, the significant emergence of the peasant army was to be a short-lived affair in Awadh as it was rapidly aborted under Shuja's successor, Asaf-ud-daula.

THE BENARAS ZAMINDARI: RECRUITING THE PEASANT ARMY

The Benaras zamindari revealed another way in which it was possible for Indian states in the eighteenth century to build up a peasant army. Here the troops were recruited through clan leaders in the countryside and it was a case of 'peasantization from below'. The Benaras army was comparable to the zamindari levies that constituted the Mughal infantry and the Maratha army where recruitment followed a similar pattern.[46] In Benaras, Mansa Ram, the founder of the Raj and the Nawab of Awadh's· amil, used his high office and his kin and clan ties in the region to carve out his independence.[47] It was in the reign of his son Balwant

[46] T. D. Broughton, *Letters Written in a Maratha Camp during the Year 1809: description of the costume, character, manners, domestic habits and religious ceremonies of the Marathas* (London, 1813), p. 103.

[47] Warren Hastings, *A Narrative of the Insurrection which Happened in the Zamindary of Benaris in the Month of August 1781 and of the Transactions of the Governor-General in that District, with an appendix of authentic papers and affidavits* (Calcutta, 1853) p. 8. Hereafter *Transactions.* Mansa Ram was the descendant of a pious Brahmin, Kuthoo Misr, of Otataria who refused worldly responsibilities offered to him by the local king. His father, Matrunja Singh, lived in Otataria and contrary to the desire of his brothers living in Jaunpur, Ghazipur and Chunar he earned his livelihood by taking up agriculture. Mansa Ram was his eldest son. Seeing the power of his kinsmen and their hostility towards his father he came to Benaras with a retinue and obtained an interview with the Governor of Benaras, Meer Rustam Ali Khan. Rustam Ali Khan had been anxious to find a man with contacts in the countryside and he loaded him with favours, and retained him amongst his personal attendants. Mansa Ram increased his retinue by attracting men of his clan, and soon became the virtual ruler of the district. Rustam Ali got him the title of Raja from the Mughal Emperor Muhammad Shah. Mansa Ram requested that this honour should be given to his son Balwant Singh. Balwant Singh was young and energetic and Rustam Ali liked him even more than his father. Mansa Ram's request was therefore granted. He and his family soon won the favour of Shuja. Rustam Ali was removed and Mansa Ram was appointed in his place as the amil of Benaras. In 1773 his grandson Cheyt Singh obtained from Warren Hastings the first legal title of property in

Singh that the Benaras zamindari expanded territorially and the Bhumihar Brahmins consolidated their power in the region.[48] The expansion of the zamindari took place by conquest of the other Brahmin and Rajput zamindaris in the region.[49]

The Benaras army played an important role in the political expansion of the Benaras Raj both through direct conquest and by its recruitment policy which built up an interest for the Bhumihar rulers in various localities. Balwant Singh's army, like the Mughal army, was syncretic and broad-based in its composition. This reduced the Raja's dependence on his immediate clansmen, many of whom had been Mughal mansabdars. But in this army the old Bhumihar élite occupied the core position with the Rajputs, Brahmins and Afghan risaldars in a secondary role. It was structured in three tiers with the Bhumihar élite and the recruits from the Bhumihar Brahmin kin network of the Raja occupying the highest position. The second tier consisted of Afghan and Rajput risaldars who were generally cavalrymen and had served in the Mughal army.[50] The rank and file was composed of the zamindar auxiliary

the land. Until this period he was only the amil who had become the acknowledged zamindar by a sanad issued by Shuja in 1773. On the succession of Asaf-ud-daula, the right of sovereignty which he held over the zamindari, was transferred to the Company.

[48] This was the name by which the clan of Mansa Ram was called because they had taken to agriculture rather than performance of priestly functions.

[49] Wilton Oldham, *Historical and Statistical Memoirs of the Ghazipur District* (2 vols., Allahabad, 1876), II, pp. 47–52. Some of the Rajput zamindars in the region subdued by Balwant Singh were as follows: the Raja of Kuntit, the head of the Gurhurwar Rajputs in the Mirzapur district, who had 1,283 square miles of land situated south of the Ganges between Chunar and the Allahabad border. He was removed from his lands by Balwant Singh in 1753. Balwant Singh took advantage of the tension that had existed between the Kuntit Raja and the Naib of Allahabad, and eventually managed to drive him out of his zamindari. The former owed a balance of Rs 90,000 to the Naib of Allahabad from the time the Raja had bought his lands. Balwant Singh accused him of defaults in payment, and made one of his bankers, Nandan Lal Shah, pay the amount to the Naib and buy the zamindari. The other Rajas defeated were the Raja of Agori Barhar and a Chandel Rajput, in the Mirzapur district, called Sambhu Shah. Bikramjit Ujjain, the Raja of Dumriaon, was driven out of some of the lands he possessed in pargana Zumaneeah in the Benaras zamindari. In 1760, the Hyobuns Rajas of Ballia were also disposessed of their lands.

[50] Fakir Khair-ud-din Khan, *Tuhfa-i-Taza (Balwantnamah),* tr. F. Curwen (Allahabad, 1875), p. 1. In the Mughal suba of Benaras, as in other subas, there was a marked number of Brahmin and Rajput risaldars who served in the Mughal army. At the commencement

forces of non-élite Brahmins, Bhumihars and Rajputs of the Jaunpur, Ghazipur and Chunar zamindaris.[51] Despite their subordinate position in the hierarchy of the army the Afghan risaldars as well as the zamindar auxiliaries were the indispensable fighting force of the army. For instance, in 1750 Sahib Zaman Khan Jaunpuri, who had been deputed by Ahmad Khan Bangash to eject Balwant Singh from Benaras, did not carry out his plan because of the influence the Afghan risaldars had over him. Instead he arranged for a meeting between Balwant Singh and Ahmad Khan Bangash.[52] Again, it was on the advice of these risaldars that Balwant Singh decided to give up the battle with Zaman Khan after Ahmad Khan had retreated. Further, it was their political manoeuvrings that determined the course of events in that year.[53]

In the manner of the Mughal army this heterogeneous force

of the reign of Muhammad Shah the provinces of Benaras, Jaunpur, Ghazipur and Chunar were conferred as jagirs on Nawab Murtaza Khan and he obtained a yearly revenue of 5 lakh rupees. In these sarkars Brahmin zamindars like Futteh Singh, the zamindar of Jakhini, Berisal Singh, and Dureao Singh, the zamindars of Majhowa, held the highest place amongst the risaldars. They paid their revenue regularly. In the initial years of Balwant Singh's reign, such risaldars and their kinsmen appear to have been accommodated in the Benaras army.

[51] Ibid., p. 24. In 1750 in a contest between Ali Quli Khan and Raja Balwant Singh, the latter's army was organized in the following way: its right wing was commanded by Babu Ramruch Singh, Lal Khan, and other Afghan risaldars; its left wing comprised of zamindari levies commanded by Hurdut Singh and Purundut Singh; in front were the infantry and camel guns and in the rear the luggage and camp followers. Balwant Singh, with some chosen troops, always stationed himself in the centre.

[52] Ibid., p. 27. Lal Khan, risaldar, and Rasul Khan, the bakshi, were sent by Balwant Singh with expensive gifts to Zaman Khan who had arrived at Allahabad and had besieged the fort. Balwant's strategy of sending Afghan envoys with gifts to Zaman Khan had the desired effect. Zaman Khan agreed to meet Balwant Singh and consequently the Benaras Raja was able to retain half his territories. The other half was given to Zaman Khan.

[53] Ibid., pp. 29, 45. For instance, risaldars Lal Khan, Rasul Khan, Mangli Khan, and others refused to fight Zaman Khan once they discovered that Ahmad Khan had left and there was not much point in continuing with the battle. Balwant Singh at first ordered his own kinsmen to continue the fight, but soon realized that this would make his Afghan followers his worst enemies. Consequently, he agreed to keep the Afghan risaldars in the forefront of the army, and on their advice the battle was soon given up. Once again in 1760, during Balwant Singh's fight with Muhammad Quli Khan, Subahdar of Allahabad, and his chief officer Zain-ul-abdin Khan, the Afghan risaldars took major decisions in matters related to the issue.

conciliated a variety of ethnic groups and also helped to keep in check various tremors of recalcitrance and protest in the Raj.[54] By giving a section of his Bhumihar kinsmen the privileged central position in the army, the Raja distanced them both from the Rajput lineages in the province and the Brahmins who emphasized their superiority over the Bhumihars. Initially, in the manner of the Mughal rulers, the Raja dealt only with military commandants and the élites. Consequently, unlike the Awadh Nawabi, the administrative institutions scattered in the sarkars and parganas were seldom engaged in direct peasant recruitment. For a similar reason, the state never attempted to create a separate 'disciplined' military world for the recruit as this responsibility devolved on the risaldars who were mostly clan leaders.[55]

After the death of Balwant Singh, his Chief Minister Ausan Singh made the officials and risaldars agree to the succession of Cheyt Singh to the position of raja. Cheyt Singh was Balwant Singh's son by a Rajput mother. His accession to the throne therefore caused immense resentment amongst the Bhumihar commandants and members of his officialdom. They objected to his descent through a Rajput mother and refused to dine with him because of the inferiority which they attributed to his origin.[56] It is interesting to note that from this, quite early, stage the Bhumihars were concerned about stressing their superior status to the Rajputs.

---

[54] Ibid., pp. 22–3. For instance, in 1749 Balwant Singh was able to seize Bhadoi fort from the zamindars only with the help of his Afghan risaldars.

[55] Ibid., p. 2. These were zamindars like Fateh Singh of Jhakini, Berisal Singh, and Duriao Singh who had been subordinated to the Benaras Raja. They served as risaldars in the Benaras army.

[56] Ibid., p. 10. The wife of Cheyt Singh's younger brother, Sujan Singh, had died. On the day of the funeral feast, when dinner was ready, Cheyt Singh summoned Ausan Singh, and ordered him to ascertain who would partake of the food and who were the people likely to refuse it. He wanted to be sure about this before he invited these people to dine, and thereby avoid the danger of being slighted by his kinsmen. All the babus (kinsmen of Balwant Singh) which included Jagdeo Singh and Pertabrudr Singh said they would dine only if Ausan Singh joined them. Ausan Singh made an excuse and refused to dine. Cheyt Singh posted guards outside the houses of Ajaib Singh and other Bhumihar zamindars who had refused his invitation. This was done to prevent ingress. On hearing of this Ausan Singh escaped to Allahabad from Ramgarh.

However, the consent and backing of the Afghan risaldars, who still commanded tremendous influence in the functioning of the Benaras zamindari, became an important factor in determining Cheyt Singh's succession.[57] This was possibly because of the close cultural links that had always existed between the Afghans and the Rajputs within the Mughal polity.[58] This not only reflected the position of power and influence of the Afghan risaldars but also revealed the key position the military enjoyed in the politics of the zamindari.

Throughout Cheyt Singh's reign the army continued to play a vital role in the transformation of the Benaras zamindari into a Hindu Raj. Having experienced the rather ambivalent attitude of his immediate Bhumihar kinsmen during his succession and the immense power of the Afghan risaldars, Cheyt Singh attempted to marginalize both these groups. He adopted a strategy whereby without completely dispensing with them, he broadened the peasant base of his army by extending his recruitment to the Bhumihar zamindaris of Benaras and north Bihar. There were perhaps as many as 100,000 Bhumihar Brahmin clansmen militarily supporting the Benaras Raja.[59] Moreover, there were as many as 200,000 Bhumihar clansmen which sustained the north Bihar zamindaris[60] and there is evidence, particularly at the time of Cheyt Singh's insurrection, showing the military support the Benaras Raja derived from them.[61] Cheyt Singh was related to many of these Bhumihar zamindaris by kinship and/or caste ties and he actively sought their assistance.[62] Fateh Sahi, the Raja of Huseypur, in the

---

[57] Ibid. p. 10.

[58] See M. Athar Ali, *The Mughal Nobility under Aurangzeb* (Bombay, 1986).

[59] Bayly, *Rulers, Townsmen and Bazaars*, p. 18. Bayly had calculated this figure from M.A. Sherring, *Hindu Tribes and Castes as Represented in Benaras* (London, 1872), p. 40, and projected it backwards in line with the assumed rate of growth for the general population. Bayly shows that the Benaras ruler had the capacity to mount an exhausting guerilla war against the Awadh camp, using his Bhumihar clan levies. This had forced the Nawab to withdraw his main force. Khairuddin Khan, *Balwantnamah*, pp. 19–33.

[60] S. G. Misra, *History of Bihar* (Delhi, 1970), pp. 19–51.

[61] L. No. 111, Charles Graeme, Collector of Saran, to Warren Hastings, Governor-General, 19 Aug. 1781, *Transactions*, p. 133.

[62] Ibid.

northwestern corner of Saran, not only received Benaras money but also letters from Cheyt Singh encouraging him to kill Europeans and their sipahis.[63] In fact, in the wake of the Benaras uprising a full-fledged alliance was formed between the north Bihar rajas of Huseypur and Majhauli, the Perrouna zamindar and the Narrowneys. Together they fielded an army of 8,000 troops and six cannon. Other Saran Bhumihar zamindars of Bagoura and Chainpur supported the rebel cause by creating obstacles for the Company's forces or by secretly assisting Fateh Sahi.[64]

To further broaden the social base of his army Cheyt Singh extended his peasant recruitment to the Rajput zamindaris of Benaras and Awadh as well. For in 1782, at the time of his insurrection, the Company officials were surprised at the military support he derived from the region and the contacts he had established in the Awadh zamindaris. Middleton, the British Resident in Lucknow, pointed out this popular enthusiasm for Cheyt Singh's army when he wrote to Hastings in 1781:

The whole country to the East side of the Ghagra was in arms and rebellion, his own troops deserting and the single companies scarcely able to join other detachments. The forts of Goruckpur, Bilma and Dumreeragunge taken from the amils by the zamindars. The town [Faizabad] has more the appearance of belonging to Cheyt Singh than the Vazir. Within these few days Sheikh Khan with nearly 1000 horse and foot has marched from here to Benaras (they were raised here).[65]

Middleton viewed with concern Cheyt Singh's popularity in Khairabad, Sylack and the country on the west side of the Ghagra between Faizabad and Khairabad. He of course reported the situation to be one of 'disorder' and noted that Cheyt Singh had sent money to Futteh Shah, Ghinu Roy, Ajeet Mull, Zalim Singh and several other Rajas so as to assist them financially in recruiting men for his army.[66]

[63] Charles Graeme, Collector of Saran, to Bengal Revenue Council, 15 Sept. 1781, BRC, Sept. 1–Oct. 23 1781, Sept. 28, No. 582.

[64] Charters Report cited in Yang, *Limited Raj*, p. 68.

[65] L. No. 6, N. Middleton, Resident at the court of Nawab, to Warren Hastings, Governor-General, 17 Sept. 1781, *Transactions*, p. 65.

[66] Ibid.

It is interesting to note that in this predominantly Hindu army not only did the local zamindars act as recruiting agents but some faujdars also extended their service to Cheyt Singh. The faujdar of Ballia, in the country of the Raja, denied grain to the Company's sipahis but also encouraged their desertion to the Raja's army.[67] Commenting on the role of the faujdar in the region Middleton wrote:

Faujdar of Tanda, Shumseer Khan a chelah of Behar Ali Khan...shot dead many of the Rajput Sepoys...Jawar Ali Khan in the Chauki of Faizabad asks every man who bears the appearance of a soldier why he goes not to Chait Singh for service.[68]

Even though this emphasis on broad-based peasant recruitment came from the internal political problems of the Benaras Raj, it may also have been prompted by a similar development taking place at this time in Awadh. B. S. Cohn has shown that the relationship between Cheyt Singh and Shuja was very delicately balanced on mutual benefits and Cheyt Singh never lost an opportunity to assert his independence.[69] So it is quite likely that the need to counter the peasant regiments of Awadh may have triggered off the organizing of similar peasant regiments in the Benaras Raj as well. A reliance on a standing army of infantry and artillery men which was assisted by zamindari levies initiated a process of direct recruitment by the Raja. This was very similar to what Shuja had attempted in Awadh. But whereas Shuja, in the absence of religious or kinship connections in the countryside, used the administrative institutions of the faujdar and amil to carry on his recruitment, Cheyt Singh utilized his clan and religious affiliations in the countryside to recruit his peasant army. As we have seen he utilized the services of his zamindars for this purpose and only on rare occasions, like at the time of his insurrection in 1781, did the faujdars involve themselves in recruiting.

In eastern Awadh and north Bihar's predominantly Rajput and

---

[67] Letter No. 4B, Affidavit of Hindu Singh, Adjutant of Buxar, 9 Dec. 1781, *Transactions*, p. 183.

[68] Ibid. p. 64.

[69] B. S. Cohn, 'Political system in eighteenth century India: the Benaras region', in Cohn, *An Anthropologist among the Historians*, p. 489.

Bhumihar zamindaris, Cheyt Singh's popular appeal arose from a variety of sources. It was true that in the war-torn conditions of the late eighteenth century the army continued to provide an avenue for furthering military and political ambitions. Cheyt Singh's army certainly provided lucrative employment; but it had the additional advantage of providing prestige. Unlike the Mughal emperors or the Nawab of Awadh, the Benaras Raja was a high-caste Hindu who had marginalized the Muslim risaldars and projected the image of a Hindu army. Cheyt Singh's army was a much larger force than the one under Balwant Singh. Before the military expansion which accompanied Cheyt Singh's insurrection against the Company, the established number of standing troops in the army was 7,690. This included 700 select troops or bodyguards both horse and foot, 1,150 sipahis, 1,800 matchlockmen, a large number of armed levies of some important zamindars, and only 1,700 Afghan cavalrymen.[70] During Cheyt Singh's insurrection the strength of the army suddenly increased to 22,190 troops. Even in this brief and spontaneous military expansion the army continued to maintain its Hindu image. In 1782, out of the 22,190 troops in the service of Cheyt Singh, the number of Afghans remained unchanged at 1,700. The rest were Hindu recruits from the various Rajput lineages and Bhumihar zamindaris of the region.[71]

Indeed the recruiting of Cheyt Singh's army seems to have been one aspect of the regime's increasing projection of itself as a Hindu Raj. For instance, the use of threats of self injury and *kurh* by Brahmins to negotiate terms on which revenue was collected, and to dispute land rights among themselves, was allowed to go on in the parganas of Bhadoi, Kantit, Ballia and Kharid. When Jonathan Duncan became Resident of Benaras he noticed that Brahmins in the city had received many forms of preferential status in law. This appeared to have been of recent origin.[72]

---

[70] *Transactions*, p. 43. The following three zamindars had the largest levies: Bullam Das: 300 cavalry, 500 infantry, total 800; Sujan Singh cavalry and infantry—500 sepoys with two guns and 340 artillery men, total 840; Muniar Singh, 700, cavalry and infantry.

[71] Ibid. p. 44.

[72] Singha, 'A despotism of law', p. 100. J. Duncan, the British Resident in Benaras, was

It also appears that in this period the practice of burning corpses at Harish Chandra *ghat* became common to high-caste Hindus. Finally, it was in these years that a growing involvement of the Benaras Raja with the Ram tradition is noticeable. P. Lutgendorf argues that these overtly Hindu credentials, particularly the royal patronage of Ramlila, reflected among other things the Raja's need to cultivate an explicitly Hindu symbol of royal legitimacy and achieve ideological as well as political independence from the Nawab of Awadh.[73] In 1782, after Cheyt Singh's insurrection had been crushed, the Company disbanded his army, puting a check on the increasing 'Hinduization' of the Benaras *zamindari*. But amongst the populace the significance of Cheyt Singh as the Hindu Raja who resisted the increasing encroachments of the East India Company, must have gained momentum when, a decade later, Duncan began to take steps to control social customs like infanticide and sati, practised by Rajputs living in the Benaras Raj.[74]

---

of the view that this practice of Brahmins killing or wounding themselves went back to the earliest times, as far as memory reaches. However, Singha shows that the earliest reference to an incident of this kind in Duncan's records dates to the reign of Balwant Singh. Allaud, a Brahmin pattidar of pargana Bhadohi, who Duncan examined in one such case, referred to an incident in Raja Balwant Singh's time in which two females of his family had taken poison and died when the amil had confined a relative for arrears of revenue. There are more incidents recounted for the reign of Cheyt Singh; see enclosure in letter from Benaras resident 26 April 1789, P/51/38, 17 June 1789, IOL.

[73] P. Lutgendorf, 'Ram's story in Shiva's city: public arenas and private patronage', in Sandria B. Freitag (ed.), *Culture and Power in Banaras: Community, Performance and Environment, 1800–1980* (Berkeley, 1989), p. 41. Lutgendorf argues that the Rajas of Benaras turned to Ram in trying to revive a Vaishnav ideal of divine worship, and a harmonious but hierarchical social order. The myth of Ram had retained a strong martial, imperial, and socio-political dimension. This was expressed most clearly in the vision of Ramraj, or the golden age of Ram's universal rule, and in the hero's role as an exemplar of *maryada*. Moreover, the Ram tradition's emphasis on social and political hierarchy and on the deferential behaviour of subjects could serve as chastening examples to the Raja's rebellious zamindars. See also S. B. Freitag, 'State and community: symbolic popular protest in Banaras's public arenas', ibid., p. 210. Freitag argues that this royal patronage of the Ramlila served other significant political ends as well. She shows that the elaboration of this public observance reinforced the Benaras Raja's relations with the lower classes of Benaras, frequently Muslim, through the emphasis on the Maharaja as the ruler of all.

[74] D. Kopf, *British Orientalism and the Bengal Renaissance, the Dynamics of Indian Modernization 1773–1835* (Princeton, 1969), p. 30.

Cheyt Singh's military experiment had a parallel in Hastings' rule, for in 1782 the Company, which had been drawing recruits from the same social groups for some years, is found emphasizing their 'Hindu status'. We now turn to the tradition of Company recruiting in the Bengal Presidency, which arose at the same time as, and later merged with, the north Indian peasant armies.

ROBERT CLIVE: RECRUITING THE BENGAL ARMY

In its early years in India, the Company did its utmost to avoid becoming embroiled in the affairs of the various Indian potentates from whom it had obtained concessions to trade. But avoiding a situation of conflict was easier said than done. The hinterland was seldom at peace. Political instability consequent on the decline of the Mughal centre and perceived threats from other European powers encouraged the Company to take steps to defend its settlements against an attack. To begin with, in its early days, this protection was largely provided by European soldiers and it was the struggle between the British and the French for the control of south India that compelled the Company to revise its military policy. In the wars of 1747, the Company found itself with an insufficient number of troops to oppose the French. It had to rely on the arrival of the British fleet with its reinforcements to save itself.

It was then that the need for a regular army on a permanent footing was realized. Major Stringer Lawrence who arrived with the British fleet in 1747 was the first to begin recruiting and organizing native regiments on the European model. Robert Clive was one of his most able assistants. When Clive arrived in Bengal in 1757 after the defeat of Nawab Siraj-ud-daulah, he emulated the example of Lawrence. In January 1757, he raised a battalion of 300–400 carefully selected sipahis, clothed them in the manner of the British army and appointed a British officer to instruct and command them.[75] This, the earliest Bengal Native Regiment, was known for many years as the Lal Paltan. Later it came to

[75] Captain A. Broome, *History of the Rise and Progress of the Bengal Army* (Calcutta, 1851), p. 92.

be called by the name of Galliez ki Paltan because it was commanded by Captain Primrose Galliez for many years.

The sipahis of the Lal Paltan were recruited in keeping with the traditions in eighteenth-century Britain which established certain criteria for military service. At this time, the ideal recruit in the British army was a country soldier recruited from the rural areas of Ireland or Scotland. There were important political and social reasons behind this preference. Jonh Prebble's work shows that in the eighteenth century military service was a means to placate the 'turbulent' highlanders.[76] By the 1830s, the Scots were found to be the best disciplined soldiers. They lived with their fellow soldiers, many of whom were their clansmen, within the regiment and the likelihood of misconduct being reported home kept a check on their behaviour.[77] Irish and English yeomen were also recruited because there was thought to be excess population in the countryside while the towns were in need of skilled labour.

The army officials viewed with concern any change in the recruiting pattern of the British army. In the mid-nineteenth century, Sir William Butler, Lieutenant-General in the British Army, anticipated a widespread change in the recruiting pattern following the increased spate of industrialization in the country. Regretting the change he observed in the 'old military order', Butler wrote:

Prior to the Crimean War...strong men were easily obtained and no soldiers equalled ours in strength, courage and endurance. That day is gone...men are now taken who would have been rejected with scorn a few years ago. We get recruits no longer from the rural districts, but from the slums of the big cities....The old soldiers were men of well-chiselled features...all I know now is that they are gone as the buffalo is gone from the prairies.[78]

In the early nineteenth century, as the urban poor grew in numbers, many more military officers expressed similar apprehensions. They feared that the social base of the British army would now switch

[76] John Prebble, *Mutiny: Highland Regiments in Revolt, 1743–1804* (Harmondsworth, 1977), pp. 97–9.

[77] H. Strachan, *Wellington's Legacy: the Reform of the British Army, 1830–54* (Manchester, 1984) p. 51.

[78] W. Butler, *An Autobiography* (London, 1911), pp. 13–20.

to the slums. The army viewed this with alarm as it was commonly believed that men from the rural areas were accustomed to bearing the vagaries of weather and, being more inured to physical fatigue, they were best suited for warfare.[79]

The British army's definite preference for agricultural labourers, highlanders, and men from the countryside, had a bearing on recruiting patterns in India. The Company officials were similarly of the view that the agricultural classes of India made the best soldiers. But very early they had begun to differentiate between India's agrarian zones. In 1750 Robert Orme had already marked out the 'martial' races of the subcontinent according to their climatic environment and dietary habits. According to his theory the population of India living in the wheat-producing zones was better built and hence more 'martial' than the short statured people of the rice-producing zones. Orme perceived the Indian *varna* system as a rigid hierarchy which served to protect what climate had already imparted or determined.[80] In practice this meant that recruitment was guided by two main considerations: the Company would only consider peasants with a well-built physique and an average height of 5 feet 7 inches; secondly, at this stage, at least, it confined recruitment to the Company's territories and established direct contact with the recruiting villages in wheat-growing areas.[81]

One might have assumed that the sipahis within easy reach of the Company were the former members of the Nawab of Bengal's army. But these did not conform to the Company's image of a 'good soldier'. The cavalry was the leading wing of

[79] Strachan, *Wellington's Legacy*, p. 53. However, the fears of the military officials were unfounded. As pay in the army and conditions of service did not conform to the expections of the better paid operatives in the civilian sector, military service continued to attract mainly agricultural labourers, and did not become very popular in the towns. Most of the recruits continued to be men from the rural areas of Ireland and Scotland.

[80] J. P. Guha (ed.), R. Orme, *Historical Fragments of the Mogul Empire, of the Morattoes, & of the English Concern in Indostan from the year MDCLIX* (London, 1782; reprint New Delhi, 1974), p. 303.

[81] Major Stainforth to R. Kyd, Sec. to Gov.–Gen.–in–Council, 9 March 1779, BMC, Consult. 17 March 1779, P/18/47, IOL. He sent him a descriptive roll of recruits stationed at Berhanpur, prepared by Colonel James Morgan who was posted in Berhanpur. Of the 37 recruits 21 were found under standard height, being less than 5' 7". Nine of them were under 5'6", and were therefore not eligible for the service at all.

the Nawab's army and was composed of urban-based Afghan and Pathan risaldars. These were supplemented by a force of about 10,000 Bengal musketeers who were stationed in different parts of the province. In the late eighteenth century, Gholam Hussein, a historian of Bengal, regretted the Company's reluctance to enlist the soldiers of the Nawab's army. He wrote:

On the other hand, out of the vast multitude of people called musqueteers, whose numbers were heretofore counted by ten thousand in these provinces, only a small number of them have obtained a livelihood by enlisting as Talingas in the English service and yet it was these two provinces that fed and paid regularly forty or fifty thousand horse.[82]

It is possible that political considerations also lay behind the decision to dispense with the predominantly Muslim soldiers associated with the former regime. The merchants and artisans, who had benefited from the high-spending cavalry army of the Nawab, were adversely affected when the Company distanced itself from former troopers. Gholam Hussein noted with concern:

Now matters go otherwise. Service for troopers and cavalry there is none at all...were the English to take into their service some thousands of that cavalry once commanded by such renowned officers as Shah-Muezeddin Qhan and Ahmed Qhan and the like, there is no doubt but these men would render them important services in their wars against the cavalry of either the Marhattas or the Sykes, especially if care was taken to attach them to the service and to excite their zeal and emulation.[83]

Immediately after 1757, not finding the Nawab of Bengal's army very useful, the Company began recruiting in the rural areas of the Bengal province. Burhanpur and Dinapur became the two important recruiting centres. However, even here the Company's recruiting parties had limited success, for most of the agricultural classes available were deemed to be undersized. This became a cause of grave concern for the commanding officers. Brigadier

[82] Gholam Hussein Khan, *The Seir Mutaqherin or Review of Modern Times, Being an History of India from Year 1118th year 1194 of the Hedjrah* (3 vols., reprint Lahore, Pakistan, 1975), III, p. 203.

[83] Ibid., p. 204; for the sorry plight of the Muslim military gentry in the Bengal Nawabi see P. J. Marshall, 'Bengal, The British Bridgehead: Eastern India, 1740–1828', in *The New Cambridge History of India* (Cambridge, 1987), pp. 138–9.

General G. Stibbert who was sent to these regions for inspection wrote to Warren Hastings:

The difficulty of obtaining recruits of the right size at this place has induced the officers commanding those battalions to enlist some men under the size that was fixed as the standard.[84]

WARREN HASTINGS AND THE BENGAL ARMY

The difficulty of obtaining the requisite recruits in Bengal led to an extension of the recruitment base westward into the wheat-growing areas of north India. This shift was accompanied by an important development. Not only did the Company look for peasant recruits in the region but it preferred high-caste peasant recruits. There were two main reasons for this—the first had to do with the Company's political strategy. The Company now recruited from areas outside its territory. It was thought that the Company should rely on the traditional high-caste warriors for loyalty and for the control they would be able to exercise over their peasant recruits. But this shift was also due to the influence of Warren Hastings' own ideas about preserving Indian caste roles in the military and civilian institutions the Company was putting in place in north India. Moreover, Hastings and his subordinates had the model of Cheyt Singh and Shuja's Hindu peasant force before them. In Benaras as well as in Awadh, the nature of military recruitment had played a significant role in consolidating the power of the regional rulers.

Hastings was critical of the indisciplined state of the Awadh and the Benaras armies. Still he was of the view that the political expansion of the Company should take place without disturbing the established institutions of the Indian polities. Until 1774, the Company could exercise only a financial pressure on the regional states. The treaty of 1773[85] and the financial pressure exercised

[84] Brigadier General G. Stibbert to Warren Hastings, Gov.-Gen.-in-Council in the Mil. Dept., 26 Oct. 1778, Mil. Dept. Procds., Jan.–June, Consult. FW 25 Feb. 1779, NAI.

[85] Barnett, *North India*, p. 91. According to this treaty Kara and Allahabad were given to Shuja on condition that the Company would be paid 50 lakh rupees in the Awadh currency. The treaty also engaged the Nawab to pay sicca Rs 2,10,000 monthly for the brigade of Company's troops that were stationed in Awadh or Allahabad for his use.

on Cheyt Singh[86] in 1778 drained a considerable amount of revenue from the region. But these Indian states continued to resist the military encroachments of the Company and did not allow it to establish recruiting centres within their territory. Not only did the Company encounter fierce resistance from Shuja to its policies of political influence and military recruitment, but until his death in 1774, Shuja continued to resist any interference with his military.[87] Cheyt Singh showed a similar resistance to financing the Company's regiments from the revenues of Benaras until 1775 when Awadh transferred the sovereignty of the Benaras Raj to the Company. For instance, the fifty troopers that he supplied to Hastings in 1773 for the Governor-General's bodyguard consisted largely of Muslim risaldars rather than peasant recruits.[88]

It was with the accession of Asaf-ud-daula and the growing influence of British Residents at the Awadh court that the Company obtained an opportunity to intervene more directly both in Awadh and in Benaras. Along with this the Company began to build up an interest in Awadh's military affairs. In 1775, the Nawab agreed to the reduction of Awadh's regiments, the deputation of British officers to his remaining regiments, and the stationing of a permanent contingent of Company troops at Faizabad, Lucknow, and Chunar which was to be maintained by the revenue of the Nawabi.[89] In the same year the grant of the sovereignty

---

[86] *Transactions*, p. 3. In July 1778, on the first intelligence of the war with France, the Company council resolved that Raja Cheyt Singh would be required to contribute an extraordinary subsidy to meet the expenses which this new exigency had imposed on the Company. The sum was limited to 5 lakh rupees for the current year. When the Raja evaded this demand, two battalions of Company sipahis were quartered in the neighbourhood of Ramnagar, and their pay was charged to his account until the whole payment was completed.

[87] Barnett, *North India*, p. 97. According to Barnett the treaty of 1773 placed Awadh within the formal command area of the Bengal Army but by no means implied control over all military activities within its borders.

[88] Lt. V. C. P. Hodson, *Historical Records of the Governor-General's Bodyguard* (Calcutta, 1910) pp. 1, 20.

[89] Barnett, *North India*, pp. 144–5. The treaty of Benaras which was signed in 1775 between Asaf-ud-daula and the Company, increased the subsidy of the Company's brigade in Awadh to Rs 31,20,000 per year. When a substantial portion of Asaf's army was placed under British officers their pay was placed, on the Company's account, at an

of Benaras by Asaf-ud-daula to the Company initiated a similar intervention in the affairs of Benaras.[90] The political weakening of the north Indian states and the swelling numbers of their un-employed military men was revealed by the success of the Company's new recruiting centres in this region. Permanent recruitment centres were established in Budgepur, Patna, Buxar in Bihar, and Jaunpur and Ghazipur in Benaras. Pratapgarh and Azamgarh in the Rajput zamindaris of eastern Awadh were also developed as important recruiting bases. Drafts of recruits from the zamindaris of Awadh, Benaras, and Bihar were sent through these centres to Bengal or wherever the need arose.[91] The difficulty experienced in the continuous movement of troops from these stations to fill drafts in Bengal was overcome with the establishment in 1779 of a permanent co-ordinating centre for such recruits at Buxar.[92] As the recruitment centres proliferated, the Company moved towards political stability. This paved the way for its eventual rise to political supremacy in the region.

In 1775, the Company introduced the *tankhah jagir* system in Awadh. The Company's military officers were granted jagirs in the zamindaris of Awadh instead of being paid salaries in cash for maintaining their contingents. Their new interest in the efficient collection of revenue on their jagirs brought them in direct contact with Asaf-ud-daula's amils. The amil's own contingent was reduced or disbanded and he functioned with the assistance of Company troops. The 'de-militarization' of the amil not only eroded his

annual charge that varied between Rs 13,00,000 and Rs 16,87,333. Along with this was the unpaid balance of Rs 41,26,971 charged to Asaf, and an army donation of 10 lakh rupees.

[90] *Transactions*, p. 10. There was pressure on Cheyt Singh to make an annual grant of 5 lakh rupees to the Company. This was to meet the cost of the French wars. The Company also forced him to agree to the financing of two of its regiments.

[91] Brigadier General G. Stibbert to W. Hastings, Governor-General, 10 Feb. 1779. The recruits available to the Company in Bengal did not conform to its military standards. This forced the Company to send recruitment officers as far west as Benaras. One such officer, Captain Lane, procured 500–600 good recruits from the Benaras region. He sent them to Burhanpur and Danapur. Here, the recruits were trained before being sent for duty elsewhere.

[92] Brigadier General G. Stibbert to W. Hastings, Governor-General, 10 Feb. 1779, Mil. Deptt. Procd. Jan.–June 1779, Consult. FW, 6 March 1779, NAI.

power but also unleashed scores of armed men across the countryside. Ironically, this earned the Nawabi the charge of maladministration and justified further intervention in the affairs of · Awadh.

However, the power of the amils was not totally eroded, and the Company continued to use their influence in the countryside to further its own interests. In some areas of Awadh, strong amils like Alam Ali Khan resisted the Company's encroachments and continued to support their own military contingents until the early nineteenth century. The Company appears to have treated them as 'independent jagirdars' and continued to function through them so long as they paid revenue regularly to the Awadh treasury.[93] The Company's cautious policy towards the amils was due to the influence of British Residents in Awadh like John Bristow, who were concerned about the more long-term effects of the slump in the status of the amil. In 1777 Bristow wrote to the government:

So considerable an office of Government as an Amil, whose character should be held up to the people in the most respectable light, to be thus disgraced must not only effect the Vizir's authority but his revenue, and is so prejudicial that it will be impossible for the Government to subsist long upon this plan.[94]

Indeed, Bristow's cautious approach towards the amil contributed to the failure of the tankhah jagir system to remit sufficient amounts of revenue to meet the Company's requirements. In 1775, Bristow

[93] L. No. 4, Abstract of vazir's reply to queries by Colonel J. Collins, 7 April 1807, BPS, Consult. 30 April 1807, P/BEN/SEC/201, IOL.

[94] Report of J. Bristow, Resident in Lucknow, 17 Feb. 1777, BSC, Consult. 13 Jan.-13 May 1777, P/A/40, The Company did not want to dispense with the office of amil altogether for it wanted to utilize the amil's influence in its aim of political expansion. However, the Company did wish to erode the basis of his power and independence so as to make the amil militarily dependent on it. The Company, at least in some areas of Awadh, achieved its objective. For instance, in 1815, Richard Strachey, the Resident at Lucknow, ordered a contingent of troops for the assistance of the amil Ehsanullah in the district of Salon. The amil's task was to identify the recalcitrant zamindars who were then approached directly by the Company. Similar arrangements were made by the amils of Sultanpur and Pratapgarh as well; see also L. No. 17, R. Strachey, Resident in Lucknow, to Captain Engleshot, Ist Regiment Native Infantry, 10 Jan. 1816, IOL, MSS Eur. D 514/3/L80/951, Strachey Papers.

had procured assignments on Rohilkhand and the Doab. But a year later Middleton, who succeeded Bristow as the British Resident in Awadh, discovered that one-fourth of this was unpaid and severe warnings to the amils were ineffective.[95] However, by the 1780s, the Company had considerably weakened its main competitors—Benaras and Awadh—in recruiting infantry regiments in north India. What used to be Shuja's field of recruitment now became the Company's recruiting ground. In the 1830s, Donald Butter, a Company surgeon posted in Awadh, called it 'the nursery for the armies of British India'[96]

But more important, the Company's service became popular in the Awadh-Benaras region because of the improved rewards and security it offered to its soldiers. A candidate before enlistment as a recruit received from the Company an allowance of only two annas per day, but after enlisting, his pay and allowances increased to seven rupees per month.[97] The Company army offered better terms than those offered by other professions in the country,[98] though the actual salaries might not have been higher than those of the Indian states. Shuja and Cheyt Singh paid their men at comparable rates and the sipahis in Ranjit Singh's army received between seven and eight-and-a-half rupees a month.[99] But what made the Company's service really sought after was the regular payment of wages, the pension benefits and other rewards enjoyed by its sipahis. In the armies of the Indian states, the soldiers' regular complaint was that their salaries were always in

[95] Barnett, *North India*, p. 151.

[96] D. Butter, *Outlines of the Topography and Statistics of the Southern Districts of Oudh* (Calcutta, 1839), (ed.) Safi Ahmad as *Topography and Statistics of Southern Districts of Oudh* (reprint Delhi, 1982), p. 156.

[97] A. Barat, *Bengal Native Infantry: Its Organization and Discipline 1796–1852* (Calcutta, 1962), p. 130.

[98] Ibid., p. 138. Barat shows that in the first quarter of the 19th century ordinary coolies in the district did not get more than 3 pice and masons and carpenters did not earn more than 2 annas a day. A field labourer in Bareli earned 2–6 rupees per month. The earnings of a carpenter in the same district varied between 5 and 10 rupees and that of blacksmiths between 5 and 20 rupees. The free male domestics in Shahabad district were usually allowed 8–16 annas a month in addition to their food and clothes. In Arrah their wages often rose to 2 rupees a month.

[99] N. K. Sinha, *Ranjit Singh* (Calcutta, 1933), p. 207.

arrears.[100] In comparison, the Company soldiers were better off because they had the advantage of being regularly paid every month. Moreover, the Company sipahis were at times granted extra allowances either in cash or in kind or both. As they were not recruited for general service, special volunteer corps were raised from amongst them whenever required, to proceed on a sea voyage, and they received an additional allowance. Besides, whenever they were sent outside the Bengal Presidency they could secure a family certificate by which a certain portion of their salary was paid to their family every month.[101] Apart from this the Company's pension benefits were novel and attractive to the soldier, promising him and his family a great deal of security after he left the service. Every soldier who had served for a minimum of twenty years was eligible to receive a cash pension at the rate of three rupees per month. But a jagir system of pensions was also in vogue by which grants of land were made to disabled sipahis.[102] Finally, the Company instituted a system of honours and rewards for its soldiers for meritorious service. Medals were awarded to commemorate participation in important battles. Some years later the Company also instituted special distinctions for the army.[103]

Along with these attractive material benefits, the Company army made an appeal to the recruit's religious sensitivity as well. Hastings' ideas about preserving high-caste roles in the army resulted in confining recruitment only to the high-caste peasants. In one of his essays on the encouragement and promotion of a knowledge of the sciences among the inhabitants of the British territories in India, Hastings expressed these views quite directly:

If unhappily any measures should be pursued to shake the religious faith

[100] For the Mughal armies see W. Irvine, *Army of the Indian Mughals* (London, 1930), p. 13; for the Awadh army see Ghani, *Tarikh-i-Awadh*, III, pp. 41–4; for the Maratha army see S. Sen, *The Military System of the Marathas* (Calcutta, 1958), p. 57; for the army of Ranjit Singh see Sinha, *Ranjit Singh*, p. 208.

[101] Barat, *Bengal Infantry*, p. 140.

[102] Ibid., p. 143. For details of the Company's pension benefits see below, chapter 3.

[103] Ibid., pp. 145–7. In 1813 the Company created the rank of Subahdar Major. Under the regulations of 1796, a native officer could only reach the rank of a subahdar.

of the Hindoos and break up these political distinctions and gradations in society we call caste and the whole male population of India be left free to follow any occupation they like, *even that of a soldier* [emphasis mine] which in the present state of things can be exercised but by a very small proportion of the whole, there is danger, that they will soon be united and embodied as an armed nation after the example of the Sikhs and become too formidable for their rulers.[104]

This policy of Hastings created a 'high caste' monopoly in the Bengal army. The high-caste overtones of the army further suited the political interests of the Company for it provided the requisite legitimacy to Company rule. Further, the Company's sedulous attempts to encourage a high-caste ethic within the army and the great care taken not to compromise caste principles, appears also to have made military service attractive in the eastern Uttar Pradesh and Bhojpur regions. Hastings and his subordinates began to promote the high-caste religious, dietary, and travel preferences which reflected the caste status of the sipahis. In 1779, when men and material from Bengal had to be moved to Bombay to fight the first Maratha war, Hastings decided that the only effective way was to send reinforcements overland.[105] This was because he believed that crossing the sea was considered offensive to the religious feelings of the Bengal sipahis. In the 1789 expedition to Fort Marlborough at Bencoolem on the north-west coast of Sumatra, sipahi volunteers of the 1st, 30th, and 32nd Sipahi Battalion themselves supervised the filling of their water casks. They were also asked to state every sort of article they wished for their diet during the voyage. The government provided the food items of their liking for this journey.[106] Finally, in this period the sipahis, at their request, were allowed to live in huts rather than in barracks in the manner of the European infantrymen,[107] so making it easier for them to maintain a strict

---

[104] Add. 29234, Warren Hastings, Copies of essays etc., Warren Hastings Papers, BM.

[105] Michael Edwardes, *Warren Hastings: King of the Nabobs* (London, 1976), p. 102.

[106] J. Williams, *An Historical Account of the Rise and Progress of the Bengal Infantry from its Formation in 1757 to 1796* (London, 1817), p. 90.

[107] Barat, *Bengal Infantry*, p. 43.

caste practice. All these factors made the Company a highly attractive employer.

CORNWALLIS AND THE SYSTEMATIZATION OF THE SERVICE

Cornwallis continued with Hastings' policy of encouraging a high-caste ethic in the army. In 1789, Cornwallis wrote to the Deputy Governor and Council at Fort Marlborough where he had despatched four companies of native troops:

> We cannot too forcibly impress on you the important light in which we view an attention to objects connected with the means of indulging these religious prejudices, and being persuaded that the most desirable good consequence would result from this detachment returning perfectly satisfied with their treatment. We recommend you to pay particular attention to the suggestion of Captain Hamilton and Lieutenant Cullock on the points. For their intercourse with different castes composing the native troops will enable them to point out in what instances an attention to the prejudices of the men becomes necessary.[108]

In the same year Cornwallis once again showed a similar concern when he wrote to Robert Hamilton, the officer commanding the troops at the Residency of Fort Marlborough:

> The Government of Bengal has studied every means to render this situation on board ship comfortable with a view to lessen and if possible to remove those prejudices which Hindus of every description entertain against going to sea. Due attention to these prejudices will be no less necessary on shore and whenever the service for which they are destined will admit of their returning to Bengal.[109]

The continuation of Hastings' policy of creating a separate religious cultural tradition within the army often created a dilemma for Cornwallis because it conflicted with his drives towards anglicization. This first became evident in 1788 when Cornwallis wrote to the Bishop of Salisbury on the subject of the spread of English education and Christian religion in India. The Bishop, encouraged

---

[108] Cornwallis to Deputy Governor and Council at Fort Marlbro, day and month not cited, 1789, London Public Records Office (PRO) Cornwallis Papers, PRO/ 30/11/184.

[109] Ibid.

by the success of the Portuguese missionaries on the Coromandel coast, had argued forcibly for the propagation of Christianity in north India as well:

It is likewise a matter for serious consideration how far the impudence or intemperate zeal of one teacher might endanger a Government which owes its principal support to a native army composed of men of high caste whose fidelity and affections we have hitherto secured by an unremitted attention not to offend their religious scruples and superstition.[110]

Hastings' military experiment was so successful in leading the Company towards political stability that the differences between Hastings' 'orientalism' and Cornwallis' 'anglicizing' intentions seem to have been temporarily ignored.

Cornwallis continued with Hastings' military policy and further systematized the recruiting procedure so as to make the recruiting officers accountable for the men they enlisted. In practice this meant that recruiting parties either camped in villages or in the Company's military stations and the people of the surrounding areas approached them directly. From now on, detailed records were required to be maintained making the recruiting officer accountable for the men he enlisted. An alternative method of recruitment was to encourage potential recruits who were friends or relatives of the serving sipahis and accompanied them from their villages so that they could be enlisted in the same regiments.

In the earlier phase of the Company's recruitment the first system was more popular. The commanding officer of a regiment recruited from the villages where his regiment was stationed. Sometimes when sufficient recruits of the desired type were not available in the region, he sent out recruiting parties to the neighbouring areas. Each recruiting party comprised an European officer, a native officer, and a doctor. The people who visited this makeshift recruiting camp were thoroughly examined by the doctor and their

---

[110] Cornwallis to Bishop of Salisbury, 1788, London Public Records Office (PRO) Cornwallis Papers, PRO/30/11/187. Later in Wellesley and Bentinck's period this was to become a major issue in the debates on the abolition of sati. See IOLR, MSS. Eur. E. 424, Typescript Copies of Documents omitted from correspondence of Bentinck by C. H. Philip.

age and social background were noted down by the commanding officer. Recruits who were less than 5 feet, 6 inches, or not in the age group of sixteen to thirty years, were considered ineligible.[111] Once declared physically fit the Articles of War were read out to the recruits and they took an oath in their native language, pledging their loyalty to the regiment. For one month the recruits were kept under observation and in this period they were not given any batta or salary except a small subsistence allowance of two annas per day. For this the recruiting officer was sanctioned a sum of Rs 80 which was adjusted every three months.[112]

After the initial month was over, the recruits found eligible for permanent enlistment were shifted to the military stations in the Presidency for training and discipline. Alongside creating a definite procedure for recruiting, Cornwallis also curtailed the freedom enjoyed by the sipahis when they went to their villages on furlough. Here, once again, Company officers were directed to maintain records of the family the sipahi lived with and to keep track of his movements outside the cantonment. For instance, the adjutant or clerk of the regiment maintained a review roll of each recruit from the information he received from the Commanding Officer.[113] This must have been a remarkably large set of records that the early colonial state possessed, comparable with their substantially detailed revenue records.[114]

By the early nineteenth century the Company had begun to show interest in the second system of recruitment as well. It came to prefer this system because the serving sipahi acted as the guarantor of the respectable antecedents and future loyalty of the sipahi recruit of the army.[115] Collectively, the two methods

[111] Minutes of Council in the Military Department of 8 Aug. 1796, BMC, Consult., FW 8 Aug. 1796, P/19/19, IOL.

[112] Ibid.

[113] Ibid.

[114] These records have not been located yet by historians interested in the subject. They presumably stayed with each regiment and could have been destroyed during the 1857 Mutiny.

[115] J. Lunt (ed.), *From Sepoy to Subedar: Being the Life and Adventures of Subedar Sita Ram, a native officer of the Bengal army, written and related by himself* (reprint Hong Kong, 1970), pp. 13–15.

of recruitment enabled the Company to enlist a large standing army. Cornwallis' measures made the Company's service more efficient and further increased the security it offered to its sipahis. Throughout the late eighteenth and early nineteenth century the Company's service continued to attract a large number of people in the north Indian countryside. Cornwallis commented on this popularity in his papers:

The army could raise an almost unlimited number of men of the best quality for native soldiers in a very short period from the populous provinces in that quarter of the Company's dominions.[116]

THE HIGH-CASTE BASE OF THE ARMY

The recruiting practice introduced by Hastings appears to have aroused an enthusiastic response from the predominantly Rajput and Brahmin zamindaris of Benaras as well as the predominantly Hindu peasant populations of Pratapgarh, Rae Bareli, Unnao, Sultanpur, Salon, Faizabad, Bahraich and Gorakhpur. The Company's service improved the recruit's economic and social position as well as safeguarded their high-caste status. In the 1840s, William Sleeman, on his travels through Awadh, noted that by 1825 Baiswara, in southern Awadh, had supplied approximately 30,000 men to the Company's army,[117] and every village had at least a member in the Company's service.[118] Here, the Company inherited the tension-ridden relationship that had existed between the Bais Rajputs and the Awadh Nawabi in the early decades of the eighteenth century.[119] It appears that military service was

[116] Marquis Cornwallis to Henry Dundas on the best mode of modelling the army in India, 1788, London, Public Records Office (PRO), Cornwallis Papers, PRO/30/11/211. Cornwallis justified the retrenchment policy by pointing to the continuing popularity of the military service.

[117] W. Sleeman, *A Journey through the Kingdom of Oude in 1849–50* (2 vols., London, 1858), I, p. 170.

[118] W. Sleeman, *Rambles and Recollections of an Indian Official* (ed.) V. Smith (reprint Karachi, 1973), p. 244.

[119] Alam, *Crisis of Empire*, pp. 94–5, 212–17. Alam has shown that since the early reign of Aurangzeb the zamindars of Baiswara had constantly threatened imperial power in Awadh. A number of villages and mahals in the district, such as Bijnaur, Ranbirpur,

used to ease out these tensions and conciliate the powerful Bais zamindaris.[120] Later in the nineteenth century, S. H. Fremantle, the settlement officer of Rae Bareli district, attributed the good and improved state of cultivation in the Brahmin tenures to the extra investments in the area from the remittances and pensions of sipahis formally recruited from the district.[121] Further, in the Pratapgarh district of Awadh, which had a large Brahmin and Sombansi Rajput population, the Company's service became very popular amongst the rural high caste. The preserving of high-caste customs, dietary, and travel preferences in the army strengthened the high ritual status of the Brahmin cultivators whereas the Rajput castes used the military service to emulate and compete with their richer clansmen in the zamindaris. In the nineteenth century, J. Sandars, the settlement officer of the Pratapgarh district, attributed the flourishing state of cultivation on the lands cultivated by Brahmins to the investment of the sipahi pensioners living there.[122]

Harsha, Unao, Deori, Balaimau, Sadauli, Parinda, Jhalotar and Dondia Khera were disturbed by zamindar revolts at the time of Aurangzeb. By the time of Farrukh Siyar, Mardan Singh, the zamindar of Jagatpur, had assumed leadership of the Bais. In 1714 under the leadership of Mardan Singh, and in 1715 under the joint leadership of Mardan Singh and Amar Singh, they demonstrated their strength against the Mughals in Jagatpur, Bhika and Shankarpur. Besides this collective defiance of the Bais there were some instances of individual revolts as well. For instance, in 1714, the taluqdar of pargana Bar, in Baiswara, had built five strong fortresses and raised an army of 2,000 horsemen. It was to a strong army under the command of Sarbuland Khan, the governor, that the taluqdar was forced to surrender.

No significant Baiswara zamindar revolted during the period after 1722. This was because Burhan-ul-Mulk, the first Nawab of Awadh, tried to make some arrangements with the Bais zamindars. He substantially increased the assessment of Baiswara and according to Alam, the military superiority of Burhan-ul-Mulk seems to have been a factor in making them accept the new arrangement. Moreover, the consistent drive of the imperial campaigns, for about forty years, against the Bais zamindars appears to have broken the strength of the rebels in the region. Finally, privileges in keeping with the zamindars' strength and influence, were extended to them so as to win them over to the side of the Nawabi and strengthen its social base. Nonetheless, the relationship between the Nawabs and the Bais zamindars always remained delicately balanced.

[120] For details of this tendency in the Company's military policy during the early 19th century, see chapter 2 below.

[121] S. H. Fremantle, *Report on the Second Settlement of Rae Bareli district, Oudh 1897* (Allahabad, 1898), pp. 18–19.

[122] J. Sanders, *Final Settlement Report of the Partapgarh District, Oudh* (Allahabad, 1896), p. 57.

In the district of Unnao, W. H. Moreland, the settlement officer, noted that a sum of Rs 88,569 from the Unnao treasury alone was still drawn annually by 1,240 military individuals who had inherited military pensions. Most of this was invested by the pensioners in land.[123]

However, Awadh was not the only recruiting depot and it was certainly not the largest supplier of recruits. For a large proportion of the Company sipahis came from Bihar. In fact the Company's military service was most popular in the zamindaris of north and south Bihar. Here, the option for service in a 'high caste' army came at a time when the claim of the Bhumihar-Brahmin peasants to a high-caste status was being denied by all the other Brahmins and rural high castes in the region. This was because the Bhumihar Brahmins had taken to agriculture.[124] In such circumstances the army's claims to preserve the 'high caste' customs of its sipahis began to be used by the Bhumihars to emphasize their own high-caste status.[125] It was for this reason that the predominantly Bhumihar northern and southern Bihar zamindaris became the 'high recruiting zone' for the Company's army.

Kolff has recently highlighted the important role that the Bhojpuri region, which included the districts of eastern Awadh, Shahabad, and the Champaran and Saran districts of north Bihar, played in the recruiting of the Company army.[126] In the 1780s, the Company had its major recruiting station at Buxar with six companies of recruits under the command of Captain Eaton. These were disciplined and kept as a nursery for supplying the battalion of sipahis at the Presidency and the several stations in Bengal. Whenever drafts were made from this 'nursery', the accoutrements and clothing of the recruits who had been sent down country were retained for fresh levies which were immeditely made in

[123] W. H. Moreland, *Final Report on the Settlement of Land Revenue in the Unao District, Oudh* (Allahabad, 1896), p. 3.

[124] See S. Saraswati, *Bhumihar Brahmin Parichai* (Benaras, 1917), p. 12. He notes the differentiation that existed in the ranks of the rural high caste in Benaras and Bihar due to the Bhumihar having taken to agriculture and associated themseves with the Mughal Empire.

[125] See for details chapter 2 below.

[126] Kolff, *Naukar, Rajput and Sepoy*, p. 160.

order to fill their vacancies.[127] Other recruiting centres were scattered over Bhagalpur, Shahabad, Monghyr, Saran, Champaran and Hajipur.[128] Brigadier Troup, who had been in the Bengal military service since 1819 and served as the Commander at Bareli in 1859, also stated that the, 'Bengal native Infantry came chiefly from the province of Awadh, Buxar, Bhojpur and Arrah.'[129] The recruits from Bihar were predominantly Rajput and Bhumihar peasants. It is not possible to give exact figures of Bhumihar representation in the Company's army.[130] But we may safely attribute the popularity of the Company's service in Bihar to the high proportion of Bhumihar peasants it had begun to attract to its regiments. For the Bhumihars were numerically the second largest community and one of the principal Hindu cultivators in the south Bihar zamindaris of Shahabad and Monghyr.[131] As tenure holders of all grades, occupancy and non-occupancy raiyats, as well as petty proprietors and tenants, they were most likely to be attracted to the Company's service. The service supplemented their income from land and improved their financial position. Again the Hindu image of the Company's army also assured these men a superior status denied to them by the Brahmins proper in their localities. This explains the great success of the Company in recruiting from the villages of southern Bihar. By 1810, when Buchanan wrote his accounts of the Bihar district, the number of men absent from Shahabad to serve in the Company's army

[127] Brigadier General G. Stibbert, Commander-in-Chief, to W. Hastings, 10 Feb. 1779, Mil. Deptt. Procd. Jan.–June 1779, Consult. FW 6 March 1779, NAI; also see Brigadier General Stibbert's plan for fixing a recruiting station at Buxar, Fatehgarh, 1 Feb. 1779, BMC, Consult. 6 March 1779, P/18/47, IOL.

[128] See chapter 2 below.

[129] PP, 1859 VIII (254) 143–46, H.C. PP. Cited in Barat, *Bengal Infantry*, p. 120.

[130] L. S. S. O'Malley, *Bihar and Orissa District Gazetteers, Shahabad* (rev. ed., Patna, 1924), p. 47. This is because records of recruiting lists began to be organized in a systematic manner only after 1857. Moreover, the Bhumihar recruits never got themselves listed separately as Bhumihars. They were always included in the Rajput or Brahmin category. In fact O'Malley, the compiler of the *Shahabad Gazetteer*, notes that Brahmanical titles such as Misr, Panre and Tewari were used by the Bhumihars along with Rajput titles of Singh, Rai or Thakur.

[131] O'Malley, *Shahabad Gazetteer*, p. 47; also L. S. S. O'Malley, *Bihar and Orissa District Gazetteer, Monghyr* (revised edition, Patna, 1926), p. 66.

was 4,680. The Ujjainya Raja of Bhojpur informed him that from the northern half of the district alone 12,000 sipahis had joined the East India Company's service.[132] The same source also noted that the Shahabad district itself had contributed at least 1,200 sipahis to the army. The importance the Company gave to Bhagalpur and Monghyr as recruiting areas was evident from the large establishment of retired soldiers it based in these districts. In 1817, Bhagalpur had 1,016 invalid soldiers settled on land,[133] whereas in Monghyr, approximately 92,243 bighas of land were settled with colonies of retired soldiers.[134]

In north Bihar there was a larger concentration of Bhumihars. The major zamindars of Saran—Maharaja Bahadur of Hathwa, the Raja of Chatapur and the babus of Manjha, Parsa and Khaira were all Bhumihars.[135] The powerful Bhumihar Raja of Bettiah in the Champaran district had colonized vast tracts of land with his clansmen and Bhumihars from Benaras.[136] Further, Darbhanga and Tirhut also had large Bhumihar settlements. The Company received large number of recruits from all these districts. Recruiting from these powerful north Bihar zamindaris served the Company well. For, as in the case of the Awadh Nawabi, the settlement of these north Bihar zamindaris was carried through by striking military contracts with their landed magnates and obtaining a large supply of recruits from the region. For instance, the most significant challenge to the initial British penetration into Bihar came from the landed magnates of the north Bihar district of Saran. These were the Raja of Bettiah and other local zamindars. But the most protracted and strong protest which kept Saran in turmoil in the last three decades of the eighteenth century, came from the ninety-ninth Huseypur Raja, Fateh Sahi.[137] Even

[132] Kolff, *Naukar, Rajput and Sepoy*, p. 171.

[133] Report to Board by Collector of the District, undated, BCBB, Consult., 1 March 1817, vol. 9 UPSA; see chapter 3 below.

[134] Enclosure No. 5 in letter from Collector of Bhagalpur to Board, undated, BRJP, Consult. F.W. 14 June 1803, Volume I, WBSA; see for details chapter 3 on the Invalid Thanah.

[135] L. S. S. O'Malley, *Bihar and Orissa District Gazetteer, Saran* (Patna, 1930), p. 45.

[136] L. S. S. O'Malley, *Bihar and Orissa District Gazetteer, Champaran* (Patna, 1938), p. 43.

[137] Yang, *Limited Raj*, pp. 62–7.

though, after Cheyt Singh's rebellion in 1781, the military superiority of the Company effectively crushed Fateh Sahi and other recalcitrant zamindars, the settlement of the region, later called the Hathwa Raj, was still not achieved. This seems to have gained momentum in Wellesley's period and army recruitment played a significant role in its progress.[138] In this period the Company signed contracts with the zamindars of the northern Bihar districts to obtain their clan levies for the Bengal Army. The zamindars of Saran were important suppliers of such levies[139] and the powerful Raja of Bettiah also sent his clan levies for the Company's service.[140] In 1815, the Company also received a contingent of troops from Raja Chutter Singh of Darbhanga.[141] Further, in Tirhut and Purnia, the Magistrates worked through local zamindars for obtaining recruits and[142] Hajipur in north Bihar became a major centre for co-ordinating such zamindari levies and bringing them to Bengal.[143] Finally, the importance of the northern Bihar Bhumihar zamindaris in the recruiting zone of the Company was also evident when the Company established one of the largest colonies of retired

[138] Ibid., p. 68. Yang sees the settlement of the region as a major consequence of the rising advantages the Company had gained on the political and diplomatic front. He argues that rebels in the interior, tenacious adversaries to overcome in their strongholds in the initial years after *diwani*, had become less formidable opponents as the Company developed its revenue-collection machinery. Their power was further weakened as the Company backed its revenue-collection machinery with enough firepower to deprive recalcitrant zamindars of their major source of funds, viz., their lands.

[139] For contracts with the zamindars of Saran see L. No. 50, C.I. Sealey, Magistrate of Tirhut, to John Adam, Sec. to Govt. Pol. Deptt, 6 Jan. 1815, Consult. 25 Feb. 1815, P/BEN/SEC/266, IOL. For details see chapter 2 below. In 1830 Rankine, a Company Surgeon posted in Saran, reported that the district supplied 10,000 recruits. R. Rankine, *Notes on the Medical Topography of the District of Saran* (Calcutta, 1839), p. 34.

[140] L. No. 31, Gen. I. Adam, Sec. to Govt., to Colonel P. Bradshaw 18 Jan. 1815, Consult. 7 Feb. 1815, P/BEN/SEC/265, IOL. See chapter 2 below.

[141] L. No. 149, parwanah to Rajah Chutter Singh, Zamindar of Darbhanga, from the Vice-President, a true copy by C. A. Molony, 23 May 1815, Consult. 20 Sept. 1815, P/BEN/SEC/273, IOL.

[142] L. No. 151, parwanah to Chowdhri Bholee Singh, Zamindar of Tirhut, from the Vice-President, 23 May 1815, P/BEN/SEC/273, IOL.

[143] W. Moorcroft, Superintendent of the horse stud, to acting Chief Sec. to Govt., 25 April 1815, Consult. 9 May 1815, P/BEN/SEC/269, IOL; see chapter 2 below for details.

sipahis in Kalyanpur, close to the territories of the Bettiah Raja.[144] These colonies of sipahis were not only to continue the dissemination of the favourable opinion of the Company in the region from where it received its recruits but were also meant to maintain a check on the powerful rajas of the region through whom the Company recruited its sipahis.

However, the success of the Company in recruiting a large number of recruits by appealing to their religious sensibilities generated a variety of economic, political and social changes in north Indian society.

Chapter 2

The Peasant Army
in the Gangetic Plains

The Economic Impact of Recruitment

The savings of the Company sipahis and the pensions drawn by its former soldiers kept the 'military labour market' alive[1] and contributed to the political and economic stability of zamindaris located in the recruitment zone.[2] For instance, in 1810, on an average about 3,920 recruits came from the zamindaris of eastern Awadh and Benaras.[3] Given

[1] Kolff, *Naukar, Rajput and Sepoy*, p. 3. This is a term used by Dirk Kolff to indicate the easy availability of peasant warriors in the Bhojpur region from the time of Sher Shah. I use it to indicate the notion of availability of peasant warriors but differ from Kolff both in the timing when this market gained prominence as a recruiting ground as well as the simplicity and ease of sale and purchase which the word market seems to convey.

I argue that the armed peasant needs to be differentiated from the professional peasant soldier which was a characteristic feature of the regional states of the 18th century. The 'labour market' in northern India became active and volatile once the regional states of the 18th century began to recruit their peasant army from the region. In the late 18th century the Company also began to tap this market for its peasant recruits. This increased the pressures on this market, and sale and purchase was not an easy affair.

[2] L. No. 39 enclosure, Captain I. Burnett, in charge of payment of remittances to families of sipahis on foreign service, to Captain A. Greene, Sec. Mil. Board, 3 March 1802, BMC, Consult., 1 April 1802, P/20/30, IOL. The amount of money entering the recruitment zone can be gauged from the sum distributed to sipahi families by Captain I. Burnett. In 1802 he distributed Rs 3,374 (an average of Rs 727 per month) to families of sipahis in Major Broughton's battalion, and Rs 1,874.5.3 to those in Major Maclean's battalion.

[3] Ibid. The break up was as follows: Buxar—600, Benaras—600, Allahabad—200,

the average remittance of each sipahi as at least Rs 2, the region obtained approximately Rs 7,840 per year from the sipahi recruits of one batch alone.[4] This did not include the remittances of high-ranking military servicemen from the region and it also excluded military pensions which were paid at high rates.[5] It was the inflow of these incomes which made the settlement officers in the Awadh districts comment on the prosperous state of peasant sipahi holdings.[6] In the mid-nineteenth century, S. H. Fremantle, the settlement officer of Rae Bareli, attributed the flourishing nature of the Rae Bareli zamindaris to the investments made by the Brahmin sipahis.[7] The same observations were made by the settlement officers of Pratapgarh and Unnao.[8]

These strengthened zamindaris now made it difficult for the Company to obtain an easy supply of peasant recruits. Many peasant families, taking advantage of the stable political and economic environment, preferred to concentrate on agricultural activity. Since military service took family labour away and hindered agricultural production, most peasant homes preferred to send only one member of the family for military service. This gave peasant families easy access to the local administration and made it possible for them to sort out their village problems amicably. For instance, Sita Ram, the son of a middle-level zamindar of Tilloi, was encouraged by his father to join the army in 1821. Years later, in the 1850s, he noted in his memoir:

Secrora—300, Futtehgarh—300, Pratapgarh—817, Sultanpur—803, Sitapur—300.

[4] M. Martin, *The History, Antiquities, Topography and Statistics of Eastern India* (2 vols., reprint Delhi, 1976), I, p. 553.

[5] Sleeman, *Rambles and Recollections of an Indian Official*, p. 448. The different categories of pensions received by retired soldiers was as follows: each sipahi obtained a pension of Rs 4 per month; Rs 8 per month after 16 years of service; and Rs 9 per month after 20 years of service. A naik or corporal obtained Rs 7 per month, a havaldar Rs 7, a jamadar Rs 13, and a subahdar Rs 25 per month.

[6] See for details chapter 1 above.

[7] Fremantle, *Report on the Second Settlement of Rae Bareli*, pp. 17–18. Also see Butter, *Topography*, p. 88. These figures of a later period are indicative of similar investments in an earlier period when the region sent a much larger number of recruits to the Company army.

[8] Sanders, *Settlement Report of Pratapgarh District*, p. 57; Moreland, *Final Report on Unao District*, p. 3.

There was a law suit impending over my father about his right to a mango grove of some 400 trees, and he thought that having a son in the Company Bahadur's service would be the means of getting his case attended in the law courts of Lucknow; for it was well known that a petition sent by a soldier through his commanding officer, who forwarded it onto the Resident Sahib in Lucknow, generally had prompt attention paid to it, and carried more weight than even the bribes and party interests of a mere subject of the King of Oudh.[9]

On many occasions the peasant's reluctance to join the army was socially sanctioned. For instance, the Bais Rajputs, who by the early nineteenth century were well represented in the army, always preferred commercial activity to military service.[10] In the early nineteenth century, when the agricultural and economic stability of the region gave a fillip to trade as well, it was natural for them to opt for commercial activities rather than enter military service.

In this social, economic, and political environment the army tried to regain its popularity by adding new strategies to Hastings' recruiting practice. Its sipahis, more than ever before, acted as recruiting agents as well.[11] They projected the adventurous world of the military into their villages. Further, the Company started utilizing its military commandants and commercial agents in north India to reach out to a wide section of the rural élite. Through its military and commercial contacts the army struck deals for military recruits with the powerful zamindars, and thereby incorporated them into its network of control. Anand Yang has shown a variety of political and administrative ways in which the colonial state delineated its 'collaborators' and established

[9] Lunt, *From Sepoy to Subedar*, p. 5.

[10] Butter, *Topography*, p. 156.

[11] GOCC 1806, *Military Records: Abstract of General Orders and Regulations in Force in the Honourable East India Company of Bengal* (Calcutta, 1812), p. 231, L/MIL/17/2/433, IOL. This order read as follows: 'The officers commanding battalions and regiments of native infantry are to be particularly careful that none but good and efficient recruits are entertained and that they are drawn as far as possible from the Company's provinces between Allahabad and Bengal. (b) Commanding officers requiring men for the prescribed complement of their Corps are to avail themselves of the service of their native officers and men going on furlough to bring recruits with them, on returning to the Corps, to the number required.

political alliances with the rural magnates of Saran for strengthening its rule in north India.[12] In the early nineteenth century army recruitment also appears to have played an important role in the 'settlement' of the north Indian countryside. Eric Stokes' work shows that it was in the interest of the Company to encourage the zamindari as an economic institution.[13] But, by the first decade of the nineteenth century, it became important to preserve the zamindari as a military institution as well.

The practice of making political alliances with the Company's ·military was always a welcome prospect for the small zamindars. Very often they used it to prosecute their village disputes at a higher level. For instance, Rang Bahadur, a Rajput zamindar of pargana Agpouri and Barrur, which formed the border with Berar, lost his zamindari because of the high revenue assessment which he was unable to pay. In 1803, when offered the chance of serving in the Company's army he agreed on the condition that he would be paid to enlist his retinue. While in the service of the Company the zamindar obtained numerous favours from his employer and finally got back his zamindari. The Company relinquished the balance of revenue due on his zamindari and authorized the Collector to conclude a new engagement for revenue. The Collector was asked to calculate the demand at a 'reasonable' rate so as to ensure future punctuality in payments.[14] In another case, Bhoop Singh, a petty raja of pargana Sikanderpur and Chaukundah in suba Allahabad, had been reduced to penury after his land had been auctioned off by the Collector to Babu Devkinandan of Jaunpur[15] at the time of the triennial

---

[12] Yang, *Limited Raj*, pp. 68, 70, 78.

[13] See E.T. Stokes, *The Peasant and the Raj: Studies in Agrarian, Social and Peasant Rebellion in Colonial India* (Cambridge, 1978).

[14] T. Brooke, acting agent to Governor General in Benaras, to N. B. Edmonstone, Sec. to Govt. in Secret Deptt., 12 Oct. 1803, BPS, Consult. 27 Oct. 1803, P/BEN/SEC/118, IOL.

[15] B. S. Cohn, 'The initial British impact on India: a case study of the Benaras region', in Cohn, *An Anthropologist among the Historians*, p. 333. Cohn shows that Devkinandan Singh was a Bhumihar from Ghazipur. His father had been an official in Allahabad and in Benaras. He controlled James Barton, the Collector, by placing his own men in the key positions of Barton's staff. When Allahabad was ceded to the Company in 1801,

settlement.[16] Babu Devkinandan then started harassing Bhoop Singh and his family. In 1804, Bhoop Singh applied to Colonel E. S. Broughton, who was encamped at Allahabad, for military service. He was enlisted along with his 200 sawars and 1,800 piadas and matchlockmen. For their salary and maintenance he was granted Rs 12,129 and a travel allowance of Rs 7,000. Soon after Bhoop Singh used his contacts with the Company to get back his zamindari. The term of Babu Devkinandan was over and the Company restored Bhoop Singh to his zamindari and also granted him Rs 700 per month in lieu of his military service. He was appointed *ijaradar* of the pargana of Sikanderpur and Chaukundah in the district of Allahabad.[17]

Political alliances with the Company's army boosted the prestige of big zamindars as well. For instance, in the year that Bhoop Singh was made ijaradar, Rajah Fateh Singh of Deo had also agreed to enlist with his retinue. He came with his men to Colonel Broughton but was refused service because by then Bhoop Singh's contingent had fulfilled the Company's immediate requirements. But Broughton was compelled to change his decision because of Fateh Shah's protestations highlighting the detrimental effect which the Company's refusal would have on his 'character and respectability'.[18]

In this period the army entered into similar political alliances with the zamindars of south Bihar as well. These regions had supplied a large number of the Company's soldiers and the sipahis' remittances and pensions had contributed to the agricultural stability

---

Devkinandan, because of his experience and wealth, was able to get employment there as an amil. In the space of a few years Devkinandan Singh acquired about a tenth of the land in the district.

[16] Due to some personal rivalry with Devkinandan he was prevented from personally attending on the Collector and from presenting a petition in support of his claim.

[17] L. No. 15, Colonel E. S. Broughton commanding Ramgarh battalion, to John Lumsden, Chief Sec. to Govt., 2 Nov. 1803, BPS, Consult. FW 12 April 1804, P/BEN/SEC/133, IOL; also see L. No. 120, N. B. Edmonston, Sec. to Govt., to Colonel E. S. Broughton, 15 June 1804, BPS, Consult. 5 July 1804, P/BEN/SEC/142, IOL.

[18] L. No. 18, Colonel E. S. Broughton, commanding Ramgarh battalion, to J. Lumsden, Chief Sec. to Govt., 22 Nov. 1803, BPS Consult. FW 1804, P/BEN/SEC/133, IOL.

of the zamindaris. For instance, in the Bhojpur region of Shahabad district, which had furnished a large proportion of the Company's best sipahis,[19] the investment of these men in land further strengthened the Bhojpur zamindari. In 1809 a survey of the Invalid Thanahs[20] conducted by W. Francklin, the Regulating Officer of Bhagalpur Invalid Thanah, revealed that the region obtained a sum of Rs 6,504 annually as allowance for wells, encampments, tree plantation, construction of bungalows, etc.[21] In 1833, M. Martin, reporting Buchanan Hamilton's findings of 1810, noted that the Shahabad district had contributed at least 1,200 sepoys to the army. On an average each man sent not less than Rs 2 per month. This gave the district an annual investment of Rs 268,00 per year.[22] But here also, as in the case of the Awadh zamindaris, the Company found it difficult to recruit fresh Bhojpuris to meet its expanded military requirements for, in the early nineteenth century, peasant families of the serving sipahis preferred to cultivate land in their village. In 1815, at the time of the Gurkha War, the Company was unable to recruit from the region, and it could only obtain a military contingent from the Raja of Bhojpur.[23]

By the 1820s, Company rule had become increasingly dependent on the military support of the big zamindars of Bihar. The Company used the services of its Horse Superintendent,[24] William Moorcroft, to strike political alliances with the powerful zamindaris of Bihar. Moorcroft (1765–1825) was a veterinary surgeon who joined the Bengal Army in 1808. He was appointed the superintendent

---

[19] See chapter 1 above.

[20] This institution designed to help pensioners will be dealt with in chapter 3 below.

[21] 'Report on the western and northern Thanahs attached to the jagirdars Invalid Establishment at Bhagalpur and Tirhut 1809 by Major W. Francklin, Regulating Officer of Thanahs Bhagalpur, Tirhut and Purnia', BMC, Consult. FW 30 June 1810, P/23/39, IOL.

[22] Martin, Eastern India, I, p. 553. The district also had a large settlement of invalids and benefited from their labour and investments.

[23] L. No. 84, W. Moorcroft, Superintendent of the horse stud, to J. Monckton, acting Sec. to Govt. in the Pol. Deptt., 13 March 1815, BPS, Consult. FW 28 March 1815, P/BEN/SEC/268, IOL.

[24] An Officer in charge of the Company's horse-breeding experiments.

of the Company's horse stud at Pusa and his theory about the improvement of the native cavalry horse by the introduction of English or Turkoman 'bone and muscle' drew his attention towards the opening of commercial intercourse between British India and the Himalayan regions.[25] Moorcroft was a popular and familiar figure in the Bihar and eastern Awadh area due to his involvement in horse-breeding experiments and organizing of horse fairs. He had established influential contacts with the Raja of Bhojpur and other zamindars of the region. He used his influence with the local rajas and zamindars to obtain Rajput recruits for the army. Clan patronage was so firmly established in the region that it was only on the Raja's call that his relations and principal tenantry brought squads of picked men of their own family on the promise that their leaders would command them in warfare. These leaders gave personal security for the conduct of their men. The Raja sent one such contingent of 400 men commanded by Mendu Khan, his favourite servant, to serve in the Company army.[26] Hajipur in north Bihar, the biggest horse-breeding centre in north India, became the co-ordinating centre for levies of recruits obtained through the rajas and zamindars of north and south Bihar.[27] Here, Moorcroft inspected recruits sent from Bhojpur and Tirhut. Only those men who were approved by him were eventually enlisted into the Company army.[28]

[25] Sidney Lee (ed.), *Dictionary of National Biography* (London, 1894), XXXVIII, pp. 337–8. During his stay in India he travelled extensively in the Punjab and Central Asia and died in 1825 during one of his travels.

[26] L. No. 84, Moorcroft, Superintendent of the horse stud, to John Monckton, acting Sec. to Govt. in the Pol. Deptt., 13 March 1815, BPS, Consult., FW 28 March 1815, P/BEN/SEC/268, IOL. There was a general understanding between the leader and his group that any man who should back out on the day of the battle would be immediately killed. Those who deserted were to be treated as outcastes from their religion, family, and country and were to be punished. The Raja favoured those who distinguished themselves on the battlefield. A few elderly men of approved character were mixed with large proportions of young men to give steadiness and confidence to the contingent.

[27] W. Moorcroft, Superintendent of the horse stud, to I. Monckton, acting Chief Sec. to Govt. 25 April 1815, BPS, Consult. FW 9 May 1815, P/BEN/SEC/269, IOL.

[28] L. No. 67, W. Moorcroft, Superintendent of the horse stud, to C.W. Gardiner, Sec. to Govt. Mil. Deptt., Fort William, 7 Jan. 1815, BPS, Consult. 7 Feb. 1815, P/BEN/SEC/265, IOL. Moorcroft raised a body of troopers in Pusa because he could not recruit

In the manner of the Mughal Emperor the Company also symbolically marked the zamindar's political incorporation into the Company Raj by honouring him with a khelat. For instance, Raja Jye Prakash Singh of Bhojpur was presented with a khelat of seven cloths, jiggas, serpaich and a string of pearls by the Magistrate of Shahabad for his military support to the Company.[29] Here, as in the case of the Mughal Empire, the ritual of granting the *khelat* emphasized the Company's superior position in the hierarchy of power in the region.

In the north Bihar zamindaris of Bettiah, Tirhut, Darbhanga, Purnia and Saran, a situation very similar to that of Awadh and south Bihar prevailed. In 1815, the magistrates of Tirhut, Purnia and Saran indicated time and again the difficulties experienced in recruiting in an area which had been a major recruitment base in the previous years.[30] C. I. Sealey, the Magistrate of Saran, was of the veiw that the people

although of a turbulent disposition and ready to join the Gohar for the purpose of contesting disputed land were not in the habit of engaging in military service. In fact they were averse to the idea.[31]

Here also, Company officials came to rely on the influence and the patronage network of local zamindars to recruit men for the army. These 'allies' were then symbolically incorporated into the Company's polity by the grant of khelats.[32] In the Champaran

---

a sufficient number of men in the Hajipur and Patna region. In Pusa he obtained six mares from the 8th Native Cavalry, and got them shoed and saddled. These were distributed to those troops of his contingent who showed a keen interest in military service and demonstrated a 'spirit of discipline'. Kalb Ali Khan, a pensioner of the Government, assisted Moorcroft in recruiting and training them.

[29] L. No. 155, C. A. Molony, Deputy Sec. to Govt., to Raja Jye Prakash Singh of Bhojpur, 1 July 1815, BPS, Consult. 20 Sept. 1815, P/BEN/SEC/273, IOL. He was conferred with an honorary dress in the name of the British Government.

[30] See Rankine, *Notes on Saran*, p. 34.

[31] L. No. 50, C. I. Sealey, Magistrate in Tirhut, to John Adam, Sec. to Govt. Pol. Deptt., 6 Jan. 1815, BPS, Consult. FW 25 Feb. 1815, P/BEN/SEC/266, IOL. Similar views were expressed by the Magistrate of Champaran to the Government and are noted in L. No. 31, General I. Adam, Sec. to Govt., to Major P. Bradshaw, Pol. Agent in Nepal, 18 Jan. 1815, Consult. 7 Feb. 1815, P/BEN/SEC/265, IOL.

[32] L. No. 149, parwanah to Rajah Chutter Singh, Zamindar of Darbhanga, from the

district the Company commandants negotiated with the powerful Raja of Bettiah for recruits. The Raja was one of those zamindars of north Bihar who, because of his crucial position on the frontier of the erstwhile Mughal suba of Bihar, had been allowed internal autonomy as long as he paid tribute to the Mughal state. This arrangement was continued by the Nawabs of Awadh. However, the Company interfered in the region and tried to keep in check the power of such powerful rajas. But its three military campaigns against the Bettiah Raja were unsuccessful, and the rebel Raja could not be politically extinguished. As early as 1786, the Company settled retired soldiers of the Ramgarh and Chittagong Regiments in the north Bihar districts, so as to establish its permanent presence close to the recalcitrant Raja. However, these sipahi settlements benefited the Raja for they converted to a populous and agriculturally flourishing region what had been forested and infested with wild animals.[33] The Raja's lands under cultivation benefited by similar sipahi settlements in the neighbouring district of north Bhagalpur and Saran.[34] This economic prosperity and social security

---

Vice President, a true copy from C. A. Molony, Deputy Sec. to Govt., 23 May 1815, BPS, Consult. 20 Sept. 1815, P/BEN/SEC/273, IOL. Also see L. No. 151, parwanah to Chaudhury Bholi Singh, a Zamindar of Tirhut, from the Vice President, 23 May 1815, BPS, Consult. 20 Sept. 1815, P/BEN/SEC/273, IOL. The influential zamindars whose patronage networks were utilized by the Company to recruit its army, and who were honoured with *khelats* were as follows: Raja Chutter Singh, zamindar of Darbhanga, honoured with a khelat of seven cloths, *jiggah* and *sirpaich* and a string of pearls; (b) Zain-ul-abdin Khan received a khelat of five cloths, jiggah, sirpaich, sword and shield; (c) Neema Singh received a pair of shawls, a *goshwarah* and sirpaich. Like the Mughal Emperors the Company also accepted *nazars* from the zamindars of Tirhut. This formalized the political alliance which they had entered into with the Company by supplying it with recruits.

[33] B. Aliney, Member, Board of Rev., to C.F. Grant, Collector in Tirhut, undated, MCR, 1786, vol. 5, BSA.

[34] Report to Board by Collector of Bhagalpur, undated, BCBB, Consult. 1 March 1817, vol. 9, UPSA. The largest colony was of approximately 12,000 soldiers settled in 22 Thanahs, over 6,993.18 bighas of land, in the Bhagalpur district. See for details chapter 3; also see, 'Report on the western and northern Thanahs attached to the jagirdars' Invalid Establishment at Bhagalpur and Tirhut, 1809' by Major W. Francklin, BMC, Consult. FW 30 Jan. 1810, P/23/39, IOL. Francklin noted that the Government invested a large amount of money in the areas where invalids were settled. The region also received considerable amounts of money in the form of sipahi pensions and salaries. Bhagalpur received Rs 995.3.0 per year, Tirhut Rs 343.11.3 per year, Bihar

made agriculture a more attractive option for the peasant families in the region. In 1815, Major P. Bradshaw, the Company's political agent in Nepal, was unable to attract peasant recruits from this area. Consequently, the military initiated a policy of wooing the powerful Bettiah Raja by entering into military contracts with him. Bradshaw agreed to give political recognition to him if he supplied the Company with 600 troops. This was a deal which he agreed to and it benefited both the parties involved.[35]

In the north Bihar district of Saran, where Yang has shown the political and administrative ways in which the Company intervened in local society, developing relations with the cadet line of the Huseypur family which later became the powerful Hathwa Raja of the district, the army was also used to having an easy access to rural élites. Here, as in Awadh and south Bihar, the reluctance of families to send more than one member for military service made the Company utilize the services of Mr MacEntry, an indigo plantation employee.[36] MacEntry used his commercial contacts in the region to encourage men to enlist in the Company army. In the early nineteenth century approximately 100,000 Company sipahis were recruited from Saran.[37] Interestingly enough, the increasing military recruitment in the district led to a situation in which MacEntry provided 'employment' of a different kind to the people of Saran.

In this way the Company's expanding apparatus of military recruitment soon involved the zamindars, a variety of Company officials and private individuals. In another instance, correspondence between the Collector of Bihar, W. Monez, and the Board of

---

Rs 650.4.0 per year, and Saran Rs 650.4.0.

[35] L. No. 31, General I. Adam, Sec. to Govt., to Major P. Bradshaw, 18 Jan. 1815, BPS, Consult. 7 Feb. 1815, P/BEN/SEC/265, IOL.

[36] L. No. 48, I.B. Elliot, Magistrate of Saran, to John Monckton, Sec. to Govt. in the Pol. Deptt., 23 Jan. 1815, BPS, Consult. 7 Feb. 1815, P/BEN/SEC/265, IOL. He reported that the younger brothers of village zamindars had been in the habit of entering Company service for some time. But military recruitment was not very popular, as despite the offer of salary of Rs 6 per month and 5 annas per month additional pay if they brought their own ammunition, not many people were willing to be recruited into the Company's army.

[37] Yang, *Limited Raj*, p. 191.

Commissioners for Bihar and Benaras regarding a disputed *altamgah* (revenue-free grant) to a person by the name of Shahbaz Beg Khan, revealed that, at times, the Company relied on Indian merchants and their contacts for recruiting its sipahis.[38] This incident also indicated that often it was possible for a trader to become a recruiting agent and eventually an officer in the Company's army. In 1816, Shahbaz Beg Khan came to Patna with a beggar in search of employment. He stopped at the door of Nurhur Singh who was the munshi of Mr Biller, the chief magistrate. The munshi, who wielded considerable power and influence in the town, first arrested him and then appointed him to the low office of a doorkeeper. But he soon realized that he was worthy of a higher position and appointed him to look after his children. Soon he loaned him Rs 500 and sent him to the town of Bihar to purchase cloth. Shahbaz Beg Khan took to business and became a very successful merchant, amassing Rs 4,000 within a few months. In 1816, when the Company army required recruits to meet the challenge of the Pindaris, Mr Biller, who was stationed at Monghyr, received instructions to raise some cavalry recruits. His munshi introduced him to Shahbaz Beg Khan, who agreed to become his recruiting agent. Khan invested his own savings of Rs 4,000 in enlisting men. He used his extensive contacts in the Gangetic basin and soon returned from Lucknow with a contingent of about 250 men. The Company honoured him by making him a non-commissioned officer and he greatly distinguished himself in several engagements.[39]

An interesting fact that emerges from the meteoric careers of men like Shahbaz Beg Khan, who rose from a doorkeeper to become a non-commissioned officer in the Company army, is that in the early nineteenth century darbans, chaukidars and doorkeepers in Calcutta and down country could be drawn from the same areas and from the same kind of migrating population

[38] L. No. 6, Monez, Collector of Bihar, to Richard Rocke, Senior Commissioner of Board and Edward Scott Waring, Junior Commissioner of Board, 8 Sept. 1818, Bengal Board of Commissioners at Bihar and Benaras, Consult. Shahabad 16 Oct. 1816 P/112/7, IOL.

[39] Ibid.

which the army tapped for its recruits. This appears to be more a feature of the early nineteenth century when the Company's recruiting teams, unable to attract peasant recruits from the Bihar and Awadh countryside, were increasingly relying on rural élites, commercial agents, and private individuals for recruiting its army. It is in this period that the Company, in a manner reminiscent of Clive's recruitment of his Lal Paltan, seems to have tapped the up-country migrants in Calcutta and Patna for its military requirements. On many occasions, as in the case of Shahbaz Beg Khan, they became the Company's recruiting agents and were eventually rewarded with high ranks in its army. The Company must have had no difficulty in finding such private individuals with contacts in the Awadh and Bihar region because, despite the economic prosperity in the region, there were always seasonal migrations of the Bihari Bhojpuri people into Bengal at times of the year when agricultural labour was not required.[40] However, the Company's military–political dependence on the zamindaris and on local men of influence resulted in the creation of a sub-military culture in the region for it strengthened alternate points of military political power in the area. This, in the long run, hindered the Company's rise to political supremacy and posed a threat to its further political evolution. It thus negated the Company's objective of establishing a monopoly of power which it attempted to achieve through the recruitment of its army.

THE POLITICAL IMPACT OF RECRUITING

The Company's claims of preserving the religious beliefs of its recruits along with the notion of well-paid service abroad began to be used by some private individuals for building their own independent militarized states. In the eighteenth century, the military requirements of emerging regional states allowed 'peasant

---

[40] Yang, *Limited Raj*, p. 191. He has shown the mobility of Saran's population in the early 19th century by retracing the steps of many of its inhabitants who joined the initial streams of emigrants to the sugar plantations of Mauritius, British Guiana, Trinidad and Jamaica. As little or no organized recruiting was conducted in the interior, many of Saran's emigrants were enlisted in Calcutta. He argues that by the late 19th century the stream of migration toward Calcutta had become well-established flows.

sub-contractors' to exercise significant political and financial power. An individual like Almas Ali Khan, amil under Asaf-ud-daula, was a case in point. Similarly, as the Company's institutions of military recruitment expanded in the north Indian countryside, another range of local agents invaded it in order to further their own interests. In the early nineteenth century, when the Company increasingly relied on chiefs and important peasant leaders for its supply of sipahis, recruiting a military force appears to have became a very lucrative profession for private individuals. Ironically, the Company's territory became a virtual 'job centre' in north India. Here, private individuals adopted the Company's rhetoric of making an appeal to the religious sensibilities of the people; sometimes they appealed to the popular reverence of cults and pirs, superstition, prophecy, and miracles to gain credibility for themselves and access to village society. At other times the private military contractors themselves were invested with religious charisma. For instance, in the Gorakhpur district, in 1807, a large assemblage of villagers rallied around a faqir at a dargah called Hanif ki Dargah. The faqir claimed he was the real Wazir Ali, pretender to the throne of Awadh, who by his supernatural powers had managed to escape from the prison where the British had imprisoned him.[41] This was enough to mobilize the villagers of the surrounding areas who offered their services to him. A worried Lewis Thomas, the Commander posted at Secrora, wrote to the Resident at Delhi:

Numbers join him by night and day on the promise of Rs 4/month for each talwar man, Rs 6/month for each matchlockman and Rs 1/day for each horseman. He is said to have been joined by Bahadur Singh, the son of Rajah Newal Singh of Bulrampur, Murdon Singh, the son of Sew Singh the Raja of Bingah, and Mandalah Singh, Raja of Acconah. His force is said to be already 1400 men.[42]

[41] D. P. Sinha, *British Relations with Awadh 1801–56: A Case Study* (Delhi, 1983), p. 333. In 1798 the Company had deposed Wazir Ali, the Nawab of Awadh, and elevated Saadat Ali Khan to the throne in his place.

[42] Lewis Thomas, commanding at Secrora, to Captain I. Baillie, Resident at Lucknow, 1808 (day and month not mentioned) GCR, Sl No. 101, Miscellaneous Letters Received, 5 July 1805 to Dec. 1808, ARA.

What is interesting about this report is that the faqir was using Company rates of pay and Company methods of recruiting. This large assemblage of villagers rallying around the faqir became violent when the Company refused supplies to the faqir. A large contingent of these men attacked, wounded, and killed ten to twelve men. Among those killed was the amil's diwan. They plundered the whole country and it was with great difficulty that the amil managed to escape. The magistrate ordered the dispersal of the crowd but did not consider it necessary to disarm them.[43]

Such private recruiting in the Company's territory increased in the 1830s when the British clamped down on the surviving Indian states. In this decade, many Indian jagirdars, like Begum Samru and Amir Khan, either died or were politically extinguished by the Company. This unleashed hordes of unemployed soldiers whose plight worsened with the economic depression of the 1830s. Their quest for employment suited the political and military ambitions of private individuals engaged in enlisting people. They used the Company's vocabulary of recruitment to draw more recruits and often furthered their interests by manipulating local religious arenas and symbols for their own purposes, gaining credibility by circulating stories claiming the fulfilment of religious prophecies at the site of the popular religious fairs.

For instance, in 1839, at the popular annual fair of Amunt Chawdus, held at Ayodhya, a large congregation collected. This year the crowd was particularly excited and large because Shivnandan 'Chuttree', a resident of Nasoolspur elaka of Tanda in the Awadh province, predicted in fulfilment of a popular prophecy, the appearance of Inderjit, the son of Ravan, on the banks of the Saryu at Ayodhya.[44] The worried acting magistrate of Jaunpur believed that large crowds would begin to enlist to witness the

---

[43] Ibid.

[44] Deposition of Shivnandan 'Chuttree', prisoner in irons, resident of Nasulapur, elaka of Tanda, province of Awadh, Son of Bisram Singh, undated, PFD P, File No. 84, Consult. 18 Sept. 1839, NAI. Shivnandan claimed to be the recruiting agent of Indivar (Ravan's son). He enlisted people in his private army on a salary of Rs 6 per month. The recruits were told that they would be presented to Indivar on Amunt Chowdus day at Ayudhya. Shivnandan claimed that Indivar, at the time of appointing him as the recruiting agent, had threatened to kill him if he did not follow the latter's commands.

rendezvous simply because they expected a miracle would take place. However, religious curiosity was just an added incentive, for Shivnandan had made himself prominent in this congregation by offering to pay the people as well. He was reported to have said:

I told the men to reach Ayodhya on 14 when Raja Inderjit would appear and give them pay at Rs 6/month. I specified no service to them, nor whether to come armed or disarmed. All classes Hindus and Muslims added their names.[45]

His success as an employer was reflected in the fact that Hindus as well as Muslims collected in large numbers to witness the occasion.[46] In three months Shivnandan had recruited 6,000 men. His popularity alarmed the Awadh government and his Brahmin friend from Tandah was arrested by some *sawars* of the government. He was soon released because no charges could be made against him. Despite his arrest the enthusiasm for recruitment continued unabated and Hindus as well as Muslims continued to enlist in his army. It appears from this story that the gathering of people assembled to witness the festival of Amunt Chowdus was being used as a recruiting ground by private individuals like Shivnandan. In fact, Raja Darshun Singh's karindah, who was sent to disperse the crowd, was told by the recruits in Ayodhya:

We have not come to fight but merely to fulfil our agreement with Sookunun-den and we will return homeward after the festival of Amunt Chowdas.[47]

The Company officials reported that the issues and symbols used by private individuals ranged over a wide variety of themes which the Company army had made popular in the region—from the promise of attractive salaries, to an appeal to the spirit of adventure, so vividly recounted by Sita Ram's uncle each time he returned to his village on furlough,[48] and often concluded with explicit

---

[45] Ibid.

[46] H. I. G. Tucker, acting Magistrate of Jaunpur, to Colonel I. Caulfeild, officiating Resident, Lucknow, 22 June 1839, PFD P 1839, Consult. 18 Sept. 1839, File No. 83, NAI.

[47] Translation of a paper of intelligence received from Faizabad, 27 Nov. 1839, PFD P. File. No. 71, Consult. 27 Nov. 1839, NAI.

[48] Lunt, *From Sepoy to Subedar*, p. 4. Sita Ram wrote in his memoirs, 'He [his uncle] would sit on the seat before our house and relate the wonders of the world he had seen,

appeals to their religious beliefs. For instance, in the Tirhut, Chapra, and Arrah regions of north Bihar, recruiting parties attempted to attract the maximum number of recruits by claiming that they were recruiting a Hindu army for the purpose of taking Mecca from the Muslims.[49] This 'propaganda' of the recruiting teams appears to have had the desired effect. For most of those who enlisted were the Rajput and Ahir agriculturists from north Bihar and eastern Awadh. However, the offer of a good salary, comparable to the Company rates, and the promise of adventure also appears to have contributed to the success of the recruiting teams for a small number of Muslims from eastern Awadh also enlisted in this army.[50]

In another case in 1839, a risaldar in Safipur (Awadh) recruited men for his private army by using the Company's method of recruitment. He promised the people a 'decent' salary if they accompanied him to release the ex-Peshwa Baji Rao from Bithur, where he had been exiled by the British, and take him to Gwalior and then to his ancestral seat of power in Poona. This is of extreme interest in view of the role of Bali Rao's heir, Nana Sahib, in 1857. Once again the risaldar was using a Hindu theme to further his own military and political interests. According to official reports the use of the Hindu Peshwa as a religious symbol to garner support brought him closer to village society and increased the people's trust in him. In a very short time he was able to recruit a large number of people from the area.

Such developments in the 'recruiting zone' created problems of control for the Company whose officials reacted in different ways. The civil authority perceived it as a 'law and order' problem. The potential peasant recruit caused as much panic to them as

---

and the prosperity of the great Company Bahadur he served, to a crowd of eager listeners, who with open mouth and staring eyes took in all his marvels as undoubted truth. None of his hearers was more attentive than myself, and from these recitals I imbibed a strong desire to enter the world and try the fortune of a soldier.'

[49] Officiating Magistrate at Tirhut to Resident at Lucknow, 3 Nov. 1839, PFD P. File No. 69, Consult. 27 Nov. 1839, NAI.

[50] Deposition of Berrack Bhut Nana, taken on 28 April 1839, and of Golab Singh Thakur, taken on 25 April 1839, before Major I. Manson and Baji Rao, PFD S, File Nos. 71- 94, July 1839, NAI.

the mercenary when he threatened colonial authority by collecting in large numbers. Village assemblages and large peasant congrega- tions gathered to witness public events, the coming true of a miracle or the fulfilment of a prophecy, became a threat to colonial authority and consequently to 'public order'. The civil power undertook to administer assemblies such as those at religious fairs, where it thought it understood the rationale of the gathering. Here, colonial authority was reinforced by a proper check on the number of pilgrims and a count of their arms.[51] But for the more 'erratic' and spontaneous village assemblages the local vocabulary of the peasant world did not conform to the colonial vocabulary of 'order and rationale'. Peasants with their weapons of self-defence when in an assemblage were considered a threat and never lightly ignored. T. H. Maddock, officiating Secretary to the Government of India with the Governor-General, reporting on the private recruitment going on under the auspices of Shiv- nandan, in Faizabad district, wrote to I. Coulfield, Resident in Lucknow:

Imprisonment with labour in irons for one or two years might be suggested to His Majesty as the most befitting punishment for these persons. It being calculated to lower them in the eyes of the ignorant people over whom they have sought to establish an influence by arrogating to themselves a degree of superior authority.[52]

But these very peasant populations, back in their own villages, were the agricultural classes the recruiting officers preferred for the Company army.

The military reacted to this threat to the Company's political power differently. It further emphasized its definition of a peasant soldier and made a distinction between a mercenary warrior and

[51] L. No. 65, G.F. Harey, Magistrate of Saharanpur, to G. F. Franco, Commissioner of 1st Div. Meerut, 19 April 1843, SCPMR Judicial Letters Issued, 14 Jan. 1842 to 30 June 1843, ARA. One such annual administrative task for the Company was the Haridwar fare. Here, chaukis were set up under guard, at different entrances to Haridwar to regulate the entry of arms and maintain a count of the number of people who attended the fair.

[52] T. H. Maddock, officiating Sec. to Govt. of India with the Gov. Gen., to Colonel I. Coulfield, Resident in Lucknow, 10 June 1839, PFD, Secret Committee, 17 July 1839, File No. 22, NAI.

an armed peasant. The professionally trained cavalrymen and infantrymen who hired out their services to the best bidder were never considered as eligible recruits. In 1816, E. Cunningham, a Company officer posted in Bareli at the time of the Bareli disturbances, reported that he had turned down many applications from Rohilla mercenaries seeking employment in the Company army.[53] The same repugnance was shown towards those mercenary soldiers of Bundelkhand and professional infantrymen from Buxar who hired out their fighting skills to the best buyers. In these regions the recruiting parties recruited from the agricultural classes rather than from the ex-servicemen of earlier polities. The Company, though concerned, took no specific measures over the recruitment of such 'mercenary' sipahis by the neighbouring Indian states.[54] But it was notably alarmed by the appearance of competitors fot its peasant recruits.

There appears to have been a delicate balance between not allowing village assemblages of armed men but encouraging the peasants to protect the recruiting ground against any outside invasion. For this the Company was willing to allow peasants to be armed for their defence because it was a cheaper way of defending its territory. However, it tried to control the flow of arms in its villages[55] and once a proper check of arms had been accomplished the peasants, particularly the populations in the frontier regions, were encouraged to defend their territory against any external or internal threat. For instance, in 1808, J.

[53] L. No. 23, E. Cunningham to W. B. Bayley, Sec. to Govt. in the Judicial Deptt., 10 Aug. 1816, BC, 1821-22, File No. 17692, Judicial No. 5, vol. 2, pp. 55–6, F/4/640, IOL.

[54] Memorandum of intelligence collected at Sarungpur and Soneira, undated, PFD P, File No. 52, Consult. 12 June 1837, NAI. In this period Bundela Rajputs continued to hire out their services to neighbouring states. In 1837 the Nawab of Bhopal sent recruiting parties to Bundelkhand, where the Nawab's recruiting agent enlisted 45 piadas, 25 of whom were Bundelas. At Shahjehanpur where 15 troopers and 100 infantrymen were entertained, 70 of the latter were Bundelas.

[55] J. E. Colebrooke, *Digest of Regulations and Laws enacted by the Governor General in Council under the Presidency of Bengal* (2 vols., Calcutta, 1807), I. p. 158. From 1795 the Company, in a bid to regulate the supply of arms, had made it necessary for all arms of a 'private nature' imported in Calcutta and passing through Benaras, to have a pass before they could be given transit.

Grant, a judge in Gorakhpur, regretted that certain thanadars had taken upon themselves to prohibit the people the use of arms. In a letter to the Magistrate, John Ahmutty, he wrote:

I am perfectly aware of the dreadful way in which the inhabitants of this part of our possessions often abuse their weapons. But I am, notwithstanding, firmly of opinion that this evil is far inferior to that which would arise by dis-arming the community, and giving them up defenceless and dispirited to the attacks of the vicious profligate both of our own and the Nawab's territories.[56]

A concerted policy of disarming the people had not been initiated. This was evident in 1815, when during the preparation for the Nepal War, the Company officials were not keen to disarm the population of the north Bihar zamindaris located in the districts of Saran, Champaran, Bettiah and Darbhanga. The Bhumihar peasants in these zamindaris, as a result of their closeness to the dangerous Tarai region, possessed arms for defending their lands. In 1815, the Company officials encouraged them to use these arms to defend the frontier against a Gurkha attack. Indeed, P. Bradshaw, the political agent to Nepal, suggested a further 'arming' of these peasant populations so as to prepare them for the impending Gurkha onslaught.[57] Once again in 1821, the Company forbade F. W. Dick, the magistrate of zillah Agra, to disarm the population of village Simree, in the Mathura district. Dick made this request after an affray between the local population of his district and the zamindar of Simree over the offerings made to a temple on the border of the two villages. The Government recognized the illegal nature of the assemblage and allowed the dispersal of the population. But it disapproved

---

[56] J. Grant, 3rd Judge, Court of Circuit Gorakhpur, to John Ahmutty, Magistrate of zillah of Gorakhpur, 24 Dec. 1808, GCR No. 101, Miscellaneous Letters Received July 1805–Dec. 1808, ARA.

[57] Noted in L. No. 48, I. Halhed, acting Magistrate of Purnia, to J. Monckton, acting Sec. to Govt. in Pol. Deptt., 23 Jan. 1815, BPS, Consult. 7 Feb. 1815, P/BEN/SEC/265. IOL. Suggestions against disarming these north Bihar peasant populations also came from the Magistrates of Tirhut, Purnia, Champaran and Saran. See L. No. 50, C.I. Sealey, Magistrate Tirhut to the Sec. Mil. Deptt., 25 Feb. 1815, BPS, Consult. FW 25 Feb. 1815, P/BEN/SEC/266, IOL.

Dick's suggestion of disarming the population so as to prevent any further affrays.[58]

The Social Impact of Recruitment

Ironically enough, in the 1820s, the gravest political and social threat to the Company came from within the army itself, and from the high-caste peasant sipahis it had hitherto encouraged in its regiments. The creation of a high-caste identity, which in a sense levelled the differentiation and tension within the different rural high castes represented in the army, was one of the most significant consequences of recruitment. In the 1820s it seems to have backfired on the Company. The Company had utilized various strategies to create this high-caste identity. Initially, as we have seen in chapter 1, Hastings and his subordinates showed great concern for the dietary preferences of the sipahis. In the subsequent years Company officials continued with this practice and further encouraged the sipahis' religious customs, particularly the celebration of festivals in the regiments and cantonments. However, while religious festivals were encouraged their form was changed. The Company made them exclusively 'military affairs' and regulated their celebration. This created a separate religious tradition in the army which projected the sipahis' high-caste status. In this way the Company thought it had created a loyal support base in its Indian regiments because its high-caste sipahis had the added privilege of wielding military power as well. This high-caste identity in the army was in a sense reinvented,[59] for

[58] L. No. 6, F. W. Dick, Magistrate of Agra, to Govt., 15 May 1821, and L. No. 10, reply from Chief Sec. to Govt., 22 June 1821, BCJ WP, Consult. 22 June 1821, P/135/2, IOL.

[59] E. Hobsbawm and T. Ranger (ed.), *The Invention of Tradition* (Cambridge, 1983), pp. 1–4. I am using here the concept of 'invented tradition' as laid down by Hobsbawm to mean 'a set of practices, normally governed by overtly or tacitly accepted rules and of a ritual or symbolic nature, which seek to inculcate certain values and norms of behaviour by repetition, which automatically implies continuity with the past. In fact, where possible, they normally attempt to establish continuity with a suitable historic past.' Hobsbawm further clarifies his argument by adding, 'invented traditions, it is assumed here, is essentially a process of formalization and ritualization, characterized by reference to the past, if only by imposing repetition.'

by providing a forum for sorting out the social tensions hinging around the ritual purity of the rural high caste, the army formalized these tensions and made them more obvious and rigid. Having being transformed by colonial institutions the high-caste status in rural north India was reinvented. But for this military recruiting, the evolution of high-caste status in rural north India would have progressed differently. We will now discuss the military diet and cantonment celebrations to show how this high-caste identity was created in the Company's regiments.

Military Diet and Social Status

The army showed its respect for the religious customs of the sipahis by promoting their high-caste dietary preferences, and by the early nineteenth century military messing was governed by an extremly complex set of rules and regulations. The sipahi came to eat food which had previously been associated exclusively with high caste and ritual purity. Not only was the diet fixed in accordance to the sipahi's choice[60] but the preparation, types of food etiquette, and manner of taking meals were guided by similar considerations. In the Company army Brahmins, Rajputs and Bhumihars were able to mark out their high-caste status much more effectively than would have been possible in their own villages. In a sense, then the Company was promoting sanskritization of the military.

According to Durga Das Banerji, a Bengali clerk attached to a native regiment in the 1830s, the general food of the soldiers was *dal* and *roti*. Meat and alcohol were excluded from the sipahi's diet. There was never any fish, meat, *pulao* (spiced rice) or curry. Even vegetables like potato, aubergine, radish and *kundru* were not included in the diet.[61] The colour or properties customarily associated with these foods were thought to have an unbalancing effect on the health and temperament[62] and they were consequently

---

[60] See Barat, *Bengal Infantry*, p. 43.

[61] Durga Das Banerji, *Amar jiban katha* (Calcutta, 1857), p. 51.

[62] For an interesting discussion on a cultural colour code influencing village life see C. A. Bayly, 'The origins of swadeshi (home industry): cloth and Indian society, 1700–1939' in A. Appadurai (ed.), *The Social Life of Things: Commodities in Cultural*

excluded from the Brahmin diet. The sipahi's daily consumption would be 125 grams of dal, one *chintank* (10 grams) of ghee, and one-fourth of a chintank of salt, which he obtained on loan from the bazaar shops. Besides this he would take two paisa to buy firewood and masala with. Only once or twice a week would the sipahi purchase vegetables, and here again a typical high-caste taste was reflected. Garlic, leeks, onions, and cooked vegetables were never purchased by any of the sipahis.[63] The cultivation of vegetables like the potato, which required deep ploughing and labour-intensive techniques was abhorred by the sipahis; according to Butter, those sipahis who, out of necessity, did eat potatoes, refused to cultivate them when they went back to their villages.[64] Durga Das Banerji observed a general contempt for potatoes amongst the Rajput, Bhumihar Hindustani sipahis.[65] Very rarely was there a demand for this vegetable in the markets.[66]

The sipahis were allowed to follow rules of caste pollution in the regiment so as to safeguard their high-caste status. Durga Das Banerji observed that the sipahis even carried their own cooking pots and each individual prepared food for himself. Not only did he cook his food on his own, once a day, but also ate alone so as to maintain his ritual purity. The place where the sipahi ate his food was freshly cowdunged.[67] The military granted the sipahis special leave from military duties for their elaborate cooking and eating rituals. This was one of the reasons why the regimental common mess could not be introduced into the Indian regiments.

It is interesting to note that this high-caste diet was formalized by the military authorities in connection with the 1789 campaigns to Sumatra and later elaborated in the campaigns in 1811 to Java and then in the 1820s to Burma. On all these occasions

---

Perspective (New York, 1986), pp. 285–322.

[63] P. V. Kane, *History of Dharmsastras* (2 vols., place of publication not mentioned, 1941), II, Part 2, p. 771. These were forbidden vegetables for the Hindu high castes.

[64] Butter, *Topography*, p. 70.

[65] Banerji, *Amar jiban katha*, p. 51.

[66] Butter, *Topography*, p. 70.

[67] Banerji, *Amar jiban katha*, p. 69. This was the 'proper' way of eating laid down in the Shastras. See Kane, *Dharamshastras*, II, p. 759.

the military authorities were concerned about the danger of sipahi resistance because of crossing the sea which was thought to compromise purity. The rigour with which these rules were enforced is borne out by the fact that many sipahis took no *pakka* food at all on ship because ritual cleanliness could not be guaranteed. Muslims and other non-caste Hindus however cooked on board and their diet included garlic, onions and turmeric which were absent from the diet of the Bhumihar recruits.[68] The General Order of 1817 declared this 'high-caste' diet to be the standard military diet for the sipahis on board.[69]

The army projected its high-caste image each time it issued orders to the local civilian authorities for arranging provisions for its high-caste sipahis. The army had two kinds of bazars to meet the requirements of its soldiers. There were cantonment or regimental bazars, which were generally at the permanent army stations, and camp bazars which were makeshift arrangements which accompanied the regiments on march.[70] The responsibility of supplying provisions to the camp bazars was given to the regional Indian rulers through whose territories the army marched. For this purpose orders were issued by the commanding officer to the local magistrates well in advance. In Awadh the local gunjs took the responsibility for supplying the army and obtained extra duties for this.[71] The gunjs of Awadh hoisted their flags next

---

[68] Arrangements connected with the expedition to Java, BC, File No. 9275, extract BMC, 25 March 1811, pp. 54–62, F/4/377, IOL.

[69] See G O of 3 and 31 Jan. 1817, D. Thompson, *Abstract General Orders from 1817–1840* (Delhi, MXCCCXL), p. 18, L/MIL/17/2/435, IOL.

[70] See L. Nos. 56–7, PFD S. Consult. 6 Sept. 1841, NAI. In both bazars the army used the system of money rations for its sipahis. According to this arrangement each sipahi purchased his victuals on a monthly account. After one month the sipahi in the presence of the chaudhury or the *musaddi* sorted out his accounts with the shopkeeper. Only when the accounts had been settled did the Commanding Officer give orders for the *bania* to be paid. The Magistrate in the town verified the cost of every item being sold in the military bazars, keeping them similar to those in the bazars outside the military areas. To encourage a regular supply of goods to these bazars the Company gave banias an extra profit of 1 anna per rupee on his sales. Moreover, the goods which reached these bazars went tax free and paid no tolls.

[71] Copy of letter from the Nabob Vizir to Colonel Morgan, 4 Rubbee (year not mentioned), PFD S 2 May–4 June 1781, Consult. FW 4 June 1781, File No. 3, appendix

to the Company flag as they engaged to supply the army camp bazars.[72] The selection of food items on sale in these gunjs was determined with a due regard to the soldiers' preferences.[73] Thus, in all these different ways, in the first fifty years of Company rule in India, the formalization of the military diet provided the sipahis a forum to emphasize their assumed high-caste status.

Ceremonies and Festivals in Cantonments

Along with promoting a high-caste diet the Company encouraged the celebration of Hindu festivals in the regiment so as to create an exclusive religious and cultural tradition in the army. The Commander-in-Chief, by the General Order of 17 March 1793, gave sanction to the celebration of Indian festivals in the cantonment. His order read as follows: 'The Commander-in-Chief has no objection to the native troops amusing themselves at the celebration of their festivals according to their respective rites and customs while they do so in a peaceable and orderly

---

E. NAI. In 1781 an order was passed that the vazir was to have the power of appointing all the officers and agents that were necessary for procuring and providing such articles as were requisite for the camp consumption of the troops stationed in his dominions.

[72] Flags of Rakab Ganj and Fateh Ganj were amongst those which were hoisted in army camps. Ibid., appendix, No. E.

[73] A typical diet provision chart sent to the civil authorities for a marching Hindustani regiment was:

	Cavalry/day (maunds)	Infantry/day (maunds)
atta	42	35
dal	6	5
gram	35	35
rice	0.5	0.5
goor	1	1
ghee	3	2
oil	1	1
salt	2	2
sugar	0.5	0.5
wheat	2	2
firewood	100	80
earthen pots	200	100

Collected from L. No. 587, Saharanpur Commissioner to Govt., undated, Judicial Letters Received from Commissioner, SCPMR, 1829–31, vol. 196, ARA.

manner. But he warns them against improper conduct lest the consequence 'should be serious to all the parties who may be concerned.'[74] This General Order gave the Company the authority to regulate the celebration of festivals in the cantonment. In practice this meant that the commanding officer of the regiment gave special permission for using firearms in these celebrations.[75] The firearms which the sipahis possessed represented the new power the Company had invested them with. Their use in festival celebrations began to merge the cantonment world and the religious world of the recruit. The Company encouraged such a convergence and very rarely denied applications for permission to use firearms. Furthermore, the Company encouraged the participation of European officers in these festivities. With their involvement in the religious celebration within the cantonment these public spectacles began to mirror the hierarchies of military command. T. D. Broughton, a commander of the Resident's escort at the court of Shinde, observed that during the Holi festival, Hindu sipahis were fond of seeing exhibitions of dancing boys: they were called *kathaks* and they as well as their attendant musicians were Brahmins. Their dress was nearly the same as that of nautch girls but their dancing and singing was in general much better.[76] The sipahis

---

[74] *Abstract General Order and Regulations*, p. 225. He called on the European officers to keep an eye on men of their Corps whilst they were engaged in the performance of festivals and ceremonies. In cases of dispute they were to 'use their utmost endeavours to suppress them before they proceed to outrageous lengths'.

[75] Ibid., p. 225, G O 13 Oct. 1793. The order was passed after the case of a Lascar who fired a musket in the Lines at night. He defended himself by claiming that he had done so while involved in the celebration of the muharram festival. The Court admitted the excuse under the plea of usage. It was then that the following order was passed: 'No native officer, sepoy lascar or camp follower shall in future upon any occasion whatever presume to let off fire arms within the lines of a cantonment or a camp without express permission for that purpose. General Abercrony, far from wishing to check the native officers and sepoys in their customary amusements, is very desirous that they should be allowed all reasonable indulgence in the celebration of their festivals and religious rites. He is confident that the commanding officer of stations, cantonments and camps will never refuse these indulgences when application shall be made to them for that purpose, unless upon occasion where the exercise of them may be judged improper.'

[76] T. D. Broughton, *Letters Written in a Maratha Camp during the Year 1809—description of the costume, character, manners, domestic habits and religious ceremonies of the Marathas* (London, 1813), p. 71.

were so fond of these exhibitions that they would often sit up for many successive nights to enjoy them and offered money to these dancers. The whole festival for them was a time of mirth and relaxation. The European officers also participated in these celebrations and the sipahis were gratified if their officers joined in their nautches; and even more if they joined with them in playing on the last day of Holi. The officers very often participated and so successful was their attempt to integrate themselves into the cultural world of the recruit that very often the names of the European officers were introduced into the Holi songs.[77]

Even more significant was the Company's encouragement of the celebration of Ramlila in the cantonments. The patronage of the Ram tradition in the cantonment appears to have been encouraged so as to further the Hindu credentials of the army. This was reminiscent, as we have seen in chapter 1, of the Benaras Raja's attempts to patronize Ramlila so as to create a Hindu symbol of legitimacy and achieve independence from the Nawab of Awadh. Cheyt Singh's patronage of a public spectacle, in which all castes and religious groups participated, was a convenient forum in which to emphasize his superior power to the variety of social groups over whom he had established his domination. In the Company's army Ramlila appears to have served similar ends.[78] The Ramlila spectacle within the cantonment provided the Company with a cultural idiom through and by which British authority could be represented in India. Such public spectacles, in which its high-status sipahis displayed the superior technology and power that had devolved to them, reinforced the Company's political superiority and added legitimacy to its rule.

For a somewhat later period we have a first-hand report of the form these celebrations took and the symbols that were deployed within them. The Reverend C. B. Leupolt, a missionary in the mid-nineteenth century, observed that the state encouraged the participation of recruits in the celebration of the Ramlila festival in Benaras, which was the model for all these celebrations.[79] Ramlila,

---

[77] Ibid.

[78] See chapter 1 above.

of course, was the anniversary of the conquest of Lanka by Ram. In 1856, Leupolt reported that the great giant Ravana was made of paper every year and placed in a court which was enclosed by a mud wall. The upper part of the wall was made of paper and this signified his castle. In former years people went inside the castle to defend it and now and then blood was shed as Ram's army, partly dressed as monkeys, stormed the castle with swords in hand and conquered the giant. The sipahis who participated in these celebrations told Leupolt, that having made progress in the art of war, instead of attacking the giant Ravana with bows and arrows, storming the castle, and cutting down the giant with swords, they would spring a mine, blow up the castle, and knock down the giant with a few six-pounders.[80]

The original myth of the victory of good over evil, which was basic to Ramlila, was manifest in the form its celebration took. In medieval times its celebration represented the victory of the medieval representations of power—the sword-bearing horseman. He symbolized the force of 'goodness' who crushed to death the 'evil' force represented by the figure of Ravana. With the establishment of the Company as a political power in India the representations of power had changed. Power which was represented in the form of superior technology, like the artillery, was now woven into the myth of Ramlila. The form of celebration therefore changed to express new power relations and create a new tradition. Further, the Company, by making the sipahis celebrate Ramlila independent of the patronage of any priestly figure, created a superior status for them. In fact they maintained that their status was higher than that of their rivals the Brahmin priests. For not only were they donors and patrons of a Hindu ritual but they also had the power to modify the celebrations by their superior military technology. It was not a suprise then that Leupolt observed that the Brahmins outside the military establishment 'regretted and bemoaned the fact that the festival

[79] Diary of Lieutenant-Colonel J. Pester, Bengal Army 1801–26, MSS. Eur. D436, IOL. The Company allowed the sipahi to be absent from parade for two days at the time of a festival.

[80] Rev. C. B. Leupolt, *Recollections of an Indian Missionary* (London, 1856), p. 78.

had lost its efficacy'.[81] The enthusiasm of the soldiers for the Ramlila celebration is evident from their voluntary subscriptions. Indeed, soldiers of all ranks made voluntary subscriptions, at high rates, for the success of the Ramlila celebration. The following were the rates to defray the expenses of the festival in 1830: subedar Rs 7, jamadar Rs 2, havaldar and naike Rs 1 and sipahi 8 annas.[82]

In 1829, Fanny Parks, who travelled extensively in north India, noted a Ramlila celebration in the parade grounds of the Kanpur cantonment. She observed that 'the sipahis themselves dressed up as monkeys with long tails to represent Ram's army and were led by one of them dressed as Hanuman.' From her comments it appears that in the cantonment Ramlila the Company encouraged the association of its sipahis with Hindu mythical figures so as to further merge their religious and military identity. The Company appears to have been successful in its efforts because the sipahis saw the regiment as supporting their religious status. This was nowhere more vividly represented than in a ceremony which Fanny Parks observed in the cantonment of Kanpur. She noted:

Here each native regiment took out its colours and made *pooja* to the standards offering them sweetmeats, flowers, rice and *pan* as they do to God. They rode around the image of the giant Ravana with the colours flying after having made *pooja* to them. At the conclusion of the *tamasha* the figure of Ravana was blown up by the conqueror Ram.[83]

Alongside Ramlila, the Company regulated other forms of cantonment recreation as well so as to further reinforce the assumed high-caste status of its sipahis. For instance, the Company supplied its sipahis only with Brahmin and Rajput prostitutes.[84] Indeed

---

[81] Ibid., p. 78.

[82] 10 L. MS. Eur. C. 29 MS 'Travels in India', Commonplace book of G. E. Westmacolt (A Cadet in 1822), p. 98.

[83] Fanny Parks, *Wanderings of a Pilgrim in Search of the Picturesque* (2 vols., London, 1850) I, pp. 108–10.

[84] Report of crime for 1850, Pre-Mutiny Kumaon Division, Judicial Letters Issued, File No. 55, vol. 40, UPSA. This had been a practice started by the Rajas of Kumaon who employed lowlanders and foreigners in their army and appear to have regarded it their duty to provide for the well-born mercenary soldiers, a distinct class of prostitutes. Rent-free villages were granted for the support of Pathans, and the protection of the

the sipahi regiments from the plains, cantoned in the province of Kumaon, kept up the demand for high-caste prostitutes. The large number of Brahmin and Rajput prostitutes at so small a place as Almora often excited astonishment.[85]

The Company did not encourage temple worship within the cantonment. Very rarely were temples allowed inside the Sepoy Lines or regiment. If cantonments developed around old forts with temples already in use, then their priests and idols were shifted outside the cantonment. It was argued that religious sites located within military areas were detrimental to cantonment hygiene for pilgrims visiting these shrines brought disease into the cantonment.

The absence of temples inside the cantonment separated the sipahis from the patronage network of Brahmin priests. This contributed to the Company's efforts to establish a caste status ·for the sipahis that was relatively independent of the Brahmin hierarchy itself. For instance, at the cantonment in Kumaon, which had developed around the fort of Almora, there were three Hindu temples. At the time of its construction the military officials pulled down an adjoining building which housed the idol of the Hindu Goddess Bhawani. Its Brahmin priest caretaker, who resided in the same building, was also rendered homeless.[86] At the time of its razing the Company promised that after the completion of the cantonment a separate house would be erected near the three temples for the use of the priest and the Goddess. But once the construction work was over, strong objections surfaced against the readmission of this idol into the fort. Lieutenant-Colonel J. W. Adams, commanding at Kumaon, was of the view that since the idol was the Goddess of war to which sacrifices of

---

rights and property of these people as well as the strict preservation of their caste and custom formed a major business of the native Darbars. Brahmins and Rajputs of respectable families were reported to have sold their daughters to bards either of the 'Rajchele' or Pathan tribe. The bards sold these women to the Kumaon army.

[85] Ibid.

[86] L. No. 2633, I. W. Adams, Lieutenant Colonel commanding at Kumaon, to Lieutenant Colonel G. H. Fagan, Adjtt. General, 6 Aug. 1815, and I. Adam, Sec. to Govt., to E. Gardner, Commissioner at Kumaon, 20 Aug. 1815, Pre-Mutiny Records Kumaon Division, Miscellaneous Letters Received, vol. 6, UPSA.

animals had to be made, the military would have to allow armed pilgrims inside the cantonment. He argued that it was against military decorum and custom to admit armed men into the interior of the garrison and therefore the room housing the idol should not be reinstated. Alongside security reasons, he also thought that pilgrim traffic to the temple would cause tremendous inconvenience to the health and cleanliness of troops.[87] The temple idol and its priest were thus removed to a house outside the cantonment at a period when the Company was very sensitive about interfering with issues and institutions of a religious nature.

The Company, anxious to ensure the loyalty of its sipahis by buttressing their assumed high-caste status, was equally concerned about the activities of Christian missionaries. For instance, in 1819, Major M. Boyd, commanding the 1st Battalion 25th Regiment at Meerut, was alarmed at the conversion of Purbdeen Pandey, a Brahmin Naik. He had been converted to Christianity by Reverend Mr Fisher and Boyd argued that this conversion was against the Company's claim to preserve the religious customs and practices of its sipahis. The government took strong note of this conversion and the sipahi was punished by his removal from the 25th Native Infantry. At the same time the government instituted a committee at Meerut, to review rules and regulations in the cantonment which could in any way interfere with the religion of the sipahis.[88]

However, outside the regiment and the cantonment, this new form of high-caste military authority came into direct contact with the Brahmin priesthood itself. But even here the military maintained its exclusive high-caste status independent of and superior to that of the Brahmin patronage networks. This was done by exempting the sipahis from certain religious obligations which reinforced the superiority of the priestly class of Brahmins.

[87] Ibid.

[88] Major Boyd, commanding 1st Battalion, 25th Regiment, to Lieutenant Colonel J. Nicol, Adjutt. Gen., 23 Oct. 1819, enclosed in L. No. 794, Adjtt. Gen. J. Nicol to Lt. Colonel W. Casement, Sec. to Govt. Mil. Deptt., 12 Nov. 1819, Parliamentary Papers, Accounts and Papers, East India China Session 1857–58, vol. XLIII, p. 163; see also L. No. 398, W. Casement, Sec. to Govt. Mil. Deptt., to Lt. Colonel J. Nicol. Adjutt. Gen., 20 Nov. 1819, ibid., p. 164.

Exemption from pilgrim dues was one such concession given to the sipahis.[89] Initially, in 1791, the government authorized the exemption from usual pilgrim dues, 'such Hindu Sepoys as volunteered in going on service of Bencoolen.' From 1793, Hindu sipahis who returned from serving on the coast of south India were also exempted from these dues.[90] Finally, in 1810, the government exempted all the Hindu sipahis from the pilgrim tax.[91] Moreover, the military regulated and monitored the activities of the sipahis when they performed their religious rituals in the temples outside the cantonments. In this way, the sipahis were shielded from the power of civil authorities, both British and Indian, at the temple site. In 1809, the Commander-in-Chief decreed:

In order to guard against public inconvenience and acts of irregularity which are liable to occur at the temple of Juggernauth for the native officers and sipahis who obtained leave to visit that temple, the Commander-in-Chief is pleased to direct that it be henceforward considered a standing order that whenever native commissioned and non-commissioned officers, Sepoys or others in the military service of Government shall obtain leave to visit the temple at Juggernauth they shall be strictly enjoined to report their arrival to the officer commanding the detachment of Juggernauth, and in all respects to conform during their stay there to such rules and directions as he may prescribe.[92]

On the occasion of taking their departure from Jagannath the

[89] For an interesting discussion of British administration of pilgrimage see K. H. Prior, 'The British administration of Hinduism in north India, 1780–1900', Ph.D thesis, Cambridge University, 1990, pp. 6–88. Prior shows that it was accepted that a pilgrim ought to pay both the priest and the Government according to his ability; 'when a pilgrim was of a particularly high social, political or religious rank it was an act of courtesy and diplomacy to exempt him from the Government dues. However, there was no similar expectation regarding the donations to the priest. The grander the pilgrim the more general the patronage of the religious institution and their functionaries ought to have been.' I argue that the Company's non-interference in donations which the pilgrims gave to priests must have suited the high-caste sipahi. He could interact with the priest in ways which suited him best.

[90] A. Seton, Collector of Bihar, to Charles, Marquis of Cornwallis, Governor General in Council, 12 March 1793, BPC, 11–29 March 1793, P/115/1, IOL.

[91] GOCC, 21 Dec. 1810, *Abstract of General Orders and Regulations*, p. 238.

[92] Ibid.

sipahis were expected to make a previous report to the officer commanding at the post and strictly conform to all the directions issued for their guidance.[93]

Moreover, the Company also distanced the sipahi from the Brahmin patronage networks at the temple sites by exempting them from payment of any kind of fee to the *purohit* at the time of *darshan* (paying of homage to the shrine). These special privileges and arrangements for the sipahis at temples and shrines outside the cantonments strengthened their high-caste status and projected them as superior devotees who wielded power sufficient to override even the sacred power and influence of the temple priest. This was a very significant development in the history of the Rajputs and the Bhumihars who had joined the Bengal Army. In fact, the Company agreed to this measure only after the sipahis asserted, by the force of their newly acquired power and authority, their superior high-caste status. The demonstration of their power disturbed public order in the city of Jagannath and threatened to affect the pilgrim traffic to the city. The sipahis not being able to make darshan in the temple of Jagannath, free of cost, went on a rampage in the city.[94] They violently interfered in the building of the *rath* of Jagannath by forcibly taking away the workmen and material. They performed acts of violence on the public officers of the temple, and attempted to set the Collector's house on fire. The alarmed Collector at Jagannath reported:

I am given to understand by several pilgrims and respectable inhabitants that they are much afraid to go about the streets and to the temple in the night for fear of being maltreated by the Sepoys which has already taken place. If nothing is done for this, pilgrims will not come in hereafter from hearing such unfavourable accounts. Likewise the officers of the temple will not be able to celebrate and bring their Gods out at Chudun Jatrah accompanied by several Maharees (dancing girls) which continues regularly for 21 days and nights as customary and will commence on the 6th.[95]

---

[93] Ibid.

[94] L. No. 42, R.M. Mitford, acting Collector Cuttack, to B. Crisp, acting President and member Board of Revenue, 30 April 1810, enclosed in a letter from Sec. Board of Rev. to BCJ, 11 May 1810, BCJ, Consul. FW 26 May 1810, P/130/16, IOL.

[95] Ibid.

On another occasion, at the Allahabad pilgrimage site, they made a similar assertion of their power. Here, the sipahis, entirely on their own, extended the exemption from pilgrim dues to their families and relatives as well.[96]

The Company's encouragement of the sipahis' superior ritual status often generated fresh problems for it. For it created points of conflict between the high-caste sipahis and the figures of religious authority outside the regiment and cantonment. In its less organized but more violent form this superior military-religious status was used by the sipahis to openly uproot and desecrate places of worship and symbols associated with the patronage and influence of civilian religious authority structures. This was evident in the case of a sipahi, Hari Prasad, of the First Battalion, Third Regiment in Benaras, who complained that he had been beaten by a villager while he was looking after the Company's camels sent out to graze in the neighbourhood. On investigation it was revealed that the sipahi had destroyed a *bur* tree so as to provide forage for his camels.[97] This tree had been held in veneration by the villagers because it was believed to be the sanctuary of the tutelary Goddess Bhawani. In the popular folklore of the locality, on many occasions, it had saved the village from fire. The sipahis had repeatedly attempted to destroy this tree despite their knowledge of its significance and very often this had resulted in violence between them and the village people. The manner in which they escaped the charges made against them at the court martial revealed that by the early nineteenth century the Company authorities had begun to regard sipahis almost as the custodians of Hindu practice. The sipahis asked the president of the court martial, who was himself a Hindu, the following question: 'Could we from our caste have permitted to cut down the bur tree if there had been an image of the Hindu saint Bhawani under it?' The question being answered in the negative, the prisoners called no further witnesses and the court verdict declared the

[96] See Allahabad Commissionary Pre-Mutiny Revenue Deptt., file 13/1815, basta 13, box 60; file 32/1827, basta 38, box 124; file 28/1814, basta 10, box 50, ARA.

[97] L. No. 4 A, Correspondence between W.W. Bird, Magistrate of the city of Benaras, and Major Wood, commanding at Benaras, 7 Feb. 1817, BRC LP, vol. 6, UPSA.

prisoners 'incapable of the offence imputed to them because it was incompatible with their religion.'[98]

It was the creation of this stereotype of the Hindu sipahi which made I. Nicol, the acting Adjutant General of the Army, reject the proposal of W. W. Bird, the magistrate of Benaras city, to provide police escorts with public cattle rather than sipahis. In 1817, in a letter to Captain A. R. Young, officiating secretary to government in the Military Department, he argued that only the Company's Hindu sipahis were in a position to understand and protect the sensibilities of the Hindu population of the region. He wrote:

The Commander-in-Chief does not agree to the above proposal. The Guards sent continuously with the cattle must, from the composition of native Corps, chiefly consist of Hindus. Consequently, though they may sometimes forget their prejudices, they must in most cases enter into the feelings of a Hindu population so as to make them more likely to protect the inhabitants against the wanton destruction of sacred places, as trees, by servants with the cattle than the police servants who are generally Musalman.[99]

Paradoxically, the very fact that the Company so forcefully created a Hindu 'sanctuary' within the cantonment made it possible for high-caste custom to co-exist with practices such as cow slaughter, which otherwise might have been regarded as unacceptable. Consequently the dietary requirements of the British officers could also be easily met within the Cantonment.[100] In

[98] Ibid.

[99] Ibid., I. Nicol, Acting Sec. Adjtt. Gen. of army to Captain A. R. Young, officiating Sec. to Govt. Mil. Deptt., 10 Jan. 1817, BCJ WP, Consult. 7 Feb. 1817, P/133/14, IOL.

[100] G.C. Gowan, Commissioner of Kumaon, to Lieutenant Colonel Andre, commanding 7th regiment Native Infantry, 24 Feb. 1837; and to G. Bushby, officiating secretary to the Lt. Gov. NWP Agra from G.C. Gowan, Commissioner of Kumaon, 27 Sept. 1837, Kumaon Pre-Mutiny Records, Judicial Letters Issued, vol. 33, UPSA. In 1815 G.C. Gowan, the Commissioner of Kumaon, on being asked by the Government to suggest possible ways of killing cattle within the cantonment, with the least possible offence to the Hindus, submitted the following report: He was of the view that the feelings of the Hindu population in the unostentatious killing of cattle in Kumaon would be pacified if this was confined to special grounds allotted for it, within the cantonment limits of Almorah, Huwal Bagh, Lahoaghat and Pethoragarh. The persons living outside the limits of the cantoment would be permitted to avail themselves of the beef from these places.

fact, having abstracted the sipahi from the constraints and hierarchy of 'Hindu' society the Company now used him to subdue the Hindu population. In 1815 the sipahi regiments were used to put down demonstrations and assemblages of Brahmins protesting against cow slaughter at the temple of Nanda Devi in Kumaon district.[101] With reference to discussions on sati reforms, in particular, it was evident that the Company could use the sipahis to control any form of protest if they did not object to infringement in 'Hindu custom'. It was for this reason that William Bentinck, the Governor-General who finally banned sati in 1828, was concerned about the sipahi reaction to the measure. For it was generally thought that the Company could deal with all other forms of protest if it had the support of its army.[102] Indeed their support was essential as a force against 'Hindu society'.

By the mid-1820s, the Company began to realize that it incurred some disadvantages by the creation of this very specific form of military Hinduism. The 1820s was a decade of mutinies and desertions. The Company experienced the severest crisis of control in this period. This had partly to do with the military retrenchment and cuts which followed the completion of the Pindari war and Burma campaigns, but it was also because of the resentment of the sipahis towards the slightest infringement of the ritual rules instituted by the Company but which had now come specifically to define their own status and identity. The number of men who deserted from the native infantry in the year 1822 was 687. In 1823, the number of deserters increased to 1,041, and in 1824 the figures soared to 5,593, while in 1825 they rose to 8,322.[103]

He argued that the Brahmins would eventually submit to what they perceived was beyond their power to obviate. The Government accepted Gowan's suggestion and allowed the slaughter of cattle within the limits of the Kumaon cantonment.

[101] Ibid.

[102] See IOLR, Typescript copies of documents omitted from correspondence of Bentinck by C. H. Philips, MSS Eur. E. 424. Discussions on sati reforms brought this out very well.

[103] File No. 21, L. No. 488, C. Fagan, Adjutant General of Military, to Sec. to Govt. in the Military Department, 17 Jan. 1829, BMC, Consult. FW 23 Feb. 1829, P/33/20, IOL. A government order for apprehending and punishing deserters was passed in 1825. Fagan attributed the high desertion rate to the cuts in furlough, absence of leave, and

The Barrackpur mutiny in 1825 was a major manifestation of the sipahi's zealous shielding of his high ritual status. At the time of the Burma campaign in 1824–5 the 26th, 47th and 62nd Regiments of the Bengal Army were ordered to march from Mathura, where they were stationed, to Barrackpur and then continue marching to Rangoon. The 47th Regiment on reaching Barrackpur refused to march further to Rangoon and this sparked off the Barrackpur mutiny. It was later disclosed by the committee, which discussed the cause of the Barrackpur mutiny, that there were two major grievances the soldiers nurtured which ultimately resulted in their refusing to march to Rangoon. The main cause, as the committee believed, was the want of carriage cattle. As we have seen, every Hindu sipahi cooked his own food and so had to carry a variety of bulky articles for its preparation. As he also had to carry essential things like uncooked food sufficient for two or three days, his arms, some linens, a carpet, a quilt, and five to six brass vessels for cooking, it had always been customary for the government to furnish hired carriage to the marching sipahi. The sipahi had to pay for this facility and it was becoming increasingly difficult for him to do so because the prices of bullocks had gone up due to the increase in the demand for carriage cattle. Being unable to cart his essentials, he was unwilling to make any journey where he might have to compromise his ritual status.[104] Moreover, the sipahis feared that they would have to board a ship for the final leg of the journey from Chittagong to Rangoon. In fact they were reported to have said that 'during their journey they would not undertake even a short passage by boat, rather they would halt in their march and proceed no further.'[105] This appears to have prompted the Company to action and its officials soon realized that their attempt to abstract sipahis from Hindu society had backfired on them. They found that they could no longer control their own sipahis, severed as they were from social bonds.

In the late 1820s, the Company reacted to this crisis with rigorous parade and discipline in the regiments.

[104] Barat, *Bengal Infantry*, pp. 212–13.
[105] Ibid., p. 204

the creation of two new figures of religious authority—the regimental pandit and the regimental maulvi. This was an attempt to rebuild the old relationship between the sipahis and traditional religious figures. Like the regimental padre in the British regiments these religious figures were to exercise control over the sipahi (plate 1). The General Order of 4 March 1825 directed that

a pandit and a maulvee be added from the Proximo to the Interpreter and Quarter Master Establishment of every Regiment of Native Cavalry and Infantry of the Line on an allowance of 8 Sonnaut Rupees/mensem each.[106]

The Company laid down specific criteria for the recruitment of such religious figures. The pandit and the maulvi were expected to be well versed in the native languages, the former in Hindi in the Nagri script and the latter in the Persian. Their duties were to act as figures of control over the sipahi. They attended all court martials or courts of inquiry and presided over the oath-taking ceremony of all sipahis. The maulvi and the pandit taught the sipahi how to read and write Hindi and Persian. For this extra tuition they received two to four annas per month from the sipahis. From 1827, their importance as teachers further increased because in that year the Company decided that it would not promote any sipahi to the rank of a non-commissioned officer in any corps of the Line if he was not competent in the knowledge of reading and writing at least one language.[107] This appears to have been a deliberate attempt to increase the dependence of the sipahi on traditional authority structures so as to exercise more control over him. It is interesting to speculate whether this measure began to increase the distance between Hindi in the Nagri script and Urdu in a Persian script which had been nowhere near as precise before.

By the 1830s, the Company's peasant army experiment had become a cause of concern to it. The Company's reaction was one of ambivalence: emphasizing its preference for high-caste sipahis

[106] GOGG in Council, 4 March 1825, BMC, Consult. FW 4 March 1825, P/31/15, IOL.

[107] Ibid. Exceptions were made only in the case of those sipahis who distinguished themselves on the battlefield.

but at the same time putting checks on the power and status hitherto enjoyed by them. It was this cautious policy which was reflected in Bentinck's concern to consult the army before going ahead with his sati reforms. These developments in the social politics of the Company's army were tidings of the graver dangers which the Company was to confront in the more well-known crisis of 1857. After the 1857 disturbances the Company fully realized the dangers inherent in its experiment of building a caste-conscious army. The Company attempted to dilute further the power and authority of its high-caste Hindu sipahis by opening its regiments to different social groups—the Jats, Punjabis, Gurkhas and the Sikhs. But the high-caste purabias continued to look towards other forums to emphasize the high status they and their ancestors had now been deprived of. From the mid-nineteenth century, British ethnographers noted that the Bhumihars emphasized their Brahmanical status in the varna hierarchy. Sherring, the British ethnographer in Benaras in the 1870s, supporting such claims wrote:

Some doubt has been thrown on the purity of blood as Brahmins. It has been said that they are Kshatriya or Rajpoot Brahmins. I have been unable to obtain any trustworthy evidence for such assertions.[108]

Once again, in the early twentieth century, Sahjanand Saraswati, the peasant leader of the Bhumihars, defended their Brahmanical status in the magazine *Bhumihar Brahmin Parichai*. In his article Saraswati emphasized their Brahmin origin and high-caste status.[109]

[108] Sherring, *Hindu Tribes*, p. 39.

[109] Saraswati, *Bhumihar Brahmin Parichai*, pp. 25–30. He attributed their non-religious functions to their association with the Mughal state. Sahjanand argued that they were the branch of Brahmins who had entered into the service of the Mughal state in various capacities. The state had granted them land and that was the origin of their zamindaris. The fear of losing their Brahmin status by being engulfed in the zamindari class made the Bhumihars substitute the word zamindar for Bhumihar. However, the divide between the Bhumihars and the purohit class of Brahmins was created because the Brahmin priests emphasized their knowledge of the Hindu texts so as to establish their superiority over the Bhumihars. The continued association with the Mughal court led to their learning the Mughal court language, Persian, and the emulation of the Mughal lifestyle, its titles and food habits, perpetuating the difference between them and the Brahmins proper who still carried out priestly functions. The zamindars acquired titles such as bahadur and rai sahib in place of Brahmin names like Pande, Misra, etc. and

At about the same time, Raghunandan Saran also tried to emphasize their superiority by establishing their links with the branch of Kanyakubja Brahmins whom he regarded as the highest and parent stock of Brahmins.[110] This need to emphasize their high ritual status was increasingly felt by the Bhumihars because by 1857 the Company, grappling with the problems its military recruiting had created, had significantly curbed the power and authority of its high-caste sipahis. Alongside this, some of the Company's military institutions had also been modified to tackle the problems arising from its pattern of recruitment.

---

chewed tobacco in the manner of Mughal courtiers.

[110] R. Saran, *Kanyakubjaon ka itihas* (Benaras, 1991) pp. 17–24. According to Saran the Kanyakubja Brahmins resided south of the river Saryu. Those who migrated to different regions in search of employment adopted the names of the regions where they settled, but they did not lose their Brahmin status. The Bhumihars, according to this theory, were Brahmins who had migrated from the south of the river Saryu and settled in different regions as cultivators and servicemen. According to Saran there could be Kanyakubj Brahmins, Saryupari Brahmins etc., depending on where the migrating Brahmins chose to settle.

Chapter 3

The Invalid Thanah

The army sustained Company power by providing it with a cultural idiom through and by which British authority was to be represented in India. The key institution in this process was the Invalid Thanah. Indeed, the army became a critical institution used by the British in India not only to expand territorially but also to legitimize their presence in the country. From 1778 onwards, new areas were colonized and pockets of influence were created in the Company's territories by settling within them retired sipahis called 'invalid soldiers'. In 1781, an invalid was defined as a sipahi who had been in the Company's service for a minimum of ten to twelve years and who was disabled by age or infirmity. Those who had not served for this length of time but had become disabled by wounds sustained in the service of the Company were also classified as invalids.[1] Those sipahis who took their discharge from the service for personal reasons and were allotted plots of land, generally near their homes, formed the third kind of invalid.[2] Settlements of invalid sipahis were called Invalid Thanahs. The word Thanah, along with its more familiar meaning

---

[1] At a council meeting attended by Warren Hastings, Governor-General and President, Edward Wheeler and Commander-in-Chief, PDS S, Consult. FW 16 Jan. 1781, vol. 45, NAI.

[2] Hutchinson's 'Report on the Invalid Thanah of Bhagalpur', 24 May 1792, BSMC, Consult. FW 27 June 1792, P/C/15, IOL. Mungulpur had a large invalid settlement of this kind.

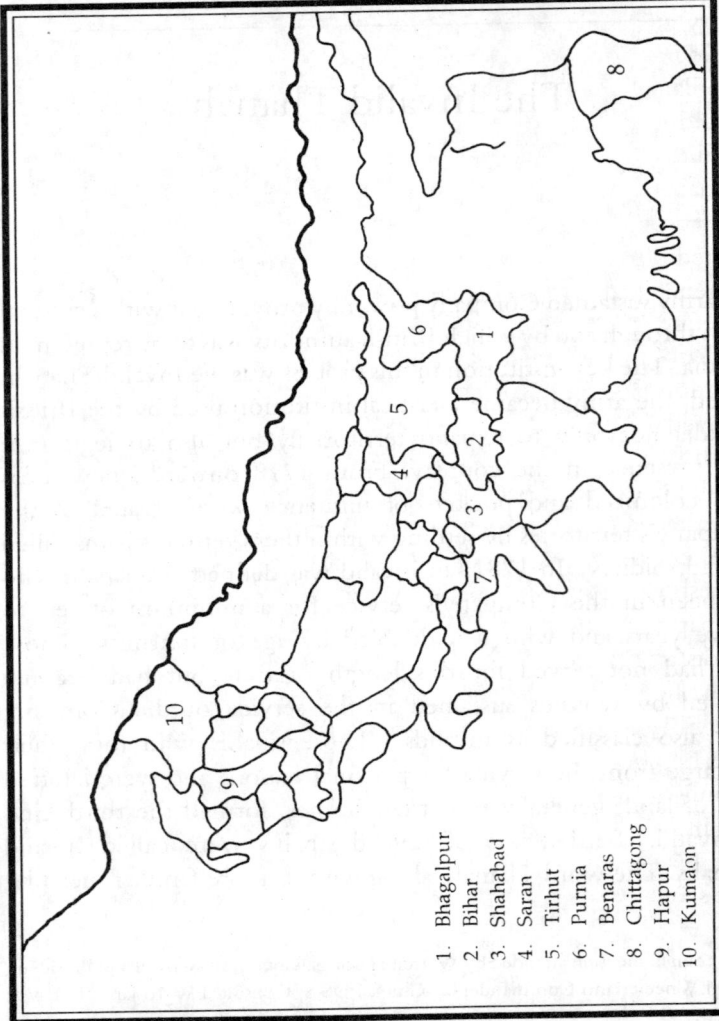

1. Bhagalpur
2. Bihar
3. Shahabad
4. Saran
5. Tirhut
6. Purnia
7. Benaras
8. Chittagong
9. Hapur
10. Kumaon

Map 2. Districts with Invalid Thanahs, Northern India.

of a police station or a military post, was also defined as 'a village or station assigned to the Company's invalid sipahis.'[3]

The Thanah performed important administrative and military functions for the Company by providing men for policing its territory and for training new recruits. This saved the Company a considerable amount of money. Moreover, the Thanah brought acres of land under cultivation and increased the amount of revenue collected by the Company in north India. But more importantly, the military exclusivity which the Company strove to create for the Thanah by separating it from the jurisdiction of civilian administration and law courts had very significant implications. For, separated as it was from civilian society, the Thanah created a very general definition of the Company soldier as one who was best defined in terms of his separation from civilian society. Finally, the Thanah performed the important social and ideological role of demonstrating the Company's benevolence towards those employed in its military service.

In the period of the Company's territorial expansion, the Invalid Thanah performed its functions very successfully. From Bhagalpur, where the first Thanah was established, the Thanahs were extended to western and northern Bihar and as far west as Benaras (map 2). Fresh lands could not be colonized in Awadh since it was not a part of the Company's territory. Here, the Company's Resident distributed pensions in cash at the rate of three rupees per month, to the invalid sipahis who volunteered to stay in their home villages.[4] The British Resident intervened in the functioning of the Nawab's officials so as to expedite the amicable settlement of family and village disputes involving the Company's pensioners living in Awadh. This interference in the administrative functioning of the Nawabi furthered the Company's efforts to reduce Awadh to the status of a subordinate ally.[5] From 1802, with the Company's

[3] H. H. Wilson, *A Glossary of Judicial and Revenue Terms and of Useful Words occurring in Official Documents relating to the Administration of the Government of British India* (London, 1855), p. 518.

[4] For pension rates see Barat, *Bengal Infantry*, p. 143.

[5] See M. H. Fisher, *A Clash of Cultures: Awadh, the British, and the Mughals* (New Delhi, 1987), p. 17. Fisher argues that ever since the coronation of Nawab Ghazi-ud-din Haider in 1819, the Company had been trying to convert Awadh into its subordinate ally and

expansion further westward, more Thanahs were established in the wastelands of what later came to be known as the Ceded and Conquered Provinces.

The Thanah experiment appears to have been very successful until the first decade of the nineteenth century. But in the 1810s and 1820s the Thanahs of Bihar suffered problems of decay and depopulation. The ecology of these thanahs was fragile. Their inherent vulnerability did not differ from that of any other institution similarly located on the fringes of settled arable land. But in the early nineteenth century their extension into uncultivable wasteland exposed the sipahis to disease and death. Consequently, the second and third generation of Thanah inhabitants refused to carry on cultivation on the Thanah lands. By contrast the invalids in Awadh and Benaras had already made significant contributions to the economy of the region. Here, the Thanahs were located in a better ecological environment. But in these regions the Company experienced problems of control caused by what it considered to be the fraudulent practices of the local people who also wanted to benefit from the Thanah.

As early as 1811, the land already colonized by the Thanahs was allowed to remain with the grantees but no fresh grants were made.[6] However, the social tensions generated by the existing Thanahs continued to pose problems for the Company. In the 1820s, these problems were exacerbated because they coincided with the general problems of control within the Company army. This prompted the Company to introduce reforms in the Thanah which enabled it to tighten its control over its peasant regiments. In the late 1820s, Bentinck's preoccupation with the sipahis and, even more so, with their families' welfare resulted in the replacement of the Thanah by several decentralized institutions to monitor the sipahi and his family. For instance, the Company assumed the right to determine the 'legal' heirs of the sipahi and to interfere in his family disputes. Moreover, Bentinck encouraged the Native Family Pensions Institution, inaugurated several offices of the Superintendent of Family, and increased

the Nawab resisted this with all his power.

[6] GOVP, 4 June and 30 July 1811, *Abstract of General Orders and Regulations*, pp. 506–8.

the number of Pension Paymasters functioning in different provinces. They distributed pay and pensions to sipahi families and also maintained written records of each family. It was through these measures that the soldier's family was linked to the institutions of the army. In 1831 the institution of the Thanah was abandoned. This marked a shift from the Company's earlier practice of emphasizing a general category of soldier who was set apart from civilian society to defining him in terms of his family and caste—a feature more characteristic of the late nineteenth century.

Comparable to the Thanah was another type of military colony of 'medically unfit' sipahis lodged in civilian society. These were sipahis confined to the lunatic asylum in Monghyr. Those sipahis whose behaviour and actions posed a problem of discipline in the regiment were declared 'medically unfit' by the Civil Surgeon and classfied as 'insane sipahis'. Institutional confinement of the 'insane sipahi' was the only treatment offered by the Civil Surgeon who also acted as the administrator of the asylum. In its social and ideological role in society, the asylum was comparable to the Invalid Thanah. Like the Thanah it projected the benevolence of the Company and was intended to make the service popular in the region. In 1831, the military, economic and political reasons that saw the abolition of the Thanah prompted the closing of the asylum as well. The Company made the sipahi's family responsible for the care of the medically unfit serviceman. This integration of the family into the functioning of the military marked a further control of a section of civilian society through the institutions of the army.

ORIGINS OF THE INVALID THANAH: BHAGALPUR

In 1778 Captain James Brown, who had been in charge of the Jungle Tarai district since 1774, submitted to the Board specific suggestions for improving the system of control over the hill areas. Towards the end of his report he suggested the role which the retired sipahi could play in this plan. He wrote:

Most of the Sepoys in the Company's service have originally been husbandmen and their families still follow that method of life beyond the Company's territories. I beg to submit to your consideration, whether it would not be for the advantage of Government to publish through the Invalid Corps of Sepoys that whoever among them will settle on the lands between the hills and sudder shall have small jagirs given for that purpose, for the subsistence of themselves and their families who are to be brought thither. This would afford the prospect of a comfortable maintenance to old soldiers worn out in our service. It would also create a militia whose possession being interspersed among those of malguzary tenants would keep the whole in safety from the mountaineers.[7]

On 10 March 1778, the Supreme Council expressed their approval of the plan, marking the genesis of the Invalid Thanáh.

In 1779, Augustus Cleveland, the Collector of Bhagalpur, was directed by Warren Hastings to set up an Invalid Thanah in the northern part of his district. This was for controlling the hill people who pillaged the southern districts. In 1782, Cleveland allotted jagirs to the invalid sipahis in accordance with their military rank. Land lying waste on the fringes of cultivated fields was purchased from the zamindars of the lower hills in return for an allowance called rusum. Generally the following distribution was made for the troopers of the Bengal infantry: commandant Risaldar of horse—300 bighas; jamadar of horse—200 bighas; first dafadar of horse—100 bighas; trooper—50 bighas.

Drummers and fifers were excluded from the establishment but they were admitted to it by special order of the Board and allowed thirty bighas each,[8] whereas in the Bihar, Shahbad, Rohtas, and Benaras districts, the invalids of the infantry regiments were allotted land at the following rates: subahdar—400 bighas; jamadar —200 bighas; havaldar—120 bighas; naik—80 bighas; sepoy—60 bighas.

Even given the fact that this was marginal land, these were considerable holdings and gave great status to those who held them. Moreover, along with the landholdings invalids also received a gratuity in the following proportion to their landholdings: those

[7] Captain James Brown, 'Description of the Jungle Terry Districts, their revenue, trade and government with a plan for the improvement of them', 15 Feb. 1778, Warren Hastings Papers MSS Add. 29210, f. 164, BM.

[8] Revenue Consultations, 24 July 1783, RPB Oct. 1788, Procds. Benares 15 Oct. 1788, Basta 22, File no. 11, ARA.

with 400 and 120 bighas, Rs 50; 80 bighas Rs 30, and 60 bighas, Rs 15.[9]

Cleveland compensated those zamindars who allowed him to allocate invalid jagirs in their zamindaris. They were paid two annas per bigha for such land which had been under cultivation and had fallen waste. However, they were not compensated for land which had never been brought under cultivation.[10] In 1786, R. Adair, the Bhagalpur Collector, identified a large quantity of wasteland extending from 'Oudomulla' westwards to 'Suregegarah' and suggested the extension of jagir land to this area. In a letter to the Board of Revenue he wrote:

The zamindars have no plans of bringing it into cultivation. One could extend the jagir lands along the side of the great Western Road which coasted the range of the hills from Rajmahal to Monghyr.[11]

Between 1786 and 1817, on his advice, the Government purchased extensive tracts of wasteland in Bhagalpur district and allotted them to invalid sipahis. By 1817, Bhagalpur had twenty-two Invalid Thanahs[12] and by the end of 1817, a total of 6.992.18 bighas

[9] Extract from the resolutions of the Governor-General in Council, 18 Feb. 1789, Letters received from the Collector of Shahabad 1789-94, vol. 40, BSA.

[10] Ibid.

[11] R. Adair, Collector of Bhagalpur, to W. Cowper, President and Members of Board of Revenue, 29 April 1786, BRR, 1786, vol. 5, BSA.

[12] The geographical distribution of Thanahs and the number of invalids attached to each of them is given below:

Land Purchased	Estb. of Thanah	No. of Men
Bhagalpur*	1783	184
Mohanpur	1796	31
Augarpur	1785	43
Goga Nulla	1784	67
Duniapur	1784	44
Shazabad	1790	32
Colgong	1785	40
Maisa Mundah 1796	1796	60
Sultanabad	1794	60
Nasibabad*	1794	45
Khawnpur	1795	65
Pialapur	1784	65
Singdawpur*	1784	20

of land had been settled by approximately 1,016 invalid soldiers.[13] In the early nineteenth century, one-fifth of the whole, i.e., 29,700 bighas of wasteland in Bhagalpur had already been purchased by the Company and only 1,000 bighas remained with the zamindars.[14] The invalid jagir became a form of intermediary tenure. The Company leased land from the zamindar and the deed of lease included the *julka*, *bunker* and *phulker* or all trees and their produce, fisheries, and pasture land in the area. The zamindars were compensated at the rate of two annas per bigha for allowing the Company to settle invalids on jagirs located in the zamindaris. This allowance was made only for land which was cultivable and the Company did not compensate them for *bunjar* or forest land.[15] The invalids held the land rent free for life after which it devolved to their heirs who were also exempted from paying rent for the first five years. However, after this period they gave one-tenth of the produce as *malikanah* to the zamindar. This arrangement continued for another five years after which they paid rent, in cash or kind, and at the current rate, to the zamindar.

Land Purchased	Estb. of Thanah	No. of Men
Mawannulla★ .	1784	–
Gaur★	1785	53
Kheri	1789	82
Chickrown★	1783	53
Jaffragunge★	1785	–
Himmuntpur	1785	90
Bindiabund★	1789	–
Hybutgunge★	1784	–
Alinagar★	1787	–

★ Only part of this district. Encl. Nos. 6–8, in letter from J. Sherburne, Collector of Bhagalpur, to Board of Revenue, 1 Nov. 1802, BRIP, Consult. FW 14 June 1803, vol. I, WBSA.

[13] Report of Collector of Bhagalpur to BCBB, undated, BCBB, Consult. 1 March 1817, vol. 9, UPSA.

[14] Martin, *Eastern India*, p. 233.

[15] Minute by a supernumerary member on the subject of invalid jagir lands in Bhagalpur, 15 Jan. 1827, BBR LP, Consult. FW 16 Jan. 1827, P/80/31, IOL. In 1783, in Bhagalpur district, the Collector paid the zamindars Rs 4,473.12 for 35,790 bighas of wastelands, at the rate of 2 annas per bigha. After the Decennial Settlement had been concluded most of the land was bought from the zamindars because they were averse to the delineation of their wastelands.

At the time of assessment, land which had not been brought under cultivation was resumed by the zamindar and he was free to grant pattas for it to whoever he liked.[16] In the case of heirless jagirdars the Company intervened more directly. Their land was made amaunat, resumed by the government, and then disposed of by public sale.[17]

SOUTH BIHAR: MONGHYR AND SHAHABAD

With the success of the Bhagalpur experiment the Invalid Thanahs became the vanguard of colonial expansion westwards.

In the Company army, unlike the British regments at home where ordinary invalid soldiers do not appear to have been settled on landholdings,[18] the Thanah became a very important military institution. It was strategically located on the fringes of the erstwhile Mughal subas. These peripheral areas of the Mughal Empire posed graver problems to the British than the core areas. Here, the Mughals had not been able to establish their administrative machinery and the power of successive Emperors represented little more than the symbolic incorporation of the hill and jungle chieftains[19] into their polity. These chiefs, called autonomous

[16] No. 4, Draft of regulation for invalids, undated, BRIP, Consult. FW 19 Aug. 1803, vol. 1, WBSA.

[17] L. No. 290, BBC BB to Collector of Bhagalpur, 20 March 1817, BBC BB, Consult. Camp Arrah, zillah Shahabad, 20 March 1817, P/111/71, IOL.

[18] The British state very often rewarded its high-ranking military pensioners with grants of land.

[19] S. Nurul Hasan, 'The position of the zamindars in the Mughal Empire', *IESHR*, vol. I, No. 4 (Delhi, 1964), pp. 107–19. I follow Hasan here in using the term autonomous chieftains to refer to the powerful, and often recalcitrant, zamindars on the fringes of the Mughal Empire. Explaining the Mughal state's attitude to such chieftains, Hasan argues that the Mughals absorbed a large number of chiefs into the administrative machinery by conferring mansabs upon them. They asserted the principle which later came to be known as that of paramountcy, i.e. they reserved for themselves the right of recognizing the successor of a deceased Raja. This made the chieftains dependent on the goodwill of the Emperor for their rights. Further, they imposed the obligation of military service even upon such chiefs as were not given mansabs. Finally, they compelled the autonomous chieftains to conform to imperial regulations, especially with regard to the maintenance of law and order and freedom of transit; see also A. R. Khan, *Chieftains in the Mughal Empire during the Reign of Akbar* (Simla, 1977), pp. 1–4. Khan shows the

chieftains, paid irregular tribute to the Mughal Emperor following armed expeditions sent from time to time. They accepted Mughal sovereignty but enjoyed internal autonomy. The Company retained this relationship with the hill chieftains but from 1779 it began to settle colonies of invalid sipahis on the peripheries of the erstwhile Mughal subas of Bengal, Bihar, Benaras and Awadh. These military colonies were intended to keep a check on the power of the autonomous chiefs. It appears that the Company had now set itself the task at which the Mughal administration had apparently proved its incompetence.

The second major invalid settlement was set up in Monghyr. Here, once again, the Company allotted jagirs close to the autonomous chieftains living in the hills and forest regions of the district. For instance, the area with the largest concentration of invalids was the small pargana of Monghyr close to the hill chieftains of Gidhaur and near the territories of the recalcitrant Raja of Kharakpur. Nestling in the Kharakpur hills, 6,864 bighas of land in this pargana were settled with invalid sipahis.[20] Towards the end of 1791 more land in the Kharakpur hills and forests of Monghyr was settled by invalid soldiers. By 1802, approximately 93,243 bighas of land, scattered over hills and forests, was either purchased by government or ceded by local zamindars for the Thanah.[21] This included patches of wasteland and forest lying in between the land under cultivation. Consequently, in Monghyr the invalid jagirs were scattered all over the district. The lands of some of the invalids of the same Thanah were at a distance of approximately sixteen to eighteen miles (seven to eight kos) from each other. Sometimes the same invalid had land in four or five different places at a distance of about six miles from each other.[22]

---

practical difficulties of imposing Mughal 'paramountcy' on the fringes of the Empire. In many regions like Bihar the chieftains resisted the payment of tribute to the Mughal Government and remained recalcitrant until Mughal armies were sent in to crush their power. It appears that the Mughals always had an uneasy alliance with hill chieftains.

[20] Enclosure in a letter from the acting Collector of Bhagalpur to BRMP, 23 July 1791, BRMP, Consult. 8 Aug. 1791, vol. 117, Part 1, UPSA.

[21] Enclosure No. 5 in letter from Collector of Bhagalpur to BRIP, Consult. FW 14 June 1803, vol. 1, WBSA.

[22] Ibid.

Another Invalid Thanah was located in the Shahabad district. This was also strategically positioned close to the land of the recalcitrant hill chiefs of the district. For instance, the forests of the Kaimur hills, in the extreme south of the erstwhile Mughal sarkar of Rohtas, had the largest concentration of invalid jagirs. In fact, in south Rohtas, close to the powerful hill chieftains of Sasaram, the government sanctioned 1,500 bighas of wasteland in the *mouja* of Dhumnowa, in pargana Sasaram, as well as land in the surrounding villages for the Thanah.[23] Further, invalids were also settled in the forests and wastelands of northern Rohtas and the erstwhile Mughal sarkar of Bihar. Indeed, by 1800, there was a flourishing invalid settlement in the hitherto forest-covered areas of Cuttahr in the pargana of Bhojpur. This was due to the efforts of I. Deane, the Collector of Shahabad, who was anxious to settle invalid colonies at Cuttahr because the jungle provided an asylum to recalcitrant zamindars and gave shelter to robbers. Deane spent Rs 1,600 to clear the jungle and this provided the Company with fresh tracts of land which were then granted as jagirs to its invalids.[24]

Alongside these three major Thanahs in southern and eastern Bihar, the other big Invalid Thanah in the east was located in Chittagong. For much of the seventeenth century the eastern coastal and river areas of Bengal had been raided by the Portuguese from Chittagong and by Maghs from the Arakan coast. In 1665, the Mughals took Chittagong and a Mughal fleet was always stationed at Dhaka to ward off raids from the Maghs which continued intermittently into the East India Company period. Like the Mughals, the Company also appears to have experimented

[23] Martin, *Eastern India*, pp. 471–80. Martin, reporting the findings of Buchanan Hamilton who toured the region in 1810–13, notes that 4,680 men were sent to the army from Shahabad. He also reported that in Shahabad invalid soldiers kept slaves but he believed them to be the adopted children of the invalids.

[24] Collector of Shahabad to Board of Revenue, 3 July 1800, BMC, Consult. 31 July 1800, P/20/7, IOL. He asked for the Board's approval for opening up the jungle tract in his district for settling invalid soldiers. The 4th article of the rules passed on 25 February 1793 empowered the Collector to have the jungle cut down after having procured a tract of land for establishing a Thanah. He was also authorized to make such embankments, reservoirs and water courses as might be necessary for the cultivation of the land of the Thanah.

with different strategies to defend this coastal frontier of the Bengal province. Marshal notes that there are indications that the process of opening up eastern Bengal was going ahead at speed in the late eighteenth century. By 1801, seven-eighths of Jessore and seven-ninths of Tippera were said to be under cultivation.[25] It appears that at about the same time the Company also began to settle the eastern hilly fringes of the old Mughal sarkar of Chittagong with invalid sipahis. Their settlements were largely concentrated in the pargana of Arrangabad which was sufficiently large for the proposed Invalid Thanah. The area was covered with forest and required great labour for clearing it. But the government made an advance of money to the invalids so that they could hire labourers for felling the woods and making the land suitable for cultivation.[26] By 1805, other areas on the fringes of this coastal district, like forty-four Kannies on the banks of the Isamati river, were populated with invalid sipahis.[27] Here, the Thanah further assisted the Company in controlling attacks of pirates and infiltrators from the neighbouring forests of Burma.

NORTH BIHAR: SARAN, CHAMPARAN, AND TIRHUT

The interesting aspect of the Thanah was that it was not directed only against small bands of roving people but also against substantial rural magnates who had never been under the control of the pre-colonial polities. This was particularly true of north Bihar which was the home of some of the well-known 'recalcitrant Rajas' of north India. North of the Ganges were located the Mughal sarkars of Saran, Champaran, and Darbhanga. Here, the people living on the fringe of settled arable land had always resisted Mughal authority. Marshal has shown that over large areas of north Bihar, what the British called the 'village zamindaris' were firmly established. These were numerous settlements of Rajputs,

---

[25] Marshall, *Bengal: the British Bridgehead*, pp. 21–2.

[26] S. Pierard, Collector Zillah Chittagong, to Board of Revenue, 14 April 1800, BMC, Consult. FW 29 May 1800, P/20/6, IOL.

[27] Collector of Chittagong to BRIP, 22 March 1805, BRIP, Consult. FW 22 March 1805, vol. 3, WBSA.

Bhumihars or ashraf Muslims who exercised the right to collect revenue from cultivators even though in some cases they themselves cultivated the land.[28] The Mughal Government had inevitably to employ intermediary collectors to handle the collection of payments from the multitude of small zamindaris. Some of these men were amils and others were chieftains of the leading clans of Rajputs and Bhumihars. In both cases there was a powerful trend towards turning their duties to collect for the government into property for themselves.[29] The Raja of Darbhanga, the Bettiah Rajah and the Bhojpur Raja were some of the powerful rural élites of the region who often resisted the regular payment of revenue to the government. It was because of the emergence of these powerful zamindars that even though Bihar was potentially a valuable province with a high target figure for government revenue, early British enquiries showed that the Nawab of Bengal had been able to exact virtually nothing from it until 1748 and only small amounts thereafter.[30] The Company again settled invalid soldiers close to the territory of the recalcitrant zamindars and rajas of Bihar so as to establish its permanent presence in their strongholds. For instance, the largest colony of invalid soldiers was set up in Kalyanpur close to the powerful Bettiah zamindari in north Champaran. On most occasions the Company's collectors identified the areas available in their district and it was on their recommendation that land was purchased

[28] Marshall, *Bengal: the British Bridgehead*, p. 57.

[29] Ibid., Marshall notes that in Bihar the process had not gone so far as in Bengal and in many cases its outcome still depended on the use of force. For instance, north of the Ganges the Raja of Darbhanga had successfully enlarged a grant made to them by the Emperor Aurangzeb. He had for all practical purposes come to be regarded as master of the whole sarkar of Tirhut. But further west the Bettiah Raja of Champaran was still locked in conflict with the Nawab's government which launched periodic forays against him. South of the river the Rajput chiefs of Bhojpur had built up a large and powerful holding; for the relationship of the Company to the Bettiah Raja see Yang, *Limited Raj*, p. 68.

[30] Bengal Select Committee Procds., 6 March 1769, range A, vol. 9, pp. 127–8. Cited in Marshall, *Bengal: the British Bridgehead*, p. 58. The British believed that the dependent rajas and zamindars were continually in arms and though these countries were rated very high, they generally compounded for the payment of half or one-third according to the situation of their possessions and their own strength.

for the Thanah.[31] For instance in 1786, on the recommendation of the Collector of Tirhut, the invalid Indian officers of the Ramgarh and Chittagong Regiments were settled on large areas of wastelands in the Darbhanga district.[32] They were allotted jagirs in the divisions of Hajipur, Darbhanga, 'Iurrooah' and Bassarah regions of the old sarkar of Darbhanga. Here, land under cultivation was intermixed with wasteland. Consequently, the arable land being used to grow crops and the lands of some invalids of the same Thanah were at a distance of fourteen to sixteen miles (six to seven kos) from each other.[33] As more and more land became habitable due to the grant of invalid jagirs the zamindars often made tenders to the government for the sale of their wastelands. They were willing to pay at the moderate rate of six to eight annas per bigha but in return wanted the Collector to procure for them an equal amount of land dependent on a village which bordered their estate.[34] In this way the distribution of invalid jagirs represented a rigorous intervention by the Company in the affairs of the zamindars which must have facilitated the collection of revenue as well.

BENARAS, HAPUR, AND KUMAON

The Benaras Thanah, like the Thanahs of Bihar, was also meant to keep a check on the Rajput chieftains and powerful zamindars on the fringes of the district. In addition, the Benaras Thanah helped the Company in maintaining its monopolistic power and authority over a commercially important and religiously significant political centre. In 1780, Jonathan Duncan, the British Resident in Benaras, settled invalids in the forested regions of his district.[35]

[31] Enclosure No. 12, Captain R. Spottiswood, Regulating Officer of the Shahabad Thanah, to Collector of Shahabad, undated, enclosed in letter No. 11, Collector of Shahabad to BRIP, 2 Nov. 1802, BRIP, vol. 1, WBSA.

[32] B. Apliney, Member Board of Revenue, to G.F. Grant, Collector in Tirhut, 18 July 1786, MCR, 1786, vol. 5, BSA.

[33] Enclosure in a letter from acting Collector of Bhagalpur, 23 July 1791, BRMP, Consult. 8 Aug. 1791, vol. 117, Part 1, BSA.

[34] Extract from a minute by G.P. Grant, 22 Aug. 1798, MDR, Extract from Procd. of Hon. Gov.-Gen. in Council in Military Deptt., 27 Aug. 1798, vol. 17, BSA.

The Thanah was localized in the extensive wastelands in parganas Kuntit, Shadeabad, Dhoosa and Chausa. Duncan, on being appointed the British Resident in Benaras, observed that in many parts of these parganas more than one half of the cultivable lands were lying waste. But what really worried him was the fact that these jungles and wastelands were providing shelter to the Rajput communities who fled there so as to escape paying revenue to the Benaras raja.[36] Even though the Company increasingly came to rely on a close relationship with the Bhumihar ruling family it had to deal with groups of these Rajput *bhaiyachara* tenures, scattered in Benaras, who resisted the rule of the Raja as well as that of the Company.[37] Moreover, their surveillance became more important because in this period Duncan began to make efforts to abolish the prevalence of infanticide amongst the Rajkumar Rajputs of the region[38]

The establishment of the Benaras Thanah in 1781 and its expansion in the period following Cheyt Singh's 'insurrection' suggests the significant role of surveillance and control the Company allocated to the Thanah. In 1781, Duncan granted Juggernath Subahdar, an ex-Commandant of the 3rd Regiment of Sepoys, the first invalid jagir in the district.[39] Soon after, on Hastings' recommendation, Bandu Khan, resident of Chunar who had shown immense valour in the battle of Pateeta, was also granted a jagir in his home village of Jelalpur in pargana Pateeta which was

[35] J. Duncan, Resident in Benaras, to Board of Commissioners, 15 Oct. 1788, RPB, Basta No. 22, Record No. 11, Procds. Benaras 15 Oct. 1788, UPSA. In this letter he notifies the availability of land for the establishment of an Invalid Thanah.

[36] Ibid. From a report on the pargana by Ramchand Pandit, an amil of the pargana, it was evident that in the Tuppah of Khurnaie there was a forest of large *pulas* and other trees and long grass which extended for two to three acres. This was also the region of the turbulent zamindaris of Khereed, Buragong and Kopah. These recalcitrant chiefs caused disturbances in the area by their internecine warfare and by their perpetual hostility with the zamindar of Bettiah. The jungle in their territories served as a refuge when escaping from the exactions of state officials and also during their fights with each other.

[37] B. S. Cohn, 'Structural change in Indian rural society 1596–1885', in Cohn (ed.), *An Anthropologist among the Historians*, p. 353.

[38] David Kopf, *British Orientalism and the Bengal Renaissance*, p. 30.

[39] Oldham, *Historical and Statistical Memoir of Ghazipur District*, p. 17.

strategically placed on the route ways of the Ganges.[40] In 1788, with the official sanction and assistance of the Board of Revenue, the forest-covered areas of Benaras became one of the biggest colonies of retired sipahis. The Company never experienced any problems settling soldiers here. Being an important recruiting base and a holy city invalid sipahis were very happy to be settled there. Very often invalid sipahis from different Thanahs applied to the the Board of Commissioners for transfers to Benaras.[41]

The Benaras experiment was encouraging but the Company could not repeat it in Awadh. Here, it found it difficult to settle its invalids on wastelands since Awadh was not part of its territory. But since a large percentage of the Company's sipahis came from Awadh, it assumed the responsibility of looking after them and their families if they chose to settle in their homeland. The British Resident in Awadh distributed pensions in cash to the invalids in Awadh.[42] This practice of making payments in cash to invalids increased after 1811 when the Company stopped making fresh land grants in Bihar and Benaras as well. Henceforth, those delcared invalid by the invaliding committee were granted six months' invalid pay of their respective ranks and were given permission to retire to any part of the Company's territory. The invalids' pay was attractive and generally they were paid at the following rates:

Subahdar	Rs 25
Jamadar	Rs 12
Havaldar	Rs 7
Sepoy	Rs 4

An additional allowance was made to those who had lost a

[40] Ibid., pp. 16–17.

[41] L. No. 34, Collector of Shahabad to Sec., BCBB, 2 March 1818, BCBB, Consult. Shahabad 3 March 1818, UPSA. This letter contains an arzi of Dinaram, Subahdar of Shahabad Thanah, requesting a transfer to his home district Benaras, because of the difficulties and expense involved in travelling from his present Thanah to his home in Benaras.

[42] Referred to in GOGG 25 Nov. 1825, Thompson, *Abstract of General Orders*, pp. 38–9.

limb or become blind or had been badly wounded while on service. This was granted at the following rates:[43]

Subahdar	Rs 15
Jamadar	Rs 8
Havaldar	Rs 5
Sepoy	Rs 3

In Awadh, the Company distributed pensions, in cash, to its invalid soldiers who had settled in their home villages. Until as late as 1825 the British Resident administered the distribution of pensions to these retired soldiers. This was in contrast to Bihar and Benaras where pensioners were settled on landholdings on the fringes of settled land and superintended by a military official called the Regulating Officer. In Awadh the Resident, with the assistance of the local Collector and military commandants, prepared the pension roll of sipahis and organized the distribution of their pensions. The invalids approached him for the redressal of their grievances.[44]

By 1800, the Company's frontier had moved up into the drier lands surrounding Delhi and here it had to combat mounted troopers—the Mewatis and the Pindaris. Here too the Thanah was found to be useful for colonizing new land so as to create strongholds for the Company in the countryside. The Thanah enhanced the Company's familiarity in its newly acquired territory and enabled it to deal with its military problems efficiently. Wastelands and forests in the parganas of Hapur, Surrawah and Garh Mukteshwar, being close to the military station of Hapur, were marked out for the settling of invalid soldiers. Here, the Government purchased about 13,500 bighas of land at the rate of eight annas per bigha.[45] At times land was given out to contractors for clearing it before it was settled with the invalids.[46] Many supernumerary

[43] Regulation 11, GOVP, 4 June, 30 July 1811, in ibid., pp. 506–8.

[44] Reference in GOGG, 25 Nov. 1825, in ibid., pp. 38–9.

[45] L. No. 21, Collector of Saharanpur to Board of Revenue, 6 March 1807, BRFW, Consult. FW 24 March 1807, vol. 31, UPSA.

[46] L. No. 11, Sec. to Govt. Rev. Deptt., to Collector in Garh Mukteshwar, 1 Sept. 1807, BRFW, Consult. FW Sept. 1807, vol. 36, UPSA. In 1807 the Company appointed

soldiers of the Sirmour Battalion were settled on land so cleared in Dehra Dun.[47] The plan was to grant them holdings in Dehra Dun while they retained their full pay for life but gave up promotion in their corps. These new engagers were allotted a 'right to the forest' in the lands granted to them. This meant that they were at liberty to cut wood for building and fires, grass for chuppers (thatched roofs), fodder for their cattle and derive any benefit they could from the neighbouring jungle.[48] In this way the Thanah had become a critical frontier institution for the Company's territories throughout the Gangetic river system.

CREATING LEGITIMACY THROUGH THE THANAH

We do know that the British state had an experience of using invalid soldiers in the army. In 1688, the British army had an Invalid Corps which had been raised by James II in preparation for the invasion by William of Orange.[49] This was basically for measures of economy. James II had intended to save some money by using army pensioners for garrison duty thereby releasing the regular soldiers, who were stationed in royal castles and forts, for more active service in the field.[50] In India, in the initial years

a contractor called Kishen Chand, to clear vast areas of land in the Garh Mukteshwar region. The land thus cleared was allotted to invalid soldiers.

[47] F.I. Shore, to Supdtt. of Police and Acting Third Member BRWP, 8 Jan. 1824, DDPMR Judicial Letters Issued Feb. 1823–Sept. 1824, vol. 34, DDRA. This battalion consisted of hill men from Sirmour who had deserted to the Company during the period of the Gurkha war in 1815. In 1820 when this battalion was about to be reduced, they preferred to remain supernumaries and forego their promotions rather than be discharged.

[48] Ibid.

[49] Michael Mann, 'The Corps of Invalids', *Journal for the Study of Army Historical Research*, vol. LXVI, no. 265 (Spring 1988), p. 6.

[50] Ibid., pp. 6–7, 19. The invalids were kept under the medical care of the Royal Hospital at Chelsea, and after being declared fit for garrison duty they were recruited into the Invalid Corps. The hospital administration supervised the administration of the Corps and continued to supply new recruits into its ranks. In 1802 it was decided to do away with the title 'invalids' which had assumed a derogatory connotation. In 1802 they were renamed the Royal Garrison battalion and those invalids who were unfit for service were given additional pensions and discharged. In 1804 they were called the Veteran Battalions and were used extensively to maintain civil peace in Britain throughout the

of Company rule, officials like Robert Clive emphasized the notion of benevolence towards their European invalid soldiers. For instance, in a painting, no. 91 in the Foster catalogue, stored in the India Office Library Records, Clive is seen receiving Mir Jafar's grant from his son Nawab Najum-ud-Daulah while pointing to a group of destitute soldiers.[51] This was the time when Clive was under attack in England and it was important for him to project an image as a charitable benefactor. From the 1770s, military officials began to demonstrate the Company's benevolence towards Indian invalids as well. This was of tremendous political significance because the Invalid Thanah, which projected the beneficent character of British rule, became an important institution through and by which the Company attempted to replace the paradigm of legitimacy established by the Mughal state.

Interestingly, the Company officials' attempt to construct a new form of legitimacy through the creation of the Thanah institution, was quite similar to the methods the Mughals had adopted to legitimize their rule in India. For the Thanah was reminiscent of the Mughal practice of granting revenue-free grants called *madad-i-mash* to religious scholars, destitutes, and people of noble lineage who deemed it below their dignity to take up any employment.[52] Even though this support base of the Mughal state included very few military personnel, these holy men and shurafa grantees, indebted to the Emperor for their landholdings which enhanced their social standing, always glorified Mughal rule in their scholarly works, and prayed for its longevity. In so doing they legitimized the Mughal state and contributed to its political stability. It was for this reason that Jahangir called them *lashkar-e-dua* or an army of prayers.[53] The Company wanted to follow a similar practice of diffusing pockets of influence in its recently acquired territories.

---

period of the Chartists and early Victorian Britain. It was not until 1843 that they were re-formed as Enrolled Pensioners; in 1867 a new form of Army Reserve was constituted and the Enrolled Pensioners were then incorporated into a second-class reserve available for home defence.

[51] See IOLR, Foster 91, painting note by B. Allen, No. 111 in C. A. Bayly (ed.), *An Illustrated History of Modern India 1600–1947*, New Delhi, p. 101.

[52] Alam, *Crisis of Empire*, p. 110.

[53] Ibid., p. 141.

Like the madad-i-mash landholdings it wanted to diffuse its land grants in society so that they would become an indicator of social status. But in the early phase of its expansion it was too sensitive to interfere with religious matters and create new religious land grants. However, despite its scepticism of carefully graded privileges, the Company followed the Mughal practice of territorial expansion—only the grantees and the nature of grants were different. The new land grands, opening up fresh territory, were made only to administrative families and the sipahis of the Company's army.

The military exclusivity which the Company strove to create for the Thanah, by separating it from the jurisdiction of the civil administration and law courts, had very significant implications. For, separated as it was from civilian society, the Thanah itself tended to create the impression that the Company soldier was a being radically distinct from civilian society. This suited the political interests of the Company for the military distinctiveness which it attempted to construct for its soldiers added an aura of invincibility to its power even as it continued to incorporate itself into Indian society. Indeed, the Thanah demonstrated the benevolent character of the invincible Company 'Bahadur' thereby contributing to the Company's attempts to add legitimacy to its rule in India.

The Regulations passed between 1766 and 1790 for the admission to and administration of the Invalid Thanah reflect the cautious policy of gradually settling invalid sipahis in civilian society together with attempting to create a distinct and privileged status for them.

The Invalid Thanah had a large number of officers attached to it who helped in the admission of invalids into the Thanah and supervised its administration.[54] The successful expansion of

[54] Some of the more important ones were as follows: the team of surgeons who medically examined the sipahis and certified them as invalids; the Adjutant-General of the invalids who prepared their character rolls and maintained a record of all those diagnosed as invalid, who also arranged for their rehabilitation on land and corresponded with the Collectors of districts where the invalids were to be settled, to arrange for the allocation of jagirs to them. The officer in-charge of the administration of the Thanah was known as the Regulating Officer. He was the immediate superintendent of the Invalid Jagir and received orders from the Board of Revenue. Initially, there was one Regulating Officer for superintending the Thanahs of Bhagalpur and Tirhut and another one for the Thanahs of Bihar district, whereas the Thanahs of Shahabad, Saran and

the Thanah prompted the Company to establish a separate Board to superintend the working of the Thanah officers, known as the Board of Invalids which functioned for a brief period of three years (from 1 November 1802 to 13 December 1805) and generated its own written proceedings. The officers regularly reported to the Board from their districts and kept it informed of their activities. They also followed its orders in all matters concerning the invalids. In 1805, when the territorial expansion of the Company was temporarily stalled, the Board of Invalids was abolished and the Invalid Thanahs were placed under the charge of the Board of Revenue in Calcutta. The proceedings of the Board of Invalids and the Board of Revenue provide us with useful material for studying the procedure for admission to the Thanah, its administration and its functioning.

The military authority held discretionary powers to admit sipahis into the Thanah. Every year the major commanding each sipahi regiment sent a record of invalid sipahis to the colonel of the brigade. The record listed the sipahi's name, village, and the number of years they had served the Company. Alongside this, the major also dispatched the sipahi's medical certificates indicating the age and nature of wounds if any.[55] The colonel of the brigade forwarded these certificates to the Commander-in-Chief who in turn presented them to the Military Board. The Board met once in every three months to consider the cases presented to it and no sipahi was admitted into the Thanah without its approval. The Military Board's decisions were made public in a general order which was sent to the paymaster as soon as it was issued.[56]

Chittagong were under the charge of a separate Regulating Officer. Later with the spread of the Thanahs westward more Regulating Officers were appointed for superintending them (No. 4 Draft of a regulation from the Governor-General, undated, BRIP 2 Nov. 1802, Consult. 14 June 1803, vol. I, WBSA). In addition each Invalid Corps had a European Adjutant with his staff attached to it. His duty was to maintain an updated general register listing all the invalids. He had a staff allowance of Rs 4 per day and Rs 50 per month for writers and stationery (9 May 1788, *Abstract of General Orders and Regulations*, p. 504).

[55] At a Council meeting attended by W. Hastings, Governor-General and President, Edward Wheeler and Commander-in-Chief, undated, PFD-S, Consult. FW 16 Jan. 1781, vol. 45, NAI.

[56] Ibid.

By the end of 1809, the sipahis of the Provincial Corps were also declared eligible for Thanah benefits. In the case of the sipahis of the Provincial Corps we have detailed information about the actual working of the policy adopted for admitting sipahis into the Thanah and interestingly enough it was similar to the one the Company followed for its regular regiments. It appears that every year the commanding officers of different regiments assembled all the physically unfit Indian soldiers at Allahabad. The officer who accompanied the invalids presented each invalid's 'character roll' to the adjutant stationed at Allahabad.[57] This document was accompanied by a certificate signed by the Surgeon attached to their corps and countersigned by the commanding officer, specifying the 'deformity' of each invalid and the reasons which had prompted the Surgeon to consider him eligible for the Thanah. The adjutant at Allahabad forwarded these documents to a committee of Surgeons, appointed by the Commander-in-Chief, and each invalid was medically examined by them.[58] The sipahis recommended by this committee for admissions into the Thanah were then sanctioned land jagirs by the military authorities.

On being admitted into the Thanah every invalid received a copy of his descriptive roll which contained his past history. This roll was his identity card which entitled him to all the benefits of the Thanah in the district where he resided. On the receipt of this roll, the local Collector was authorized to extend the benefits of pay and pension to him. In 1796, when the Company decided to extend the privileges of the Thanah to the family and heirs of the invalids, the descriptive roll of the sipahi became the link between the military and civil authority.[59]

[57] L. No. 27, Rules established for the admission of native commissioned officers and privates of Provincial Corps who may become entitled to the benefits of the Invalid Thanah, extract Bengal military letter, 27 March 1809, BC, File No. 7524, p.1. F/4/326, IOL. This was prepared and signed by the commanding officer of the Provincial Battalion and stated the regular Corps in which the invalid formerly served, the particular service on which he was employed at the time of getting wounded, and the number of years of service he could have performed if not disabled.

[58] Ibid.

[59] L. No. 4, Draft of regulation of 1796, BRIP, Consult. FW June 14 1803, vol. 1, WBSA. By the regulation of 1796 the state took over responsibility of the heirs of the

The Company also extended the Thanah benefits to the native commissioned and non-commissioned officers of the Provincial Corps. Those found eligible for admission to the Invalid Thanah were relieved from service on the pay of their respective ranks. An advance of six months' pay was allowed to enable them to retire to their homes.[60] Once they were admitted to the Invalid Thanah these rates were adjusted in accordance with the quantity of land assigned to them as jagirs. The rates of pay and portions of land allowed to jagirdars invalided from the Provincial Corps and admitted to the benefits of the Thanah was as follows:[61]

Rank	Rs	Land in Bighas
Subahdar	16	80
Jamadar	6	40
Havaldar	3.8	25
Naik	3	20
Sepoy	2.8	1.8

The military maintained its exclusive position in civil society by creating a separate administration for the Thanah which was placed under the charge of the Regulating Officer. He punished and checked disobedience in the Thanah and solved the internal disputes of the invalid soldiers. He also had the authority to call a court martial for settling all sipahi disputes brought to his notice.[62] In this way the Thanah administration kept the invalid soldiers out of the reach of the civil and criminal law of their district. However, in 1803, the expanding jurisdiction of the civil and criminal courts curtailed the authority of the Regulating Officer

invalid after he died. The rule was that if the original grantee died within seven years of his being put into possession of his lands, his heir continued to hold them rent free for seven years. After this period the heirs paid malikanah to the proprietor of land for five years, and then they paid rent at the current rate.

[60] Ibid. Their pay was as follows: Subahdar, Rs 30; Jamadar, Rs 10; Havaldar, Rs 6; Naik, Rs 5; and Sepoy, Rs 3.

[61] Ibid.

[62] L. No. 12, Collector of Bhagalpur to BRIP, 28 April 1804, BRIP, Consult. FW 8 May 1804, vol. 2, WBSA.

considerably. His judicial duties were curtailed and the invalid sipahis were brought within the jurisdiction of the local courts.[63] But even now the invalids retained their distinctiveness because the *vakil* of the government pleaded for the invalid sipahis, free of cost, in the local courts of law.[64] Similarly, even though the Regulating Officer was answerable to the local Collector of his district the authority he exercised over his Thanah made him a powerful figure in the locality and he dealt directly with the invalid sipahis who came to report their daily problems to him.[65] Thus the military exclusivity which the Company strove to maintain for the Thanah also created a very general definition of the Company soldier as one who was best defined in terms of his separation from civilian society.

THE FUNCTIONS OF THE THANAH

In its actual functioning the Thanah came to perform a variety of roles. The Thanahs in the Company's territories opened up fresh areas and drew the Company closer to the local population. The Thanah also assisted the local administration in many ways for the invalid sipahis from Awadh and Bihar performed a variety of civilian jobs in Bengal. Their presence as chaukidars and garrison troops in Bengal marks the early pattern of migration from Bihar to downcountry.[66] This migration of sipahi pensioners was particularly useful for the Company because it saved it a considerable amount of money in raising separate contingents for guard duties in the towns. For instance, the invalids were posted as watchmen outside kachehris and gaols and guarded convict labour while they worked on the roads.[67] Similarly in 1773, an entire contingent

---

[63] Ibid. Bengal 1793 regulation, re-enacted in 1804. Those invalid sipahis who were guilty of heinous crimes were sent to the magistrate to be dealt with as other civilians.

[64] Regulations for invalids, 1793, BRIP, Consult. FW 19 Aug. 1803, vol. 1, WBSA.

[65] Ibid.

[66] Yang discusses this migration pattern for the mid-19th century in great detail. Yang, *Limited Raj*, p. 191.

[67] Orders by Colonel Richard Smith, Commander-in-Chief, 17 Sept. 1768, BMC, Consult. Jan. 1778, P/18/45, IOL. A decade before the establishment of the Invalid Thanah a somewhat similar plan had been implemented in Bengal. By the orders of

of native invalid soldiers from Awadh and Benaras, which included ten subahdars, seven havaldars, nine naiks and fifty-eight sipahis, were placed under the Town Major of Calcutta for the performance of town duties.[68] The Pargana Battalions performing garrison duties in the city were disbanded and the invalid sipahis substituted in their place.[69] Further, by 1785, invalid sipahis from the military stations of Monghyr, Patna, and Buxar were sent regularly on garrison duty to various parts of the Bengal Presidency. They furnished escorts for military stores and accompanied treasure being transported by water.[70] In the same year the services of the invalid sipahis stationed at Monghyr were used in the faujdari, revenue and commercial departments in Tirhut. The Pykes and Barkandaz establishment was replaced by a contingent of one havaldar, one naik and twenty-three sepoys from the Monghyr Thanah to perform the duties of thirty Barkandaz.[71] The Thanah also helped the Company to make a considerable saving on the training of regular recruits. The invalid sipahis trained the new recruits stationed close to their Thanah in the use of arms. In this way the Company was able to acculturate its new entrants in Indian surroundings rather than placing them in the company of 'alien' British commandants.

The Company's pensioners played a significant political role in undermining the authority of the princely states. This proved particularly useful in the early nineteenth century when the Company was trying to remove any threat to its paramountcy by encouraging Awadh and other regional powers to proclaim their

---

Colonel Richard Smith, Commander-in-Chief of the forces under the Presidency of Fort William, the retired soldiers were given a cash pension of Rs 8, in return for which they performed garrison duties in their districts. Artillery invalids at Budge Budge had been assigned the lighter garrison duties. This was true for the invalids in the Madras Army as well. Colonel Richard Smith reported the existence of 150 invalid soldiers performing garrison duties in Madras.

[68] Minute of Brigadier General R. Barker on the subject of reconstructing the sepoy corps, undated, PFDSP, Consult 28 Jan. 1773, vol. 23, NAI.

[69] Ibid.

[70] Commandant of artillery to W. Hastings, Governor-General, 30 July 1777, BMC, Consult. (?) Jan. 1778, P/18/45, IOL.

[71] E. Hay to R. Bathurst, Collector in Tirhut, 1 March 1789, MC, 1789, vol. 7, BSA.

de jure independence from the Mughal emperor. Since this offer suited the political ambitions of the eighteenth-century Indian rulers they supported the Company. In Awadh this led to the imperial coronation of Ghaziuddin-Haider in 1819.[72] However, as Fisher shows, this policy generated problems for the British because the 'independent' Indian rulers refused to be treated as subordinate allies dependent on the Company.[73] In the years following 1819, the Resident finally succeeded in demonstrating the Company's superiority by personally placing the crown on the Awadh ruler's head. By the extension of extra-territorial protection, administering of guaranteed pensions, and by the provision of honours and preferment the Resident attracted a circle of important dependants and made himself the centre of a new cultural world at the Awadh capital.[74] Interestingly, in this period the Company's pensioners living in Awadh also contributed to the gradual erosion of the authority of the Awadh state, for the British Resident and military official monitored the functioning of Awadh officials—the darbar agent and the local chakladar—so as to sort out all cases of land allotment or property disputes involving the Company's pensioners. He often forced the Awadh administrative staff to take speedy action and on several occasions pressurized them to take decisions in favour of the sipahis. For instance, the invalids settled in Awadh had the privilege of complaining about their grievances to the Awadh Nawab through British officers.[75] So sought after was this favour that in 1838 I. D. Shakespeare, Assistant to the British Resident in Awadh, was of the view that this was one of the main reasons for the popularity of the Company's army in Awadh.[76] In 1839 he observed:

[72] Fisher, *A Clash of Cultures: Awadh, the British, and the Mughals*, p. 18.

[73] Ibid.

[74] Ibid. Fisher argues that extraterritoriality, or the exemption of individuals from the jurisdiction of the sovereign in whose territories they were, enabled Europeans to exempt not only themselves but their individual collaborators as well from the authority of the local sovereign. The extraterritorial protection enabled the Resident to recruit a constituency loyal to, and dependent on the Company from amongst the administrative and social élite of Awadh.

[75] See PFD P, Consult. 19 Dec. 1838, File No. 73, NAI.

[76] Report of I. D. Shakespeare, Assistant to the Resident in Lucknow, to Lieutenant

Generally, the British Officer who received the petition of an invalid regarding any grievance, sent it to the Agent of the Durbar. The Agent wrote a letter, emphasising the need for its immediate redressal, to the local officer of the area. When the invalid sipahi produced this letter to the Chakladar he was sure to have his problems resolved favourably.[77]

Where the local Awadh administration delayed expediting the cases of the invalids in solving the village disputes, a regulation made it binding for the Awadh government to intervene directly in resolving these cases. Very often the invalid soldiers took advantage of this provision. In instances where the Awadh government was compelled to intervene directly, a special procedure was adopted. On receiving a complaint against the local chakladar, the Darbar Agent of the Awadh court issued a letter of warning to him. On its receipt the chakladar normally speeded up his proceedings. But if the Darbar Agent had to write to him for a second or third time, for the same case, it was considered an act of insubordination on the part of the chakladar. The Darbar Agent took action against him and intervened personally in solving the sipahi's dispute. This suited the sipahis as the direct action of the Darbar Agent meant that the king sent a *sazawal* (a horse-man, camel sawar, *chuprasi* or foot soldier) along with the invalid soldier to the local administration for speeding up the process of investigation. Shakespeare reported that in many cases the invalids abused this privilege and did not go with the letter of the Darbar Agent to the chakladar. Without the 'whip' from the Darbar Agent the chakladar either took his own time to deal with their requests or many times shelved it altogether. This gave the invalid an oppportunity to complain to the Darbar Agent and he intervened directly in sorting out the sipahi's problems. In his report to the government, Shakespeare noted the way in which the civil authority very often submitted to the unjust demands of the sipahi:

but the Sepoy prolonged the discussion by insisting that they were right and continuously sending in their Urzees. The local authority pounded by the continual pressure from his own Government in the shape of repeated

Colonel Low, Resident in Lucknow, Dec. 1838, PFD P, Consult. 19 Dec. 1838, File No. 74, NAI.

[77] Ibid.

injunctions and incessant petitions poured in by the Sepoy and continuous annoyance experienced from Suzawuls, frequently found it his last policy to settle the case by at once dispossessing the dependant and submitted to all the unjust demands of the Sepoy.[78]

The Thanah had very significant economic consequences as well. In the early phase of the Company's expansion hitherto neglected areas of Bihar and Bengal were developed at very small expense. This was the result of the invalid sipahi investing his labour and savings in cultivating the rent-free jagir granted to him. The pioneer invalids often encountered difficult circumstances to begin with. Despite these hardships and the fact that the number of men involved in developing the Thanah was not very large, the local economy benefited from the Thanah which, in effect, created an active landholding group. The invalid sipahi was like a new and wealthy zamindar in the region and he used his power and influence to put together a band of cultivators whom he directed and supervised besides carrying on cultivation himself. For instance, Hulaus Roy, an invalid subahdar of Thanah Pialapur, complained to his Regulating Officer that, 'many lives were lost in consequence of the ferocious animals and the dacoits living in the jungles in his jagir.' Roshun Bukht, the zamindar in whose domain these jungles were, was given the option either to cut down the jungle himself or grant a sanad to Hulaus Roy to clear it and cultivate the land as his jagir. The zamindar agreed to the latter and Halaus Roy was granted a sanad for the jungles, hills, rivers, barren land and parts of the jungle that were fit for cultivation in mouzah Ahkerpur. Hulaus Roy invested all his savings to make the area habitable. He advanced money to the raiyats and encouraged them to cultivate and live on these lands. By 1803 the land was in a flourishing state of cultivation and Hulaus Roy regularly paid a fixed annual jama of twenty-five rupees.[79]

The investment of money and labour by the invalid sipahis very often resulted in the development of small urban centres

[78] Ibid.

[79] Enclosure No. 4, translation of petition of Hulaus Roy, undated, enclosed in letter of F. Hamilton, Collector of Bhagalpur, to BRIP, 29 June 1805, BRIP, Consult. FW 23 August, vol. 3, WBSA.

in the Thanah. In such small towns the houses were built by the invalids themselves on the *milkiyat* land and the government met the expense of clearing the ground and marking out the streets. At times the labour of the *faujdari* prisoners, who had been condemned to work on the roads either in Bhagalpur or in the neighbouring districts, was used for clearing the ground and assisting the invalids in building their houses.[80] The invalids when involved in such managerial and supervisory roles were comparable to the *jotedars* of Bengal who performed similar functions.[81]

CONFLICTS BETWEEN INVALID SOLDIERS AND ZAMINDARS

The emergence of this privileged class of 'military landlords' created some tensions in society. The nature and range of grievances the sipahis solved by using the army connection reflected the position of power and superiority which even a retired army sipahi wielded in his locality. He emerged as the 'influential elder' who was respected yet envied. The locality's most intractable problems were resolved for him and he could demand and obtain the restitution of several villages yielding perhaps many thousands of rupees of revenue per annum to the government. At times the sipahi might demand compensation for considerable sums of money which he claimed had been plundered from his house; on other occasions he might ask for a distribution of either cattle or property to make up arrears of revenue for relatives or friends killed in any affray with government troops. The invalid sipahi might even have the village disputes of distant relatives and acquaintances solved by introducing them as his brothers. People generally of the same caste were the beneficiaries of this practice. In many cases the sipahi abused these privileges and even had the relatives of rivals imprisoned and punished.[82]

---

[80] See RPB, Oct. 1788, Rev. Consult, 24 July 1783, Basta No. 22, Record No. 11, ARA.

[81] Rajat and Ratna Ray, 'Zamindars and Jotedars: a study of rural politics in Bengal', *MAS*, No. 9, Part 1 (February 1975), pp. 81–102. Jotedars were a class of men who owned sizeable portions of village land which they cultivated with the help of share croppers, tenants-at-will and hired labourers.

[82] Ibid.

This exercise of power by ex-servicemen in their localities made I. Low, the British Resident at Lucknow, remark:

The invalids have become habitual tyrants in their neighbourhood. In case of a quarrel with a neighbour nothing is more common than for an invalid sepoy to threaten his opponent with vengeance through the Resident at Lucknow. This is often brought about by a false complaint being lodged by the invalids. This causes immense injury to the unfortunate villagers against whom it is made, as the falsehood of the complaint is not discovered for a long period of time.[83]

The people of the locality reacted to the activities of such sipahis in different ways. The invalid sipahi was respected and envied yet also dreaded and often detested. These reactions cut across religious and caste considerations. There were instances where the local population compromised with the invalid sipahi but the occasions of open hostility were also very common. In 1838, I. D. Shakespeare, Assistant to the Resident in Awadh, reported the case of Gholaum Jalani, an ordinary non-military resident of a village in Awadh, which reflected the enviable position the invalids enjoyed in the kingdom. On seeing the growing influence and resourcefulness of the invalid sipahis and their families settled around his locality, Jalani procured for himself an old cavalry uniform which allowed him to pass himself off as an invalid soldier for about fifteen years. During that long period he gave in petitions about various grievances in the Resident's office and the last but one secured him a zamindari.[84] Many zamindars unable to achieve this enviable status maintained good terms with these influential colonies of sipahis. In 1799, during a joint inspection of the eastern Bihar Thanahs, the invalids presented a case that the lands proposed to be attached to them as jagirs were totally unfit for cultivation and they declined to accept them. It was decided to remove them to a place called Bauroon, situated on the New Road, a great distance from their earlier location. On the removal of the Thanah a number of zamindars of the area

[83] Resident at Lucknow to Foreign Department, 17 Sept. 1836, PFD, Consult. 19 Dec. 1838, File No. 73, NAI.

[84] I. D. Shakespeare, assistant to the Resident in Lucknow, to Sec. to Govt. Pol. Deptt., 17 Sept. 1836, PFD, Consult. 19 Dec. 1838, File No. 74, NAI.

waited on G. Cruttender, the assistant to the Regulating Officer of the Thanah, and petitioned to prevent the removal of the Thanah. They argued that

it had contributed to their happiness and to the preservation of their property by keeping in check the numerous gangs of bandits, for which the neighbourhood of Burthushean was well known.[85]

On their appeal, the shifting of the Thanah was postponed and the Military Board decided that the invalids with no jagirs or deficient jagirs were to be put on full pay till this deficiency was remedied.[86]

Nevertheless, the social equilibrium of the locality was often disturbed when the interests of the contenders clashed. This happened on occasions when the sipahis tried to promote their status by using their connection with the army and abusing their power. For instance, in 1791, the zamindars of pargana Monghyr complained about invalid soldiers encroaching on their lands. They were concerned because they had already given 6,864 bighas of land to the Thanah and the Collector had exempted them from making any further grants.[87] In another case, some invalid sipahis, with Imam-ud-din and Saifulla Commandant, got by force 991 bighas of zamindar Badrinath's land in pargana Mungelpur, dependent on Chakla Akbernagar, measured off for their Thanah. They disregarded the orders of the Bhagalpur Collector which allowed the appropriation of only such uncultivated land as had not been included in the jama for at least ten to twelve years. According to the zamindar, out of his 991 bighas, approximately 521 bighas of land had not been in an uncultivated state for more than two or three years. Moreover, it had been part of his jamabundi. On the zamindar's complaint and consequent interrogation by the Collector the sipahis said that they would pay the *khazana* (treasury) with the proceeds of whatever cultivated land they had taken from the raiyats and that having collected

[85] L. No. 6 D, G. Cruttender, assistant to the Regulating Officer in Bihar, to F. Hawkins, Collector of Bihar, 11 Dec. 1797, BMC, Consult. FW 11 Feb. 1799, P/19/52, IOL.

[86] Ibid.

[87] Arzi from Zamindars of Monghyr, undated, enclosed in a letter from acting Collector of Bhagalpur to Board of Revenue, BMC, Consult. FW 8 Aug. 1791, IOL.

resources for the payment they would relinquish the land in *bhaudon* (month of the post-monsoon season). However, they never kept to any of these promises and acquired another eighty-five bighas, twelve cottas of newly cultivated land with a jama of Rs 62.6.2.[88]

The zamindars often reacted to the invalids' power by using the local civil authority to redress their grievances. They manipulated cases and duped the civil authority to get possession of Thanah land. This was often accompanied by the surfacing of military-civilian tensions in the locality. In one case, the Collector of Bihar ordered the invalids to vacate about fifty bighas of land which they had brought under cultivation. At the time of their settlement nobody had disputed the proprietary right to this land. But once it was brought under cultivation its ownership was challenged by a zamindar who actually never turned up after making this claim. The disputed ownership of land was a cause of concern to the civil authority of the region and as soon as the matter was referred to the magistrate he ordered the Regulating Officer to remove the invalid sipahis from that land. Consequently the invalid sipahis were removed from this Thanah and settled on a new jagir in the neighbourhood.[89]

On other occasions the hostility of the zamindars took the form of open violence against the invalid sipahis. The tensions became most acute in regions which were fertile and consequently attractive possessions. This was best represented in the 1797 conflict over the Dyarra tract of alluvial land in Bihar. The Dyarra land originally assigned to the invalid sipahis of Thanah Burrye belonged to the village of Burrye which was separated by the Ganges from the neighbouring prosperous villages. It had never been the subject of dispute because about 5,600 bighas of it were absolutely impossible to cultivate. But by 1797, the Ganges had changed its course and the Thanah lands now bordered the fertile zamindaris on the banks of the Ganges. The prosperous state of the Thanah

[88] Arzi of Beijenath, Zamindar of Pargana Mungulpur, 19 Feb. 1789, BRMP, Consult. FW 5 Aug. 1791, vol. 117, Part 1, 1–8 August 1791, BSA.

[89] R. Greene, of Thanah Englishabad, Zillah Bihar, to Lieutenant Colonel W. Scott, 20 Feb. 1798, BMC, Consult. 28 May 1798, P/19/43, IOL.

lands made them very attractive for these zamindars and they made attempts to annexe them. Moreover, the shift in the course of the Ganges adversely affected the zamindaris on the opposite side of the river. Now these zamindars also looked towards the Dyarra land for support. One such zamindar was Ram Devra whose lands were washed away by the Ganges and he now claimed a part of the Dyarra land as his own. In such struggles the hostility of the zamindars was invariably directed towards the invalid sipahis. In one such outburst of violence the invalids were assaulted by an armed body of men from the village of Jaintpur and one of the invalids' son was seriously wounded.[90] On yet another occasion in 1797, invalid sipahis settled in Behia and Dinwar parganas of Shahabad district complained of a considerable portion of their jagirs having been withheld from them by the zamindars of the area.[91]

The Collector of Hapur also reported acts of open hostility against the invalids. Here the lands of the invalids were mixed with those of the zamindars and the latter discovered that most of the land they had given to the Company for the Thanah had been left uncultivated. The Collector considered that this was either due to the poor state of the soil or due to the reluctance of the invalids' heirs to cultivate them. This often prompted the zamindars to resume this land and they often complained about the neglected state of invalid jagirs to the local Collector. But for fear of exacerbating the existing tensions the Collector decided to continue with the invalid jagirs and not to interfere in the distribution of lands.[92]

The civil administration's attempts to resolve these disputes was complicated by the absence of definite boundaries demarcating the jagirs of the invalid sipahis. This was because very often the invalid sipahis, taking advantage of the surveyor's ill health or

---

[90] A. Tufton, Collector in Shahabad, to W. Cowper, President and Members of Board of Revenue, 8 July 1797, SDR, 12 March 1797 to 10 Aug. 1797, vol. 26, ARA.

[91] Ibid.

[92] See for a discussion on this kind of rural tension Pre-Mutiny Revenue Correspondence, vol. 4, Letters Received from Government by the Board of Revenue, Oct. 1820–April 1822, UPSA.

absence, carried on their own measurement at the time of allotment of land. However, the authorities remained duly concerned about the harassment of invalid sipahis in these disputes. In most cases they openly condemned the zamindars for having seized the crop and the land of the invalid sipahis.[93]

The social tensions cut across religious considerations. This was demonstrated in instances where the invalids mobilized townspeople to demonstrate their strength to the state as well as to the other residents of their locality. The sipahis were aware of the sensitivity of the Company to conflicts of a religious nature. For this reason they sometimes took up religious issues and used religious gatherings in order to bring their collective strength to bear on the local civilian authorities with whom they were contending. In one such instance, invalids stationed in Allahabad, who were predominantly Hindus, organized violent demonstrations of townspeople outside the *kachehri*. They demanded action against a kotwal who had been abused by a member of a Muslim Moharrum procession and had arrested him. The invalid sipahis used this as an occasion to buttress their influence in society. They demonstrated their strength by inciting the townspeople to further action after they were returning satisfied with the assurances of the kachehri that the kotwal would be suspended and that later a proper inquiry would be instituted.[94]

The tensions between invalid sipahis and zamindars remained largely confined to the class of landed élite in the locality. However, the involvement of the invalids in the land disputes made them more contentious since it drew a new and powerful political authority into the disputes. On the rare occasions when they were directed against the Company they were too weak and uncoordinated to make any impact. But on all occasions they gave the Company an opportunity of emphasizing its presence in the small world around the Thanah. This it did by backing

[93] L. No. 7, Report on disputed Dayyara lands by Captain Geo Cruttender, officer of invalid jagirdars, 23 March 1797, BMC, Consult. 26 June 1797, P/19/31, IOL.

[94] G. Mercer, acting Magistrate of Allahabad, to Sec. to Govt. in the Ceded Provinces, 20 May 1803, Bengal Revenue Board, Judicial, Ceded Provinces, FW 26 May 1803, UPSA.

directly or indirectly the cause of the invalid sipahis. It resolved most of the conflicts by either granting them sanads to confirm their rights[95] or else purchasing the disputed lands for the invalids.[96]

DETERIORATION OF THE BIHAR INVALID THANAHS, 1810–20

Between the 1810s and 1820s the Thanahs of Bihar suffered problems of decay and depopulation. The ecology of these Thanahs, located as they were on the fringe of settled land, was fragile. They were subjected to periodic flooding and disease as well as the depredations and attacks of wild animals. By the second decade of the nineteenth century the further extension of the Thanah into uncultivable swampy land increased its vulnerability. Consequently, the new generation of invalids expressed their inability to cultivate Thanah lands and requested the Company to convert their land jagirs to pensions in cash.[97] Whenever land was available and no major practical difficulty in these transfers existed the Company acceded to the requests. But by the 1810s most of the cultivable wasteland in the Bihar districts had already been allotted to the sipahis. Any further grants extended beyond the areas where the Thanah had been confined and this created discontent amongst the invalids. For instance, in 1810, H. Worsley,

[95] L. No. 45, R. Cavendish, political assistant on deputation to Bihar, to Earl Cornwallis, 1 Nov. 1789, BRR, 1789, vol. 8, BSA.

[96] I. Hutchinson, Collector in Bhagalpur, to Charles Swindland, Collector in Tirhut, 1 March 1796, BMC Consult. 14 March 1796, P/19/14, IOL. He suggested the purchase of disputed land in Purkeak, Tirhut district, which the government purchased.

[97] B. Crisp and C. Butter to Lt. Gen. Hewett, Vice-President-in-Council, Fort William, 13 March 1810, Bengal Rev. Board of Commissioners, 2–27 April 1810, appendix for April 1810, E *vide* consult. 13 April 1810, No. 23, UPSA. He sent a petition from two invalids, named Futteh Muhammad Havaldar and Gurudat Singh Naik, who wanted to relinquish their jagir in the district of Purnia and receive the reduced pay of their rank, the former at Nattore and the latter at Benares; see for more petitions of a similar nature Proceedings of the Board of Commissioners, Lower Provinces 1801–1807; see also translation of a petition presented by Sheikh Gulam Ali, Subahdar of the late Brigade commanded by Sheikh Kalb Ali, written on 1 Nov. 1807, translated by I. Wauchope, 20 Nov. 1807, BCJ, Consult. FW 20 Nov. 1807, P/129/40, IOL. He was from Patna and wished to be transferred back to Patna. Similar requests were also made by the *purabia* sipahis who were disinclined to settle on the wastelands in Hapur.

the Adjutant-General of the army, showed concern over the resentment that followed the allotment of land to the Company's ex-servicemen. He noted:

Not satisfied with their jagir lands these people waited for lands like in the zillah of Sarun. They sometimes asked for reduced invalid pay and returned to their homes.[98]

Worsley suggested the establishment of more Invalid Thanahs either between Allahabad and Fatehpur or on the banks of the river Ganges.

In 1810, Major W. Francklin, the Regulating Officer of the Bhagalpur Thanah, conducted a survey of the Thanahs in Bhagalpur, Tirhut, and Purnia and observed that these Thanahs were deserted. The few Thanah invalids he came across complained of periodic flooding and annual losses.[99] From what he saw and heard in the region he concluded that the expansion of the Thanah into swampy and marshy terrain infested with wild animals and disease, had prompted the invalids to desert. Further east, Francklin noticed a similar decay and depopulation in the eastern Thanahs which were located on the route which stretched from Bhagalpur to Rajmahal and extended up to Gaur. Here, the mortality rate was very high. For instance, in Sikiagully Thanah, one of the oldest Thanahs established in 1784, out of the original 125 native officers and sipahis only ten males and forty widows survived in 1810. A similar high rate of mortality prevailed in Thanah Kopakuttie in the Purnia district. In 1789, the year the Thanah was inaugurated, 114 people (invalids and their families) were settled in the region. In 1810 only fifteen males and fifty-five widows survived. In the neighbouring Thanah of Singrampur, out of the sixty-four original inhabitants only seventeen males and forty-eighty widows were alive. Most of the surviving members

[98] L. Nos. 17–20, Adjtt. Gen. to John Adam, Sec. to Govt. Military Deptt. 21 Jan. 1810, BMC, Consult. FW 30 Jan. 1810, P/23/39, IOL.

[99] 'Report on the western and northern Thanahs attached to the jagirdars' invalid establishment at Bhagalpur and Tirhut 15 Dec. 1809 by Major W. Francklin, Regulating Officer of Thanah Bhagalpur, Tirhut and Purnia', BMC, Consult. FW 30 Jan. 1810, P/23/39, IOL.

were willing to relinquish their land if the Company gave them a charitable allowance.[100]

Francklin also observed that in some Thanahs the invalids were abandoning agriculture and engaging in more profitable trades. For instance, in the Gaur Thanah, in Purnia district, the surviving twenty-three men and sixty-three widows derived considerable profit from their mulberry fields which extended along the banks of the Bhagirathi river. They earned eight to twelve annas per bigha from the sale of the mulberry leaves to the neighbouring zamindars and to the Company's silk manufactory at Malda.[101] Francklin was concerned about the decay of these Thanahs and the neglect of agriculture in the region. He suggested an influx of 6,000–7,000 invalid sipahis to repopulate them:

> The greater and useful purpose of this institution, whether it be for establishing a provision for our worn out soldiers in the evening of their lives or securing the attachment of their posterity by bringing forth a body of men for the service of the state in times of eventual difficulty or distress, these motives surely plead powerfully in favour of the preservation of the institution and for replacing the jagirdars in their former situations of ease and comfort, a measure which at the same time contributed to the fertilization of the Honourable Company's lands in those districts where the invalid jagir establishment prevails.[102]

The Company took serious note of Francklin's survey. But its efforts to encourage sipahis to settle in the Bihar region were in vain. For the hardships encountered in the fringe areas deterred the invalids from accepting any offer to settle there. Thus by the early 1820s, the Thanah experiment, at least in the Bihar region, appears to have failed. But even though the Thanah declined the Company was still saddled with the task of distributing pensions

---

[100] 'A survey of the eastern Thanahs from Bhagalpur to Rajmahal to Gaur, Nichintpur and Muldah, in zillah Purnia, from thence to Mungulpur and Bencuttie and return by Aurangabad, Rajmahal to Bhagalpur, by Major W. Francklin, Jan.–Feb. 1810', BMC, Consult. 27 March 1810, P/23/44, IOL. In the Thanahs of Deriapur, Pialapur and Colgonge the invalids complained of poor soil and asked permission to relinquish their jagirs. They requested to be placed on the charitable allowance for life.

[101] Ibid.

[102] Ibid.

to the invalid sipahis and their families who lived in their home village, in the more habitable parts of Bihar.

PROBLEMS OF CONTROL IN AWADH AND BENARAS, 1810–30

In the 1810s, in contrast to the Thanahs of Bihar, the invalid settlements in Benaras and the pensioners residing in the better ecological environment of Awadh appeared to be prospering. They had made significant contributions to the economy of the region and Francklin reported that the sipahi landholdings in the fertile and cultivable lands of Awadh and Benaras were in a good state of cultivation.[103] But the visible benefits of the Thanahs in Benaras and the privileges the pensioners enjoyed in Awadh increased the power of the pensioners in their locality and made it difficult for the Company to control their activities. The beneficiaries, their relatives, and heirs resorted to illegal practices to derive the maximum advantage from the Company's pension benefits. In 1818, I. Fagan, Adjutant to the native invalids, reported to Lieutenant Colonel James Nicol, Adjutant-General of the army, that the pay roll of Subahdar Dewan Singh was presented to him by an elderly man who first tried to pass himself off as that individual but later on being questioned stated that Dewan Singh had died a few days before. He claimed to be his brother and said he had brought his son with him. Fagan sent a *harkarah* (intelligence officer/runner) with them to the said village to verify the story. But the two men separated from the harkarah after travelling some distance. The harkarah finally traced the subahdar's house in the village and found out from his wife that he had died five years previously. It was soon evident that on the subahdar's demise these imposters had somehow got possession of his roll.[104] In another case of fraud reported by Fagan, it was found that a man called Buldi Singh was illegally receiving the pension of a deceased naik called Lal Singh. The Board of Commissoners

---

[103] Ibid.

[104] I. Fagan, Adjutant native invalids in Allahabad, to Lieutenant-Colonel James Nicol, Adjtt. Gen. of the Army, 2 Feb. 1818, Consult. Camp Jullalabad 7 April 1818, Bengal Revenue Board of Commissioners 27 March–21 April 1818, P/93/27, IOL.

for the Lower Provinces was concerned about such cases of deceit and punished the guilty whenever they could discover the fraud. But the problem was widespread and in most cases the Company officials remained helpless spectators.[105]

In 1817, I. H. Shakespeare, the magistrate of zillah Allahabad, complained of similar fraud and deception amongst the invalids stationed in Allahabad, Kanpur, Furrukhabad, Gorakhpur, Benaras, and Arrah. Evidence of such fraud was obtained from the local people. Lal Singh, an inhabitant of Muligunge, in Allahabad, stated that he knew many men currently resident in the zillah, who regularly received the stipend of subahdas, jamadars, havaldars, naiks and sipahis at Allahabad, Kanpur, Furrukhabad, Benaras, and Arrah. He also reported the case of a woman who had long been in receipt of a pension obtained on the false declaration that her husband had been killed by an explosion at the power works in Allahabad. They were never married or connected in any other way.[106] The most notorious of such characters reported by Shakespeare was a man called Bheek Singh who was a resident of pargana Shewram. In 1817 Shakespeare noted:

He received the half pay of a Sepoy here, Rs 3 at Benaras, the pension of a Subedar Rs 25 at Farrukhabad, that of a Jamadar at other places. Besides these he enjoyed the shares of 9 deceased pensioners' stipends whose rolls he surreptitiously obtained after their death and distributed to 9 of his accomplices who regularly received the pensions thereon recorded at the stated periods of payment at Benaras.[107]

In the Thanah of Awadh and Benaras, the sale and purchase of pension rolls became a common practice. In 1817, Dhunneah, the widow of pensioner Ram Golam, reported that the same Bheek Singh, 'a notorious character of her village', had obtained the pension roll of sixteen men and sold them to Baiju and Raghu who lived in her locality. They had bought three and two rolls respectively and now received the stipends of pensioners

---

[105] Ibid.

[106] L. No. 30, H. Shakespeare, Magistrate in Allahabad, to W. Bayley, Sec. to Govt., 9 Oct. 1817, BCJ LP, Consult. FW 2 Dec. 1817, P/133/18, IOL.

[107] Ibid.

at Allahabad, Kanpur, Farrukhabad and Arrah. Bodhi Ahir, a discharged havaldar at Karah, purchased three rolls and received pensions on them at the stations of Benaras, Gorakhpur, and Arrah. Similarly, Bhawani Baksh purchased a roll for Rs 30 and received a pension in Benaras. Many more people testified to the purchase of pension rolls from Bheek.[108]

The relatives of the deceased sipahis also engaged in fraudulent deals to retain their pension benefits. Very often they deprived the legitimate heir of the sipahi of his Thanah benefits. In one such case Ranjit Naik of the 2nd Regiment had died several years earlier but his brother Lawluck retained his pension roll and received the stipend to which his deceased mother was entitled.[109] In another case the brother of Tajee Singh, a sipahi of the 2nd battalion, took possession of his pension roll after he died. He received Tajee Singh's stipend at the rate of three rupees per month.[110]

Another kind of abuse which threatened the Invalid Thanahs which were doing well in Bihar and Benaras was that of illegal heirs. The land and monetary pensions given to the invalid sipahi were very attractive and many people tried to become the beneficiaries. In cases where the sipahi died without heirs, imposters tried to inherit his wealth illegally by claiming that they were his heirs. Most of the time such claims were made on the grounds of being adopted sons or daughters of the sipahi. In 1822, I. W. Sage, Collector of Bhagalpur, reported the case of a sipahi of the regular corps, who claimed to be the adopted son of Ramu Jamadar and wished to be put in possession of the invalid jagir of Ramu. On examining the claimant Sage discovered that not only was he no relation of the deceased sipahi but was also of a different sect. He was a 'Kussee' and Ramu was registered with the Company as a Sayyid.[111] Even though the Company

---

[108] Ibid.

[109] Ibid.

[110] Ibid.

[111] L. No. 8, Collector of Bhagalpur to BRIP, 9 Feb. 1822, Bengal Rev. Consult. Customs at Bihar and Benaras 12 March–9 April 1822, Consult. 22 March 1822, P/42/58, IOL.

officials cancelled pension benefits each time they discovered any fraud yet the problem was widespread and throughout the early nineteenth century it remained a major cause of concern for the Company.

FROM INVALID THANAH TO FAMILY SUPPORT, 1820–30

The disaffection in the Thanahs of Bihar and the abuses that had crept into the pensioners' establishment in Awadh came at a time when, as we have seen in chapter 2, the Company's sipahis were causing concern to it by reacting violently to any infringement on their assumed high ritual status. In response the Company experimented with different methods of curbing the power and authority hitherto wielded by the sipahis. In the same way the social problems created by the decline of the Thanah prompted the Company to introduce major reforms in its working. One significant shift in the Company's policy towards its pensioners was the heightened interest in the soldier's family. The Company now began to monitor the soldier's family as well as the individual sipahi and thereby attempted to exercise a firmer control over its increasingly 'disaffected' peasant regiments.

The importance the sipahi gave to his family was always recognized by the Company. As early as 1796 furlough privileges were introduced in the army. This enabled the sipahi to visit his village and attend to his family duties and social functions.[112] There also existed a provision of leave of absence and permission to obtain a permanent discharge from the army. The Company also had an elaborate arrangement which enabled the sipahis to remit their savings to their families. The local Collector distributed to the sipahi families the *hundis* dispatched by their relatives in the army.[113]

---

[112] Barat, *Bengal Infantry*, p. 141. Each native soldier was allowed leave with pay once in five or six years. Under ordinary circumstances, at any one time ten or fifteen sipahis and a corresponding proportion of commissioned and non-commissioned officers from each regiment were permitted to be absent on furlough. But the commanding officer had the right to call any of them at any time, if circumstances so demanded. While on furlough the native soldier enjoyed his pay but not the garrison batta.

[113] I. Lumsden, Resident in Lucknow, to G. H. Barlow, Sec. to Govt., 22 Aug. 1797, BMC, Procds. 8 Sept. 1797, P/19/34, IOL.

Again, in 1790, special provisions were made to enable the sipahis employed on foreign service to remit money to their families. The Commanding Officer of the sipahi battalions distributed tickets with the name and the rank of the soldier along with the amount of money he wished to remit. These tickets were then dispatched by the sipahi to his family. They helped the local Collector to identify the recipient who received the stated sum from his treasury.[114] Evidently the flow of large quantities of cash and credit into the military districts was itself a major force in the integration of rural areas into the commercial economy.

The Company had also made provisions for the exchange of correspondence between the family and the sipahi while he was on foreign assignment. The Adjutant-General of the army monitored the passage of mail ensuring its collection from the Collectors and its delivery to the Commanding Officer of the battalion who then distributed it to the sipahis.[115] Moreover, from 1808 we also have evidence of the existence of a Superintendent of Family Money who maintained records of money remitted by the sipahis and letters dispatched by them to their families.[116] However, until 1825 there was only one office of the Family Superintendent at Barrackpur which dealt with the soldiers' families residing in the Collectorships of any of the three Presidencies of Bengal, Bombay and Madras. Captain I. Read, the Superintendent of the Family Money in 1825, described the extensive duties of his office when he wrote about the nature of his job:

The 40th or any other regiment have 800 family certificates in payment and the amount of the abstract is perhaps 3,000 Rupees a month. 500 of this are paid at Barrackpore to the families adjacent, and the remaining five-sixths are to be distributed in portions of Rs 2 and Rs 3 or from 8 annas up to a moiety of remitter's pay, to every Collectorship throughout the Presidencies in which these families reside.[117]

[114] Regulation of 3 March 1790, H. C. Grace, *Code of Military Standing Regulations of the Bengal Establishment* (Calcutta, 1791), p. 339, L/MIL/17/2/438, IOL.

[115] Ibid.

[116] Reference in GOGG 29 Aug. 1818, Thompson, *Abstracts of General Orders*, pp. 22–3.

[117] L. No 1475, I. Read, Supdtt. Family Money, to Lieutenant-Colonel C. Casement, Sec. to Govt. Mil. Deptt., 25 Sept. 1825, BMC, Consult. 9 Dec. 1825, P/31/38, IOL.

Read's jurisdiction also extended beyond the Company's collectorships. This was evident when he wrote to Lieutenant-Colonel C. Casement, Secretary to government in the military department, about the far-flung places to which he had to remit money:

besides to other places where there are no Collectors and so on with every Corps Detachment and Establishment on foreign service. Hence I am in constant correspondence with 29 Collectorships exclusively of the various Residences and Regulating Officers of invalids and Commandants of various descriptions as well as with the officers to whose Company or establishment the grantees may belong.[118]

In the early nineteenth century one significant result of the social changes generated by the Thanah was the heightened official interest in the family of the sipahi and the Company's increased concern to define family relationships and if necessary to determine inheritance within military families. As the Company stepped in to check what it saw as the increasing cases of fraud related to illegal adoptions it assumed the responsibility of defining the 'legal' heirs of the sipahi. Regulation I of 1804 had given permission to invalid jagirdars to adopt sons to succeed as heirs.[119] From the second decade of the nineteenth century, the Company officials verified all adoptions made by the sipahi before the local administration considered applications for any claims.[120] They used a religious, caste and sect-based classification to define the 'legitimate' family relationship of the sipahis. Any relationship or adoption which did not conform to this pattern was declared illegal. In 1817 the adoption of Purshaud by Umrao Singh, an invalid jagirdar, was declared illegal by the zillah Judge in consequence of their being of different castes. The land he had inherited

---

[118] Ibid.

[119] Reference in J. S. Ward, 'A regulation for declaring the right of invalids, being Hindus on the jagirdar institution, to adopt heirs to succeed them in the possession of their jagir tenures and for prescribing rules for the observance of this class of people in case of adoption and for the proper registry of the same', 11 Oct. 1828, Bengal Sadar Board of Revenue, Consult. 13 March 1829, P/80/74, IOL.

[120] L. No. 8, Collector of Bhagalpur to Board of Revenue, Bihar and Benaras, 9 Feb. 1822, Bengal Rev. Consult. Customs at Bihar and Benaras, Consult. 22 March 1822, P/42/58, IOL.

was reverted back to the zamindar.[121] Once again in 1822 the Company declared the adoption of a child by Ramu Jamadar, an invalid jagirdar, illegal because the adopted son was not of Ramu's religious sect. Ramu was a Sayyid and his adopted son being of the 'Kussee' sect was denied any succession rights to Ramu's lands.[122] Moreover, on 21 June 1822, the Board of Commissioners for Bihar and Benares resolved that the inheritance rights of even the 'legally adopted' heirs were entirely at the discretion of the government. In a letter to the Bhagalpur Collector the Board wrote: 'Adoption though according to the legal forms conveyed to the party adopted no title to inherit lands of invalid jagirdars.' In the same year, on the Board's order, the practice of allowing adopted children to succeed to invalid jagirs was discontinued.[123]

In 1828–9, concerned with the growing problems of controlling the discontent among its peasant sipahis the Company sanctioned inheritance rights to the adopted heirs of only the Hindu invalid sipahis. The Regulation of 1828 read as follows:

It is hereby declared that the adoption of a son by an invalid jagirdar with the view to his being admitted a share to a jagirdar under the rules of the institutions shall be recognised as a title of inheritance only in cases of Hindoos and not unless the adoption may be proved to the satisfaction of the Collector and Regulating Officer to have been made in the regular and legal form prescribed by the Hindoo Law.[124]

In order to monitor and control its Hindu peasant regiments

---

[121] L. No. 320, R. U. Tilghman, acting Secretary to Board, to Collector of Bhagalpur, 15 June 1817, Bengal Board of Commissioners Bihar and Benaras, Consult. 10–30 June 1817, P/111/74, IOL.

[122] L. No. 8, Collector of Bhagalpur to Board of Revenue, Bihar and Benares, 9 Feb. 1822, Bengal Revenue Consultations Customs at Bihar and Benaras, Consult. 22 March 1822, P/42/58, IOL.

[123] L. No. 10, I. Pattle, Member Sadar Board of Revenue, to Sec. to Govt., 13 March 1829, Bengal Sadar Board of Revenue, Consult. 13 March 1829, P/80/74, IOL.

[124] J. W. Ward, 'A regulation for declaring the right of invalids, being Hindus on the Jagirdar Institution, to adopt heirs to succeed them in the possessions of their jagir tenures and for prescribing rules for the observance of this class of people in case of adoption and for the proper registry of the same,' 11 Oct. 1828, Bengal Sadar Board of Revenue, Consult. 13 March 1829, P/80/74, IOL (hereafter 'Right of invalids').

more effectively, the Company did not give the adopted heirs of the invalids the right to adopt sons with the intention of their becoming heirs to the invalid jagirs.[125] This was contrary to the practice of splitting up inheritance into small portions, prevalent for instance in the *bhaiyachara* revenue holdings. But the more significant and interesting aspect of this practice was the fact that, contrary to the accepted notion that in the mid-nineteenth century the Company was abandoning control to local society and intervening only at the higher echelons of society,[126] here we find the Company intervening directly in the minute domestic details of relatively humble people's lives. The sipahis were definitely an exceptionally prized and important part of local society and the Company exercised a more pervasive control over them. In 1829, the Company further systematized its procedure for determining legal and illegal adoptions and maintained detailed records of all adoptions the sipahi made. Within the first three months of adopting a child the sipahi was expected to notify the Collector and Regulating Officer of his district about the details of his case. These officers after verifying his report sanctioned the adoption and registered it in a book maintained by the Regulating Officer of the Thanah. No adoption conveyed a hereditary right to an invalid jagir unless it was recorded in the office of the Regulating Officer in the manner above directed.[127]

In 1825, after the Barrackpur mutiny, as the Company experienced more problems of control within the peasant army, it further increased its surveillance of the sipahi and his family. It expanded the existing Office of the Pension Paymaster and Office of the Family Superintendent, and created some new decentralized branches of these offices locally. I. Read, in a letter to Lieutenant-Colonel Command Casement suggested greater regularity in the monthly distribution of stipends throughout the Presidency. He also wished to fix specific days for these payments so as to regulate and monitor the recipients. By making things easier for them he hoped to win them over to the Company's

---

[125] Ibid.

[126] Yang, *Limited Raj*, pp. 70–89.

[127] Ward, 'Right of invalids'.

rule. In a letter to Casement he expressed this concern when he wrote:

And trifling as [it] may at first view appear, it will not be considered so on examination by his Lordship when he learns of its importance to the wife, the child or the mother of the man on foreign service who after coming 10–20 miles to receive the monthly stipend of Rs 2–3 is gratified to find that it is instantly paid.[128]

In 1825, on Read's recommendation the Company expanded the office of the Superintendent of Family Money.[129] In the same year the Company established a new office of the Superintendent of Family Money in Awadh. So far pensions in Awadh had been distributed by the local Resident and supervised by Read's office located in Barrackpur. In 1825 Lieutenant Fitton was appointed as the first Superintendent of Family Money and Pension Pay-master of Awadh. His office was at Lucknow but he travelled all over his province to survey the invalid families and supervise the distribution of money and pensions to them. He maintained a register of all invalid pensioners within his circle of payment and kept it up to date with all periodical transfers and new entrants recommended annually by the invaliding committee.[130] Again in 1827 the Company appointed Captain Goldies as the Superintendent of Family Money and Pension Paymaster for the stations of Benaras, Dinapur and Monghyr.[131]

In 1827 Bentinck established separate offices for the Pension Paymaster in Bihar, Benaras and Awadh. Hitherto the distribution of pensions by the Collector had been supervised either by the one general paymaster or, from 1825, by the Superintendent of Family Money in Awadh and Bihar. Now the paymaster communicated directly with the soldier's family and maintained records of these transactions. Bentinck argued that this arrangement resulted

[128] L. No. 228, Supdtt. Family Money to Lieutenant-Colonel C. Casement S. B., Sec. to Govt. Mil. Deptt., 16 Aug. 1825, BMC, Consult. FW 9 Dec. 1825, P/31/38, IOL.

[129] L. No. 230, Lieutenant-Colonel C. Casement, Sec. to Govt. Mil. Deptt., to Mil. Auditor General, 9 Dec. 1825, BMC, Consult. FW 9 Dec. 1825, P/31/38, IOL.

[130] GOGG, 25 Nov. 1825, Thompson, *Abstract of General Orders*, pp. 38–9.

[131] General Orders by Governor-General, 23 Feb. 1829, BMC, Consult. 23 Feb. 1829, P/33/20, IOL.

in a saving of Rs 94,074.9.6.[132] However, despite Bentinck's efforts to justify military reforms by claiming to reduce military expenditure, he was still prepared to pay large sums as pensions to the invalids where the vital interests of surveillance and monitoring of the sipahi and his family was involved. Every soldier was entitled to the pension equivalent to his rank in the army provided he had served in such a rank for at least three years.[133] Before he reached that stage he was entitled only to the pension of the rank immediately below his present one. A sipahi received Rs 4 per month, a naik Rs 7 per month, a havaldar Rs 7 per month, a jamadar Rs 13 per month and a subahdar Rs 25 per month. After forty years of service a subahdar was entitled to Rs 50 per month.[134] These rates were rather high and reflected that pensions were approximately seventy per cent of the salary the soldier had earned when in service.

In 1827, the 'military reforms' of Bentinck decentralized the Thanah administration so as to maintain a tighter control of the regiments. He established local Invaliding Committees in each district in place of the three big ones at Allahabad, Benaras and Monghyr.[135] This was accompanied by a further tightening of control over the sipahi families as well. In 1833, the Company codified family relationships for its soldiers so as to further narrow down the definition of the family. Only those who conformed to these set relationships were regarded as the rightful heirs by

[132] L. No. 57, Minute by Bentinck (?) 1829, BMC, Consult. FW 23 Feb. 1829, P/33/20, IOL. The total expenditure on the pay for the invalid establishment from 1824–7 was: 1824, Rs 97,094; 1825, Rs 108,746; 1826, Rs 53,664.4; 1827, Rs 1177,792.8. The total for four years was Rs 376,298.6.

The expense of a pension paymaster was met by discontinuation of the salary of the Fort Adjutant at Monghyr, who drew a salary of Rs 100 per month for himself and Rs 100 per month per establishment.

[133] L. No. 137, members of the Clothing Board forwarding copies of the Board's proceedings touching clothing in wear of pensioners with a view of obtaining publication of GO on that subject, Clothing Board Office, 22 Aug. 1834, to C. T. Metcalfe, Vice-President-in-Council, 30 Sept. 1834, in circulation, BMC, Consult. FW 30 Oct. 1834, P/34/69, IOL.

[134] Sleeman, *Rambles and Recollections*, p. 644.

[135] L. No. 7, GO by Gov.Gen. in Council, 23 Feb. 1829, BMC, Consult. 23 Feb. 1829, P/33/20, IOL.

the Company. These codified relationships which defined eligibility for succession were applied to all the sipahis irrespective of their religion and its inheritance laws. In this manner the Company created a separate succession and inheritance procedure for the army. Only the heirs who stood in one of the following relationships to the sipahi were considered eligible for the pension benefits: these were sons, daughters, father, and mother. The sipahi was supposed to nominate his heir only from this list. The name was entered in the official register of the corps or department concerned. The pension lapsed on the demise of the heir to whom it may have been granted. These pensions were referred to as the Native Family Pensions.[136]

Through the excessive concern the Company showed for its retired sipahis and their families it not only increased its surveillance, control, and knowledge of local society but was in effect introducing rigid conceptions of family. The significant fact was that such notions were emerging in this period for financial and political reasons rather than for ideological ones. However, what was still missing in the early nineteenth century were exclusive notions of martial race, and caste. These were to emerge later in the century when the writing of census reports and compiling of district gazetteers codified and formalized a rigid notion of family, caste and race. All this changed the recruiting practice in the mid-nineteenth century and regimental officers approached the family heads for information and supply of recruits.

Interestingly enough, in the 1840s, Lord Grey and the colonial reformers compensated for the reduction of British regiments and the raising of local militia in New Zealand and South Africa by settling invalid British soldiers with land in these colonies. The men were settled in villages under the control of their officers and relieved the regular forces on garrison duty.[137] The inspiration for this general imperial policy appears to have been drawn from

---

[136] GOGG 12 Dec. 1833, Thompson, *Abstract of General Orders*, p. 13. Monthly pensions were paid to the heirs at the following rates: Subahdar, Rs 26; Jamadar, Rs 8; Havaldar, Rs 4; Naik, Rs 3; Drummer, Rs 2; and Sepoy, Rs 2.

[137] W. P. Morrel, *British Colonial Policy in the Age of Peel and Russell* (Oxford, 1930), p. 476.

the Indian Thanah experiment where, as we have seen, invalid sipahis were used for the political expansion and consolidation of the East India Company. As money was saved and the families of the pensioners were absorbed into the colonial community, Lord Grey always defended this experiment and claimed that it was a great success. However, it was generally believed that the experiment was a failure and could never be expanded.[138]

THE MONGHYR LUNATIC ASYLUM

In 1795, the East India Company established for its Indian sipahis the first native lunatic asylum at Monghyr.[139] The timing of its founding was significant because it took place at the same time when in Britain the care and the cure of the insane was left to the family and community. The social segregation and confinement of the insane, a new feature of Enlightenment England, remained ad hoc, indeed largely private, and no comprehensive policy for madness emerged in Georgian England.[140] Until as late

[138] Ibid. p. 476.

[139] L. No. 23, Isaac Humphrey, Sec. Mil. Board, to Captain Hook, Sec. to Govt. in the Mil. Deptt., 5 Sept. 1800, Bengal Public Consultations, Consult. FW 6 Nov. 1800, P/5/15, IOL. In 1800 the Governor-General extended its facilities to non-servicemen also, but by the end of the year this order was revoked. Those civilian lunatics who had been admitted earlier remained in the asylum, but henceforth the asylum remained exclusively for native sipahis.

[140] Roy Porter, *Mind-forg'd Manacles: a History of Madness in England from the Restoration to the Regency* (London, 1987), p. 111. See also R. Porter, 'Medicine and the enlightenment in 18th-century England', *The Society for the Social History of Medicine*, Bulletin 25 (Dec. 1979), pp. 32–5. Porter has shown that the English Enlightenment brought about three basic changes in the evaluation of medicine and health. The first was its secularization—17th-century 'deviants' had been religiously stigmatised; 18th-century 'deviants' came to be defined in medical categories. Thus, in the 18th century, overcoming religious opposition, hospitals for reformed prostitutes and lock hospitals for venereal disease sufferers were founded. Secondly, the 18th century saw the expansion of medical institutions. Thirdly, Enlightenment medicine moved from the practice of care to the goal of cure.

These patterns affected attitudes towards insanity as well. The Enlightenment 'discovery' of mental disorder had three consequences. First, in England on a very small scale, there was a movement to isolate the insane in special institutions. The total number confined in England remained very small because most madhouses were private and fee-paying and hence for the affluent: lunatic asylums for paupers were to be a feature

as 1808, the local authorities did not have the power to establish asylums and Parliament did not require counties to found asylums until 1845.[141]

This lack of concern both from the state as well as within the medical profession was mirrored in the Company's attitude towards the European lunatics in India. E. Waltraud has shown that as late as the 1810s, the Company did not perceive lunacy provisions as a necessary state responsibility.[142] According to D. G. Crawford, there had existed a lunatic asylum in Bombay as early as 1745 and in Calcutta some time prior to 1787, while in Madras it is dated to 1794.[143] But these were privately owned madhouses and the insane were either sent there, or else left under the care of their relations and friends, or confined to gaols and regimental hospitals. In 1787, Assistant Surgeon W. Dick, of the Bengal madhouse, offered his medical services and the lease of his private asylum to the Government of Bengal. The

---

of the next century. Secondly, the optimism of the Enlightenment deemed madness to be a curable disease. Lastly, madness was to be cured not by manacles or medicine but by psychology, by management and later on, by 'kindness'.

[141] Porter, *History of Madness*, pp. 111–17. He shows that in 1660 and still largely in 1800, the English state involved itself with madness in three basic ways, one of which was a residual expression of feudal paternalism: from medieval times, the judiciary had provided a facility of trusteeship for idiots or lunatics in legal matters relating to property, contracts, estate, and inheritance. The Court of Wards and later the Chancery carried out these functions for the insane. The second field in which the state encountered the mad was criminal trials. The Parliament Act of 1800 provided that if a person charged with treason, murder, felony was found insane at the time of commission of such an offence and hence acquitted, the Crown ordered such a person in custody. The third way public authority regulated the lives of the disturbed was in the domain of public order. The 1714 Consolidating Act authorised two or more Justices of the Peace to secure the arrest of any person furiously mad and to have him locked up in a secure place.

[142] E. Waltraud, 'Treatment of European Lunatics in India', PhD thesis, SOAS, 1987. According to Waltraud, one reason for official and medical apathy was the preoccupation with the treatment of tropical disease that threatened the very existence of the European population in India; for Company policy towards native civil lunatic asylums which were established in 1812 see L. No. 21, R. Levy, Sec. Mil. Board to Sec. Medical Board and G. Dowdeswell, Sec. to Govt. in the Judicial Deptt., 11 May 1812, BCJ, Consult. FW 16 May 1812, P/130/51, IOL; see also BC, File No. 15373, F/4/617, IOL.

[143] D. G. Crawford, *A History of the Indian Medical Service 1600–1913* (2 vols., London, 1914), II, pp. 400, 415, 429.

1. Hindu priest garlanding the flags of the 35th Bengal Light Infantry at the presentation of colours. IOLR Add. Or. 741.

2. Cleveland's hill soldiers. Painting by William Hodges, *c.* 1790.
Sotheby's Catalogue, 1991, p. 71.

3. Recruits on Skinner's farm: Hurdut and Kohar. IOLR Add. 1271.

4. Procession of Emperor Akbar II. IOLR Add. Or. 2609

5. Skinner's Horse at exercise. Painting by John Reynolds Gwatkin, c. 1840. National Army Museum, London.

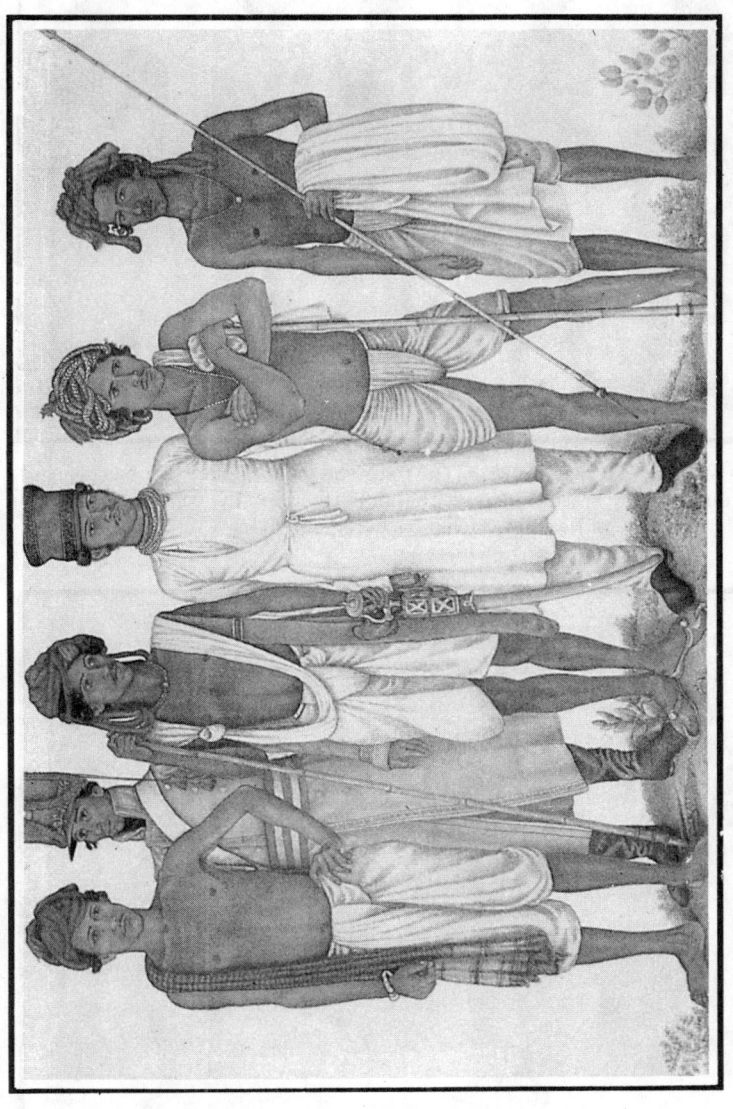

6. Recruits to Skinner's Horse. From right: Adh Ram, a Jat of Village Blan Bwanah; Lakhoo from district Panipat ; Roop Ram, a Gujar of Bhanknee village in the Mewat hills; Phulu, a Jat of Chidamah, district Sohanan, Haryana; Ramy, a Rajput of Laharu village, district Hansi; and Ram Dayal, a Jat trooper, of Nurwanah village, Hissar district. IOLR Add. Or. 1261.

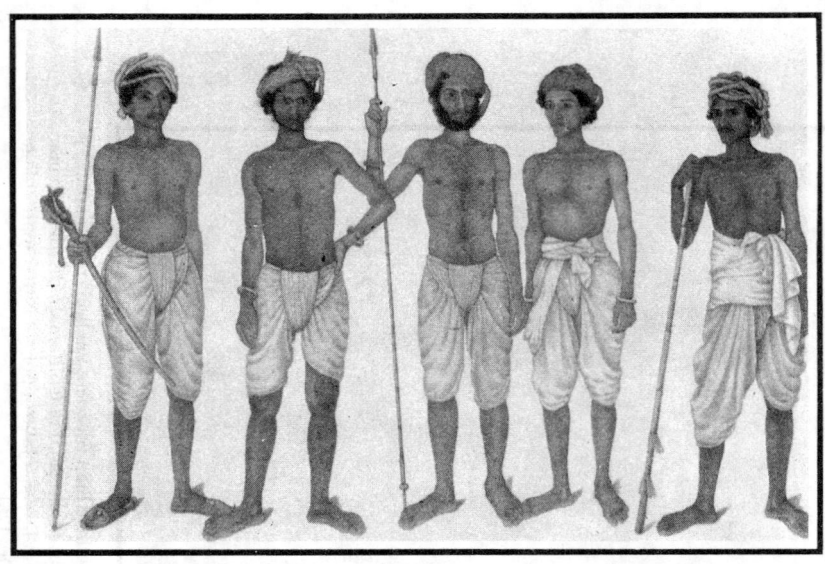

7. Five recruits, Haryana , *c*. 1815. The figure on the extreme right has been identified by Fraser as Umee Chand. Formerly in the collection of Baroness Helen Bachofen von Echt.

8. Three recruits, Haryana , *c*. 1816. The figure on the middle has been identified by Fraser as Umee Chand. Formerly in the collection of Baroness Helen Bachofen von Echt.

9. Portrait of Sayyid Mirza Azim Beg with his staff. IOLR Add. 1265.

Ghaonda. Chiefs and Soldiers

10. Gurkha Irregulars. IOLR. Add. Or. 1260.

Company accepted the offer and, from 1802, it made the private contractor of the asylum a government employee and the military commissariat provided food supplies for the patients. The institution was examined every month by the Medical Board and the chief magistrate, who prepared a report on its management and also maintained the case history of every patient. However, in the early nineteenth century, financial advantages, private corruption, contemporary medical theory and the government policy of immigration restriction introduced a policy of large-scale deportation of European lunatics to their homes. This remained the most popular practice throughout the nineteenth century.[144]

Quite in contrast to this was the concern displayed by Company officials for the insane sipahis of the Indian regiments. In 1795, the Company spent a total amount of Rs, 15,395.8.0 on the construction of the asylum at Monghyr.[145] Besides the initial costs, the Company spent an additional Rs 120 to Rs 125 on the repair work of the asylum every year.[146] In addition, a monthly sum of Rs 235 was spent on the salaries of employees.[147] The asylum consisted of four main buildings and sprawled over a vast military estate.[148] But it had a limited capacity of twenty cells

[144] Waltraud, 'European Lunatics', pp. 48–9.

[145] L. No. 20, 'Report of a committee of survey assembled by order of Major General Horston Brisco on the hospital for insanes at Monghyr', 1 Jan. 1798, BMC, Consult. FW 13 Feb. 1798, P/19/40, IOL.

[146] Captain P. D. Auvergne, Fort Adjtt. Monghyr, to Ross Moore, Assistant Surgeon Monghyr, 22 June 1801, BMC, Consult. FW 9 July 1801, P/20/20, IOL. In 1800 in order to accommodate the increase in the number of patients the Company spent Rs 1,144 to cover the veranda which surrounded the asylum. L. No. 81, Enclosure in H. Brisco's letter to I. Humphrey, Sec. Mil. Board, 16 Dec. 1800, BMC, Consult. FW 19 March 1801, P/20/15, IOL.

[147] L. No. 31, A. Campbell, Sec. to Hospital Board, to I. H. Harington, Sub Sec., 20 April 1795, BMC, Consult. FW 24 April 1795, P/19/1, IOL. The following establishment of servants was allowed: one European Sergeant as Superintendent, one compounder of medicine at Rs 8 per month, 1 cook at Rs 5 per month, 1 *bhishti* at Rs 5 per month, 1 washerman at Rs 5 per month, 2 sweepers at Rs 4 each and 1 cooley for every 2 patients at Rs 4. The surgeon was allowed to draw Rs 200 per month. With this money and the salary sanctioned for the pay of the patients he was expected to provide them with their daily diet, and fund them in every necessary item. This excluded European medicines which he was permitted to indent from the Company's dispensary.

[148] L. No. 20, 'Report of a committee of survey assembled by orders of Major General

which accommodated twenty patients.[149]

The oddness of establishing an asylum only for sipahis at a time when no similar state provisions existed for other sections of the population either in England or in India, suggests that the asylum was meant to maintain discipline and contain insubordination in the Indian regiments. Furthermore, it was very likely that some of the inmates of the asylum were also suffering from venereal disease, since the proneness of sipahis to dementia and mania, the two most common symptoms on the basis of which they were classified as lunatics, are also symptoms of syphilis of the nervous system,[150] or the last stage of gonorrhea. Moreover, this was the decade when the state was concerned about the spread of venereal disease in the army. Significantly, the founding of the Monghyr asylum coincided with the establishing of lock hospitals in the Bengal, Bombay and Madras Presidencies.[151] These hospitals were meant to check the growing incidence of venereal disease amongst European soldiers by monitoring Indian prostitutes and locking them in their wards until they were cured.[152] Unable to control the liaisons of Indian sipahis, especially when on leave in their villages, the asylum appears to have segregated the 'diseased' sipahi from the regiment and reduced the risk of the disease spreading amongst the women of the regimental bazars and the cantonment.

The sipahis' behaviour, both within and outside the cantonment, was of prime interest to the Company since it was through them that it projected its benevolence and superiority in Indian society. Any behaviour which threatened to demean the Company in

---

Horston Brisco on the hospital for insanes, Monghyr, 1 Jan. 1798', BMC, Consult. FW 13 Feb. 1798, P/19/40, IOL. Constructed around the old Monghyr fort the main building was 222 feet long by 27 feet broad and 15 feet high. Besides this there were twenty cells or apartments, each 12 feet by 10. The dimensions of the two cookrooms were 16 feet in length and 14 feet in breadth. The two privies were on a 10-foot square foundation.

[149] Ibid.

[150] See below for details

[151] K. Ballhatchet, *Race, Sex and Class under the Raj: Imperial Attitudes and Policies and their Critics, 1793–1905* (London, 1980), pp. 11–15.

[152] Ibid.

the eyes of the indigenous population was a cause of concern. For this reason the Company had put restrictions on the consumption of *bhang* and toddy, as this incited the sipahis to violent behaviour, thereby bringing a bad name to the Company. Designating some sipahis as insane appears to have provided another useful means of controlling their errant behaviour. The three major criteria for diagnosing a sipahi as a lunatic were the sipahi's proneness to 'dementia', 'mania' and 'violence'. Each of these categories was used to weed out sipahis whose behaviour was contrary to military decorum and threatened to undermine the 'civilized' image which the Company was attempting to create for itself. Soldiers who were found incapable of performing their military duties due to physical weakness but were neither physically invalid nor eligible for old-age pensions were diagnosed as demented. Those whose behaviour was detrimental to military decorum and the tranquillity of the regimental station were classified as manic. The symptomatic diagnosis which declared them 'unfit' was made after the Civil Surgeon had personally observed their behaviour. Any action not conducive to military decorum was perceived as 'abnormal' and the patient was recommended to the asylum. This method of controlling sipahi behaviour appears to have been particularly useful because by emphasizing its excessive concern for the insane sipahi the army was also promoting the benevolent image the Company was trying to create for itself.

Significantly, each time the Company encountered general problems of discipline in its sipahi army the number of persons assigned to the asylum increased substantially. From this point of view the diagnosis of insanity appears to have been a safety valve which was used to release tensions building up within the military establishment. Thus in its earliest years, 1795–1802, the asylum accommodated very large numbers of inmates: from twenty in 1795 the number swelled to 196 in 1799 and to 226 in 1800.[153] This reflected the military discontent which characterized

[153] Enclosure No. 80 in L. No. 79, from Captain I. Humphrey, Sec. to Mil. Board to H. Brisco, Major General Commandant, Monghyr, 6 Dec. 1800, 'Monthly return of natives in the hospital for insanes at Monghyr from Jan. 1799 to Jan. 1801', BMC, Consult. FW 19 March 1801, P/20/15, IOL.

Cornwallis' era of army reorganization, the period 1795–1802. In this period the Company had reason to doubt the trust it could place on its sipahis—in 1782 and again in 1795 there had been two major occasions of disobedience of orders over the question of the sipahis being transported by sea for the campaigns in Bencoolen and in Madras.[154] To avert this crisis Cornwallis introduced his military reforms of 1796, which merely generated further resentment and dissatisfaction amongst the native officers and men.[155] The military retrenchment of 1802 also aggravated the problems of military control.[156]

From 1802 till 1818 there was relative stability in the native regiments due to their being occupied on the war fronts, and very few sipahis were admitted to the asylum. But between 1820 and 1828, when the Company experienced further threats from its army the figures soared once again. The 1820s were years of mutiny[157] and desertion in the Bengal Army. C. Fagan, the Adjutant-General of the Army, attributed this to the inability of the new recruits to cope with military discipline, the curtailment of furlough, leave of absence, and the refusal of discharges because of the many wars the Company was engaged in.[158] In this period

[154] Barat, *Bengal Infantry*, p. 187.

[155] P. Manson, *A Matter of Honour: An Account of the Indian Army, its Officers and Men* (London, 1974), pp. 172–3. These reforms curtailed the responsibility and power of the native officers by grouping the battalions into regiments and placing them under the direct command of European officers. These reforms maintained the distinctions in pay in the rank hierarchy of native officers, but levelled the distinctions on account of power and responsibility which each rank held.

[156] Barat, *Bengal Infantry*, p. 190. By 1802 military recruitment was completely stopped and every Sepoy battalion was reduced to a strength of 700 men. A reduction of 200 men per battalion took blace.

[157] The gravest munity of the period was the Barrackpur mutiny of 1825 which necessitated army reorganization. Immediately after this mutiny the Company introduced regimental pandits and maulvis in its native regiments so as to curtail the high-caste sipahis' power and authority it had hitherto encouraged.

[158] L. No. 21, Adjtt. Gen. of the Mil. to Sec. to Govt. in the Mil. Deptt., 17 Jan. 1829, BMC, Consult. FW 23 Feb. 1829, P/33/20 IOL. The period saw the highest level of desertions in the army. The number of men who deserted from the native infantry in the year 1822 was 687. In 1823 this figure had reached 1,041, in 1824 it was 5,593, and in 1825 it had reached 8,322. This high level of desertion led the Company to issue the General Order of 1824 for the apprehension and punishment of deserters. But this did

the Monghyr asylum received its maximum number of patients. In 1831, of the twenty-nine patients transferred from Monghyr to the lunatic asylum at Benaras the following trend was evident: the average age was between twenty-nine and fifty-two; dementia was the diagnosis for seven, mania for nineteen, and three were considered to be idiots. Of these, twenty-three were sipahis, three havaldars and three naiks. Of the twenty-nine insane sipahis, twenty-two were admitted in the period 1820–31, and as many as sixteen were admitted between 1824 and 1831. In the period of military stability, 1814 to 1820, only seven sipahis were admitted. In 1831, the state of these sipahis was reported to be peaceable or occasionally violent.[159]

The details of the ten sipahis transferred from the insane hospital at Monghyr to the civil lunatic asylum at Patna reflected a similar pattern: the average age was beteen twenty-six and thirty; the diagnosis was dementia in four cases, mania in another four, and two idiots. Of the ten patients in the report, nine were admitted in the period 1821–30 and only one in 1817.[160]

The linkage of military control and insanity was also reflected in the architectural layout of the asylum. In its design and construction the asylum resembled a gaol rather than a hospital for the sick. To avoid the risk of fire the asylum was built of pakka material. It consisted of ten rooms which were enclosed by a verandah. Each room was ten feet by twelve feet and had one window with strong iron bars and shutters. The asylum and the other three rooms which were used by the superintendent, the cooking room and store room were all enclosed by a wall eight feet high.[161] Great emphasis was laid on the height and thickness

---

not solve the problem of desertion. In 1829 Bentinck discharged men who wished to leave so as to curb desertion.

[159] Roll of sipahis transferred from the insane hospital at Monghyr to the civil lunatic asylum at Benaras, Monghyr, 1 Nov. 1831, sent by Colonel W. Casement, Sec. to Govt. Mil. Deptt. and I. Moose, Assistant Surgeon, and C. Fagan, Adjtt. Gen. of the army, enclosure in L. No. 349, Adjtt. Gen. of the army to BCJ LP, 18 ultimo, BCJ LP, No. 2 Extract Mil. Deptt. 2 Dec. 1831, P/139/74, IOL.

[160] Ibid.

[161] L. No. 31, Sec. to the Hospital Board to I. H. Harington, Sub. Sec., 20 April 1795, BMC, Consult. FW 24 April 1795, P/19/1, IOL. Description of the building furnished

of the walls which surrounded the complex as well as the one which partitioned the cells.[162] The entire architectural layout of the asylum revealed that the army's major concern was with segregating the sipahi from society and confining him in a building from which he could not escape easily.

We do not know the precise cause of the prevalence of 'mental derangement' in the army. One of the explanations, we have seen, had to do with the way the military commandant perceived sipahi behaviour in the context of military decorum and discipline. But it seems there was an important medical aspect attached to this diagnosis as well. We have noted that dementia and mania were the two most common symptoms on the basis of which the sipahi was locked in the Monghyr asylum. Both these 'behavioural disorders' are defined as a form of mental derangement or insanity with loss of intellectual power due to brain disease or injury.[163] Venereal diseases like syphilis are amongst the most common causes of organic disease of the brain and the spinal cord leading to insanity.[164]It thus seems probable that the manics,

to Governor-General for the reception of 20 native insane soldiers.

[162] L. No. 20, Report of a committee of survey assembled by the orders of Major General Horston Brisco on the hospital for insanes at Monghyr, 1 Jan. 1798, BMC, Consult. FW 13 Feb. 1798, P/19/40, IOL. The partition walls were 13 feet high and 2 feet broad. The centre wall was 219 feet long, 2 feet thick and 13.5 feet high. The area or compound walls were 304 feet in length and 104 feet in breadth. Besides this, greater security was ensured by 1.5 foot broad foundation which was 2 feet above ground, 1 foot 3 inches thick, by 8 feet in height. Each room had one window with strong iron bars. Both the doors as well as the windows were properly secured by locks to the former and bolts to both. The beams, bungahs, door and windows were painted a chocolate colour.

[163] R. E. Allen (ed.), *The Pocket Oxford Dictionary of Current English* (Oxford, 1984), pp. 446, 193.

[164] H. W. Bayly, *Venereal Disease: Its Prevention, Symptoms and Treatment* (London, 1920), p. 35. As early as 1737, Jean Astruc, physician to Louis XVI, the King of France, had noted that the behavioural disorders normally associated with a 'diseased' brain or nervous system were some of the major symptoms of venereal diseases as well. He observed that spasms, convulsions, epilepsy, tremor of the limbs, and heaviness of the head were all symptomatic of venereal disease. More specifically, the symptoms of cerebral syphilis which included rheumatic pains, staggering, stumbling, slurring and loss of balance along with mental depression or excitement (mania), loss of memory, irritability, lack of confidence or concentration and incoherence also reflected mental derangement (Bayly, *Venereal Diseases*, pp. 36–7; and J. Astric, *A Treatise of the Venereal*

idiots, and demented sipahis of the asylum were in fact suffering from venereal disease. This speculation seems to have some substance because the Company's concern for the 'demented' sipahis came at the same time that it was establishing hospitals to check the spread of venereal disease amongst its European soldiers. By the end of the eighteenth century, the Governor General-in-Council had authorized the building of 'hospitals for the reception of diseased women' at Berhampur, Kanpur, Dinapur and Fatehgarh. Although the term 'lock hospital' was not used, patients were forbidden to leave these hospitals until they had been certified as cured. The kotwal of the regimental bazars sent all women whose conduct was found 'disorderly' to the hospital. Similarly, on the recommendation of the Provincial Commander-in-Chief, hospitals for 'diseased public women' were established at Agra and Mathura in 1807.[165] Unable to control the more far-flung nature of the sipahis' interaction with women, especially when on leave or furlough, it must have been more feasible to control the 'diseased' sipahis by locking them in the asylum. This not only removed them from the regiment but also reduced the risk of the contagion spreading to the women within and outside the cantonment with whom the sipahis interacted. Moreover, once on furlough, an infected sipahi could spread the disease in an epidemic form in the village he visited.

The classification of different categories of insanes in the asylum was quite contrary to the caste, religion or gender specific classification of inmates in the native and European civil lunatic asylums of the early nineteenth century.[166] The Monghyr asylum emphasized the general category of soldier and classified the sipahis according to their symptoms. This further suggests the significant role it played in maintaining military discipline, and reveals its

Disease (2 vols., London 1985), II, p. 7).

[165] Ballhatchet, *Race, Sex and Caste under the Raj*, pp. 11–15. He shows a similar policy leading to the establishment of lock hospitals in the Madras and Bombay Presidencies in the first decade of the 19th century.

[166] BC, File No. 15373, extract Bengal Judicial 28 Aug. 1818, pp. 53–202 and pp. 209-47, F/4/617, IOL. In the civil lunatic asylum at Dacca, Murshidabad, Patna, Benaras, and Bareli the classification of patients was based on caste, religion, tribe and gender.

crucial importance in checking the spread of 'contagious disease' in the Indian regiments. Those sipahis who were classified as 'idiots' were placed in a separate building very close to the Monghȳr gaol. Outside the Monghyr fort was a separate house for those classified as demented. A long narrow building at a great distance from the fort accommodated the worst-affected insanes—the 'maniacs' who were housed in cells.[167] There were two cook rooms in the asylum complex and one cook who prepared the food for all the inmates. There is no evidence to suggest that there were separate cook rooms and cooks for the Hindu and Muslim inmates[168] as there were in the civil lunatic asylum.[169] Here, all the inmates irrespective of religion and caste were sanctioned a common 'military diet', a high-caste Brahmin one of vegetables, fruits, ghee, rice and dal[170] which the high-caste sipahis had asked for and obtained at the time of recruitment. The government granted to each sipahi sonaut Rs 3 or sicca Rs 2.14 annas from which his food, clothing and all his wants were expected to be supplied by the Surgeon. The sipahis were so habituated to their assumed high-caste 'military diet' that in 1831, G. Angus, the Civil Surgeon in charge of the civil lunatic asylum at Benaras, asked the magistrate of Benaras for an indulgence in the diet allowed to the twenty sipahis transferred from Monghyr. He wrote:

I will also ascertain if any indulgence is to be allowed to the Sepoys in particular of diet over the other patients. At Monghier they appear to have received a daily allowance of ghee. An article not supplied here, the withdrawal of which seems to have caused great discontent.[171]

---

[167] L. No. 22, the Commissioner of Circuit of the 12 or Monghyr Division to J. Thompson, Deputy Sec. to Govt. in the Judicial Deptt., Fort William, 9 Nov. 1831, BCJ LP, Consult. 22 Nov. 1831, P/139/73, IOL.

[168] L. No. 31, Sec. to Hospital Board to I. H. Harington, Sub. Sec., 20 April 1795, BMC, Consult. FW 24 April 1795, P/19/1, IOL.

[169] See BC, Extract Judicial Letter from Bengal, 19 Dec. 1822, F/4/823, IOL.

[170] Captain H. E. Page, Fort Adjutant Monghyr, to C. Fagan, Adjtt. Gen. of the Army, 9 March 1829, BMC, Consult. 15 May 1829, P/33/26, IOL. In 1829 on the inability of the surgeon to provide these provisions within the sanctioned amount, made the government give responsibility to the military commissariat for supplies to the asylum.

[171] G. Angus, Civil Surgeon, to D. B. Morrieson, Official Magistrate of Benaras, 7 Dec. 1831, BCJ WP, Consult. FW 20 Dec. 1831, P/140/1, IOL.

The government conceded to the request for this particular batch of sipahis. It was however decided that subsequently all the sipahis transferred to the asylum would obtain the usual diet of the hospital.

As has been shown in the earlier section on the Thanah and in chapter 2, the 1830s were characterized by a strengthening of state control over the sipahi and his family. The military cuts of the decade accompanied by a rigorous control of the now much reduced Indian and European regiments made the lock hospitals seem an additional expense and the asylum unnecessary. Bentinck abolished the lock hospital in 1830[172] and the Monghyr asylum in 1831.[173] As in the case of the Thanah, the Company began using the sipahis' family as a unit responsible for the care and the protection of the insane sipahi. All the composed and peaceable patients were made over to the care of their families and friends. All those in an incipient state of insanity were transferred to the civil lunatic asylum at Patna and Benaras. This category also included the insane who were violent and required to be kept under restraint. These transfers were generally made to asylums located close to the insane sipahis' homes, where they were expected to be medically treated (which invariably meant confinement until the time the soldiers' behaviour became conducive to military decorum). For the 'cure' was said to have been completed when the soldier became 'peaceable and composed' and 'was not likely to endanger the safety of himself or others'.[174] The 'composed' soldier was then handed over to the further care of his friends or family.

By devolving the responsibility of the 'mentally sick' sipahi on the family, the Company created a permanent link with it. Records of all such families were maintained which were regularly monitored. In an effort to forge a permanent contact with the family of 'insane' soldiers an annual pension was allotted for the sipahi's maintenance. Those who by length of service were entitled to the benefits of the Invalid Pension Establishment, were provided a pensionary support according to their rank. To those whose

---

[172] Ballhatchet, *Race, Sex and Caste under the Raj*, p. 16.

[173] GOVP, 5 Aug. 1831, Thompson, *Abstract of General Orders*, p. 13.

[174] Ibid.

period of service gave them no claim to pensions, a provision of three rupees per month was sanctioned. These stipends were payable to the friends or relatives under whose protection they were placed. The Company's military Pension Paymaster maintained the record of the insane sipahi's family and distributed the pensions.[175]

[175] Ibid.

Chapter 4

The Military Experiment
with the Hill People

By 1772 the extension of the Company's rule in Bengal brought it in direct contact with the Jungle Tarai on the western frontier of the province. For the first five years the Company controlled this region with regiments of the Bengal Infantry. However, in 1779, Augustus Cleveland, the Collector of Bhagalpur in charge of the Jungle Tarai, assumed the responsibility of recruiting 'tribal' soldiers on the frontier. This marked the beginning of another distinct military tradition of raising 'tribal' troops, thus incorporating their military skills in the Company's army. Cleveland's recruitment of hill 'tribals' was a significant development since it took place at the same time as Hastings' recruitment of high-caste Rajputs, Brahmans and Bhumihars on the plains of Bengal. The methods of recruitment and organization of these hill regiments provide a contrast with Hastings' experiment on the plains. Whereas on the plains of Bengal the Company disbanded the military levies of zamindars[1] and was sceptical of carefully graded Mughal service grants, on the frontier it continued, with greater scrutiny, the Mughal *ghatwalis*[2] and zamindari levies. Moreover, the Mughal system of pacifying zamindars and chieftains by contracting with

[1] K. W. Firminger (ed.), *The Fifth Report from the Select Committee of the House of Commons on the Affairs of the East India Company*, 28 July 1812 (Calcutta, 1917), I, pp. cxxxviii–xii.

[2] Landholdings granted by frontier zamindars to their clansmen for military service.

them to supply recruits, in lieu of which they were paid in cash or land jagirs,[3] was extended to the hills of the Jungle Tarai as well.

The divergence of the Company from its established military practice was the result of a compelling necessity to tame the frontier. This was important not only for protecting the regular flow of revenue collection from the plains but also for extending the Company's political control into these turbulent areas. It was for this reason that in a period when the Company was trying to establish its paramountcy it was still willing to compromise its military and executive authority in the Jungle Tarai by sharing it with local notables.[4] The study of the Company's interaction with the frontier adds a new dimension to the analysis of state formation in early modern India and of the very nature of the Company state.

THE MUGHAL AND LATER NAWABI BENGAL FRONTIER

The western frontier of the Bengal province was called the Jungle Tarai. This was a name loosely applied to the whole country which extended from the Kharakpur hills on the west to the Rajmahal hills on the east and from the Bhagalpur plains on the north to Ramgarh, Pachet and Birbhum on the south.[5] The region can be divided into three zones: the hills, ghats (passes), and the plains. Located as it was on the fringes of the settled

---

[3] Ali, The Mughal Nobility under Aurangzeb, introduction.

[4] T. K. Ravindran, 'The Kurichiya Rebellion of 1812', Journal of Kerala Studies, vol. III, part I (March 1976), pp. 532–44. In the 1790s, in dealing with the Palassi Raja on the Malabar frontier, the Company attempted to recruit the Kurichiya and Kurumba 'tribals' into its locally raised militia so as to 'placate' the 'turbulent' Malabar jungles. However, the Company was unsuccessful in its efforts and it was only after the suppression of the Palassi rebellion in 1805 that these 'tribals' were temporarily controlled by the force of British regiments and a revenue settlement which treated them harshly. However, later in the 1820s, Outram was more successful in applying the Jungle Tarai experiment to 'tame' the Bhils on the Gujarat frontier. His well-known Bhil Corps, organized on the pattern of Cleveland's Hill Corps, continued well upto the mutiny of 1857.

[5] Buchanan Hamilton, Journal of Buchanan Hamilton, kept during the survey of the district of Bhagalpur in 1810–1811 (ed.) C. E. A. W. Oldham (Patna, 1930), p.1.

plains of the Mughal and later Nawabi Bengal, the Jungle Tarai stretched beyond the pale of their administrative institutions.

H. McPherson, a later settlement officer of the Santal Parganas, reported that only a fringe of the Rajmahal district acknowledged the supremacy or the authority of the Mughals and nine-tenths of it had never been explored or surveyed by them.[6] Even their revenue authority was limited to the east of the hills. The country within the hills, which was a part of Rajmahal sarkar, was gifted by mansabdari grant to the Manihari Katawris but was never included in the Mughal revenue surveys. From Akbar's time, when the first sanad was granted, to 1765 when the British received the diwani of Bengal, it stood at the same jagir valuation of Rs 11,250. The south and south-west portions of the district .formed part of the zamindaris of Birbhum and was barely explored by the Mughals. In 1720, the Bengal Nawabi had to be content with the tribute it received from this area. However later, Alivardi Khan, the Nawab of Bengal, managed to subdue it with the support of the British and doubled its assessment.[7]

Even though the plains, ghats, and the hills that comprised the Jungle Tarai were beyond the pale of the Mughal and later Nawabi administration, they had contributed to the power of these polities. For instance, the zamindars on the plains, who were in closest proximity to the settled society of Bengal, defended the frontier passes against Maratha assaults and attacks by hill men from the surrounding Rajmahal hills. The Mughals granted them sanads which recognized their significance in policing the Mughal frontier. The policing arrangements of the zamindars were well planned and proved effective in defending the frontier against external threats. Their most characteristic feature was the ghatwali tenure.[8] The ghatwali tenures were landholdings granted by the zamindars to their clansmen for military service they were expected

---

[6] H. McPherson, *Final Report on the Survey and Settlement Operations in the District of Santal Parganas 1898–1907* (Calcutta, 1909), p. 24.

[7] Ibid.

[8] 'Description of the Jungle Tarai District, their revenue, trade and Government with a plan for the improvement of them by James Browne, 1778', submitted to Warren Hastings, British Museum (BM) Add. 29210, Warren Hastings Papers. Hereafter Browne's Report.

to perform on the frontier. These service grants were permanent and hereditary in nature and the grantees were called ghatwals.[9] This was a name they derived from their regional location on the ghats or valley of the Rajmahal and Kharakpur hills. Generally the ghatwali tenure was assessed at a very low rate and the grantees were expected to use its revenue to maintain a specified number of men to help in revenue collection and guard the passes in the hills. Sometimes this number amounted collectively to 2,000–3,000 men. The ghatwali tenure remained a part of the zamindari and the ghatwal was responsible to the zamindar for any robbery which might occur within the limits of his ghats.[10] Rights and obligations similar to these regulated the relations between the ghatwal and his retainers. The ghatwal assigned on an average about fifteen bighas of land to each retainer who cultivated it while he discharged his military duties.[11] When the crops failed he diversified to non-agricultural pursuits like the manufacture of charcoal.[12] The ghatwals generally co-operated with each other in their everyday functioning but fighting often broke out if the interests of different ghatwals clashed. The hostility was often directed against the patron zamindar or against the ghatwal chiefs in the region.[13] Very often the Jungle Tarai was rocked with

[9] Sometimes the zamindar himself acted as the ghatwal.

[10] Information from contents enclosed in the Nizamat Adalat Register of 25 April BCJ, Consult. FW 2 May 1815, P/131/60, IOL.

[11] M. Roychoudhury and P. R. S. Shastri, 'A Sanad of Captain James Browne, Military Collector of Zilla Jungle Tarai (1776 A.D.)', *IHRC*, Baroda session, vol. XVII (December 1940), pp. 150–1. A copy of a sanad issued by Raja Qadir Ali, of taluq Kakwara, to his ghatwal chiefs defines the duties, rights and obligations of the ghatwals, who were designated as permanent ghatwals on a rent of Rs 245.12.15 and made answerable for the defence of the frontier. Similar arrangements existed in the frontier zamindaris of Rajshahi and Birbhum.

[12] L. No. 25, Bhagalpur Magistrate to Henry G. Tucker, Sub. Sec. to Governor-General-in-Council in the Judicial Deptt., 30 July 1796, BCJ LP, Consult. FW 30 Sept. 1796, P/128/29, IOL. There was a heavy demand for charcoal in the neighbourhood of the Jungle Tarai. This was used for the iron-smelting and manufacturing processes carried on in Singhbhum and Hazaribagh, and in the neighbourhood of the hills.

[13] Roychoudhury and Shastri, 'A Sanad of Captain James Browne', pp. 156–8. The case of the Kharakpur zamindari was a classic example of the ghatwal directing his hostility against the zamindar. Lakshmandeo, the ghatwal chief, had the strong support

violence because the zamindars used the ghatwali levies to solve their disputes with the neighbouring zamindars.[14]

Moving from the ghats into the interior of the Jungle Tarai it is important to understand the variety of forms in which chief-tainship was established and manifested in the forest-covered hills of the Rajmahal and Kharakpur districts. This understanding is essential for any study of the Jungle Tarai because the hill polity was very different from the constituted authority the British were dealing with on the plains. In the Jungle Tarai every hill chief was in charge of a unit, comprising a number of hills called the *tuppah*, and their subordinate chiefs, called manjis, were in charge of one hill each. The sardar manji or chief of the tuppah received no contribution from any village except his own and there were no well-defined rules laid out for his responsibilities. The chief had the power to assemble several manjis with their adherents on any offensive or defensive operation but he could not compel them to fight if they disapproved of his motives.[15] In the absence of well-defined codes of administration, the wrongs and injuries committed by the inhabitants of one village on that

---

of his soldiers. Using his military base he often expressed open hostility to Muzaffar Ali, the Raja of Kharakpur. He supported the Nawab of Bengal and often led his campaigns against the Kharakpur Raja. But the loyalty of the ghatwals fluctuated, for Lakshmandeo's adopted son, Juggunnathdeo, squandered the funds of his father and defied the Nawab's government. Sometimes the same kind of fluctuating loyalty was replicated at the level of the ghatwals' dependants. For instance, Juggunnathdeo's babus (clan title for the dependants of the ghatwals) often refused to pay him anything for the landholdings they held and even declined military service to him. Their independence was best reflected when they sent an independent delegation to the Nawab of Bengal, Mir Kasim, who had sent a battalion of troops to quell the recalcitrant Juggunnathdeo who had not paid his annual revenue. They said they were willing to pay the same tribute as had been paid by Lakshmandeo. After they had successfully warded off the immediate danger they plundered and drove out the Nawab's amils and sipahi guards from their territory and regained their country for themselves. In another instance, on the southward boundary of Curruckdea, close to Ramgarh, was the strong zamindari of 'Duchawns'. Its zamindar was Sheepdut Singh and he was in a state of perpetual warfare with the neighbouring Bhuiya zamindari rajas. Indeed it was this continuing warfare which cemented the bonds between him and his soldiers.

[14] Lt. T. Shaw, 'On the inhabitants of the hills near Rajmahal', *Journal of Bengal Asiatic Research*, vol. 4, pp. 102–3.

[15] Browne, 'The Jungle Tarai District'.

of another were in general decided by the sword. But disputes and differences with regard to property or other causes between inhabitants of the same village were always settled by the manji and his officers—the *kotwal* and the *faujdar*. These informal and flexible arrangements in the hills led British observers to believe that 'plunder', 'loot' and open violence were some of the more common tactics adopted for the solving of disputes in the Jungle Tarai.[16]

In these hills the chiefs as well as the manjis derived their authority from their patronge of elaborate rituals conducted by the forest priest called the Demauno. Evangelical Christian observers of the late eighteenth century reported these ceremonies as a form of 'devil worship'.[17] But these rituals accompanied the

[16] Shaw, 'The inhabitants of the hills near Rajmahal', pp. 84–5. When a man of one village had any claim upon an inhabitant of another village it was not uncommon, if the latter denied it and refused to have the matter brought to trial, for the complainant to apply to the chief of his village. The chief got together a few more chiefs, to whom presents were made in proportion to the nature of any dispute brought to their notice. The dependants of these chiefs were assembled so as to plunder the village where justice was denied and to carry off the offender. The division of the booty was done according to rates fixed separately for the manjis, their officers, and vassals. In such troublesome times much was not taken as all property, not of immediate use for domestic purposes, was usually concealed. The chiefs could therefore only have the first choice of the utensils and apparel which fell into their hands. The relations of the accused and the chief of the village which was plundered, sent a present to the complainant. They acknowledged the demand and promised to abide by the award which arbitrators would give on the release of the prisoner. After the prisoner was released he and his relations had to make good the loss sustained by the inhabitants of the plundered village as well as pay the cost of arbitration.

[17] Shaw, 'The inhabitants of the hills near Rajmahal', pp. 46–69. Shaw was of the view that of the innumerable public spectacles in the forest the most revealing was the Maug or Phagun annual festival, when the manji of every village sacrificed a buffalo, having fixed a day for the ritual when his vassals were obliged to attend, each of whom contributed a portion of grain, oil or spirits for the festival. Provisions were collected on the day appointed, and the manji directed his followers what to do. Some cooked while others went and cut a large branch of the *muckmum* (or *sicwa*) tree, which was brought and planted before the manji's door. The manji sat on a stool under the shade of the branch. He financed the ceremony, and organized his people for the festival rites, thereby reinforcing his power in the locality. The participation of the forest priest—Demauno—gave the manji the authority and credibility that he needed for ruling the hills. There was a separate ceremony through which the priest symbolically ratified the power of the manji. The Demauno sat on the ground and prayed for the well-being

performance of annual sacrifices which characterized the 'tribal' religion in the Jungle Tarai. For instance, William Hodges, a British traveller and painter, observed the annual performance of the buffalo sacrifice to please the local deity on the hills.[18] Moreover, since the chief derived his power from his clansmen and subordinate manjis, there were many public celebrations which underlined his relationship with these social groups and reinforced chieftainship in the region. One such public ceremony was patronized by the chief manji (head of several hills) who, every year, mobilized his clansmen and village people to pray for sufficient rains for their crops. The chief determined the time and the date of the ceremony and then sent for all the manjis who attended the ceremony with twenty to thirty men. This assemblage of dependants reinforced the power of the chief and the Demauno, by presiding over the ceremony, gave it legitimacy. A buffalo was sacrificed and the ceremony continued as long as the provisions, which were presented to the several manjis, lasted.[19]

However, the hill chieftaincies did not function in isolation in the Jungle Tarai for there were certain political rituals which symbolically integrated the hill chiefs with Mughal sovereignty.

---

of the manji and his descendants. After the prayer he gave the manji a handful of unboiled rice, which he scattered close to the muckmun branch. Soon after this ceremony was over the manji symbolically displayed his power and authority to his people. Shaw reported this was done in another ritual during which the manji beat the drum and collected all the men who were possessed of devils. The buffalo was hamstrung by the manji, its head was cut off under the branch of the muckmun tree, and the chief along with the Demauno feasted on it, while those who were possessed by the devil licked its blood. The ceremonies towards the end of this ritual distributed the power and authority of the chief among his followers. The adherents came forward with their offerings of rice, oil and spirits and received a blessing from their chief. The next morning they assembled to feast on the buffalo and other things which the manji furnished. After 5 days a foal was immolated and its blood sprinkled on the muckmun branch. This branch along with the buffalo's horns and some bones were fastened on the roof of the manji's house where they were left to decay.

[18] W. Hodges, *Travels in India during the Years 1780, 1781, 1782 & 1783* (London, MDCCXCII), pp. 88, 92–3. Hodges noted that their manners were very different from those of the Hindus of the plains. He was of the view that they were Hindu outcastes who lived in the more mountainous parts and occasionally came down to commit 'depredations' on the defenceless people of the plains.

[19] Ibid., p. 56.

This symbolic link was maintained through the zamindars based in the foothills of the Jungle Tarai. In the absence of Mughal administrative machinery the zamindars of the plains who owed allegiance to the Mughal administration, were perceived as the representatives of the Mughals by the hill men.

Symbolic gift exchanges with the zamindars amounted to the acceptance of Mughal sovereignty and complemented the legitimacy the manjis derived from their forest. Every year at Dussehra the chief of each tuppah along with the manjis living under his administrative jurisdiction, visited the zamindar in his foothills. The zamindar renewed his oath of allegiance to the Mughal government and the other manjis pledged their loyalty to the zamindar. Each manji was presented with a turban, acceptance of which symbolised the sharing of zamindari suzerainty.[20] The zamindars, as we have seen, were integrated into the Mughal policy and the acceptance of their suzerainty amounted to the recognition of Mughal sovereignty.[21]

The Jungle Tarai hills also contributed to the economy of the settled polities on the plains of Bengal. In 1792, Thomas Shaw, the Company's revenue surveyor in the Jungle Tarai, reported on the manufacture of 'small and common Hindustani bedsteads by the highlanders which they brought down to the plains for sale'. Wood for making furniture, as well as for fire, charcoal, rudely-shaped wooden ploughs, and planks shaped with a hatchet were also brought down for sale. Apart from timber and its products, bamboo, cotton, honey, plantains, sweet potatoes and, occasionally, small quantities of grain were added. These articles were bartered for the products of the plains like salt, tobacco, iron heads for arrows, hatchets, crooks and other forms of iron implements. Except for bedsteads no other articles were manufactured in the hills and even the earthen pots were obtained from the plains. Very often women participated in the bamboo and wood trade, carrying these items to the market in the foothills

[20] J. Fombelle, Magistrate of Bhagalpur, to H. St. George Tucker, Sub. Sec. to Govt. in the Judicial Deptt., 27 Sept. 1797, in K. K. Datta, *Selections from Judicial Records of Bhagalpur District Office 1792–1805* (Patna, 1968), pp. 227–8.
[21] Ibid.

and exchanging them for salt and tobacco. Charcoal also had a ready market in the plains. Whenever the rains failed, causing a scarcity of grain in the hills, charcoal was bartered on the plains for grain.[22] In all these ways a political and economic link, albeit loose and flexible, connected the Jungle Tarai to the settled polities of the surrounding plains.

THE COMPANY AND THE GHATWALIS: 1772–1818

The flexible and loose political and economic relations that existed between the hill chiefs, the ghatwals, and the zamindars were considered an aberration from the political assumptions of the British about 'proper societies' which were manifested even in the early stages of Company rule. This ideal norm was already deeply influenced by the Enlightenment tradition. But the Company's officials explained these aberrations in sociological terms as well.[23] An instance of these explanations is seen in the colonial explanation for the hill man's aberrant habit of raiding the plains. This was explained finally with reference to the manner in which hill chiefs had been treated earlier by the zamindars. Thus in 1779, Colonel Brown, in his account of the region sent to the government, observed

that it was about 15 years since the hill people had any Government among themselves of a general nature; during which period they had become dangerous and troublesome to the low country; that their ravages had been the more violent as they were stimulated by hatred against the zamindars for having cut off their chiefs by treachery.[24]

Again in 1792, T. Shaw explained the behaviour of the hill men in the pre-British period as being prompted by the zamindars:

It was a common practice for the the zamindars on the skirts of the hills to invite the Chiefs in their vicinity with their adherents, to descend and

---

[22] Shaw, 'The inhabitants of the hills near Rajmahal', p. 96.

[23] For a similar trend in the early 19th-century colonial ideology in the Company's interaction with the Bhils, see A. Skaria, 'A forest polity in western India, the Dangs 1800–1920', Ph.D thesis, Cambridge University, 1992.

[24] Shaw, 'The inhabitants of the hills near the Rajmahal', p. 102.

plunder the neighbouring zamindaris for which and for the passage through their lands, the mountaineers divided the booty with them. Thus, at one time, from repeated acts of treachery by the zamindars, the mountaineers were provoked to take ample vengeance on them and their happy ryots; and at other times, from their engaging the Chiefs to make predatory incursions to which they were strongly incited, no less from a desire of plundering their more opulent neighbours, than from a difficulty of obtaining salt and tobacco from the hauts.[25]

Shaw was of the view that the raids of hill men had depopulated the plains skirting them and made travel in the region very difficult.

'Raiding' was a recurrent feature of the relationship between the hills and the plains, contributing both to the economy as well as the political power of the polities of these regions. However, the British found it difficult to accept it because it was contrary to their notion of 'public order'. Finding it even more difficult to control these raids they made the local zamindars their scapegoat. They were accused of conniving with the hill men, thereby making it easy for them to attack the Bengal plains.

The logical consequence of such explanations was to curb the power of the zamindaris that skirted the Jungle Tarai. It was believed that once they had been deprived of their zamindar mentors the hill chiefs could be easily 'tamed'. This was first attempted by militarily crushing the power of the zamindars. In November 1773, departing from the usual British norm of rigorous-ly dividing military and civil authority, Hastings declared the Jungle Tarai a military collectorship. An infantry regiment under the charge of the Council at Calcutta and commanded by Captain Robert Brooke was placed in the Jungle Tarai. It corresponded with the Board of Revenue on the business of revenue collection and followed the orders of the Board's president in its military operations against the 'refractory' zamindars and hill men. James Browne, who succeeded Brooke in July 1774 and remained in charge of the Jungle Tarai for about six years, continued Brooke's policy with greater vigour. But realizing the practical difficulties

[25] Ibid., pp. 102–3.

in conducting military operations on the jungle-covered hills he initiated a conciliatory programme as well.[26]

Initially the Company confined its presence to the foothills of the Jungle Tarai. Here, it preserved the military service grants (ghatwali tenures) it found in existence. In a report submitted to the government in 1776 Captain Browne laid out the significance of this preservationist policy. Emphasizing pragmatic considerations for the continuation of these grants he wrote:

Because they being disarmed is what they would oppose almost at the price of their total extirpation. Also if you did succeed in disarming them you would thereby uncover your whole frontier towards the Marathas, the natural enemies of the state who might be opposed to great advantage by these feudal soldiers if attached to our interests. But if dis-armed and utterly disgusted, their places must be supplied with regular troops of whom a prodigious force would be necessary to guard the principal passes .... Since none but the natives can live in these mountains ... it seems a proper management would make them useful subjects as any belonging to the state.... Also the devoted attachment they have to their Chiefs enables you by conciliating them to your interest to secure the whole district.[27]

But if the grants were continued their nature was changed. While the rights and obligations laid out in the Mughal sanads were confirmed the performance of the duties they specified was also insisted on. Flexibility, looseness, and implicit mutual compromises based on a sharing of power, which had characterized the functioning of these tenures, were anathema to the Company. For most of the 'aberrations' from the code of conduct laid in the sanads the zamindars were held responsible. It was argued that they had mismanaged the jagirs and made them resorts of 'lawlessness'.[28]

The Company wished to insist that it alone had inherited what was now perceived as an undivided Mughal sovereignty. Therefore it attempted to bring the ghatwals under its administration and deprive the zamindars of their vital military support. Initially the presence of the military Collector's contingent overawed the zamindars

[26] Datta, *Selections from the Judicial Records of the Bhagalpur District*, pp. vi–vii.

[27] Browne, 'The Jungle Tarai District'.

[28] J. Fombelle, Magistrate of Bhagalpur, to Sir John Shore, Gov. Gen. in Council, 5 Sept. 1795, in Datta, *Selections from the Judicial Records of the Bhagalpur District*, pp. 162-3.

and ghatwals and ensured that they carried out all the service obligations specified in the sanads they had received from the Mughal Emperor or the local rajas. But when the Company renewed these sanads, the ghatwals were made directly answerable to its Collector.[29] In 1802, the ghatwals, now under the control of the Company's Collector, were used for policing the Jungle Tarai and the regular regiments were withdrawn from the region to fight the Maratha war. The same year the Company tried to dissociate the ghatwals from the power and influence of the zamindars by separating their land grants from the administrative jurisdiction of the zamindars and maintaining them as military jagirs under the authority of the Company's magistrate. Henceforth all fresh ghatwal recruits were appointed only with the approval of the magistrate who also had the power to remove them for any negligence or misconduct in the discharge of their duty. The magistrate soon appointed a tehsildar who collected rent on a regular basis from the ghatwal jagirs.[30]

Further, the Company's magistrate solved all cases of disputed claims and rights that were brought to his notice only after consulting the ghatwal's rights and obligations as specified in their Mughal sanads.[31] In this way the Collector and magistrate in the Jungle Mahals, by defining more emphatically and enforcing by its administrative machinery what had been loose rights and claims, reconstructed the history of the Jungle Tarai. They transformed the ghatwali tenure from a privileged tenure based on a sharing of power with the zamindar to a landholding with a fixed right to property. The strict enforcement of ownership rights as stated in the Mughal sanads restored many dispossessed grantees to the lands of their ancestors. The ghatwals of Bunati were one such

---

[29] Roychoudhury and Shastry, 'A Sanad of Captain James Browne', p. 154; see translation of Captain Browne's sanad. The sanad granted to the ghatwal of taluq Kakwara by Captain Browne had exactly the same terms and conditions as the sanad he had held from Raja Qadir Ali, the zamindar of Kharakpur, the only difference being that this sanad made the ghatwal answerable to the Company's military Collector.

[30] L. No. 2, W. Blunt, Magistrate Jungle Mahals, Bencooah, to BCJ, 11 July 1807, enclosed in the Nizamat Adalat Register, BCJ, Consult. FW, 2 May 1815, P/131/60, IOL.

[31] Ibid.

beneficiary who, once restored to the land of their ancestors, were always favoured by the Company.[32] Moreover, in some areas, like Birbhum, it led to the creation of new ghatwalis.[33] The act of restoration not only conciliated the ghatwals but made the ghatwali jagirs pockets of influence for the Company. Many restored ghatwals performed police duties and acted as the Company's spies and informants in the Jungle Tarai. For instance, some of the ghatwals of Sarhet were given a lease of ghats for supplying the Company with information on the hill region.[34] Sometimes they also helped the Company's magistrate to trace, chase, and capture dacoits taking shelter in their hills.[35] However, not all the ghatwals of Sarhet benefited from the Company's presence in the Jungle Tarai. The landholdings of those who had not had their Mughal sanads renewed and recognized by the Company were regarded as illegal. Many of them were sued in court and eventually dispossessed of their jagirs by men

[32] L. No. 14, Birbhum Magistrate to George Dowdeswell, Sec. to Govt. in Judicial Deptt. Fort William, 16 Aug. 1813, BCJ, Consult, FW 28 Aug. 1813, P/131/21, IOL. The Bunati ghatwals were in conflict with Bishendeo, the ghatwal of Rohni, over four *mouzas* which the latter had obtained from the Collector at the time of the decennial settlement. This was claimed by them as part of taluk Bunati and their chief, Nawab Singh, said it was the property of his nephew, Kirpal Singh, who was then a minor. The tensions were eased by the intervention of the Collector of Bunati. The Bunati ghatwals were restored to their lands and were favoured by the Company. Kirpal Singh, son of Purshaud Singh, ghatwal of Bunati, was acquitted by the Court of the charge alleged against him of supporting his uncle in his conflict against the ghatwal of Rohni.

[33] L. No. 55, enclosure in letter from the Sec. to the Board of Revenue to BCJ, 5 Jan. 1796, BCJ, 15 Jan.–29 April 1796, P/128/27, IOL. The new tenures were created in the Birbhum district. They were granted by the magistrate with a view to protecting ryots from the depredations of the hill people. The Collector reported that these tenures were new and approximately 12,600 bighas of land was assigned to them along with 65 peons and barkandazes. The engagement taken from them was that they would watch over the safety of the ryots and prevent any depredations from the hill people. They were held responsible for any robberies committed within the boundaries of the parganas under their charge and were considered as servants of the Company removable at the pleasure of government or of the zamindar.

[34] L. No. 3, D. Morrieson, Birbhum Magistrate to G. Dowdeswell, Sec. to Govt. in Judicial Deptt., 15 Jan. 1813, BCJ, Consult., 20 Feb. 1813, P/131/13, IOL.

[35] Ibid.

who purchased their land but refused to pay because of the illegal nature of their landholding.[36] The Company further eroded the zamindar's power and undermined his authority by its interference in the political rituals of the region. It insinuated itself as the donor and patron of royal rituals which had hitherto been patronized by the local zamindars. The zamindars who had been involved in these ceremonies and had derived their authority from them now began to depend on the Company for their political survival, *naukari* and status. For instance, as previously shown, Dussehra was celebrated in the hills under the patronage of the zamindars of the plains. They financed the celebrations and participated in them along with the hill people, thereby carving out a position of authority and high social standing for themselves. But from the late eighteenth century the Company began to preside over these celebrations. So successful was this substitution of authority that in 1796, when the Collector of Bhagalpur temporarily stopped funding these celebrations, it was resented by the chiefs as well as the magistrate. The magistrate, J. Fombelle, suggested making an advance to the chiefs from his funds while the matter was under discussion. However, the Collector soon yielded to the pressure and made the payment.[37] Years later in 1810–1, Buchanan

[36] L. No. 13, Birbhum Magistrate to G. Dowdeswell, Sec. to Govt. in Judicial Deptt., 18 Nov. 1812, BCJ, Consult. FW, 26 Nov. 1812, P/131/7, IOL. Since they had not got their sanads recognized by the Government, the purchasers of their land took advantage of this, sued them and dispossessed them of their lands. Several ghatwali tenures were abolished and several others were partially resumed.

[37] J. Fombelle, Magistrate of Bhagalpur, to George Dickinson, Collector of Bhagalpur, 18 Sept. 1797, Bhagalpur Judicial Records, vol. 431, cited in Datta, *Selections from the Judicial Records of the Bhagalpur District*, pp. 225–6. Fombelle reported that for many years the hill people of pargana Sultanabad had received the annual sum of Rs 100 from the Kurratch zamindari to enable them to celebrate Dussehra. But in the Company period the Collector gave money for the celebration. In 1797 Haru Kuhar, a ghatwal, made a petition to him that the Collector had refused the payment for this celebration. Fombelle thought that this was a breach of custom and wanted the matter to be decided by the Governor-General. But in the meantime he wanted to make an advance payment to the chiefs; also see letter from J. Fombelle to Henry St. George Tucker, Sub. Sec. to Govt. in the Judicial Deptt., 27 Sept. 1797, Bhagalpur Judicial Records, cited in Datta, *Selections from the Judicial Records of the Bhagalpur District*, pp. 227–8. Here once again Fombelle stated that many of the zamindars had paid for these celebrations from time

Hamilton, who travelled through the Jungle Tarai, also noted the erosion of the authority of local zamindars. The people residing in the hills close to the Teliyagarhi pass reported to him

that formerly they were subject to the zamindars of Teliyagarhi and made him presents of grain and honey. But since the estate has been mostly sold they decline any interference of new men and give no presents.[38]

Close to the ghatwali areas, in the foothills of the Jungle Tarai, the Company intervened to control the pattern of trade. Augustus Cleveland established *haths* and encouraged the settlement of colonies of craftsmen and artificers. They were given incentives to build boats from the wood which was found abundantly in the vicinity. At Foodkypur, located in the foothills of the Jungle Tarai and famous for its good quality wood, he established a bazar and built sixty houses, bringing 1,000 bighas of land under cultivation. In 1782, more than 100,000 maunds of wood were reported to be ready for transportation to the plains.[39] Cleveland considered that the control of these foothills would smooth the path for any future intervention in the hills of the Jungle Tarai. In a letter to Hastings he wrote:

I am at present engaged in establishing a village at this place the situation of which from its vicinity to the Ganges and the hills renders it peculiarly well adapted for opening a communication with the inhabitants of the interior parts of the hills.[40]

Thus in the first ten years of its rule in the Jungle Tarai, the Company had insinuated itself in the social and political role hitherto performed by the local zamindars. The Company

immemorial. But when the Company established itself in the foothills, its Collectors disbursed money for the celebration. The only exception were the two to three years when the pargana was held khas, during which period the money was advanced immediately from the treasury. He pointed out to the Government that in 1794 when Moch Singh, the zamindar, attempted to finance and patronize the celebration of Dussehra in the hills he was reprimanded.

[38] Oldham (ed.), *Journal of F. Buchanan Hamilton*, p. 102.

[39] From A. Cleveland, Collector of Bhagalpur, to W. Hastings, Governor-General, Foodkypur, 16 May 1782, IOR C. Nesbitt Thompson Papers, MSS Eur. D 1083, Letters from A. Cleveland 1782–3.

[40] Ibid.

gradually eroded their power and began to intervene in the hills proper.

THE COMPANY AND THE HILL CHIEFS, 1779–84

Cleveland and the Creation of the Hill Corps

The erosion of the power and authority of the zamindars was accompanied by the Company's efforts to control the now vulnerable hills. In 1777, Augustus Cleveland (1755–84), the Collector of Bhagalpur, was deputed the task of 'taming' the 'turbulent' hills. Cleveland, a cousin of Sir John Shore, first Lord Teignmouth and Governor-General of India, was an Indian administrator of exceptional ability. One of his most judicious steps was to 'raise a Corps of Sepoys out of the wildest of the mountaineers and to make the greatest freebooter their Captain.'[41] The Company administration was always indebted to him because he was said to have saved the lowlands from the 'incursion' of the hill men.[42]

Initially, Cleveland resorted to a rigorous military patrolling of the hills. But this was not an easy task in the Jungle Tarai and it was made more difficult by his not having independent charge of the military regiments stationed in the region. These regiments were commanded by James Browne, the first Collector of the Jungle Tarai, and followed only his order. Browne resented the merger of his district with Bhagalpur and consequently was always reluctant to supply military contingents to assist Cleveland.[43] While complaining to Hastings against James Browne, a distraught Cleveland wished to obtain independent charge of a contingent to be called the Hill Corps:

The services for which a military force could have been required here when the Jungle Terai was under Capt. Browne must in a great measure have arisen from the disturbances in those districts and he was certainly

[41] L. Stephen (ed.), *Dictionary of National Biography* (London, 1887), XI, p. 49.

[42] Ibid.

[43] L. No. 246, A. Cleveland, Collector of Bhagalpur, to W. Hastings, Governor-General-in-Council of Rev. at Fort William, 20 Nov. 1779, BRC, Consult. FW, 12 May 1780, P/50/24, IOL.

the best judge of what was necessary to be done to secure this country from depredations. But now the case is very different—the whole is under my authority and unless I have the immediate knowledge and direction of every military operation as well as civil transaction, I can't pursue with any degree of confidence or spirit such plans as may to me appear necessary to adopt.[44]

He sent an estimate of Rs 29,440 per annum to the East India Company for the total expense of the Hill Corps. However, Cleveland had little success because the Company refused to sanction this money on account of the high expenditure involved.[45]

To pursue his case and bring to Hastings' notice the urgency of his military requirements, Cleveland used the phraseology of the 'uncivilized hills' which had been made popular in his time by the social philosophy of the Scottish Enlightenment.[46] In a letter to Hastings written in 1780, he deliberately emphasized the 'civilizational role' the Hill Corps would play in 'taming' the hills:

Nothing will be so conducive to the civilization of the inhabitants as to employ a number of them in our service.[47]

In the decade when Hastings' ideas of recruiting Rajput, Brahman, and Bhumihar peasant soldiers, conforming closely to his views of preserving Indian caste roles dominated the Company's policy, the approval of Cleveland's proposal was not an easy matter. However, Cleveland did not abandon his scheme and continued to emphasize the atypical behaviour

[44] L. No. 257, A. Cleveland, Collector of Bhagalpur, to Warren Hastings, Governor-General, 21 April 1780, BRC, Consult. FW, 12 May 1780, P/50/24, IOL.

[45] L. No. 105, BRC to A. Cleveland, Collector of Bhagalpur, 23 June 1780, BRC, Consult. FW, 23 June 1780, P/50/25, IOL.

[46] P. J. Marshal and G. Williams, *The Great Map of Mankind: British Perception of the World in the Age of Enlightenment* (London, 1982), p. 136. In the second half of the 18th century the ideas of the philosophers of the Scottish Enlightenment were very popular in Britain. This philosophy was studied at Edinburgh or Glasgow by David Hume, Adam Smith, Adam Ferguson, etc. These philosophers plotted societies on a scale of civilization and pointed to environment as the main causative agent for this range.

[47] L. No. 257, A. Cleveland, Collector of Bhagalpur, to Warren Hastings, Governor-General, 21 April 1780, BRC, Consult. FW, 12 May 1780, P/50/24, IOL.

of the hill population so as to justify the recruitment of the Hill
Corps. In a letter to Hastings he wrote:

A race of people hitherto little better than savages, who will in course
of time become useful members of the community in the very heart of
your dominion and of the confidence which the inhabitants of the adjacent
country would enjoy when they were no longer apprehensive of continuous
devastations and murder.[48]

Cleveland's persistence had an impact on Hastings who personally
expounded his political philosophy in terms of Enlightenment
concepts. In the absence of any other option in controlling the
Jungle Tarai, Hastings compromised with Cleveland. At first the
former only approved Cleveland's plan of co-opting the chiefs,
leaving the defence of the country in their hands, and 'civilizing'
the hills through them. He rejected the grandiose and expensive
army contingent planned by Cleveland but the Bengal infantry
regiments of Browne were removed from the Jungle Tarai. In
a letter to Cleveland he wrote:

They ought to be answerable each for his own district and the whole
for the division. On this condition we are disposed to allow each Chief
a reasonable pension.[49]

Cleveland was quick to execute this plan and he sent the Company
an estimate of Rs 550 per annum. This included the expenses
of the pension which was to be distributed to twenty-six chiefs
and fifty-eight deputies at the rate of Rs 10 per month and Rs
5 per month respectively. These chiefs were given mochulkas which
were bonds making them responsible for the 'peace and good
order' of their respective districts.[50] Indeed, Cleveland used the
headway he had made with his plans to bargain for a further
expansion of his power. He highlighted to the Board the reluctance
of some chiefs, whose hills were contiguous to the pargana of
Ammar and Sultanabad, to enter into the Company's conciliation

[48] Para 41 of Sutherland's report, 8 June 1819. Cited in L. S. S. O' Malley, Bihar District
Gazetteer, Santal Parganas (Patna, 1938), p. 45.

[49] L. No. 105, W. Hastings, Governor-General, to A. Cleveland, Collector of
Bhagalpur, 23 June 1780, BRC, Consult. 23 June 1780, P/50/25, IOL.

[50] L. No. 599, A. Cleveland, Collector of Bhagalpur, to W. Hastings, Governor-
General, and Board, (?) July 1780, BRC, Consult. 22 Aug. 1780, P/50/28, IOL.

programme. According to Cleveland, these chiefs were disinclined to enter the Company service because their hills were continuously threatened by the inroads of hill men from Ammar and Sultanabad hill chieftaincies which were still of a 'refractory' disposition. This made it difficult for them to accept the responsibility of maintaining 'good order' in the region. Cleveland used the complaints against the chiefs of Ammar and Sultanabad to further emphasize their 'uncivilized' behaviour and urged the Company to extend his jurisdiction to their hills as well. In 1780, he wrote to the Board:

I have already taken up the Board's attention with my representations respecting the necessity of annexing the Purgunnahs of Ommar and Sultanabad to my Collectorship. I am convinced nothing but proper encouragement is wanting to bring the hill people in those Purgunnas into the same peaceable state that I have with so much success brought to those in my own district.[51]

In the same year he once again used the complaints being made against these chiefs to bargain for the Hill Corps experiment. He not only emphasized the benefits of such a corps in the 'savage zone' but pointed out the approval he had obtained from the Commander-in-Chief, Sir Eyre Coote, for his proposal. In a letter to Hastings on this issue he wrote:

I have been further induced to say this much on the subject in consequence of the very flattering approbation my plans in general had the honour to meet with from Lt. Gen. Sir Eyre Coote in several conversations I had with him on his way both up and down the country. As my proposal for raising a Corps of Archers as, represented in my address of 25th April, was particularly approved by him, I take the liberty of recalling your attention to this circumstance. Also being persuaded of the good effects it will have in bringing the hill inhabitants to a speedy state of civilization add to which the great service that they may be of in military operations at a future period.[52]

Perhaps Coote's experience of south India where the incorporation of 'tribal' archers and pikemen into the Company's local militia units was important to its everyday functioning, made him sympathetic to Cleveland's proposal. In 1779, Cleveland's persuasive

[51] L. No. 803, A. Cleveland, Collector of Bhagalpur, to BRC, 19 Sept. 1780, BRC, Consult. 19 Dec. 1780, P/50/28, IOL.
[52] Ibid.

strategies eventually led to Hastings' sanctioning of the Hill Corps experiment. But this approval came on the condition that Cleveland would make up the loss in the revenue that would be incurred by money spent in recruiting and organizing the Hill Corps.[53]

Cleveland's military plan used the local chiefs as recruiting agents and made them responsible for the levies they supplied to the Company. This was very different from the Company's method in the Gangetic plains of directly recruiting peasant soldiers from their villages. The acceptance of Cleveland's plan, different as it was from the Company's recruiting practice, may have been influenced by the confidence Hastings had in Cleveland because of his connections with the family of John Shore and his willingness to invest his time and money in the project.[54] For instance, Cleveland incurred a personal expense of upwards of Rs 20,000 in raising the Corps and in other sundry expenses. Due to the strained nature of the Company's finances he did not urge the Board to reimburse him.[55] But, as was typical of the Company officials of the time, Cleveland spent his time and money in establishing a new military patronage in the Jungle Tarai and soon requested Hastings for a completely independent command with regard to the Hill Corps. In 1780, Hastings granted him this request and the Hill Corps soon became the means for further strengthening Cleveland's power and fulfilling his ambitions in the Jungle Tarai.[56]

[53] L. No. 203, BRC to A. Cleveland, Collector of Bhagalpur, 19 Dec. 1780, BRC, Consult. FW, 19 Dec. 1780, P/50/28, IOL.

[54] See J. Shore, *Memoirs of the Life and Correspondence of John Lord Teignmouth, by his son John Shore* (2 vols., London, MDCCCXLIII) I, appendix II, pp. 489–94. Cleveland was the cousin of John Shore and a favourite of both Shore and Hastings. On his death, Shore wrote a monody, while Warren Hastings wrote the epitaph for his grave; see Keith Feiling, *Warren Hastings* (reprint London, 1966), p. 237.

[55] L. No. 173, A. Cleveland, Collector of Bhagalpur, to BRC, 8 May 1783, BRC, Consult. FW, 13 May 1783, P/50/46, IOL.

[56] L. No. 203, BRC to A. Cleveland, Collector of Bhagalpur, 19 Dec. 1780, BRC, Consult. 19 Dec. 1780, P/50/28, IOL.

Recruiting the Hill Corps

Initially Cleveland enlisted all those hill men who offered to serve as archers for the Company. These hill soldiers were allowed to reside with their families and Cleveland won the goodwill of their wives and chiefs by sending them presents and medals respectively. Hodges observed that Cleveland was affectionate towards their children, 'caressing them whenever he saw them and decorating them with beads'.[57] Cleveland's military experiment was very similar to the Mughal military system where hill leaders had been incorporated into the Mughal polity by the grant of military ranks called mansabs. In a similar manner Cleveland placated the hill chiefs by placing them in high positions in the newly formed Hill Corps. Their first commandant was a person called Jaurah who had been called a bandit by the British sources. He was the first inhabitant of the hills to enter the service of the government.[58] The length and duration of service of such chiefs was not specified but was left to the discretion of the recruits.

In 1779, to further promote his policy of 'pacifying' the hills by incorporating the 'recalcitrant' chiefs into his Hill Corps, Cleveland created the new office of *sazawal* in the Jungle Tarai. This figure, variously defined as 'a native collector of revenue; an officer specially appointed to take charge of and collect the revenue of an estate from the management of which the owner or farmer has been removed; a land steward, a bailiff, an agent appointed by a landowner or lessor to compel payment of rent by tenants or leaseholders',[59] performed the additional role of a military contractor in the Jungle Tarai. The duty of the sazawal was to identify the hill chiefs and specify their rights and duties concerning the maintenance of law and order and the supply of recruits. Abdul Rusul Khan was appointed as the first sazawal in the Jungle Tarai. In a petition to

[57] Hodges, *Travels in India*, p. 90.

[58] O' Malley, *Bihar Gazetteer*, p. 46. Jaurah remained throughout his life an active and faithful servant of the Company. He conducted several campaigns against the outlaws both in the Ramgarh Hills and in his own mountains.

[59] Wilson, *A Glossary of Judicial and Revenue Terms*, p. 473.

the Company, in his defence against the charges levelled against him by the hill people, he specified the terms and conditions of his office:

He [Cleveland] appointed me sazawal of the hills and promised me that if the hills are settled and brought to a conclusion I shall report the same to the Council and you will get your livelihood forever. Your heirs and you will be endowed with jagirs and high dignity for your trouble and labour.[60]

We do not have evidence of the existence of a similar figure in the Mughal Jungle Tarai. But the sazawal's title and functions suggest Mughal antecedents. As a 'monitor' of the hill chiefs and the 'bailiff' commissioned to collect arrears of rent or revenue,[61] he is comparable to the Mughal faujdar who performed similar functions.[62] Indeed the appointment of a Muslim to this position further suggests the possible incorporation of family members belonging to the erstwhile Mughal faujdar into the frontier defence arrangements of the East India Company. Marshall shows that the most powerful Muslims in the countryside were likely to be the Bengal Nawab's faujdars. The jurisdiction of these men was largely confined to the frontier areas and with the establishment of British rule the surviving faujdaris were largely concentrated along the frontier districts on both the western and eastern borders of the province.[63] It is quite likely that Abdul Rusul Khan belonged to one such powerful Muslim family. This seems a possibility because a large number of his family members, in a manner similar to the families of Mughal faujdars, served in various public capacities in the Jungle Tarai. While he was the chief sazawal, the deputy sazawal in the Suddar establishment of the hills was Roshunya Khan. In 1813 he had succeeded his father, a brother-in-law

[60] L. No. 26, Petition of Abdul Rusul Khan, Hill Sazawal of Bhagalpur, 14 Dec. 1819, BCJ LP Consult. FW, 1 Jan. 1819, P/133/53, IOL.

[61] 'Extracts from the diary of Emily, wife of John Talbot Shakespear, Bengal Civil Service', *Bengal Past and Present*, vol. VI (July–Dec. 1910), p. 145.

[62] Alam, *Crisis of Empire*, p. 266. The Mughal faujdar maintained law and order in the Mughal provinces by monitoring zamindari levies, often utilizing them to police his faujdari and organizing the collection of revenue.

[63] Marshall, *Bengal: the British Bridgehead*, pp. 33, 50.

of Abdul Rusul Khan, to this office. When still a child, more than twenty-eight years before, he had already become the naib sazawal of the Dighi Thanah and had been the police *Darogha* as well. Similarly in the *mofussil* establishment Dighi Thanah the naib sazawal, Lushkhum, was married to Abdul Rusul Khan's niece.[64]

Again like the Mughal faujdars, who by the early eighteenth century had ceased to follow the dictates of Delhi and had become mere agents of the local Mughal subahadar,[65] the sazawal also represented Cleveland's interest in the Jungle Tarai even though theoretically he was only an employee of the Company. Indeed he became the basis of the Collector's power and helped the latter in the execution of his administrative powers in the Jungle Tarai. Like the Mughal faujdar in the plains, he organized revenue collection by identifying revenue defaulters and 'chastising' them to pay regularly. Alongside these functions, once again like the Mughal faujdar, he also helped in the maintenance of 'law and order' in the Jungle Tarai. The Collector in the Jungle Tarai always deputed the sazawal with his staff and a detachment of the Hill Corps to quell any disturbance that was reported to him. The trial of the parties involved in any dispute was ordered and a decision was arrived at only after receiving the sazawal's report about the case. For instance, in 1795 there were disturbances in the Hindua and Bailputtah hills in Birbhum and the sazawal identified the trouble-makers and the cause of the disturbances. It was primarily on his recommendation that John Fombelle, the judge magistrate of Bhagalpur, suggested to the government the establishment of a police thanah at Noony in Hindua.[66] He argued that this would guard the ghats and chaukis and prevent the

---

[64] Enclosure No. 4 in Sutherland's report, 'Statement establishing the details and other particulars relative to the establishment at present authorized of the hills and the same of an amended establishment. Suggested by Sutherland, Joint Magistrate together with one provision entertained for that purpose', BC, 27084–27107; 1827–8, File No. 954, pp. 246–56. F/4/954, IOL.

[65] Alam, *Crisis of Empire*, pp. 70–1.

[66] John Fombelle, Judge Magistrate of Bhagalpur, to Mr G.H. Barlow, Sub. Sec. to Govt. in Judicial Deptt., 5 May 1795, Bhagalpur Judicial Records, vol. 421, cited in Datta, *Selections from the Judicial Records of the Bhagalpur District*, pp. 123–5.

outbreak of any disturbances in the future.[67] This was soon sanctioned and it helped in controlling the region for a long time.

However, unlike the Mughal faujdar, the sazawal had the additional responsibility of playing a crucial role in recruiting the Company's hill soldiers. Initially, he identified his chiefs of repute and influence and persuaded them to accept the responsibility of supplying recruits to Cleveland. He prepared a hill roll of such chiefs and each of them was given a pension at the rate of Rs 10 for their services as the Company's recruiting agents.[68] In this way a total of 557 hill chiefs were reconciled to British overlordship and made responsible for the peaceable deportment and conduct of the recruits supplied. Once drawn into the Company's policy they were considered 'loyalists' and were expected to deliver all 'delinquents' and 'disturbers of public peace' within their jurisdiction to the Collector. These convicts were then tried in the hill assembly either in Bhagalpur or Rajmahal.[69]

The chiefs and manjis who commanded respect and influence in the Jungle Tarai were generally preferred as recruiting agents. The sazawal approached them for hill recruits since they were able to supply men with ease and regularity.[70] Abdul Rusul Khan

[67] Ibid., pp. 123–5. Initial arrests were made by the sazawal in Bailputtah. They were then tried by the hill assembly. For more instances of this kind see letter from J. Fombelle to G. H. Barlow, Sub. Sec. to Govt., 26 May 1795, Bhagalpur Judicial Records, vol. 421, cited in Datta, *Selections from the Judicial Records of the Bhagalpur District*, pp. 128–9.

[68] J. Fombelle, Magistrate of Bhagalpur, to H. St. George Tucker, Sub. Sec. to Govt. in the Judicial Deptt., 5 May 1798, Bhagalpur Judicial Records, vol. no. 481, BSA.

[69] Shaw, 'The inhabitants of the hills near Rajmahal', p. 104.

[70] The sazawal dealt with the hill chiefs of the following Tappas:

Tappa	No. of Hills	Sardars	Manjis	Naibs
Manihari	66	1	61	4
Manjhwe	27	1	26	5
Madhuban	31	1	25	5
Garhi	34	1	29	–
Yamini	41	1	78	6
Chitailiya	55	–	–	–
Kangjiyala	46	2	9	4
Mawas	29	–	–	–
Ambar	80	2	34	4
Payer	32	1	32	–
Parsunda	46	1	44	4

never had any difficulty in finding chiefs who were willing to enter into Company service. For dealing with the sazawal brought them closer to the Company and increased their power and social standing in the Jungle Tarai. But at times the hostility of some of the big chiefs who ruled a large number of hills and commanded tremendous political power in the Jungle Tarai, was directed against him for the sazawal posed a political threat to their power. In his petition to the Company, Abdul Rusul Khan complained of being attacked several times by the 'hill tyrants' before they were conciliated by him and employed in Cleveland's Hill Corps.[71] However, most of the time he never experienced any major problems in recruiting and the Company's service drew enthusiastic response. In 1781, Cleveland reported to the Board of Revenue:

So well pleased are the mountaineers in general with the service proferred to them that my only difficulty now is to frame excuses for not entertaining more than the prescribed number.[72]

In the 1780s, Hodges reported that the Jungle Tarai was still recovering from the loss of people, and the fall in agricultural production and manufactures that accompanied the devastating famine of the 1770s.[73] In this hostile climate, Cleveland's Hill Corps appears to have provided a ready and immediate source of income to the hill people. It was for this reason that the Company's service

Tappa	No. of Hills	Sardars	Manjis	Naibs
Barcope	3	1	34	1
Dhamsaing	43	1	22	1
Sumarpali	21	–	20	1
Kumarpali		3	12	1
Dangarpali	–	–	6	1
Sarmi	1	1	3	1
Haranpaher	43	–	42	1
Total	631	17	477	37

Ajay Pratap, 'Paharia Ethnohistory and the Archaeology of the Rajmahal Hills', PhD thesis, Cambridge University, 1987, p. 79.

[71] J. Fombelle, Magistrate of Bhagalpur, to H. St. George Tucker, Sub. Sec. to Govt. in the Judicial Deptt., 5 May 1798, Bhagalpur Judicial Records, vol. 481, cited in Datta, *Selections from the Judicial Records of the Bhagalpur District*, pp. 246–8.

[72] A. Cleveland to BRC, 16 Feb. 1781, BRC, Consult. 3 Aug. 1781, P/50/34, IOL.

[73] Hodges, *Travels in India*, p. 95.

attracted a large number of recruits in the Jungle Tarai. In a much depleted population, which Hodges thought had been reduced by famine deaths and emigration to a few hundred only,[74] the Hill Corps had a strength of about 1,000 at the time of its establishment.[75]

Disciplining the Hill Recruits

The hill men of the Jungle Tarai were generally accustomed to the use of bows, arrows and sabres. Commenting on their military tactics Hodges reported:

They were unable either to attach or to withstand regular troops with firearms. By lying in wait like a tiger in the woods, they frequently cut off the travellers or stragglers.[76]

Initially Cleveland incorporated their weapons of war as well as their military skills into his regiments. But after the first two years he began to introduce elements of western military drill and discipline into his Hill Corps. He also dressed his hill soldiers in uniforms which were similar to those of the peasant sipahis of the plains. It is these hill soldiers who are seen in Hodges' picture in the Sotheby catalogue (plate 2). Soon the hill sipahis had to leave their private dwellings and live in a camp three miles from Bhagalpur, which could accommodate about 1,000 men.[77] However, even then they were not completely removed from their home environment for their families also resided with them in this camp. At about the same time Cleveland armed them with firelocks and introduced the practice of regular drill.[78] Further, in 1783 they were provided with muskets[79] and by 1785 they were supplied with fusils in the manner of the European and native peasant sipahis. Indeed, in 1785, 700 fusils used by

[74] Ibid., p. 95.

[75] Shaw, 'The inhabitants of the hills near Rajmahal', p. 104.

[76] Hodges, *Travels in India*, p. 88.

[77] Ibid., p. 90.

[78] Ibid.

[79] L. No. 173, A. Cleveland, Collector of Bhagalpur, to BRC, 8 May 1783, BRC, Consult. 13 May 1783, P/50/46, IOL.

the artillery to protect their guns were supplied to the Hill Corps and these were fitted with bayonets as the ones without them were too heavy for the sipahis to carry.[80] Hodges noted the popularity of the Hill Corps in the Jungle Tarai and reported:

Vain of their newly acquired knowledge, these new soldiers soon imparted the enthusiasm to the rest of the nation, who earnestly petitioned for the same distinction.[81]

Encouraged by this widespread enthusiasm to join the Hill Corps Cleveland intensified his 'civilizational' process by establishing a hill school for teaching the recruits how to read and write.[82] It appears that this was a good way of indoctrinating the hill soldiers in military ethics.

The hill sipahis were recruited with the intention of 'settling' the Jungle Tarai and initially no formal agreement existed between them and the Company regarding the nature of their duties and the areas where they could be posted.[83] But they regarded the hills as their home station[84] and lived along with their families in small huts, which they made themselves both in the hill stations and within Cleveland's military camp.[85] Here, they performed various kinds of local services, but it is important to stress that

[80] L. No. 39, Gov.–Gen. to BRC, 1 April 1785, BRC, Consult. Fort William, 1 April 1785, P/50/58, IOL.

[81] Hodges, *Travels in India*, p. 90.

[82] Bishop Heber, *Bishop Heber in Northern India: Selections from Heber's Journal* (ed.) M. A. Laird (London, 1971), p. 100.

[83] J. Fombelle, Magistrate of Bhagalpur, to G. H. Barlow, Sub. Sec. to Govt. in Judicial Deptt., 23 June 1795, Bhagalpur Judicial Records, vol. 418, cited in Datta, *Selections from the Judicial Records of the Bhagalpur District*, pp. 131–2. According to the rules and regulations of the Corps they were not entitled to any batta or additional allowance if they were detached on distant duty.

[84] J. Fombelle, Magistrate of Bhagalpur, to G.H. Barlow, Sub. Sec. to Gov.–Gen. in Council in the Judicial Deptt., 17 July 1794, Bhagalpur Judicial Records, vol. 415, cited in Datta, *Selections from the Judicial Records of the Bhagalpur District*, pp. 62–3.

[85] Oldham (ed.), *Journal of Buchanan Hamilton*, p. 5. Buchanan observed one such establishment of huts, occupied by the Hill Corps, in Karnagarh. This was originally a low hill around which a square ditch and rampart had been drawn. The hill was then levelled so as to leave a parapet, and the whole land within was as high as the rampart. He reported that the 'quarters of the Corps were tolerably neat huts and the hill soldiers had with them many women who were tolerably clean and neat.'

they do not appear to have been used in any of the Company's major campaigns. This is a fact which further emphasizes the social rather than military functions of this corps. For instance, the sipahis assisted the Company in quelling the disturbances caused by their own clansmen in the hills. In 1783, Cleveland dispatched four companies of the Hill Corps, under their commandant Jaurah, to apprehend some hill chiefs dependent on the Sultanabad zamindaris who had caused disturbances in Radshi and plundered some villages in that district.[86] The corps performed its job satisfactorily and returned with the prisoners. In a letter to Hastings, Cleveland commended the hill sipahis on their success:

Since the establishment of the Corps of Hill Archers this is the 3rd time I have had occasion to employ them against their brethren and they have always succeeded in the business they have been sent upon.[87]

On the recommendation of Cleveland the Company increased Jaurah's pay from Rs 10 to Rs 20 per month and also agreed to allot 400 bighas of land as jagir to his eldest son.[88] In another instance, in 1784, three companies of Hill Rangers were dispatched against Budhu Khan, a manji and faujdar of Tatahparra on the borders of Jammoni. He had been threatening rebellion in the hills at the time of Cleveland's departure. The detachment brought Budhu Khan also along with forty-three others as prisoners to Bhagalpur.[89] Once again in 1784, C. Chapman, the Collector of Bhagalpur, dispatched a contingent of 200 hill soldiers against Shah Mudgnvo—a noted chief from the Morung hills. He had appeared near the Malda factory with 700 armed followers and the Collector sent the Corps, fearing that the whole district was in danger of being laid under contribution.[90]

---

[86] L. No. 163, A. Cleveland, Collector of Bhagalpur, to BRC and reply, 14 July 1782, BRC, Consult. 6 May 1783, P/50/45, IOL.

[87] Ibid.

[88] Ibid.

[89] L. No. 235, C. Cockrell, Acting Collector, Bhagalpur to BRC, 31 Jan. 1784, BRC, Consult. FW, 20 July 1784, P/50/52, IOL.

[90] L. No. 240, C. Chapman, Collector of Bhagalpur, to the Board of Revenue, 10 June 1784, BRC, Consult. 20 July 1784, P/50/52, IOL.

THE SOCIAL AND POLITICAL IMPACT OF RECRUITING

The Jungle Tarai had approximately 631 'hills' and a total population of 10,000 people.[91] By 1819, at least 557 hills supplied recruits to the Hill Corps.[92] Here, as we have seen earlier, 'hill' appears to have been a territorial division referring to the private dominion of an individual and the people living under his patronage. In all there were fifty-five chiefs who received an allowance from the government in consideration for their assistance in the maintenance of peace in the Jungle Tarai and supplying a quota of recruits for the Hill Corps.[93] We do not possess population figures of the individual hills but the involvement of more than three-fourths of the hills and a large number of chiefs and manjis in the recruitment of the Hill Corps indicates that recruitment extended over an extensive area.

The widespread nature of military recruiting had important social and political repercussions in the Jungle Tarai. One of the most significant results of the Hill Corps, experiment was the introduction of considerable amounts of money into the Jungle Tarai. Money may have been in circulation in the Jungle Tarai prior to the Company's presence. But, by and large, trade, as we have already seen, was carried on through the barter system as late as the 1790s. Once the Company began to recruit its Hill Corps we have evidence of a substantial inflow of cash into the Jungle Tarai. The hill chiefs, with whom military contracts were made, were paid a monthly pension on account of their services as military contractors. The hill chief of a tuppah received Rs 10, their naibs Rs 3 and the manjis Rs 2. The monthly amount of pensions in the Jungle Tarai amounted to Rs 1,373.[94] Further, the sazawal and his office staff were well paid and their allowances added to the money in circulation in the region. After the first phase of the identification of hill chiefs was complete

[91] 'Diary of Emily', p.144.

[92] L. No. 26, Petition of Abdul Rusul Khan, Hill Sazawal of Bhagalpur, 14 Dec. 1818, BCJ LP, Consult. FW, 1 Jan. 1819, P/133/53, IOL.

[93] 'Diary of Emily,' pp. 144–5.

[94] J. Fombelle, Magistrate of Bhagalpur, to H. St. George Tucker, Sub. Sec. to Govt. in the Judicial Deptt., 5 May 1798, Bhagalpur Judicial Records, vol. No. 481, BSA.

and the so-called 'hill roll' had been drawn up, Abdul Rusul Khan, in a ceremony reminiscent of the Mughal times, was granted a robe of honour, a khelat of a pair of shawls, and Rs 500.[95] In the permanent employment of the Company, the salary of the *sazawal* was fixed at Rs 101 per month. He was allowed a proper administrative staff which consisted of a naib, two mohurirs and seven barkandazes at the sadar. For this he was given an allowance of Rs 48 and was also allowed a mohurir and two barkandazes in tuppah Munnehari (in pargana Talka Jumni, district Kharakpur). He had similar establishments in pargana Bailputta, Horawa, Kharakpur and in pargana Ambar and Sultanabad. In all he had five small establishments for which he received Rs 17–18 per month each. He was also allowed seven *bundwasis* or interpreters who understood both the language of the hill people as well as that of the plains. For this he obtained an allowance of Rs 2 per month.[96] In addition, a considerable amount of cash flowed into the Jungle Tarai in the form of salaries and pensions of hill soldiers. Each recruit obtained a salary of Rs 3 per month and from 1811, the sipahis of the Hill Corps were also entitled to the benefits of the Invalid Thanah. They received monthly pensions at the rates of Rs 7 for subahdars, Rs 4 for jamadars, Rs 3 for havaldars and naiks and Rs 2.8 for sipahis and drummers.[97]

The involvement of a large section of the hill population in the Hill Corps and the introduction of substantial amounts of money into the region restructured the role of the chiefs in the Jungle Tarai. Military service with the Company and money became the new determinants of social status in the hills. For instance, on Cleveland's death in 1782, the hill chiefs, sazawal, and zamindars made cash contributions to the Company for erecting a memorial. The total subscription amounted to Rs 2,800.[98] This was an effective

[95] Ibid.

[96] J. Fombelle, Judge Magistrate of Bhagalpur, to Sir John Shore, Gov.-Gen. in Council, 2 April 1794, Bhagalpur Judicial Records, vol. no. 417, cited in Datta, *Selections from the Judicial Records of the Bhagalpur District*, pp. 54–5.

[97] Regulation 11, GO, 4 June and 30 and July 1811, *Abstract General Orders and Regulations*, pp. 506–8.

[98] C. R. Wilson (ed.), *Indian Monumental Inscriptions*, vol. I, Bengal (Calcutta, 1896), pp. 239–41. Serial No. 932 has details of subscriptions made by government amlas and

way for the subscribers to emphasize their superior status in the redefined idiom of power and authority in the Jungle Tarai. Another such instance was a bribe in cash offered by the chiefs to the sazawal so as to escape the arm of the law in the event of possible arrest for petty crimes.[99] Often the same means was also used to get employment.[100]

CLEVELAND'S LEGACY OF CONFLICT, 1784–1818

The subsequent Collectors of Bhagalpur continued with Cleveland's military experiment and the popularity of the Corps increased. But even though the Hill Corps was maintained, the Company attempted to move it closer to its well-disciplined peasant regiments. There were many reasons for this shift. First, this practice appears to have gained momentum once the Collectors realized that the Jungle Tarai had been adequately 'pacified'. The Company was now no more willing to diverge from its established norms of military recruitment and ethics. For instance, in 1804, on the issue of granting to the Corps the right to keep the loot collected during the Benautli campaign, precedent was set aside and the practice was not allowed by the magistrate on the ground that the hill magistrate of Bhagalpur argued that:

They could not be allowed what had been permitted by Cleveland, to keep up with their 'wild and predatory' habits because the Corps has been so long since reduced to that discipline and obedience that they ought not to require any such spur to their activity as the hope of plunder on such an occasion as the present, and instead of the unusual depredations that formerly prevailed, a very recordable number of hill people had reverted to their predatory way of life for comparatively a very short space of time.[101]

---

zamindars.

[99] J. Fombelle, Judge Magistrate of Bhagalpur, to Sir John Shore, Governor-General-in-Council, 29 June 1795, Bhagalpur Judicial Records, vol. 418, cited in Datta, *Selections from the Judicial Records of Bhagalpur District,* pp. 154–6. In the disturbances of Bailputtah, in Birbhum, Abdul Rusul Khan was offered Rs 12 to Rs 52 from the various hill chiefs of the region.

[100] Ibid.

[101] J. Fombelle, Judge Magistrate of Bhagalpur, to Sir John Shore, Governor-General-in-Council in the Judicial Deptt., 28 July 1795, Bhagalpur Judicial Records, vol. 418,

Consequently the property 'looted' was restored to the people from whom it had been taken. Secondly, in the first decade of the nineteenth century, the narrow and specialized nature of duties which the Corps could perform made it unsuitable for the Company's wider military needs. For instance, when the hill sipahis were posted in the plains and placed under the charge of Company officials who did not know the hill language, it was soon obvious that these officers could not communicate with the hill men they commanded. This made it very difficult to pass on military orders to the Corps or train them further in the Company's military ethics. To resolve this problem the Collectors in the Jungle Tarai attempted to dilute the Hill Corps with peasant sipahis recruited from the Gangetic plains. J. Wintle, the magistrate of Bhagalpur, suggested alterations in the composition of the Corps. He wrote:

At present it consists of too great a proportion of hill people to the Hindustanis. The former, the good parade soldiers, want an example and stimulus to rouse them into activity and make them what soldiers ought to be. They invariably fall asleep on guard and are otherwise negligent when off the Parade and not understanding any but their own language are totally unfit for sentinels at the Magistrate's *cutcheri*.[102]

Wintle suggested that there should be one-third Hindustanis and two-thirds hill people in the Hill Corps and hoped that this would prompt the hill soldiers to learn the superior military skills of the well-trained peasant sipahis. Further, in 1811, in order to establish permanent links with the hill soldiers, the Company extended the benefits of the Invalid Thanah to them as well.[103] Finally, in the early nineteenth century when the Company realized

cited in Datta, *Selections from the Judicial Records of the Bhagalpur District*, pp. 154–6.

[102] From J. Wintle, Magistrate of Bhagalpur, to J. Lumsden, Chief Sec. to Govt. in the Judicial Deptt., 15 Aug. 1803, Bhagalpur Judicial Records, vol. 485, cited in Datta, *Selections from the Judicial Records of the Bhagalpur District*, pp. 335–6.

[103] Regulation 11 GOUP, 4 June and 30 July 1811, *Abstract General Order and Regulations*, pp. 506–8. The rates of pay of the invalid hill recruits differed from those of the Hindustani recruits in the Hill Corps. Hill men were paid: a subahdar—Rs 7; a jamadar—Rs 4; a havaldar and naik—Rs 3; a sepoy and drummer—Rs 2.8. Hindustani recruits were paid: a subahdar—Rs 18; a jamadar—Rs 9; a havaldar, naik and native doctor—Rs 5.8; a sepoy, drummer and behishti—Rs 3.8.

that the hill experiment had paved the way for the emergence of powerful local leaders like the sazawal, its attempts to dilute the Hill Corps with peasant soldiers gained further momentum. The sazawal in the manner of the Mughal faujdars of the eighteenth century,[104] now posed a political threat to the Company. From its very inception the office of the sazawal had an ambivalent relationship with the hill chiefs as well as with the Company's magistrate. The sazawal used his influence to erode the power of both the magistrate and the hill chiefs, thereby becoming the most powerful and influential figure in the hills. This, as we have seen, often incited the fury and resentment of the powerful hill chiefs. Yet, in the redefined social hierarchy of the Jungle Tarai their credibility was dependent on the sazawal because it was on his recommendation that the hill chiefs could get into Company service.[105] Moreover, many chiefs offered bribes to him to conceal their crimes[106] or have their names registered in the

[104] For the political threat of the faujdar in Awadh see Alam, *Crisis of Empire*, p. 210. In Bengal also the faujdar had become an appointee of the Governor, and the Nawab felt a political threat from him. The inevitable challenge to Siraj-ud-daula, Nawab of Bengal, came from Shaukat Jang, the faujdar of the virtually autonomous district of Purnia. He was brought to battle by Siraj-ud-daula and killed in 1756. Marshall, *Bengal: the British Bridgehead*, p. 75.

[105] L. No. 25, I. C. Sutherland, Magistrate of Bhagalpur to Govt., 5 Dec. 1818, BCJ LP, Consult. FW, 1 Jan. 1819, P/133/53, IOL. These tensions increased in the high period of military expansion that characterized Wellesley's Governor-Generalship. In 1818 a petitioner, Asaf Khan, a relative of the sazawal Abdul Rusul Khan, made a complaint against him based on the following allegations: 'The sazawal appropriated to himself the salaries of the establishment allowed to him. He intentionally allowed his naibs and other subordinate officers to levy an annual sum of money from the ghatwals and produce from the hill people. He himself participated in a portion of their illegal collections and levied from each of the manjis of the 557 hills, yearly Rs 1 and a vessel of honey or its value. The sazawal, it was alleged, after distributing the pensions illegally appropriated money from the hill people. It was stated in the petition that the sazawal in his roll, handed in to the Government, had included uninhabited hills and the names of deceased hill people. Obviously the sazawal denied all these charges. But the magistrate suspended him from office and the government ordered an investigation into the charges. However, the magistrate's demand for the abolition of the office of sazawal was not met by the Government in this year.

[106] Mr J. Fombelle, Magistrate of Bhagalpur, to Sir John Shore, Gov.-Gen.-in-Council, 29 June 1795, Bhagalpur Judicial Records, vol. 418, cited in Datta, *Selections from the Judicial Records of the Bhagalpur District*, pp. 354–5. In the famous disturbances of

Company's official hill roll.[107]

Like the hill chiefs, the Company's Collector and magistrate also held an ambivalent attitude towards the sazawal. Although the sazawal was his sole informant in the Jungle Tarai, the magistrate suspected him of abusing his power. In 1817, reports on the irregularities committed by the sazawal and his establishment in the distribution of gratuities to the chiefs made C. W. Steer, the Collector of Bhagalpur, suggest that each person who received a gratuity should be furnished with a descriptive roll from his office. This was meant to prevent any alteration being made in the official hill roll without the knowledge of the Company's Collector. These measures annoyed the sazawal to such an extent that he exerted his influence on the people assembled and persuaded them to refuse their pensions if obliged at the same time to receive a descriptive roll.[108] Steer complained to the Board of Commissioners about the political threat that the sazawal posed in the Jungle Tarai:

I have reason to believe that the arrangement framed and carried into effect by Mr. Cleveland for the civilization and management of the hill people has been perverted, and that the lands asisgned to persons, denominated

Bailputtah, in Birbhum, Abdul Rusul Khan had been commended for his efficient handling of the riots. He himself reported to the magistrate of Bhagalpur the large sums of money he had received from the hill chiefs to conceal their crimes and set them at liberty. He said he was also promised a sum of Rs 1,000 if he would release them. Abdul Rusul Khan received the money, put his seal on it, and paid it into the court as soon as he returned. The money obtained from some of the chiefs was as follows: Soneful and Sachend—Rs 52; Teep—Rs 49; Nehaul Mundle—Rs 50; Nutra—Rs 12; Chedum Mundle—Rs 23; Nehaul Soondy—Rs 12; Total—Rs 146.

[107] L. No. 39, W. Armstrong, Magistrate of Bhagalpur, to G. Dowdeswell, Sec. to Govt. Judicial Deptt. Fort William, 9 Dec. 1806, BCJ, Consult. FW, 1 Jan. 1807, P/129/32, IOL. In 1807 the Magistrate of Bhagalpur found a great difference between the hill chiefs' list in the office and that for which payments had been made by the sazawal. The sazawal explained the discrepancy due to the death of chiefs and the recruitment of some into the Hill Corps. But the magistrate was not convinced by this explanation. This was because no alterations to the list could be made without his approval. He refused the payment to chiefs not in the official list.

[108] C. W. Steer, Collector of Bhagalpur, to K. Chamberlain, Sec. to Commissioners for the Province of Bihar and Benares and districts of Bhagalpur and Shahabad, 27 Sept. 1817, BC, 1827–28, File No. 27082, extract Bengal Judicial Consult. 11 Aug. 1818, pp. 70–7, F/4/953, IOL.

ghatwals, to be held in perpetuity exempt from the payment of rent in consideration of services to be performed by them in protecting their respective ghats and in giving efficiency to the general system of the police establishment with respect to the inhabitants of the hills, have been resumed and are now generally possessed by the sazawal and his dependants.[109]

In 1818–19, the Company, concerned at the innumerable complaints against the sazawal, asked C. C. Sutherland, the Collector of Bhagalpur, to prepare a report on the role and affairs of the sazawal. In his report, Sutherland revealed that the Bhagalpur magistrate relied on the reports of the sazawal before taking any decision to solve the disputes that were brought to his notice. But Sutherland argued that these decisions were not always fair because his evidence suggested that the reports of the sazawal were biased and were often influenced by acceptance of bribes from the hill people. The dispute in the Bunkur Mahals,[110] over a section of forest land in the foothills, between the hill people and the local zamindar was a classic case of a wrong decision taken by the magistrate because of his reliance on the sazawal's fraudulent reportage. The hill sardars of tuppah Chetolia, in the Bunkar Mahals, and the zamindar of the surrounding plains had a dispute over the possession of the forest lands of the hills and the land which bordered the zamindari. The zamindar, it was alleged, had extended his possessions to the forest lands of the hill people and the land which bordered his zamindari. On the sazawal's report which referred to some non-existent deeds, Mr. Samford, the magistrate of Bhagalpur, issued an order to the zamindars to withdraw their claims over the disputed land.[111] Sutherland investigated the case in 1819 because he received petitions from the son of the Raja of Bunkur Mahals who wanted the Company to redress the decision.[112] Sutherland cross-examined no less than fourteen individuals and some of these were selected

---

[109] Ibid., p. 75.

[110] Located in Bhagalpur district.

[111] Enclosure No. 3, Sutherland's Report on certain cases extending to the corrupt collusion of the sazawal in instigating hill people and natives of the mountains, BC, 27084-27107, 1827- 28, File No. 954, pp. 68–153, F/4/954, IOL.

[112] Ibid.

by the mukhtiyar of the zamindars and some by Sutherland himself.
They included Baijnath Ghir, Ram Junnu and three others. He
also employed three mohurirs, who had been employed in making
the collection of the rent and kept accounts of receipts and dis-
bursements of the same, and also obtained particulars of the case
from Kanjeyla, Chetolia and Jumuni. On the basis of evidence
collected from all these sources, Sutherland exposed the widespread
nature of corruption in the sazawal's office. In Chetolia, Sutherland
discovered that the original lease in the name of Rajnathgir Gossain,
Shivnath Roy, and Rampurshad Misr was cancelled and made
out to Ram Junnu. This was because he had bribed the sazawal
by a payment of Rs 50 and after his death the sazawal transferred
the land to his son. In the pargana of Jumuni, Sutherland carried
out investigations with the assistance of Bhugu Roya, 'a respectable
man of the locality', and found that Salabut Khan, the adopted
son of Abdul Rusul Khan, had himself prepared a lease for the
disputed land at the kachehri. On its execution he took from
the grantee a sum of Rs 25 as a present for his uncle and Rs
5 for himself. It was also discovered that Abdul Rusul Khan
collected money from Junnu when he visited his area on hunting
expeditions.[113]

The political threat the sazawal posed became particularly acute
when in connivance with the military commandant of the Hill
Corps he bypassed the power of the Collector. This brought
the military–civil tensions in the Jungle Tarai to the surface.
For instance, in 1804, J. Wintle, the Collector of Bhagalpur,
was concerned at the exercise of independent power by Captain
D. Sloane who was the Commandant of the Hill Corps. With
the support of the sazawal, Sloane ignored the official list of
hill chiefs prepared by Cleveland and used his own discretion
to dismiss old chiefs and appoint new ones as recruiting agents.[114]

[113] Ibid. For a discussion on corruption in the Company's administration in the Guntur
district see R. E. Frykenberg, *Guntur District 1788–1848: a History of Local Influence and
Central Authority in South India* (London, 1965), p. 11.

[114] From J. Wintle, Magistrate of Bhagalpur, to Captain D. Sloane, in charge of Hill
Rangers, 21 July 1804, Bhagalpur Judicial Records, vol. 485, cited in *Selections from the
Judicial Records of Bhagalpur District*, pp. 354–5. The Magistrate stated that many of the
chiefs appointed by the Commandant had no influence in the hills. Their only claim to

The magistrate alleged that many manjis identified by the Commandant as chiefs were not ratified by him and many were neither chiefs of influence nor did they command a large following. For most of them their only claim to be put down as manjis was a little hut on an uncultivated hill. By the second decade of the nineteenth century these military, social and political reasons had made the Company's hill experiment a liability for it.

RESOLVING OF TENSIONS, 1818–30

In 1819, on Sutherland's recommendation, the Company suspended Abdul Rusul Khan and began to make its arrangements directly with the hill chiefs.[115] The office of the sazawal was not officially abolished until well after 1823, but the withdrawal of Company support reduced it to insignificance. The Company expanded its police stations, which were located on the fringes of the hills, and established several new police outposts in the region. Through all these measures it attempted to maintain a direct control of the Jungle Tarai.[116] This inaugurated an era when the Company, having 'settled' the Jungle Tarai, no longer felt the need to compromise its political and executive authority. By the 1820s, the frontier had been 'pacified' and the raids had been controlled though minor 'disputes' over grazing rights and pasture lands still erupted between the zamindars and the hill people.[117] In this period of temporary stability the wider interest of the Company to establish its monopolistic executive authority and homogeneous army became primary concerns. Moreover, the wider fiscal, military and political problems of the 1820s demanded a smaller but more disciplined army which could be used more flexibly anywhere on the subcontinent. As these concerns triumphed, the Company finally resolved its points of tension with the hill military experiment

be manjis was a little hut on an uncultivated hill.

[115] L. No. 17, W.B. Bayley, Sec. to Govt. to Magistrate of Monghyr, 1 Jan. 1819, BCJ LP, Consult. 1 Jan. 1819, P/133/53, IOL.

[116] Extract, Judicial letter from Bengal, 26 July 1826, BC, File No. 27082, pp. 12–13, F/4/953, IOL.

[117] W. S. Sherwill, 'Notes upon a tour through the Rajmahal hills', *Journal of the Asiatic Society of Bengal* (Calcutta, 1851), p. 547.

by further diluting the Hill Corps with peasant soldiers, disarming the ghatwals and placing them under the complete jurisdiction of its Collectors. This was accompanied by the Company's attempts to extend its control over the language spoken by the recruits. In 1823, the Marquis of Hastings, then Governor-General, revived the hill school Cleveland had established to teach the sipahis how to read and write. Here, he encouraged the teaching of the regional language which was in the Kaithi script.[118] This facilitated a greater control of the sipahi as military instructions and ethics were more meaningful to the soldier if they came in his own language. However, the danger was that this would perpetuate the problem of the narrowness and specialized nature of duties to which the Hill Corps could be assigned. Bishop Heber, who visited the hill school in 1825, was critical of this apparent act of 'benevolence' which fostered regionalism and made the hill sipahis misfits in other parts of the country. He wrote:

No increase of knowledge or enlargement of mind, beyond the power of keeping their accounts and writing a shop bill can be expected from it, in as much as there is no book printed in it, except Mr Rowes' spelling book and no single Hindoo work of any value or antiquity written in it.[119]

In the 1820s, when the Company's reformers began levelling the diverse military traditions of the Bengal Army, the unsuitability of the Hill Corps to function beyond the Jungle Tarai hastened its eclipse. In 1828 Bentinck reduced the Corps to 700. A garrison of these mountaineers which was then kept up at Sicligully was discontinued and the Corps was reduced in number and quartered at Boglipur and Berhampur.[120] Bentinck continued the policy of mixing the hill sipahis with the sipahis of the peasant army. In the late 1820s, when the peasant army ultimately triumphed, of the 700 recruits of the Hill Corps, 200 were Hindus of the plains.

In the 1830s, the hill experiment was abandoned and in the now 'pacified' hills the Company's paramountcy was cultivated

[118] Laird (ed.), *Bishop Heber in Northern India*, p. 100.
[119] Ibid.
[120] Ibid. p. 98.

by strengthening its administrative presence in the region. In 1832, the Company further segregated the hills from the plains by erecting a 295-mile masonry wall enclosing the Rajmahal hills. All land within the pillars was held by the government and given to the hill men on the condition of their continuing with their 'good behaviour'.[121] In the valley and level land outside the hills, but within the masonry wall, the Company began to settle Santals who paid a light land tax for this land. This Santal settlement was regarded as a separate administrative unit called the Daman-i-Koh or skirt of the hills.[122] The division of the Jungle Tarai into these rigidly defined administrative units and the settlement of migrant groups not only ensured a more rigorous administrative control of the region but had other significant repercussions as well. In the subsequent years, the Company state's special treatment to each of these zones, and its reward and punishment policy integrated the Jungle Tarai into the Company's administrative mainline but relegated it to the cultural fringe in a manner it had never experienced before. Interestingly, even though the hill experiment was discontinued for the time being it was revived again later in the nineteenth century, as chapter 7 will show, in the form of the Gurkha military tradition in the Nepal hills. In the late nineteenth century, the recruiting of hill soldiers gained further momentum when the supposed special physical qualities of mountain people once again drew the attention of military officers.

---

[121] Shaw, 'Tour through the Rajmahal hills', p. 547.
[122] Ibid.

Chapter 5

Recruiting Cavalry
in Upper India

From 1802, the East India Company expanded its territory into the central and western Doab, which was later known as the Ceded and Conquered Provinces. This expansion was accompanied by an increasing necessity to recruit cavalry regiments, for the Company needed to control these revenue-bearing territories as well as meet the challenge of the mounted armies of the Marathas, Mewatis, and Pindaris from whom this part of the Doab had acted as a buffer zone. The Company's relocation of the social base of the Indian military culture to the Gangetic valley, and the introduction of a distinctive method of recruitment, however, created a dilemma for it when it confronted, first, the troopers of the erstwhile Muslim conquest states[1] of Farrukhabad and Rohilkhand in its newly-acquired territory, and later the

---

[1] Bayly, *Rulers, Townsmen and Bazaars*, pp. 23–4. I borrow this term from Bayly for whom 'these states differed in a number of ways from both the new Hindu dominions and breakaway satrapies of the Empire, such as Awadh. They did not spring from a dominant land-controlling clan in local society. They offered nominal allegiance to the Mughals and took pride in using symbols of legitimacy with which they had been endowed. Unlike the Hindu rajas in the lower Ganges or the great Maratha and Jat movements, these Muslim conquerors were not supported by powerful bodies of clansmen among the cultivating communities who could in turn command deference from subordinate villagers.' Bayly shows that these states took various measures to buttress this weaker political position. First, they tried to raise their status within north Indian Muslim life and the Mughal diplomatic system and often sought to throw off the stigma of base origin by marrying into gentry families of Pathan origin.

ex-servicemen of Mahadji Shinde and Begum Samru, who had consolidated their hold on the region in the 1780s after the collapse of the Farrukhabad and Rohilkhand Nawabi.

The Mughal style trooper and Mughal military ethic had continued to play a crucial role in the political expansion and consolidation of these states.[2] This was particularly true of Farrukhabad and Rohilkhand where the fortified *Qasbah* town constituted the life line of the polity.[3] In contrast to these Indian states, the Company found it hard to adjust to the Mughal military ethic. It found it even more difficult to accommodate Mughal ex-servicemen in the high positions which they had enjoyed in the armies of the Indian states. Moreover, it insisted on commanding the exclusive loyalty of its recruits which, given the political uncertainties of the late eighteenth century, was quite a new element in the traditions of military service in this area. The Company attempted to resolve this dilemma by attracting to its regular regiments Afghans and Rohillas who were men of wealth and resources. By charging an entry fee at the time of recruitment it hoped to stabilize the troopers' loyalty. Obviously, such an appeal was only likely to attract the rich, who were few in number given the economic vicissitudes of the region. Consequently the regular cavalry regiments of the Company remained limited and it increasingly relied on the Indian state of Rampur for its cavalry requirements.

The Farrukhabad Nawabi, 1713–71

Muhammad Khan Bangash, the founder of the Farrukhabad state, maintained a large military establishment to meet the challenge of Awadh, his powerful neighbour. His army not only fought wars but also integrated the Afghan ruling house with the Rajput society and economy which it had subordinated to its rule. Muhammad Khan's army was multi-tiered with the Nawab as its chief patron. The core of his following were the Afghan families of high pedigree who had migrated from Afghanistan and settled

---

[2] This differed from Awadh and Benaras where, as we have seen in chapter 1, the Indian rulers had distanced themselves from the Mughal troopers and recruited peasant soldiers.

[3] Bayly, *Rulers, Townsmen and Bazaars*, pp. 23–4.

in the city of Farrukhabad.[4] Next in importance were the Afghan and Rohilla ex-servicemen of the Mughal Empire who, once recruited, were encamped in the various towns of the Nawabi.[5] Finally there was the rank and file of locally recruited Rajput peasants many of whom were converts to Islam.[6] The Nawab's recruiting officers had orders to procure Hindu boys between the ages of seven to thirteen who, when they grew up, were placed in his police or army or were appointed to manage the Nawab's private affairs.[7] In the lifetime of Muhammad Khan Bangash, the soldiers were called *tifle-i-sarkar* or sons of the state. The Nawab had a system of educating the recruits and a teacher, Kali Miyan Shah, was appointed for the boy *chelas*. When a·boy could read and write he was taken before the Nawab. The Nawab granted him a khelat thus symbolically granting him a share in his sovereignty. Later the Nawab selected 500 youths from among the recruits of eighteen to twenty years of age and these were trained to be an élite regiment.[8]

Muhammad Khan used aspects of Afghan 'tribal' customs as

[4] W. Irvine, 'The Bangash Nawabs of Farrukhabad: A chronicle (1713-1857)', *JASB*, parts I and II, nos. 47 and 48 (1878 and 1879), I, pp. 259–383. Muhammad Khan remitted large sums to Farrukhabad and induced a colony of the Bangash 'tribe' to emigrate. From among them he selected 18 leaders, giving them the rank of Jamadar (high-ranking military officer) in his army. The Nawab depended on these Bangash officers, and his daughters were given in marriage to many of them. Land was given to them, on the side of the city nearest to the Ganges, to build their houses. This area, to this day, bears the name of Bangashpura.

[5] Ibid.

[6] Ibid. The sons of Rajputs and Brahmins were seized and converted to Islam. Some were obtained by consent, and some were bought after making money payments to their families or leaders. Many of them were the sons of revenue defaulters who were arrested and often converted to Islam. In this manner thousands of boys were obtained and taught the precepts of Islam. The Nawab selected officers for his army from amongst these men, and some were deputed to collect land revenue for the Nawabi.

[7] Ibid. Whenever an amil had a fight with a troublesome village he seized all the boys he could get, and despatched them to the Nawab. By these means every year 100–200 boys were converted to Islam, and by the end of his life Muhammad Khan Bangash had 4,000 *chelas* (pupils or clients).

[8] Ibid., p. 341. They had firelocks of Lahore, and accoutrements of Sultani broad cloth. They also possessed powder horns, each holding two-and-a-half seers of powder, and a pouch with 100 bullets.

well as the indigenous Rajput and Mughal military practices of his recruits to strengthen the fragile bonds which knitted together this heterogeneous group of soldiers. For instance, one Afghan tribal custom, very popular in his army, was a regular ceremony held in the audience hall of the Nawab's house. The Nawab, 'dressed in the clothes of the commonest stuff', would take a meal with his Pathan soldiers. The carpet was covered with rows of simple mats and on these the Pathan soldiers and all persons high and low dined. The Nawab sometimes sat on a cushion and sometimes without one. As the Pathans presented themselves, they uttered an '*auji Nawab salam alaik*' and then sat down in rows.[9] In the Farrukhabad Nawabi, such Afghan tribal customs were encouraged because they created a sense of oneness amongst the heterogeneous soldiery and their alien foreign ruler. But these ceremonies shocked visitors from Delhi and they were surprised at the contrast between the Nawab's great wealth and power and the simplicity of his personal habits.[10]

But if some 'tribal' customs were continued, the Mughal and Rajput military practices were also adopted. In the manner of the Mughal Emperors, the Bangash Nawabs symbolized their successful conquest by making urban investments and encouraging town building. The most classic example of urban sites which exemplified successful conquest, was the city of Farrukhabad itself. This was built on the fifty-two Bamtella villages in the Thakur zamindaris of Bundelkhand district.[11] Town building reinforced the social hierarchies in the army and defined the political culture

[9] Ibid., pp. 337–8. At meal times 500–600 Pathans ate together. Very often groups of Pathans ate from the same plate. Each Pathan was given two unleavened cakes of half a *seer* each, with a cupful of meat and a flat dish of pulao. All the Pathans, including the Nawab, received the same set diet and ate together.

[10] Ibid.

[11] Ibid., pp. 275–7. The towns of Kaimganj, which was southwest of Mau within the lands of Chalali, Mau Rashidabad, Kuberpur and Subhanpur were built to mark the successful conquest of the lands of the Raja of Anupshehr and the Raja of Meda. The same year the town of Muhammadabad, 14 miles south-west of Farrukhabad, was founded. This included the lands of five villages—Kilmapur, Kabirpur, Rohila, Muhammadpur and Takipur—which had initially belonged to the Raja of Khor who had given them to the Kharowah Kayasths who lived in his village. The town of Muhamadabad represented the successful conquest of the Afghans over the Kharowah Kayasths.

of the Nawabi, for the building of ganjs, towns or constructing any masonry structure was the privilege of the Nawab and his close coterie of clan élites. The Nawab allowed the recruits to collect money, goods or jewels during the campaigns on the condition that in adversity loot thus collected could also be used by the state. But he retained the right to initiate urban building which was the outward manifestation of political power. Any recruit who built a masonry structure in any village was at once removed from the service of the Nawab. However, the soldiers were given permission to build a single brick room for which they were allowed to use only sun-dried bricks and mud mortar. Only special chelas or soldiers who won the favour of the Nawab by their military feats were given permission to build ganjs or rural grain markets. For instance, Daler Khan, a Thakur by birth and an important military commander who had been recruited during one of the plundering campaigns in Bundelkhand, established Dalerganj nine miles north-west of Farrukhabad on the road to Kaimganj.[12] Similarly, Brahmins and Rajputs, who were often kidnapped from the Bundelkhand region[13] and appointed as amils or bakhshis, sometimes won the favour of Muhammad Khan Bangash and were allowed to invest in urban building. For instance, Jahanganj, in pargana Bhojpur, was founded by Jahan Khan who was the Nawab's bakshi.[14]

[12] Ibid., pp. 341–5. Daler Khan also raised 1,700 men on his military jagirs of Sehand in the Banda district, and Maudah which was located in the Hamirpur district.

[13] Kidnapping members of the vanquished population, and making them serve the ruling house was a popular practice in Afghanistan. Here, it appears to have reinforced the power of the conqueror. Ahmad Shah Abdali, during his invasion of north India, was reported to have carried away many Hindus from Mathura, and used them as slaves in Afghanistan. See M. Elphinstone, *An Account of the Kingdom of Caubul* (2 vols., reprint, Karachi, 1972), II, p. 289.

[14] Irvine, 'The Bangash Nawabs', *JASB*, I, pp. 341–5. Irvine gives a list of 43 important chelas and their urban investments. For instance Yaqut Khan, a chela who had no children, was allowed to establish several ganjs because it was thought that he had no heirs and after his death his property and buildings would pass on to the Nawab. Yaqut Khan established Kasganj, also called Yaqutganj, and Aliganj, in the pargana of Azimnagar, in Eta district. Kauriyaganj, in pargana Akbarabad of Aligarh district, and Khudaganj on the left bank of Kalinadi in pargana Bhojpur, of Farrukhabad district, were some of the other important ganjs established by him. Apart from these he also set up Nabiganj in Mainpuri district, Yakutganj, in pargana Bhojpur of Farrukhabad district,

The integration of Afghan 'tribal' customs with Mughal political practices reinvented the Mughal military tradition in a new form which suited the political interests of the Nawabi. The striking contrast, with the Mughal military system was the creation of a military household with the Nawab as its chief patron and, as we have already seen, his multi-tiered army organized around his person.[15] It appears that the Nawab himself played the role of the Mughal mansabdar who had been the focus around which regiments were organized in the Mughal army. In the Farrukhabad army, loyalties were organized around the Nawab's military household and the soldiers were expected to uphold its traditions.[16] Since it was from this military household that the soldiers derived their social standing they were always willing to preserve it.

Muhammad Khan's successors, Imam Khan and Ahmad Khan Bangash (1750–71), continued to emphasize the important position of the military household in the Nawabi. But in this period the patronage of the military household expanded further to incorporate the sword-bearing tradition of the settled societies which it now dominated. Like other rulers of the times the Bangash Nawabs also needed to build up an infantry corps. In the early phase of the expansion, the standing army or the 'picked regiment' of Muhammad Khan Bangash, comprised young boys of eighteen to twenty years of age, who had been abducted from settled peasant societies. They were held in contempt because of their use of the sword.'[17] This was in sharp contrast to the Mughal

---

and Daryaganj in pargana Azimnagar of Eta district.

[15] The Bangash Afghan clansmen of the Nawab, as we have seen, formed the core of this household and the locally-recruited Afghan–Rohilla ex-servicemen of the Mughal Empire formed its inner coterie. The outer fringes were made up of Rajput peasant levies.

[16] This was different from cultivating loyalty to the regiment, a characteristic of the European armies of the time, which became a common practice in Shinde's army, possibly because it was commanded by European officers. Loyalty to the regiment remained the most distinctive feature of the Company army.

[17] Irvine, 'Bangash Nawabs', p. 341. One day the picked regiment of the 'slave boys' of Muhammad Khan Bangash were drawn up along the Jamuna bank under the fort at Delhi while the Mughal Emperor was seated on the fort wall. Muhammad Shah ordered them to fire at some moving object on the river, and was so delighted with their performance that he asked for the gift of the whole corps. Muhammad Khan was

and Rajput aristocratic traditions. In Muhammad Khan's times, the bow and arrow was considered the more advanced form of equipment by the ruling class because of its glorious tradition in the earlier history of Muslim conquest where the horse archer was the key figure.[18] By 1735, after Dalel Khan's war with the Bundelas, the expanding Afghan 'tribal' tradition had incorporated the local warrior practices of the region. This was revealed in the works of some contemporary Hindi poets of 1735. Verses in praise of Dalel Khan found in the works of Shakir Muhammad, called Lahori, reflected the incorporation of the local sword-bearing tradition into the Afghan army. One song had the following words:

> Muhammad Khan's son was Dalel, he scattered the Bundela, many swords were drawn, there was no delay. From bravery their liners burst their clothes. Their armies met, they bravely fought. Though pressed hard they would not give way before those hosts. Sword in hand, Dalel Pathan went forward, twirling his moustache.[19]

More revealing were the verses handed down as Dalel Khan's answer to the Musalmans of Maudha when they entreated him to leave the battlefront:

> My name is Dalel Khan, how can I retreat. The good name of Bangash is in my hand, on me is the hand of Muhammad Shah whose is this sword. This Pathan honour have I bound round me. I will fight face to face. Through your youthful strength the Pathans will enter the hottest

---

reported to have said to the Emperor that 'they were a lot of Brahmins and Rajputs who could do nothing but talk a rustic patois and use their swords.' The Emperor withdrew his request, but nevertheless sent Rs 1,000 to be distributed amongst them.

[18] Ibid., pp. 323–33. The Afghan Sheikhzadas were perfect masters of the art of archery and possessed arrows of every sort. They were also good horsemen. Sheikhpur, a village close to Kamalganj on the Kanpur road 8 miles south of Farrukhabad, and Siroli Chand Thok, in pargana Shamsabad east, were celebrated for the manufacture of bows and arrows. Some of the arrows cast and used in the region were: the *lais*, which was capable of tearing the flesh, and was very expensive to make; the *kalandra*; the *kohar* ; the *ghera*, which had a head three fingers in breath and inflicted a severe wound; the *nukta*, which had no head, inflicted a blow but did not wound; the *thults*; the *ankridar*, which had a bent head, like a saddle-maker's needle; and the *nawak*, which was a kind of pipe and had a flute-like cylinder attached to the bow.

[19] Ibid., pp. 370–1.

of the struggle. 'They fear not the fray' said brave Dalel boldly in the battlefield call 'Ali Ali' as Hindus call Hanuman.[20]

Moreover, in order to keep pace with the growing military power of Awadh, the Farrukhabad Nawabs expanded their military and also began to obtain more modern firearms. By the 1750s, their army was armed with firelocks obtained from Lahore, gunpowder, and pouches with a hundred bullets each. By the era of Nawab Kaim Khan (1745), cannon foundries were set up, and in the reign of Ahmad Khan Bangash (1750–71), 500 large and small guns were always ready for service. It was said the local production of powder and ball went on without intermission. It is then not a surprise that out of an expenditure of five lakhs a month the government spent three lakhs on soldiers' salaries, and one lakh on elephants, horses, camels and the artillery establishment.[21]

This diversification into new types of military accoutrement was accompanied by a considerable change in the ideology which had welded together the Afghan army. A weakened Mughal Emperor now dependent upon the Farrukhabad Nawabi bestowed high honours, including the position of the imperial Bakshi, on Nawab Ahmad Khan Bangash. Greater proximity to the Mughal court increased emulation of the Mughal darbar, and Mughal political ceremonies and celebrations began to be adopted so as to promote the social standing of the Farrukhabad court. Mughal political customs established the invincibility and charisma of the Emperor by separating him from the rank and file of the army and of Indian society in general. The adopting of Mughal ceremonies by the Afghan Nawabs had a detrimental effect on their polity and military which was delicately balanced around the person of the Nawab. Ahmad Khan Bangash emulated the Mughal processions, celebrated his birthday with the pomp and show of the Mughal Emperor and used these political rituals

[20] Ibid.
[21] Ibid., p. 371; see also Sir J. Strachey, *Hastings and the Rohilla War* (Oxford, 1892), pp. 17–18. In 1750 Ahmad Khan used a strong military force to crush the Awadh armies which had occupied Farrukhabad. It was only with the help of the Marathas the following year that Safdar Jang, the Nawab of Awadh, could avenge this defeat.

and celebrations to construct a new form of kingship to replace the diverse traditions and ideologies of the earlier period. This distancing of the Nawab from the Afghan troopers and the *tifle-i-sarkar* led to a weakening of the patronage system. The different layers of political obligation and responsibilities which had formally constituted the state were consequently weakened.

The Afghans adopted different ways to protect and defend their identity. For some it took the form of protection and support of their patron Ahmad Khan Bangash.[22] For others this identity was emphasized by the assertion of independent power.[23] Corporate bodies of Afghans dispersed from Farrukhabad in search of new patrons strong enough to provide them the *izzat* they derived from military service. The defeat of the Farrukhabad state in the 1774 war with Awadh considerably reduced the military establishment that had integrated the foreign ruling house with Indian society and led to more migrations. By the 1780s, the Afghan conquest state had dispersed into a range of powerful bands of Afghans on the move in the defence of their tribal *izzat*, searching for the high social and military status they had hitherto enjoyed in the Farrukhabad state.

THE ROHILLA STATE, 1760–74

The relative importance of trade and merchant capital in state formation was the major point of comparison between the Bangash and the Rohilla state. The Rohilla state, which consolidated its hold in the upper Doab, could be called a military entrepreneur state. The definition of the military entrepreneur state is derived from Fritz Redlich's concept of eighteenth-century European military 'enterprisers'.[24] According to Redlich, this stage of military

---

[22] Attempts were made to rally support to place him on the throne and thus increase their own political and military power. Irvine, 'Bangash Nawabs', pp. 163–4. Islam Khan, a chela, gave this explanation for mustering and rallying around him thousands of Pathans.

[23] Ibid., p. 164. The three men known as Nawabs were: (1) Ahmad Khan himself, known as *Barre* Nawab; Zulfkar Khan, called *Manjhle* Nawab; and Daim Khan called *Chhote* Nawab.

[24] Fritz Redlich, *The German Military Entrepreneur and his Workforce: A Study in*

organization is closely linked to the development of a money economy which enables the adventurers to become part of the work force of an enterpreneur who pays or promises to pay them wages along with a share in the spoils. In its fully developed form it is characterized by three functions: contracting, extending credit networks, and trading in weapons, arms, and military accessories.[25]

From Daud Khan, the founder of the Rohilkhand state, to the era of Hafiz Rahmat Khan, one can discern a transition from the mercenary warrior stage of military organization to the emergence of a military entrepreneur state. One of the reasons for this transition was that Rohilkhand became the major beneficiary of the re-routings of the long-distance trade routes of the mid-eighteenth century.[26] The income generated by trade allowed the rulers to give regular cash salaries to their soldiers and enabled them to move from the mercenary warrior phase to the military entrepreneur stage.

Daud Khan and the Phase of Mercenary Warriors

Daud Khan, the founder of the state of Rohilkhand, was the adopted son of Shah Alam Khan, the father of the famous Rohilla leader Hafiz Rahmat Khan. Daud was educated by Shah Alam Khan who committed to his charge the management of the family estate in Tooroo and Shahamutpur in Afghanistan. But Daud, being of an ambitious nature, determined to seek his fortune in

---

European Economic and Social History (Wiesbaden, 1964–5), p. 4. He calls all men of any European nationality who in the late middle ages and in the early modern period upto 1800 provided the services of organization, management and maintenance of troops in battle, for the sake of making a profit, military entrepreneurs.

[25] Ibid.

[26] J. Gommans, 'Legitimacy and conquest in late Mughal India: Afghan state formation in Farrukhabad and Rohilkhand 1707–1774' (MA Thesis, Leiden University, 1987), p. 27. Long-distance trade between Bengal and the Agra–Delhi region was transferred because of the Jat and Bundela disturbances to the north, and now moved along Benaras, Awadh, and Bareli, and then towards Delhi. In western India too things were changing. In the 17th century the Punjab had functioned as the cross-roads of trade routes in this area. The silting of the Indus had already affected its position. This was amply compensated by the east–west trade between Persia–Afghanistan and the Gangetic delta.

Hindustan, quit his master, and proceeded to Kutheir or Rohil-khand. In India, the death of Aurangzeb in 1707, and the disputes between his sons for the succession to the throne, had weakened the central government. A body of local Rajput zamindars had taken possession of the province of Kutheir. Daud with a few other Afghans reached Kutheir and began his career by entering the service of these rebel zamindars. He soon collected a body of 200 men and joined Mardan Shah, the zamindar of Mardha, in the province of Budaoun.

Daud Khan's force represented the 'mercenary warrior' stage at which there was no formal contract between the leader and his troops. He recruited on his own account and risk, and delivered his contingent to the highest bidder. He paid his soldiers by distributing amongst them the goods they plundered in battle.[27] Very often he looted horse merchants and traders to provide his men with horses and accessories for fighting.[28] Throughout his stay in India, his mercenary band remained loose and free floating and no formal service engagements involving payment of salaries in cash on a regular basis existed between him and his troops. His power was established by 'violence, assassination, treachery and corruption'.[29] With this loosely-knit band of followers, Daud Khan hawked his services to the best bidders, and while in the temporary service of Devichand, the Raja of Kumaon, he finally lost his life.[30]

[27] C. A. Elliott, *The Life of Hafizool-Moolk, Hafiz Rahmut Khan Written by his Son, the Nawab Moostayab Khan Buhadoor and Entitled Goolistan-i-Rehmut* (London, 1831), p. 7. Elliott noted that as these zamindars were constantly in a state of hostility with each other, each trying to dispossess the other, Murdan Shah dispatched Daud with his party to attack the village of Bankouli which was located in pargana Chow Mehla. From this expedition Daud obtained a large booty which was distributed amongst his recruits and he took many prisoners.

[28] Ibid., pp. 8–9. Daud Khan had purchased some horses from the merchants at Shahjahanabad for which he had neglected to pay the stipulated price. The merchants seized and confined his father, Shah Alam, on his arrival at Delhi. They refused to liberate him even though he offered to leave all his own property as a pledge for repayment of the debt. Weary of confinement Shah Alam Khan passed the whole night in prayer, and in the morning the horse merchants on their own released him. He then returned to Kutheir, procured the money from Daud Khan, and remitted it to the merchants.

[29] Strachey, *Hastings and the Rohilla War*, p. 11.

[30] Elliott, *The Life of Hafizool-Moolk, Hafiz Rahmut Khan*, pp. 9–10. In India Daud Khan

Ali Muhammad Khan: From Mercenary Bands to Standing Army

Merchants and trade formed the focal point around which Daud's son, Ali Muhammad Khan, introduced more permanent and stable ties in his band of 'mercenary warriors'. The political context of war, particularly the danger from Awadh, made Ali Muhammad increase the strength of his army to 15,000 troopers.[31] This created a demand for horses and military accoutrements and attracted trade to the Rohilla state. Rohilkhand was already located on the long-distance trade route for horses from Afghanistan to the Deccan and the demand created by Ali Muhammad's army further enhanced its importance. Ali Muhammad Khan concentrated on establishing towns in areas where trade in horses, sugar, tobacco, cloth and foodgrains could be taxed. Indeed the first book he wrote dealt with his early town-building activities.[32] In the following years the financial advantages of establishing a commercial entrepôt for the sugar and rice of Rohilkhand, as these made their way to supply the markets of Agra and Delhi, were understood by the supposedly predatory Rohilla Pathans when they founded the mart of Chandausi in the Moradabad district.[33] Charles Hamilton, the translator of a nineteenth-century chronicle, *History of the Rohillas*,

---

quit the service of Murdan Shah, and was entertained by Devichand, the Raja of Kumaon. He placed under his charge the force stationed in the pargana at the foot of the hills. Azmatullah Khan was about this time sent from Delhi, with a body of royal troops, to take possession of Kashipur and Rudrapur. The Raja marched with his army from Almora to support Daud Khan. But Daud Khan, who had in the meantime taken a bribe from Azmatullah Khan, in the first action deserted his master and the Raja was defeated. Daud then actually made an attempt to seize his master as a hostage for the payment of arrears due the troops, which was foiled by the fidelity of the hill people. The Raja retreated to Kakurdurra and, pretending ignorance of Daud's treachery, invited him to the court to receive his pay. Daud fell into the trap; on reaching Kakurdurra he was put to death by the Raja's order.

[31] C. Hamilton, *An Historical Relation of the Origin, Progress and Final Dissolution of the Government of the Rohilla Afghans in the Northern Provinces of Hindustan* (London, 1787), pp. 40, 54.

[32] S. Altaf Ali, *Hayat-i-Hafiz Rehmat Khan* (Badaun, 1933), pp. 329–33.

[33] E. T. Stokes, 'Agrarian society and the Pax Britannica in northern India in the early 19th century', in E. T. Stokes, *The Peasant and the Raj: Studies in Agrarian Society and Peasant Rebellion in Colonial India* (Cambridge, 1978), p. 68. The mart of Chandausi was established by Ibrahim Khan, a Rohilla chief, in 1769.

noted the rhythm of economic life that the Rohilla military generated:

He [Ali Muhammad] employed the income of his lands in raising troops, purchasing artillery and military stores and above all in securing the friendship of many of the principal personages in the preference, by a judicious and well-timed liberality. Neither was he remiss in cultivating the attachment of the lower orders by the same practices as enabled him to succeed with their superiors.[34]

Trade brought a predictable income which assured the loyalty of troops as they were paid at regular intervals. This more stable income from trade introduced a major change in the Rohilkhand army. The basic difference between the army of Daud Khan and that of Ali Muhammad Khan was the emergence of a more formal military establishment in which, like the Farrukhabad army, the soldiers were accountable to the Nawab. However, here, their loyalty to the Nawab was formalized by a system of contract signed between the Nawab and his soldiers. Ali Muhammad promised to make regular payments of salaries in cash to his troopers as long as they continued to serve him. Hamilton appreciated the introduction of this contract system and was of the view that it had created stability in the Rohilla army:

Through these regular payments Ali Muhammad tightened the loose ties that had existed between Daud and these troops. He took an acknowledgement from every individual by which each solemnly bound himself to stand by and adhere to the cause of the Rohilla family. This was the contract entered in the form of pledges and acknowledgements many of which were locked in the tosha-khana or Chancery under the care of Futteh Khan Khansamah.[35]

Hafiz Rahmat Khan and the Military Entrepreneur Rohilla State

Hafiz Rahmat Khan continued with Ali Muhammad's policy of encouraging a regular and stable income from trade to maintain a strong and regularly paid army. Indeed, his war with Awadh made him considerably increase his military establishment. For

[34] Hamilton, *History of the Rohillas*, pp. 54 and 40; see also Gholam Hussein Khan, *The Seir Mutaqherin*, pp. 3, 232–4.

[35] Hamilton, *History of the Rohillas*, pp. 91–2.

instance, in the 1774 war with Shuja, he possessed 24,000 horse and foot, 4,000 rocket men, and sixty pieces of cannon.[36] The enlarged military establishment generated a greater demand for arms, food and clothes and thereby attracted more traders, artisans, leather workers, metalsmiths and craftsmen to Rohilkhand. Hafiz encouraged this flow of artisans and craftsmen and in the 1760s built himself a beautiful capital at Pilibhit and adorned it with a mosque, a temple, schools and mansions. Well protected *pakka* markets were built and merchants and bankers were encouraged to settle there with incentives such as the paying of very low transit duties and cesses.[37] The increase in trade and artisanal production suited the Rohilla chiefs as it brought additional income and consequently they encouraged the urban and rural artisans to live in Rohilkhand. Indeed many expert Pathan craftsmen were settled on landholdings in Rohilkhand[38] and the Rohilla army kept alive many such colonies of skilled and unskilled craftsmen. For instance, the dependence of the army on mounted swordsmen led to the emergence of a flourishing sword industry in the region. Years later, in 1816, J. Wright, the Company's officiating magistrate of zillah Farrukhabad, noted that this sword industry had declined because its main buyer, the Rohilkhand cavalry, had ceased to exist.[39] The Rohilla artillery also ceated a demand for cannon and gunpowder and gave a fillip to the local economy. We have evidence of cannon being cast in Aonla, Shahjahanpur and Rampur even before 1774.[40] F. Wendel and Comte de Modave, French travellers who toured Rohilkhand between 1760 and 1776, commented on the boots, doublets, helmets, saddles, swords and daggers which they saw on display

[36] Ibid., p. 231.

[37] Elliott, *Life of Hafizool-moolk, Hafiz Rahmat Khan*, p. 35; Strachey, *Hastings and the Rohilla War*, p. 31. He was reported to have abolished taxes of every denomination both on exports as well as on imports.

[38] The gift of fifty bighas of tax-free land to Chand Kamangar (bow-maker) by Azim Khan of Ujhani in Badaoun. Vide Document No. 2300, dated 8 July 1782, NAI Calender of Acquired Documents III.

[39] Home Miscellaneous 776, Judicial, Furrukhabad No. 22 in No. 2 Bengal Secret Letters 13 Jan. 1816, IOL.

[40] Maulvi Sadruddin, *Tarikh-i-Shahjahanpur* (Lucknow, 1919), p. 74.

in the towns of Rohilkhand.[41] Moreover, Hafiz Rahmat Khan himself controlled the production of gunpowder and in 1774, prior to the battle of Miranpur Katra, production of these items was stepped up and all the chieftains had to report to him to collect their share of cannon and gunpowder.[42] It was in this period of heightened economic activity that the Rohilla chiefs began advancing cash to sugarcane processors so as to control the trade in sugar as well.[43]

Moreover, the expansion of the army also extended the Rohilla trading networks to distant lands. Rohilla cavalrymen provided a ready market for the horses bred by Rajput zamindars of Rohilkhand and many of them participated in the horse trade themselves. In 1811, W. Moorcroft, the Company's horse Superintendent, reported that in the days of Hafiz Rahmat Khan Rohilla merchant-soldiers purchased horses from the local Rajput zamindars when they were eighteen to twenty months old. They fed them well until they became three years of age and then resold them to the soldiers of the Rohilkhand army in the markets of Rampur.[44] The Rohilla merchant-soldiers often travelled to Bhatinda, in Punjab, and Sindh to purchase good quality horses for which there was a great demand at home. They either bought their horses directly from the individual breeders[45] or else bargained

---

[41] J. Deloche (ed.), *Les Memoires de Wendel sur les Jats, Pathans, et les Sikhs* (Paris, 1979), p. 131; J. Deloche (ed.), *Voyage en Inde du Comte de Modave, 1773–6* (Paris, 1971), pp. 326–7, cited in I. G. Khan, 'Revenue, agriculture and warfare; technical knowledge and the post Mughal elites in northern India, from the mid 18th to the early 19th century', Ph.D thesis, SOAS, 1990, p. 140.

[42] Mustajab Khan, *Gulistan-i-Rahmat*, MS 584, IOL, f. 1386, cited in Khan, 'Revenue, agriculture and warfare', p. 139.

[43] C. A. Bayly, 'India and West Asia c. 1700–1830', *Asian Affairs*, XIX, OS, vol. 7, part I (February 1988), p. 13.

[44] Enclosure No. 80, W. Moorcroft, Superintendent Horse Stud, to Maj. W. Fitzgerald, acting Sec. Board of Superintendence, 9 Oct. 1811, enclosed in L. No. 79, W. Fitzgerald, acting Sec. Board of Superintendence, to W. Gardiner, acting Sec. to Govt. Mil. Deptt., 9 Oct. 1811, BMC, Consult. 15 Oct. 1811, P/24/42, IOL (hereafter Moorcroft Report).

[45] Ibid. Moorcroft reported that the dealers from Rampur annually visited the neighbourhood of Bhatinda as well as the other parts of the Lakheri jungle for their purchases. It was said that the breeders in the Lakheri jungle seldom sent their best colts

for the best horses in the horse fairs held in Dadri and Haridwar.[46] Rohilla horse dealers also visited the fairs in the Rajput states from where they brought back many good colts. With these horses many of them went looking for lucrative military service in the Deccan and very often sold their horses at good prices in the Deccan markets.[47]

The growing military establishment and the demands it generated not only integrated the foreign Rohilla ruling house into the local economy but also brought it closer to the Rajput society which it had subordinated to its rule. For instance, to meet the growing demand for horses to supply his cavalry Hafiz began to encourage the Rajput zamindars to engage in horse-breeding. In 1811, Moorcroft reported that in the lands between the left bank of the Ganges and the Kumaon and Nepal hills, prior to Hafiz Rahmat's reign not a single district was in possession of a breed of horses fit for European military purposes. But by the reign of Hafiz Rahmat Khan things had changed. He encouraged breeding horses in this province and frequently gave stallions to Rajput zamindars. The Rajput zamindars had no religious prejudices against keeping stallions, but they mated them with their own mares and allowed them to serve those of their relatives and friends. Hafiz Rahmat's military demand for horses began to redefine status in the Rajput society of Rohilkhand. In 1800, the new symbols of power and status were most evident when the Nawab of Awadh's amils penalized the zamindars of Rohilkhand for the non-payment of revenue by seizing over 300 mares and colts. After they paid their revenue twenty-five of the best of these horses were retained and the rest were returned.[48]

---

to Haridwar but reserved them for the Rampur and other dealers who came for them annually. The itinerant Rohilla merchant-soldiers fed the breeders stories of the fluctuations of the outside market and the partiality of Europeans to Arabian horses. All this influenced the breeder to sell his horses at low prices to the Rohilla merchant.

[46] Ibid. A small number of colts, aged from twenty months to three-and-a-half-years, were annually brought to the fair at Haridwar from the Punjab and the vicinity of Bhatinda. Those under age for cavalry were brought up by the merchants of Rampur.

[47] Ibid.

[48] Moorcroft Report. Moorcroft further reported that during the Rohilla rule breeders in Mehrabad, pargana Kundhar, near the confluence of the Bygood and Ramgunga,

In all these ways the expanded military establishment gave a fillip to the local economy and attracted more trade to Rohilkhand than before. It brought ready cash to fight wars and pay the standing army on a regular basis. This not only helped Hafiz to maintain his central army but also provided the smaller Rohilla chiefs with cash to maintain their contingents. For they taxed goods and trade caravans which passed through their territory and used the cash thus collected to pay their soldiers. This was nowhere better demonstrated than in the general outcry among Rohilla chieftains when, in 1763, Hafiz announced that all *rahdari* (transit) cesses were to be abolished.[49] The chieftains protested that they would not be able to maintain their military contingents if they were denied these cesses. Their fears were quelled by the ruling house which reminded them of the profits they could make from the increased presence of *mahajans* and traders that this law would attract to Rohilkhand. It was also brought to their notice that this would increase the number of markets in the area and increase the volume of *tehbazari* (or market day) cesses.[50]

In this way the Rohilla chiefs, merchant-warriors, artisans, and Rajput peasants of Rohilkhand provided the fiscal base for the transition of the mercenary warrior system of Daud Khan to the professional military of Hafiz Rahmat Khan. In Hafiz Rahmat's army the links between him and his soldiers were further formalized. Salaries in cash were paid on a regular basis but service duties, responsibilities, discipline and professional efficiency were also clearly spelt out. In the 1760s the soldiers of his standing army were also given a uniform to wear. This consisted of a long coat and a turban which was low over the temples and high on the forehead

---

had approximately 500 broad mares. The demand for young stock was so great that advances were made for the produce long before they were foaled. The animals purchased by the people were generally lame or blemished. A zamindar having broad mares sent for a Bhat and his horse. He fed them whilst they stayed at his house and paid a fee of Re 1 for a mare being put to the horse three times with the privilege of sending her a fourth time, if there should appear a necessity for it. But if the mare was sent to the house of a Bhat the zamindar sent an extra rupee to him.

[49] Saadat Khan, *Gul-i-Rahmat*, MS 155 KBOPL, f. 173b, cited in Khan, 'Revenue, agriculture and warfare', p. 101.

[50] Ibid., ff. 173–5.

so as to act as a helmet. In war time the soldiers were given a lance to add to their dress weapons which consisted of sabre and dagger.[51]

It was this long and gradual process of transition of the mercenary 'tribal' bands of Rohillas into Hafiz Rahmat's uniformed professional cavalrymen that confused the eighteenth-century British observers. In 1774, William Francklin was ambivalent in his views about the Rohillas when he wrote:

They are a hardy warlike race, equally capable of arms and husbandry...but withal in common with other Afghans they are crafty, treacherous and revengeful. This characteristic national spirit, aided by the impetuous follies of a ferocious and uncivilised mind renders difficult the governance of this race. Hence frequent revolutions, civil broils at home and wars abroad have constantly marked the Rohilla Government under its different rulers...yet it has been evinced in more instances than one that by kind and proper treatment even this generally considered ferocious tribe may be rendered tractable.[52]

The changed political and military context of the 1780s considerably reduced the military strength of the Rohillas. The defeat of the Rohillas in 1774 was accompanied by the interference of the Company in the region and the disbanding of the Indian armies. The reductions in the military began to weaken the Rohilla ruling house as it had integrated itself to the local economy and society through its army. In 1816, J. Wright, the officiating Magistrate of zillah Farrukhabad, commented on the decline of military opportunities in the region and observed that this had a detrimental effect on the flourishing sword industry of Mau. Swords from Mau had supplied the native armies of Rohilkhand and Farrukhabad and with the disbanding of these Indian armies the manufacture of swords petered down and the cloth weaving industry became more important.[53]

[51] Deloche, *Les Memoires de Wendel*, p. 131, cited by Khan, p. 110.

[52] W. Francklin, *The History of the Reign of Shah Alam, the Present Emperor of Hindustan* (London, 1798), p. 60.

[53] Home Misc. 776, Judicial, Furruckabad No. 22 in No. 2 Bengal Secret Letter 13 Jan. 1816, IOL. He also commented that the Pathan population of Mau, Kaimganj and Shumsabad took up service in the native states, beyond the Jamuna, because of the decline of service opportunities in the region; also see S. H. Cherry, Resident at Kathmandu, to Sir J. Shore, Gov. Gen., (?) March 1796, B.C. File No. 714, Extract

The Rohillas reacted to the weakening of their polity in different ways. The Afghan risaldars who had enjoyed high positions of respect and honour in the state did not reconcile themselves to the idea of taking service elsewhere. They continued to live a retired life in Rohilkhand and associated with the *ashraf* and literati of society with whom they had always shared urban tastes and manners. However, the younger generation of Rohillas who never held high posts looked for military employment elsewhere. For instance, Busawan Lal, the *munshi* and biographer of Amir Khan, notes that Muhammad Hyat Khan, Amir Khan's father, continued to serve the Rohilla Nawab Ali Muhammad Khan until 1774. After Ali Muhammad's death he retired to *sarai* Tureena which was his birthplace. Here, he associated with nobles like Ghulam Muhel-ud-din Khan and honoured and learned men like the famous Sheikh Yayha. He obtained his livelihood by renting the land these people held in perpetuity. He was distinguished for his knowledge of arithmetic, algebra, astronomy and for his understanding of the Hindu Shastras and other branches of literature and science. Quite in contrast to his attitude was that of his son, Amir Khan, who in this period offered his service to the highest bidders.[54] Similarly, many young Rohillas, like Fazil Khan, served in the armies of Shinde and others flocked for employment to the territory of Begum Samru and Zebta Khan in the Meerut and Saharanpur districts respectively.[55] Many eventually joined the Company's service.

A few migrating Rohilla warriors, like Amir Khan, found employers who provided them with enough latitude to create their own independent principalities. Amir Khan used his 'tribal' and religious ties to create cohesive armies of Rohilla-Afghans which was reminiscent of the manner in which his ancestors had functioned in Rohilkhand and Farrukhabad. But the character

---

Bengal Pol. Consult., (?) March 1796, F/4/9, IOL. In 1796, he reported that a large number of Rohillas had enlisted in the Gurkha army.

[54] Busawan Lal, *Memoirs of the Pathan Soldier of Fortune, the Nawab Ameerood-doulah Muhammad Ameer Khan* (Calcutta, 1832), pp. 2–3.

[55] Broughton, *Letters Written in a Maratha Camp*, pp. 50–1; W. Francklin, *Military Memoirs of George Thomas* (Calcutta, 1803), p. 219; H. Compton, *A Particular Account of European Adventurers in Hindustan 1784–1803* (London, 1892), pp. 47, 63.

of Tonk state was different from these northern Muslim conquest states of the late eighteenth century. We shall now discuss this state and the position the Afghan and Rohilla troopers of the erstwhile Rohilla and Farrukhabad state held in it.

AMIR KHAN IN TONK, 1780–1818

In the late eighteenth century, the younger generation of Rohilla–Afghans, enthused with the fervour of adventure and military service, took employment as soldiers in places as far as Nepal,[56] and the Deccan[57] and with the Marathas and the army of Tipu Sultan.[58] In the service of these states, many of them enhanced their power and carved out their independence. In the late eighteenth and early nineteenth century, they became the new patrons of the Muslim warriors and artists dislocated after the decline of the courts in Delhi, Bareli, Farrukhabad, and Lucknow. Amir Khan, the Rohilla chief, was one such patron. In his jagir at Tonk, which he obtained from Holkar in 1802, he created his own independent kingdom using the troopers and military traditions of his parent state, Rohilkhand. Tonk eventually became one of the last Muslim states where the Afghan troopers could enjoy high military and social status.[59]

In Tonk, the military practices of the ex-servicemen of Rohilkhand and Farrukhabad state were continued. But if the army continued to be organized on the pattern of the Muslim conquest states the character of the Tonk state was different. Tonk

[56] G. H. Cherry, Resident at Lucknow to Sir John Shore, Gov. Gen. (?) March 1796, BC, File No. 714, extract Bengal Pol. Consult., (?) March 1796, F/4/9, IOL.

[57] Gholam Hussein Khan, *The Seir Mutaqherin*, p. 123. Haider Naik, the Commandant of the Deccan sovereign Nizam Ali Khan, had Mughal, Persian and Indian troopers in his service. To this numerous body he added 70,000 musketeers armed with flintlocks whom he trained in European fashion.

[58] See N. M. de la Tour, *History of Ayder Ali Khan Nebab Behadur* (London, 1784).

[59] Amir Khan had been employed by Holkar who, in 1801, pleased by his service in the Maratha war gave him the jagir of Tonk, Seronj and Perawa. These three jagirs together yielded an annual revenue of Rs 4 lakhs. L. No. 40, A. Seton, Resident at Delhi, to Charles Lushington, acting Chief to Govt. in the Pol. Deptt., undated, BC, File No. 7664, extract Bengal Pol. Consult., 16 June 1810, F/4/335, IOL.

had definite Muslim overtones which suited the interests of the predominantly Muslim ex-servicemen of earlier polities and enhanced their social standing. In a period when the East India Company was viewed as the mortal enemy of the independent Muslim states it appears that Amir Khan tried to project his Muslim credentials so as to garner popular Muslim support and portray himself as the last Muslim leader resisting the encroachment of the East India Company.

For this reason Amir Khan forged his bonds with his troopers by reiterating his belief in the 'will of God', faith in maulvis, belief in miracles and 'holy men'. Busawan Lal, Amir Khan's biographer, reports that in one of his moments of financial stress he was asked by a maulvi to repeat the name of God every day a hundred times. Amir Khan claimed that as a result of this penance he was helped by God. That very day he was employed by a pandit who had been sent by the Marathas for collecting *chauth* in Surat and had been turned out of the city by the English. Amir Khan assisted him in the collection of chauth. When the pandit expressed surprise that the task could be achieved by Amir Khan and his small contingent of 200 men, he is reported to have said: 'Victory is in the hands of God and does not depend on numbers.'[60] In this way he expressed his complete submission to the will of God and thereby projected himself as a devout Muslim commandant. On another occasion, when out of favour with the Nawab of Bhopal, Amir Khan gave charity to a *durvesh* and hoped for his restitution.[61] Moreover, he often visited the shrines of Muslim holy men, like Murtaza Ali,[62] and contained insubordination and unrest in his army by reminding his soldiers of the prophecy which Shah Zuhur Ullah, a durvesh who lived in seclusion at a gunj near Seronj, had made about 'him being a master of territory and of many servants, of much state ....'[63] Amir Khan's use of popular Islam to reinforce

---

[60] Busawan Lal, *Memoirs of Amir Khan*, pp. 17–18.

[61] Ibid., p. 22–3.

[62] Ibid., p. 36.

[63] Ibid., p. 38. Most Rohilla families had connections with the Naqshbandi *silsila* of the Sufis.

his power was best reflected in his comments to Holkar who, after his success in the 1803 war, offered to share his *masnad* with him. Amir Khan replied:

The musnud here was your father's. I give you joy of its possession, but sit myself on the musnud of faith and reliance on the providence of God, aiming even at higher objects, but biding my time.[64]

This encouragement to Muslim holy and learned men in the jagir of Tonk made it a seat of attraction not only for the Muslim warriors, who derived immense pride associating with such religious figures, but also to the Muslim and Hindu literary scribes. In a period when the traditional patrons in north India had declined, Amir Khan emerged as a great patron of the north Indian literati. For instance, Busawan Lal, a Kayasth native of Bilgram in Awadh and the naib munshi and author of Amir Khan's memoir, migrated to Tonk in 1815–16. Henry Prinsep, the translator of the memoir, attributed his migration and the compilation of the memoir to the entreaty of Amir Khan and his son Nawab Vazir-ud-daula who he said were 'men of considerable literary attainment'.[65] After 1818, in the period of peace which followed the Pindari war, Tonk emerged as a major centre of learning and the arts. In the 1830s Busawan Lal noted:

His [Amir Khan's] days are spent in the enjoyment of domestic happiness and in the performance of all religious observances, such as listening to the reading and interpretation of the Koran or joining in social and instructive discourse with the learned and pious, who have found in his court an asylum and honoured retreat.[66]

After the decline of the Rohilkhand and Farrukhabad states the Marathas and the indigenous independent jagirdars like Begum Samru competed with Amir Khan to enlist Rohilla-Afghan troopers. They tried to incorporate the military men of the erstwhile Muslim polities thereby giving a fillip to the military labour market and horse trade which these Indian states had sustained. However, these later regimes represented a more advanced stage of political

[64] Ibid., p. 103.
[65] Ibid., Introduction.
[66] Ibid., p. 485.

formation and consequently their armies were organized in a manner very different from that of the Farrukhabad and Rohilkhand military formations. We shall now discuss their military organization and the position the ex-servicemen of earlier Muslim polities held in them.

STATE FORMATION AND THE ARMY OF SHINDE, 1784–1802

The weakening of the Bangash and the Rohilla states coincided with the expansionist phase of Mahadji Shinde's career. From 1784, Shinde began to recruit an increasingly large number of cavalrymen of the Mughal, Rohilkhand and Farrukhabad states into his army.[67] John Pemble shows that until the nineteenth century the irregular cavalry remained the largest component of Shinde's army.[68] Apart from the troopers from Rohilkhand and

[67] Broughton, *Letters Written in a Maratha Camp*, pp. 50–1. Broughton reported that the Maratha Corps in Shinde's army was a mixture of Maratha peasants and Afghan and Rohilla ex-servicemen of former Muslim states. One of his famous, exclusively Maratha, contingents was a *Risalu* (troop) called the Baruh Bhaees or twelve brothers from the twelve leaders who commanded it. The Baruh Bhaees received a small monthly pay in cash. Shinde was always worried about their plundering activities and very often dispatched cavalry regiments against them. Shinde also had a contingent of troops that was led by a Rohilla chief called Fazil Khan who had taken service with Shinde after the decline of Rohilkhand. Thomas Pennant, in *A View of Hindustan* (2 vols., London, 1798), II, p. 170, estimated that about 17,000–18,000 Rohilla men and their families had migrated to the west of the Ganges, into Shinde territory, after the defeat of the Rohillas at the battle of Miranpur Katra. According to W. Francklin, *Military Memoirs of George Thomas* (Calcutta, 1803), p. 219, most of the Rohillas initially joined the forces of Zabta Khan, in Saharanpur district, which in 1800 included about 1,500 Rohillas. Many Rohillas joined either the army of Shinde or else the regiments of Begum Samru, and others formed brigades of Pindaris who hired out their services to the highest bidder. See also Compton, *A Particular Account of European Adventurers in Hindustan 1784–1803*, pp. 47, 63 and B. K. Sinha, *The Pindaris 1778–1818* (Calcutta, 1971).

[68] See Pemble's introduction to Compton, *European Adventurers in India*, p. x. Shinde's regular infantry numbered 20,000 men, and along with 360 artillery men the total number of soldiers was estimated at 22,000. The Hindustani cavalry amounted to no more than 4,000 men. Pemble considered that Compton had underestimated, at 35,000, the size of Shinde's irregular cavalry. Lewis Ferdinand Smith, an ex-Maratha officer, reckoned that Shinde had 45,000 Maratha horse. Sir John Malcolm who appeared to have had access to detailed returns calculated that the number was 43,000 (excluding freebooters and Pindaris) when the corps was much depleted by desertion and casualties; see also L. No. 70, R. Strachey, Resident with Shinde, to General Hewett, Vice

Farrukhabad, it also included bodies of irregular infantrymen and troopers, chiefly Muslims, who had migrated to Shinde territory following the disbanding of the cavalry forces in Awadh.[69] As in the case of Farrukhabad and Rohilkhand, the assimilation of Rohilla–Afghan troopers into the expanded military establishment of Shinde created a market for horses and integrated Shinde's territory with the wider networks of horse trade in the region. George Thomas, an Irish mercenary who worked for Shinde, observed that Shinde encouraged the trade in horses. This appears to have extended his influence to the jungles of Sindh from where the best supply of horses was obtained. In 1803, after the defeat of Shinde in the second Maratha war, Thomas noted the decline of the horse trade in the region of the Lakheri jungle in Sindh, which had been one of the major supply bases for Shinde.[70]

However, apart from the horse trade, Shinde's army was organized on different principles from those of the Rohilkhand and Farrukhabad states. These polities were perceived by their predominantly Rajput, subordinate populations as alien conquest states and were based on profits derived from trade. In contrast Shinde used his military might to collect land revenue through local intermediaries with relative ease and regularity. A steady flow of land revenue brought a more stable and predictable income than trade, so that Shinde from the very beginning of his rule could maintain a large standing army. But land revenue was often not sufficient to meet all these expenses, and Shinde was very often in arrears with the soldiers' salaries. The more striking

President in Council, 5 Oct. 1811, J. Sarkar (ed.), *Daulat Rao Sindhia and North Indian Affairs, 1810–18: English Records of Maratha History: Poona Residency Correspondence* (14 vols., Bombay 1951), XIV, p. 91. He observed that at the Dussehra spectacle in Shinde's army the number of cavalry regiments far outnumbered the infantrymen.

[69] Broughton, *Letters Written in a Maratha Camp*, p. 66. The Aligols were one such contingent. These were bodies of irregulars, largely Muslim, armed as they wished. They were not considered very disciplined regiments. They had acquired their name from their habit of charging the enemy in a *gol* or mass, and they invoked the aid of Ali before they charged.

[70] Add. 13579. Abstract of George Thomas Papers, Part I, on the North West parts of India, BM. Hereafter Thomas Papers; see also Moorcroft Report. In 1811, Moorcroft made similar observations and attributed the decline in the horse trade to the gradual eclipse of the royal court of Shinde.

difference with the erstwhile Muslim conquest states was that Shinde was not tied to his freshly recruited Rohilla-Afghan cavalrymen by 'tribal', regional or religious bonds. Consequently, he strengthened his otherwise fragile bonds with his troopers by settling them on land and thereby established permanent links with them. Shinde established in Hapur[71] an elaborate system of landholdings for the disabled or worn-out soldiers of his force.[72] Retired soldiers colonized fresh land for Shinde and increased the flow of land revenue which was used to pay his standing army. Shinde's moves in this direction may have been influenced by the Company's Invalid Thanahs in the Bengal and Bihar provinces. But they were in contrast to the regional states of Awadh and Benaras which made no such arrangements, possibly because there was no need to rehabilitate soldiers of the old military class since recruits were now increasingly of peasant origin.

Once again, unlike the Rohilla and Afghan states, Shinde employed European officers to train his troopers in military drill and parade and teach them the use of advanced military technology involving the use of matchlocks and pistols. But Mughal military practices were not entirely given up. From 1780 onwards, in the manner of the Mughal mansabdars, the European officer obtained a jagir to muster and finance his contingent. Like the Mughal mansabdar, he administered his jagir and his contingent assisted him in the collection of revenue. For instance, in 1784, De Boigne, a European officer in Shinde's service, began recruiting two brigades of infantry and artillery for Shinde. To carry on this project he was granted a substantial jagir, which included fifty-two parganas yielding an income of sixteen lakhs of rupees in the fertile Doab region between Aligarh and Delhi. Soon he employed other junior officers to assist him in discharging his duties.[73] In the manner of the Mughal mansabdar, he and his

[71] This formed part of the jagir of General Perron.

[72] H. R. Nevill, *Meerut: A Gazetteer, vol. 4 of the district gazetteers of the United Provinces of Agra and Oudh* (Allahabad, 1904), p. 235. This was a practice adopted by the British for many years. In the Meerut records there are numerous papers giving details of the contracts for clearing waste lands or jungle for the benefit of invalid pensioners who had been settled on landholdings.

[73] Ibid. De Boigne fixed the pay of a sepoy at Rs 5.5 per month. He also offered

staff collected revenue and superintended every detail of their new force. He examined and passed recruits, drilled the raw levies, organized the companies and divisions and selected and appointed native officers. When the muster was complete he chose appropriate uniforms and provided them with armaments. The synthesis of Mughal military practices with European military decorum and fighting skills was most evident in the dress of the Mughal troopers who served De Boigne. They were dressed uniformly in green broadcloth but this was tailored into a Mughal-style long coat which was called *angarkha*.[74] The troopers rode in typical Mughal style on country saddles, which were called *bairarees*, equipped with saddle cloths. But, unlike the average Mughal trooper, they were armed with small matchlocks, troopers' pistols and broadswords, and wore European belts and boots.[75]

Shinde never had any problem hiring European officers because his service was financially attractive for European mercenaries and they were always willing to join his army. Some of these European officers engaged in non-military functions and made extensive profits on their jagirs. For instance, De Boigne derived approximately thirty lakhs of rupees from his jagir and in addition to this raised considerable amounts of money from local salt and customs taxes and from tribute extorted from surrounding chiefs. Moreover, he directly drew a salary of Rs 10,000 a month from this jagir and in addition received a personal commission of two per cent on all revenue collection. In 1797, when he returned to Europe, he carried his personal savings which amounted to Rs 400,000.[76] The extent of the military and economic development in De Boigne's jagir was commented on by Wellesley when he compared

---

attractive incentives to European officers, and many joined his service. Sangster who had recently left the Rana of Gohad's service because he had submitted to Shinde was one of the first to do so. The Scotsman was a man of considerable ingenuity and skilled at casting; in Shinde's service he turned out excellent artillery and soon organized a small army. Fremont, a Frenchman, and the Dutchman, John Hessing, were other Europeans employed by Shinde.

[74] Major Palmer, Resident with Shinde, to Bengal Political Board, 6 Jan. 1796, BC 1796–7, extract Bengal Pol. Consult., 22 Jan. 1796 F/4/9, IOL.

[75] Ibid.

[76] Compton, *European Adventurers in Hindustan*, pp. 68–9, 92.

the jagir to 'an independent French estate on the most valuable part of the Company's frontier'.[77] It is then not a surprise that Shinde's officers always welcomed the setting up of European indigo factories in the Aligarh and Farrukhabad region. This definitely increased the possibility of their making personal profits.[78]

Shinde allowed the European mercenaries to exercise considerable independence of command within the regiments they commanded and this made his army very different from that of Rohilkhand or Farrukhabad. In Shinde's standing army, like the British and French armies of the late eighteenth century, attempts were made to cultivate a strong loyalty to the regiment, and it was the regiment which specified the duties and responsibilities the soldiers were expected to carry out. Grant of landholdings to military pensioners further reinforced, by making more permanent, the links between the soldier and the regiment. This marked a break from the traditions of military service in the region where royal military households forged the loyalty of the soldiers around the person of the Nawab. But this change in military organization suited the troopers of the erstwhile Muslim states of Rohilkhand and Farrukhabad who had taken service with Shinde, for it further promoted their social standing by settling them on landholdings. Moreover, the training they obtained in the use of advanced European technology enchanced their military worth in the region.

BEGUM SAMRU IN SARDHANA, 1780-1830

In the 1760s, the Mughal Emperor Shah Alam gave Sardhana, in the modern district of Meerut, as a jagir to his Austrian military officer Walter Reinhart Sombere. When Reinhart died, this jagir, which yielded an annual revenue of about 90,000 pounds sterling was handed over to his wife Begum Samru.[79] In the 1780s, Begum

[77] M. Martin (ed.) The Despatches, Minutes and Correspondence of the Marquis of Wellesley during the Administration of India (3 vols., London, 1828), III, p. 211.

[78] Stokes, 'Agrarian society and the Pax Britannica' in Stokes, Peasant and the Raj, p. 67.

[79] M. M. Kaye (ed.), The Golden Calm: An English Lady's life in Mughal Delhi—Reminiscences by Emily, Lady Clive Bayley and by her father Sir Thomas Metcalfe

Samru competed with Shinde in recruiting Rohilla-Afghan troopers for she too needed cavalrymen to fight the mounted warriors which included the Mewatis and unemployed bands of Rohilla mercenaries in the region. Even after the decline of Shinde in 1803 Sardhana flourished as an important 'job centre' in north India. The Company allowed Sardhana to continue as an independent jagir on the condition that it would supply cavalrymen to the Company army whenever the need arose. The Begum, taking advantage of this independence, expanded her army and extended her jagir by incorporating additional lands in the Panipat region.[80]

The Begum's political formation in Sardhana was very similar to that of Shinde's polity. Here also, unlike the Rohilla and Afghan conquest states, the army was not hurriedly assembled in the specific political context of war. Once again, like Shinde, the Begum, believed to be of Kashmiri origin,[81] was not perceived as an alien conqueror but was seen as an indigenous ruler exemplifying the tastes and manners of the higher echelons of north Indian Muslim society. Indeed she emphasized her 'Indian' cultural moorings to garner greater social acceptability so as to effectively integrate her ruling house into local society.[82] The emphasis on purdah travel in closed palanquins, the use of Persian and Urdu, and expensive and luxurious silk and brocade attire were some of the external symbols of high status of the upper echelons of society. The Begum adopted all these and not only dined with European male officers clandestinely[83] but also kept her liaisons

---

(Delhi, 1980), p. 111.

[80] H. Wilkinson, *Two Monsoons: The Life and Death of Europeans in India* (London, 1987), pp. 140–3; Compton, *European Adventurers in Hindustan*, pp. 400–10; for an interesting account of Begum Samru see also B. Banerji, *Begum Sumru* (Calcutta, 1925). During the 1790s the Sardhana forces included six infantry battalions, comprised 3,000 men under European officers, several hundred cavalry, and fifteen artillery cannons.

[81] Kaye, *The Golden Calm*, p. 111.

[82] J. Jain, *Begum Sumroo* (Surat, 1976), p. 25. He notes that the Begum always dressed in expensive attire and seated in a palanquin, accompanied her troops to the battle front.

[83] Banerji, *Begum Sumru*, p. 47. On one occasion when Lord Lake, as a gesture of friendship, kissed the Begum's hand, his action was perceived by the army as contrary to notions of Muslim morality and conduct. The Begum saved the situation by her

a closely guarded secret. Her affection for her Irish officer George Thomas was kept secret for fear of the disapproval it might cause among her soldiers. Her liaison with the French officer in her service called Le Vaisseau was enough to incite a major mutiny in her army.[84]

Her popularity in her territory was evident from the considerable regularity with which she managed to extract land revenue[85] and collect tolls. She used all these resources to support her standing army. For instance, approximately one-third of the land revenue supported Sardhana's army. This was a sprawling establishment of 3,371 officers with forty-four guns and was composed of infantry, artillery and cavalry. Three battalions of infantry 1,550 strong were usually stationed at her frontier station in Hansi and Ranya. Her artillery was stationed at Sardhana and the monthly cost of the establishment was about Rs 12,000.[86] The Begum added to her income by collecting tolls and transit duties on goods that passed through her territories by land or by water.[87] These were also spent on maintaining her army.

If the Begum's polity was comparable to that of Shinde, her

presence of mind, remarking to her sipahis, 'Look, this is the way Europeans show respect to their women.'

[84] Ibid., pp. 27–9. The soldiers rallied around an officer called Liegeois who fanned this discontent to his advantage. They determined to defeat both the Begum and her lover. The general disaffection in her regiments made her flee Sardhana along with Le Vaisseau. The rebel troops placed Zafar Yab Khan, the son of Samru by his first wife, as their leader. In this flight from Sardhana, Le Vaisseau at one stage thought that the Begum, to avoid disgrace, had shot herself. He therefore committed suicide.

[85] She collected revenue from Jat cultivators by compulsion as well as credit advances to push the cultivation of cash crops to their limit. Stokes, 'Agrarian society and the Pax Britannica' in Stokes, The Peasant and the Raj, p. 67.

[86] Banerji, Begum Sumru, pp. 140–1.

[87] Abstract statements: Political Consultations 18-6-1832, No. 87, compiled by Rahmat Khan and submitted to Government in 1832, enclosed in letter from W. Fraser, Assistant to the Gov. Gen. to Sec. to Gov. Gen., 31 Aug. 1832, Pol. Consult., 8 Oct. 1832, cited in Banerji, Begum Sumru, p. 141. The net receipts for duties collected on land and water traffic from 1826–7 to 1830–1, after deducting the pay of collecting officers, was as follows: pargana Jewar, land Rs 8, 719. 150 and water Rs 10,062.80; pargana Tappal, land Rs 9,836.11.3 and water Rs 6,465.3; for the ghats of two parganas of Jewar and Tappal the tolls collected amounted to Rs 3,644.3.11; for Kutana they amounted to Rs 822.8.7.

army was also organized in a manner very similar to that of Shinde's regiments. Indeed Begum Samru, like Shinde, had to integrate the 'foreign' Afghan, Rohilla, and Mughal ex-servicemen of earlier polities into the predominantly Hindu society of Jat cultivators she had subordinated to her rule. For this reason she also encouraged her troopers to settle on landholdings. This strengthened her bonds with her troopers and helped in colonizing new land which increased her supply of revenue. In the 1830s, I. K. Hutchinson, the Commissioner of Meerut, noted the decisive superiority of the Begum's jagir to the other jagirs in the area. He attributed it to the encouragement the Begum gave to the cultivation of cash crops like sugarcane.[88] T. C. Plowden, the settlement officer in Meerut in 1840, was also impressed by the jagir of the Begum. He showed that in the last twenty years of her rule the demand averaged Rs 5,86,65 and her collections were Rs 5,67,211.[89]

The Begum's military–political establishment at Sardhana offered another means of acquiring the status which the Afghan and Rohilla ex-servicemen had once acquired in the Mughal Empire or in the Rohilkhand and Farrukhabad states. But more importantly, her army became the vehicle for the upward social mobility of the large population of semi-pastoral and herdsmen communities of Jats, Gujars and Ahirs who lived on her estates in Sardhana, Baraut, Barnawa, Kutana, Budhana, Jawar, Tappal, Dankaur and Pahasu in the Doab, and Badshahpur and Hansi on the western side of Ranya. Some of these communities had settled on land during the Mughal period but still lived with the stigma of their pastoral origin. Being on the lower rungs of both Hindu and Muslim society, political power was a route to higher social standing for them.[90] The Begum's military service, which provided the

[88] L. No. 21, I. R. Hutchinson, Esq., 1st Div. Meerut, to R. H. Hamilton, Meerut Collectorate office, Sardhana, 9 Feb. 1836, Meerut Collectorate Pre-Mutiny Records, Series Part 2, Basta No. 3, vol. 26, Register Copies of Letters submitted to Government Board and Commissioners, July 1834 to Aug. 1835, ARA.

[89] E. T. Atkinson, *Statistical, Descriptive and Historical Account of the North Western Provinces of India* (3 vols.,. Allahabad: NWP and Oudh Govt. Press, 1875–1876, *Gazetteer of North Western Provinces*), III, p. 295.

[90] For the Jat zamindars' aspirations to share political power with the Mughal Emperor

recruits with landholdings, political power, and social status, became a major attraction for these groups.

Her military service became even more popular because the Begum clearly manipulated the aspirations of her recruits who valued the status they and their predecessors had enjoyed in earlier Muslim polities. She adopted Mughal practices so as to be perceived as the restorer of the troopers to the high social status they had always aspired for. In her jagir at Sardhana she recreated the Mughal political ritual of the darbar as the ultimate source of legitimacy. The court was held in one of her many palatial residences at Sardhana, Jalalpur, Meerut, Kinria and Delhi. In these residences she held her darbar and conducted administrative work from behind a curtain. Her recruits sat on the other side to hear her commands.[91] This symbolic arrangement helped to reinforce the relations of power which were further strengthened by the distribution of about five lakhs of revenue on the salary and other expenses of the recruits. The darbar ritual symbolically restored the trooper to his sought-for position in a political structure and thereby strengthened his adherence to the ruling house.

But if Mughal practices were emulated, European military ethics were zealously encouraged as well. Begum Samru, like Shinde, introduced European-style regiments, which emphasized military drill and discipline, and dressed her soldiers in standard uniforms. These were made of dark blue English broadcloth and tailored in the Mughal fashion. To this was added yellow vests with scarlet turbans and waist bands.[92]

Thus Shinde and Samru's military formations marked a break from the Rohilkhand and Farrukhabad states where, as we have seen, loyalties and military discipline were forged around the royal

---

and then to use this power to challenge the state see S. Chandra, 'The 18th century in India: its economy, and the role of the Marathas, the Jats, the Sikhs and the Afghans', S. G. Deuskar Lecture on Indian history, 1982 (CSSS, Calcutta, 1986); R. P. Rana, 'Agrarian revolt in northern India during the late 17th century and early 18th century', *IESHR*, nos. 3 and 4 (July–Dec. 1981), pp. 287–326.

[91] For a description of the darbar see Francklin, *Military Memoirs of George Thomas*, p. 58; also see A. Deanes, *A Tour Through the Upper Provinces of Hindustan Comprising the Period between 1804–1814* (London, 1823), p. 149.

[92] Deane, *Tour through the Upper Provinces*, p. 149.

household. These more advanced political formations further increased the social standing of the Rohilla and Afghan ex-servicemen of earlier polities by not only granting them landholdings and restoring them to the high social status they valued but also training them in European ethics which emphasized the regiment as the basic unit around which loyalties were forged.

THE RECRUITMENT OF REGULAR CAVALRY, 1802–30

In 1802, Company power expanded into the lands of Shinde in the central and western Doab and shared its borders with Samru's estate in Meerut. It soon realized that a peasant army recruited on the basis of an assumed high-caste Hindu identity was less relevant here. There were important military and social reasons for this. First, the new neighbours of the East India Company included the mounted armies of the Marathas, the Pindaris, and the pastoralist and semi-agriculturalist population of Mewatis. In 1802, the Company's increased interference in the regional polities had uprooted these groups from the positions they held in the Indian states of Rohilkhand, Farrukhabad and Shinde territory. A peasant army was not suited to meet the immediate problems of their political conciliation and control and was therefore ineffective in controlling the Company's newly-annexed territories. Secondly, in the 1770s, the Company had opted for a high-caste peasant army because it recruited from territories outside its possessions. At this time recruiting from a peasantry with no previous history of military service avoided the danger of the Company's military techniques being passed on to its enemies. In 1803, R. Frith, the Major of the 4th Cavalry Regiment, expressed this fear when he wrote in his military memorandum about the recruitment of Indians in the Company's artillery corps:

I confess that the very strong and general objection to the employment of natives in the corps of artillery appear to me to rest solely upon one of those maxims which were formed upon correct principles prevalent in the infancy of the Empire in India, and which continued to be received upon trust although they have become inapplicable to the state of that power under its present circumstances....At that early period when British dominion was confined within narrow limits, and were surrounded by powerful and hostile states, with which we were at war,...we had soldiers who were consequently prone to desertion, and who upon quitting the British service, at all events, were likely to return to their native countries and carry with them whatever knowledge they might have acquired of our discipline.[93]

By 1802, the problem was the reverse. The drying up of employment opportunities in the Rohilkhand and Farrukhabad areas due to the decline of the Rohilla and Bangash Afghan states, and the Company's reliance on peasant soldiers had led to a migration of the troopers of these polities into the Maratha territory. The Company could not ignore the flow of men and military knowledge from its territories to the Maratha army, for the Marathas were one of its important political and military competitors. Their reliance on an irregular cavalry not only forced the Company to take cavalry more seriously but it was also necessary to pre-empt the Marathas from recruiting from its territories. The Company attempted to check the migration of troopers to the Maratha army by holding out attractive pay and pension benefits to them.

But more importantly, the events of the first decade of the nineteenth century made the Company reconsider the reliance and trust it placed on its carefully recruited peasant armies. This was a decade of mutinies.[94] The Vellore mutiny in 1806 was followed by the Java mutiny in 1816.[95] In the Bareli riots of 1816 it was the cavalry regiments which proved most useful.[96] The peasant army was gradually being viewed with greater scepticism. Finally, the social structure of the newly acquired region was very different from that of Awadh, Benaras and Bihar. The scanty population and the far-flung nature of revenue holdings made the task of revenue collection and protection of trade routes very difficult. Here, recruiting a peasant army was not a feasible proposition. Besides, the attempt to create a high-caste Hindu

[93] Add. 13856, Wellesley Papers, 'On Military Establishment 1802–1805', BM.

[94] See Barat, Bengal Infantry, pp. 187–290.

[95] For the Vellore mutiny see P. C. Chinnian, The Vellore Mutiny, 1806 (Madras, 1982).

[96] See BC, File No. 17692, Judicial No. 5, vol. 2, 'Report of the committee appointed to enquire into the origin and causes of the disturbances which occurred in the town of Bareli in the beginning of the year 1816 in consequence of the introduction of the Chaukidari system'. Henceforth 'Report on disturbances'.

identity for the army as a basis of popular appeal was less applicable in the Ceded and Conquered Provinces. The relatively small population of Brahmins and the weaker nature of Hindu social hierarchy had made other forums of social mobility more popular. In a region inhabited by Muslims and Hindu pastoral communities, the patronage of nobles and social movements such as Bhakti devotionalism provided a much more appropriate vocabulary of respectability.

The recruiting of a cavalry force was not an easy task for the Company officials. They found it difficult to assimilate the mounted warriors of the Ceded and Conquered Provinces into their regular regiments because it was very difficult to include men with loose and fluctuating loyalties into the Company's tradition of military exclusivity. Moreover, it was particularly difficult to place ex-servicemen of earlier polities at the core of its army. Yet these were the best troopers available for its much-needed cavalry regiments.

From 1802, the Company, very reluctantly, began to assimilate into its military establishment those troopers who had sufficient financial resources to offer securities.[97] In the political turmoil which followed the Rohilla defeat in 1774, the Company had granted Faizulla Khan, the son of Hafiz Rahmat Khan, a jagir in Rampur and most of the wealthy Rohilla aristocracy had migrated to Rampur.[98] Consequently, in 1802, Rampur became an important recruiting zone for the Company.

The flight of the Rohilla capital through its military and craft personnel had transformed Rampur into an important urbanized Rohilla citadel.[99] Hamilton was of the view that the prosperity of Rampur was above all because of

[97] Banerji, *Amar jiban charit katha*, vol. III, p. 58.

[98] Hamilton, *History of the Rohillas*, p. 284.

[99] I am indebted to Dr Ian Derbyshire for information on this section. He sees this as the main cause of Rampur's urbanization. According to him the population of Rampur began to build up to 80,000–100,000 during the early 1790s while the other centres declined. In such circumstances the region's urban profile, which during the 18th century had been unusually balanced at its upper level, became more pronounced; see also E. I. Brodkin, 'British India and the abuses of power: Rohilcund under early Company rule', *IESHR*, vol. X, No. 2 (June 1973), p. 99; W. Hamilton, *A Geographical, Statistical and*

the superior population and consequent cultivation and wealth it derived from the accession of subjects within the three before mentioned years from the circumjacent country as it is natural for men to fly from famine and its inevitable consequence, oppression, to a mild and equal Government and abundance...and in the same proportions as the territory of Fyzoola Khan gained by this circumstance, that of the Vizier lost in its population and consequently in its cultivation and revenue.[100]

Elliott also praised Faizulla Khan for having adopted every means in his power to improve the state of cultivation in his lands. He wrote:

In a few years he so improved the country that the produce was treble or perhaps quadruple the former amount, being prudent in his expenditure. His coffers were well filled and he was enabled to entertain a large proportion of the Afghans of Bareilly, Pilibheet, Ownlah etc., all of whom eagerly flocked to his standard. He secured the affections of his subjects and soldiery during a reign of 21 years and some months.[101]

The political and economic vicissitudes of the late eighteenth century made the Company's military service an attractive option for the Rohilla-Afghans of Rampur for, from the 1790s, Rampuri merchants had suffered losses as the overland trade route from Afghanistan and Persia which passed through the Punjab, Rohilkhand and Rampur to Awadh, the Maratha lands, Jaipur, and the Deccan began to dry up.[102] With declining mercantile opportunities, many of the Rohillas began to invest in land,[103] and service in the Company's army also became very popular. But the Company rarely recruited the small-time merchant-soldier into its cavalry regiments. E. Cunningham, the Captain commanding the 2nd Cavalry Regiment sent to suppress the Bareli

---

Historical Description of Hindustan and the Adjacent Countries (2 vols., London, 1820), I, pp. 429 and 445.

[100] Hamilton, *History of the Rohillas*, p. 284.

[101] Elliott, *Life of Hafiz ool-Mulk*, p. 130.

[102] This was because of the drying up of the royal markets in Awadh and Shinde's country and the Company's increased reliance on Arabian horses from the Persian Gulf; see chapter 6 below for dislocation of trade routes.

[103] E. I. Brodkin, 'Rohilcund from conquest to revolt, 1774–1858', Ph.D thesis, Cambridge University, 1968, pp. 152–3.

riots of 1816, expressed the Company's repugnance for such Rohilla troopers when he wrote:

The Rohillas collected said ... we were once men of consequence. We are now in want of bread and they certainly seemed to think they either did or would possess power to better themselves...I have daily, I may say hourly applications for admission into my Corps from men of the above description. If I tell the applicant there is no vacancy but that he may if he choose wait till there is one which may occur in 3-4 months, he is perfectly satisfied. He will wait that period and longer mortgaging what will be his pay perhaps for two months to the amount of Rs 40 or Rs 50 to support himself at home. But he looks on himself as being provided for. When I marched to Goruckpur in Nov. 1815, I had at least 100 following me without any promise whatsoever.[104]

Once again in 1818, the Collector of Shahjahanpur, recruiting in the Bareli region, refused to enlist those Rohillas who did not possess sturdy horses or an equivalent amount of money. One such Rohilla, Imam Buksh Khan, was refused enlistment because he did not have a horse and on the Collector's insistence that he produce one as a prerequisite for recruitment he produced a 'tatto' (pony).[105]

The Company was keen only to employ Rohillas of wealth and status in its regular cavalry regiments. Durga Das Banerji, a Bengali clerk attached to a Company Regiment, commented on the procedure of cavalry recruitment:

The sawar would have to be present before the English Commander himself and would pay for his recruitment. At the time of making petitions the Commandant would look at him from head to foot. After this searching look the English soldier would ask him, 'Rupiaya maujood hai' [do you have money]. The person would answer, 'Jee khudawund maujood hai' (Yes Lord I do have). If he said he had no money or had less amount he would be turned away. Only being sure about the money the Commander would send him to the Doctor, who would then do the medical test for him.[106]

[104] L. No. 23, E. Cunningham to W. B. Bayley, Sec. to Govt. in the Judicial Deptt., 10 Aug. 1816, BC, File No. 17691, Judicial No. 5, vol. 2, pp. 55–6, F/4/640, IOL.

[105] From Collector of Shahjahanpur to W.H. Trant Esq. Junior, Commissioner of Bareli, 10 May 1818 BRRC, Consult. Farrukhabad 10 Aug. 1818, P/93/33, IOL. He was refused and in his place a sawar, Haqiqat Singh, was appointed. The Company approved of this arrangement.

Durga Das explained the significance of the often repeated phrase 'Rupiaya maujood hai'. According to him every applicant for the job of a sawar brought approximately Rs 250–375 in cash and was expected to buy his own horse. The government did not spend its money on buying a horse for the sawar. If the sawar received a horse from the government he paid Rs 200 for it and an additional Rs 70-80 for the accessories. The government was always willing to give small loans to the recruits to meet their expenses of buying the accessories and the recruit subsequently repaid such loans from his salary.[107] This method of recruitment resulted in most of the troopers being wealthy Rohillas and Afghans of Rampur. This was reflected in the social background of two Rohilla cavalrymen of the 2nd Rohilla Cavalry Regiment, who were involved in suppressing the Bareli riots of 1819. The two brothers, 'Woadd' Khan and Nujoo Khan, were grandsons of Sheikh Qubir, a jagirdar of Etawah, and their father lived in Rampur. During the Bareli riots these brothers were praised for their loyalty and fidelity to the Company.[108]

The Company never experienced any difficulty in attracting the landed class of wealthy Rampuri Rohillas who, once in Company service, used their political connections to protect their wealth in Rampur. However, a recruitment method which looked for the wealthy and the rich was bound to attract only a limited section of the Rohillas. From 1795, when the cavalry troops were first formed into regiments, till 1824, the strength of the regular cavalry regiments had increased only from six to eight. The proportion which the cavalry bore to the infantry in 1824 remained one to eight.[109] This was by no standards sufficient to meet the requirements of the region.

However, the Company's friendship with the Nawab of Rampur proved very useful and compensated for the deficiency in its cavalry

[106] Banerji, *Amar jiban charit katha*, III, p. 58.

[107] Ibid., p. 58.

[108] E. Cunningham, Captain commanding 2nd Cavalry, to Sir E. Colebrooke, Bart., C. Elliott and T. Perry, 10 Aug. 1816, BC, File No. 17692, Judicial No. 5, vol. 2, 'Report on disturbances in Bareli', p. 47.

[109] Maj. Gen. Shahid Hamid, *So They Rode and Fought* (Kent, UK, 1983), pp. 16–17.

regiments. For the Company relied on the support of the Rampur state cavalry in case of any eventuality. The Rampur state's Rohilla cavalry displayed its outstanding show of loyalty and support to the British during the 1857 mutiny. Yusuf Ali Khan, the Nawab of Rampur, not only suppressed the Moradabad and Bareli rebels but virtually ruled these two districts. In 1857, the Rampur state army and the Company's loyal cavalry regiments, which had hither-to remained on the fringe of its military set-up, played a crucial role in quelling the disturbances caused by its disaffected peasant soldiers.

Chapter 6

Irregular Cavalry, Eurasian Officers and the Company, 1802–1840

The Company yielded the most to indigenous military practice in the regions around Delhi where the charisma of Mughal authority was still very strong. Here, its growing demand for irregular cavalry[1] was met by incorporating the Rohilla and Afghan troopers, some of whom had served Shinde and Begum Samru, as well as through the recruiting practices of the Mughal Empire. To a great extent the Company's policy was influenced by the prevalence of a similar practice in the contemporary Indian states of Shinde and Samru. Major R. Frith, the main architect of the military experiment in the Ceded and Conquered Provinces, observed that the Company was trying to compete with these Indian states in recruiting the soldiers of the erstwhile Muslim polities. In 1802 he wrote:

The Company's service holds out more substantial and permanent advantages to military men than any other in India or in the world. Of this the natives are by no means insensible. When the points are conceded to them of allowing them to ride, dress and accouter themselves in their own fashion we should entice back many of the inhabitants of our own country who now fill the armies of the native princes. For few of them would remain in a foreign service who could obtain more advantageous employment at home.[2]

[1] In military terminology 'irregular cavalry' referred to a contingent of troopers hurriedly assembled for war. They were not employed permanently and were dismissed once the need for them was over. But the Company, as this chapter shows, used the irregulars to settle its newly-acquired territory after their military function ended.

[2] Add. 13856, Wellesley Papers, BM.

Frith was optimistic that the incorporation of the ex-servicemen of Samru and Shinde would 'also supply the Company with the local knowledge of these countries. This would be of greatest use in times of war against these states.'[3]

These concessions to Mughal military custom also stemmed from the Company's perception of Afghans and Rohillas as offshoots of oppressive Muslim states. As late as 1820, William Moorcroft, the horse superintendent of the Company and a key figure in recruiting the irregular army in the western and central Doab, expressed such ideas about Muslim warriors. He noted in his journal:

Musalmans who came into the country as conquerors and reaped the fruits of the soil by the bands of Hindu peasantry disdain other occupations than the sword.[4]

To ensure their loyalties it became essential to relocate them in their indigenous military tradition and give them a secure basis of subsistence.

From 1802 the Company began to shape the military culture of the Ceded and Conquered Provinces to suit its military and political requirements. In this process it benefited most from the services of European and Eurasian officers who had served the late eighteenth-century Indian states and were experienced in dealing with Mughal troopers. George Thomas, James Skinner and William Gardner were three such officers who formed the bridge which connected indigenous military convention to the Company's military practice. Even though Thomas was never directly employed by the Company he assisted it indirectly by laying the foundation of a military tradition in the Aligarh–Haryana region which was later expanded by Skinner. But changing circumstances enabled Skinner to extend these practices of recruitment and resettlement over a much larger area. This was because from 1802, after the defeat of Shinde, the Company was saddled with the task of

---

[3] Ibid.

[4] W. Moorcroft, 'From Srinagar to Nahr', from February 4 to 23, pp. 84–5, MSS Eur. D 236 A (I) 1820, Journal No. 1, IOL.

resettling vast tracts of land in Haryana and Skinner's troopers were best suited for this task.

GEORGE THOMAS IN INDIA, 1781–1804

George Thomas was a pioneer in the re-creation of the Mughal military tradition in the Delhi area. He first arrived in India in a British warship in 1781–2 and was in service with Begum Samru from 1787 till 1792. In 1793 he worked with Appakandarao, a Maratha chief who had separated from Shinde, who granted him the parganas of Panipat, Sonepat, and Karnal as military jagir. From the revenue of these parganas he maintained a contingent of 2,000 infantry, 200 cavalry and sixteen pieces of field artillery.[5] In 1798, after a disagreement with the Maratha chief, Thomas left his service and settled in Jyjur in the Haryana district.

His hitherto unused private papers were written during his stay in India in the 1790s. They contain valuable information which throw light on developments around Delhi in the period which followed the decline of the regional courts of Rohilkhand, Farrukhabad and Shinde. In 1802, Thomas handed his papers to William Francklin for organization. But he did not live to see the work finished. Soon after Thomas' death in 1804, Francklin passed these papers to the British government and they are now held in the British Museum.[6]

These papers reveal that it was in Haryana that Thomas started re-creating the link between military service and landholding. Haryana was strategically located on the borders of the fertile tracts of Punjab and the land of the Islamicized Jat tribe of Bhattis and shared the frontier with the Lakheri jungle. In the period of the Delhi Sultanate and the Mughal Empire, Haryana had enjoyed agricultural prosperity. The canal irrigation of Firoz Shah Tughluq had been continued by the subsequent Mughal Emperors

[5] Francklin, *Military Memoirs of George Thomas*, p. 48; see also M. Hennessy, *The Rajah of Tipperary* (London, 1971).

[6] Add. 13, 579, Abstract of George Thomas Papers, Part I, on the north-west parts of India. These were papers delivered to Government and committed to the charge of William Francklin by the late George Thomas for organization, BM. Hereafter Thomas Papers.

and this had made the district agriculturally very productive.[7] Mughal Haryana yielded an annual revenue of approximately fourteen lakhs of rupees.[8] Moreover, Haryana straddled the principal trade route from the north-west to the southern provinces and this had contributed to the income of the land.[9] However, in the late eighteenth century, Haryana was in a state of political and economic flux. In this period the Jat power in Haryana and western Doab was threatened by the growing strength of the Marathas who by 1770 had annexed the greater portion of the Gangetic Doab. Meanwhile another enemy appeared in the person of the Mughal minister, Najaf Khan. In 1774 the Jats suffered a defeat at his hands and they were expelled from their territory in the western Doab. These political disturbances adversely affected the traffic on the trade route which passed through Haryana and the western Doab region. The maintenance of the canals which the Mughals had built was also neglected. In the 1790s, Thomas reported that they were in ruins and the people dealt with the scarcity of water by digging wells in the district.[10] But this shortage of water had a detrimental effect on the district's agricultural prosperity and in 1802 the annual revenue slumped to one lakh per annum.[11] However, the pastures in Haryana were good because of a special grass which was very healthy for the cattle. Thomas reported in his papers that 'the region produced the largest supply of forage to be seen in any part of Asia.'[12] This continued to sustain its pastoral community of Jats and Ahirs who were always well armed with lance, sabre and matchlock to brave the incursions

---

[7] Extract, Pol. Letter from Bengal, 7 Feb. 1809, BC, File No. 7014, pp. 27–8, F/4/305, IOL.

[8] Thomas Papers.

[9] Ibid.

[10] Ibid. People had resorted to digging wells as deep as 120–50 feet. Each district had one or two tanks as well for the storage of water. The number of wells varied according to the requirements of each village and the investment the inhabitants were willing to make. At Hissar there were 300 wells, at Hansi 30, at Mahim 100, at Suhana 6 and some smaller villages and towns had two to five wells.

[11] Ibid.

[12] Ibid.

of their 'unsettled' neighbours—the Gujars, Mewatis, Bhattis, and the Rohilla and Afghan mercenaries.[13]

Thomas realized the benefits he could derive from a region so constituted. His estimate was that a proper investment in Haryana would increase the revenue to six crores and five lakhs of rupees. In addition, he was optimistic about the recruitment of the indigenous population for his army and the use of the region as a buffer against invaders from the north-west. He wrote in his papers about the projected role of his army:

Our force augmented without incurring any new expense to Government 50,000 Regular Infantry and like number of Cavalry. We crush all our enemies beyond a possibility of their being able to hurt us in future. We complete a strong western frontier almost impregnable to an invading army ... we obtain a certain and plentiful supply of bullocks, horses and camels for the future demand of our armies in India.[14]

All these advantages made Thomas choose Haryana as his home. The country he possessed extended approximately 200 miles from north to south and the same distance from east to west. To the north it was bounded by the possessions of the Jat chieftains Sahib Singh and Lal Singh, on the north-west by the recalcitrant Bhatti 'tribe'[15] and on the west by the dominions of Bikaner. South-east of his lands was the pargana of Dadri and north-east were the cities of Rohtak and Panipat. Thomas chose Hansi as his capital.[16]

A region surrounded by hostile 'unsettled' and recalcitrant neighbours was best settled by the army. Even the Mughals had based their power on the fort of Hansi and had projected their influence into the surrounding region. In the late eighteenth century Thomas revived this policy. He noted in his memoirs:

[13] Ibid.

[14] Ibid.

[15] Ibid. The Bhattis were Rajputs and Jats whose ancestors had migrated from Jaisalmer about 600 years earlier, accepted Islam as their religion, and settled as agriculturists and pastoralists west of Haryana. They had chosen Fatehabad as their capital. But this shift towards a sedentary existence had not changed their habits; they occasionally foraged in neighbouring territory for food, cattle and fresh pasture land.

[16] Ibid.

I rebuilt the walls of the city ... and repaired the fortifications...as for the last 16 years they had been entirely deserted ... procured 5,000–6,000 people to whom I allowed every lawful indulgence.[17]

He soon built a strong army and manufactured his own military equipment. Narrating his achievements in his papers he wrote:

I now judged that nothing but force of arms could maintain me in my authority....I therefore cast my own artillery, commenced making muskets, matchlocks and powder, purchased large quantities of ammunition and in short made the best preparation for carrying on offensive and defensive war. Till at length having gained a capital and country bordering on the Seikh territories, I wished to put myself in a capacity when a favourable opportunity should arise of attempting the conquest of Punjab and aspired to the honour of planting the British standard on the banks of Attock.[18]

In the 1790s, Haryana became a 'military labour market' for the Jat, Rohilla and Pathan aspirants. Thomas' service drew an enthusiastic response from the Jat and Rohilla men as it provided military employment very close to their native villages. Moreover, the opening of this new employment centre increased their bargaining position in the armies of Shinde and Amir Khan. In this period, Thomas was reported to have an army of eight battalions of infantry amounting in all to 6,000 men. In addition he possessed fifty pieces of cannon, 1,000 cavalry and 1,500 Rohillas with about 2,000 men who garrisoned his different forts.[19] He created a permanent link with the sipahis by granting pensions to the widows, children, and nearest relations of soldiers who died or were killed in service.[20] These pensions, amounting to Rs 40,000 per annum, were paid every six months to the nearest relative of the deceased officer or soldier.[21] The granting of pensions on a regular basis benefited his territory as the sipahis invested their money in it and colonized new lands.

The presence of Thomas in Haryana had other important consequences as well. One of the most significant of these was that

[17] Francklin, *Memoirs*, p. 93.
[18] Thomas Papers.
[19] Francklin, *Memoirs*, p. 219.
[20] Ibid., p. 94.
[21] Ibid. The pension was about half the soldier's pay.

communications were established with the neighbouring 'tribe' of Bhattis.[22] This was of extreme significance because in the late eighteenth century, the Bhatti raids had made this region a virtual *terra incognita*. The cordiality which Thomas established with the Bhattis curtailed their raids into his land. The nature of the agreement between Thomas and the Bhattis is not very clear; nevertheless, it is significant because later Skinner further developed this contact. Moreover, the accommodation with the Bhattis brought to light the significant role the Bhatti lands could play in the development of Haryana. It was soon obvious that their territory was fertile and could serve as an important resource for forage and supplies for an army based in Hansi. The new cordiality with the Bhattis and the consequent investments of the sipahis who were encouraged to stay permanently in Haryana, revived the region. In the first decade of the nineteenth century, the revenue of the region which had slumped from a Mughal high of rupees fourteen lakh per annum to a low of one lakh rupees in the late eighteenth century, showed an upward trend;[23] it yielded an annual revenue of over two lakh rupees and 253 villages were reported to be inhabited.[24]

JAMES SKINNER, 1778–1841

In 1802, when Britain declared war on Shinde and the peasant armies of the Gangetic plains proved incapable of meeting the cavalry onslaught of the Marathas, the Company began to enlist officers of British origin, including Eurasians, serving Indian powers. The idea was to use their expertise to organize its irregular cavalry.[25] The Company had belatedly accepted the fact that hereafter British as well as Eurasian irregular officers were to be in the forefront

[22] Thomas Papers. Thomas invited the Bhatti Raja for talks, who accepted the invitation and stayed with Thomas. This initiated a friendly dialogue with the hitherto unknown 'unsettled' Bhatti 'tribe'; see also BC, File No. 7014, F/4/305, IOL.

[23] Francklin, *Memoirs*, p. 53.

[24] Thomas Papers. The total number of villages inhabited in the Mughal period was 950.

[25] James B. Fraser, *Military Memoirs of Lt. Col. James Skinner* (2 vols., London, 1955), I, pp. 251–8.

of imperial expansion. Hereafter it never experienced any problem in recruiting Eurasian officers for its army, for the war with the British had made Shinde and his French officers suspicious of men of British origin serving in the Maratha army and many of them were sacked. This made a pool of officers available to the Company.[26]

James Skinner, the son of a Scotsman married to a Rajput woman, was one such officer who left Shinde's service and joined the service of the East India Company. The use of Eurasians like Skinner in the forefront of imperial expansion in the Delhi–Haryana region presented a strong contrast to their marginalized existence on the fringe of mid-nineteenth century British society in Bengal.[27] The comparatively small European population in the Ceded and Conquered Provinces made the narrow racist bias against Eurasians less common and made it possible for them to find employment in the Bengal Army.[28] As a matter of fact, the regions where European racial exclusiveness had not yet taken hold coincided with the areas of high Mughal culture and tradition— the core of the Mughal Empire in Delhi and its surroundings. These were the regions where the shadow of the Mughal Empire still lingered and Mughal military ethic, which had placed troopers in the core of the army and had accorded their commandants high status in the royal court society, was still much valued. In such circumstances it was quite natural for Skinner to begin using

[26] Ibid.

[27] Ballhatchet, *Race, Sex and Class under the Raj*, p. 6. He argues that racial feeling among the British became more explicit and aggressive in the course of the 19th century and reached its peak during Lord Curzon's viceroyalty (1899–1905).

[28] See Laird (ed.), *Bishop Heber in Northern India*; T. Twining, *Travels in India a Hundred Years Ago* (London, 1893); M. Archer and T. Falk, *The Arts and Adventures of James and William Fraser 1801–35* (London, 1989). This is the impression which emerges from the accounts of travellers like Bishop Heber and William Twining who travelled from Calcutta into the Ceded and Conquered Provinces. They saw east India as the centre of British culture but noted that this was not true of the Ceded and Conquered Provinces. In these regions the Europeans were more acculturated in the manners of high-class Muslim society and had adopted many of their customs, especially the hookah and Mughal cuisine. This was an impression which also emerged from the fact that in 1815 William Fraser, an Englishman of 'pure blood', could travel around and relate with friendliness to Eurasians like James Skinner.

Mughal practices in building his military corps in the region. His period of service in Shinde's military establishment, where similar Mughal practices were already being emulated, drew his attention to their potential. But in the Company's service Skinner was often disappointed in his plans. This was because the Company remained biased against Eurasian officers and these prejudices surfaced each time it had to give its approval to any request or suggestion put forward by Skinner. For instance, in 1803, Skinner's request for a jagir in Aligarh was turned down. This was because the Court of Directors, sceptical of the Eurasians, regarded him as a Britisher and thus not eligible to possess a jagir in India.[29] Instead of the jagir he was awarded a pension of Rs 300 per month. A disappointed Skinner wrote in his memoirs:

I got a letter from Col. Malcolm that as I was a British subject, Sir George Barlow would not allow me to hold lands. I was thus deprived of the reward which I had so dearly gained. Lord Lake with great difficulty got me the pension of a Lt. Col. which was Rs 300 month and my brother Rs 120 .... I gave myself to despair and began to exert myself with the small sum I had saved and began to trade.[30]

It was ironic that here the Company chose to enforce the regulations of service applicable to British officers even though it refused him a commissioned rank because of his Eurasian status.[31]

Skinner's frustrations were compounded when, in the period of comparative peace in 1803–8, his contingent was reduced in size. In this period the Company, weary of the roving bands of unemployed Rohilla-Afghan troopers, began to direct their energies to agriculture. The Governor-General's regulation of 1805 asked all subjects of the Company's newly acquired territory who were in the military service of foreign Indian states to return to the Company's dominions.[32] It also promised to compensate

[29] Photo. Eur. 173, James Skinner 1778–1841, p. 125, IOL; hereafter Skinner's Memoirs.

[30] Ibid.

[31] It was only after 1828 that Eurasians were considered eligible for commissions or for high military honours like the Order of the Bath.

[32] Draft of regulation 1805 by A. Seton, Agent to Gov.-Gen. in Ceded Provinces, 7 June 1805, extract of revenue letter from Bengal in Deptt. of the Ceded and Conquered

them adequately for any loss they might suffer in making this transfer of residence. The compensations included attractive offers of landholdings or payments in cash. The same year Lieutenant Colonel J. Malcolm, the Resident in Delhi and a staunch supporter of this policy, wrote to Wellesley:

The aggregate number of horse that have come over from the enemy and are now in the employment of the English Government in Hindustan may be estimated at about 6,000. With this body are many officers of high reputation for whose liberal provision the British faith is already pledged. Several of those leaders who came over at an early period have already obtained jaidads to support their quota. I would recommend jaidads should be given for the maintenance of most of the remainder.[33]

Later in the year, the Court of Directors sanctioned this plan and allotted the ex-servicemen of earlier polities jagirs which yielded revenue estimated at six lakhs and fifty thousand rupees per annum, in the districts west of the Jamuna.[34] In 1806, a Committee met to decide the claims of those risaldars who had fought for the Company during the 1802 war. It decided to grant them landholdings in lieu of personal pay and compensation for horses killed during the war. Landholdings were granted in the districts of Panipat, Delhi, Agra and Dehra Dun and military colonies of Muslim warriors were permanently settled in these regions.[35]

Provinces, 7 June 1805, BC, File No. 3526, extract Bengal Rev. Consult. 23 July 1806, p. 31, F/4/183, IOL.

[33] Extract of a letter from Lieutenant-Colonel Malcolm, Resident in Delhi, to Marquis Wellesley, 28 June 1805, Home Miscellaneous Series 88, pp. 171–82, IOL. Malcolm justified his plan and was of the view that the wasteland west of the Jamuna would be considerably improved if the Company settled troopers in the region. He suggested that lands should be given at a computation of Rs 15 or Rs 20 to each horseman on condition that if they were called out for military service an additional Rs 10 would be paid monthly to each man as long as the service continued.

[34] Ibid.

[35] Proceedings of a committee held by order of Lord Lake, the Commander-in-Chief, to investigate and report on claims for remuneration for horses lost by irregular troops in the service of Government agreeable to general orders 22 Feb. 1806, submitted by Lieutenant Colonel R. Frith to Board of Rev., 24 March 1806, BRWP, Consult. Delhi 15 August 1825, vol. 56, UPSA.

However, in 1809, the social and political dynamics of the Ceded and Conquered Provinces once again turned the tables in favour of the experiment of raising irregular forces through Skinner. The Company soon revoked its decision to settle unemployed troopers of earlier polities on land as it soon realized that it needed these troopers to meet its requirements for cavalry warfare in the region. Between 1809 and 1824 the Company fought mounted armies of Pindaris and Marathas. All these war fronts centered on the Ceded and Conquered Provinces and efficient cavalry regiments were required to fight all these enemies. Moreover, in 1809, the settlement of Haryana and parts of the Aligarh district recently conquered from Shinde became a major concern for the Company. The acquisition of these lands extended the Company's borders to the Punjab. Its territory now incorporated the lands of the Bhattis and stretched as far as Bhatinda. The defence of this new frontier became even more important due to the Company's hostility to Ranjit Singh. Until 1809, the Company had supported the local chief of Haryana, Abdus Summund Khan, in the management of the district and had left the frontier defence to him. But now it disbanded his army and occupied the military outpost of Hansi extending its hold as far as Karnal. In this territory the Company stationed its own military to face the threat of Punjab, Sindh and the Bhattis.[36] A. Seton,

Particular statement showing the grants made to native chiefs lately in the service of the British Government.

Risaldar	Village	Total provision by jagir (bighas)
Faizulla Khan	Dhansauli in Panipat	2,142
Meer Fazal Ali	Sikri & 5 villages in Sonah	2,185
Meer Hassan Ali	Culwaka & 2 villages in Sonah	1,749.5
Kullundar Shah Khan	Mandepur & 2 villages in Kandli Palun	1,552
Meer Rustam Ali	Agra Kheera & 3 villages in pargana Panipat	1,631
Azim Khan	Agra Distt.	2,600
Ghulam Mohi–uddin Khan	Agra Distt.	3,000
Khwajah Amaunullah	Agra Distt.	2,230
Meer Karimullah	Poohunpur in Haveli Paullum	1,200
Khuda Baksh Beg	Agra Distt.	2,000
Shaikh Mullu	Saharanpur Distt.	3,850
Arab Shah Khan	Village of Sahaika in pargana Sukerpur in Doon	1,800

[36] Extract. Pol. Letter from Bengal, 7 Feb. 1809, BC, File No. 7014, p. 31, F/4/305, IOL.

the first British Resident in Delhi, in a letter to his assistant, E. Gardner, suggested the important role Skinner could play in the Company's new military build-up in Haryana. He wrote:

Captain Skinner who commands a Corps of Irregular Horse in Kurnaul is directed to meet Gardner at Rohtuck ... augment his Corps to 800 men as a species of troop best calculated for service in that country and affording means of employing some of the warlike inhabitants of the districts to be occupied.[37]

The first indication of Skinner's surfacing from political obscurity came in 1809 when Seton converted his pension, which he received in cash, to a jagir grant in Aligarh. This was soon followed by Skinner being asked to recruit a force in the Saharanpur district so as to meet the Sikh threat. From 1809 to 1816 Skinner was very actively recruiting troopers from the districts of Aligarh, Saharanpur, Agra, Delhi, Rohilkhand and the western Doab.[38] From Aligarh region alone he recruited as many as 1,700 troopers.[39] Throughout these years Skinner's jagir in Aligarh and his military headquarters in Hansi formed the base of his activities.

Soon Skinner's regiments came to perform an important ideological role as well. They became a significant forum through which Skinner began to build a new form of legitimacy for Company rule. Ironically, Skinner constructed this legitimacy by incorporating into his regiments symbols of legitimacy which the Mughals had popularized in the region, and which had continued to provide credibility to the eighteenth-century Indian polities. Over a period of time, the images of Mughal courtly splendour, valour, ritual, deference, deportment, decorum and etiquette had come to define rank and social status in north India. Further, Mughal political rituals had continued to legitimize the rule of the Indian polities that had mushroomed after the decline of the

---

[37] Ibid., 19 April 1809, p. 44.

[38] 'Skinner's Memoirs', pp. 111–12. Skinner reported that he recruited 1,700 troopers from Aligarh. Most of them were his old comrades from Perron's service, who had now returned to their homes in the western Doab; also see, A copy of correspondence and proceedings on the use of Skinner's Horse and similar Irregular Horse, Mil. Records File No. 30 A, L/MIL/5/378, IOL.

[39] Ibid.

Mughal court in Delhi. Skinner, similarly, showed a keen interest in Mughal political rituals and cultural norms.

In re-creating the military–political tradition of an earlier era Skinner clearly manipulated the aspirations of his troopers who measured *izzat* and martial status against that held by their predecessors in earlier polities, and in particular, the Mughal Empire. He adopted both the images of Mughal courtly splendour, decorum, and etiquette as well as Mughal military skills and techniques of warfare. The criterion adopted by Skinner for the restoration to rank and status in this military tradition at Hansi was similar to the one adopted by the Mughal mansabdar. Rank and status were not only determined by the clan leadership of the recruits but also by the number of troopers and horses a recruit brought with him. He gave the rank of risaldar to anyone who came with 100 horses and that of naib risaldar to one who brought with him sixty horses. Those with thirty and twenty horses were designated jamadár and *dafadar* respectively.[40] In this sense Skinner's organization proved to be a middle stage between the Mughal military system and the system of ranks adopted later in the British cavalry regiments. These risaldars were stationed on Skinner's estate which stretched from the district of Aligarh to Hansi in Haryana. In 1809, there were twenty-two risalas stationed on Skinner's estate with a combined strength of 3,000 troopers.[41] On an average, the monthly expense of each risala was Rs 2,433[42] and approximately Rs 53,526 was spent on Skinner's regiments every year. But the region benefited from this military establishment because much

---

[40] *Between Battles: The Album of Col. James Skinner (with introduction and notes by M. Archer)* (London, 1982), introduction. This system was similar to the Mughal system of assigning rank in relation to the number of troopers a mansabdar could muster.

[41] A. Seton, Resident in Delhi, to Mil. Deptt., 21 Aug. 1815, extract Secret letter from Bengal, 21 Aug. 1815, a copy of correspondence and proceedings on the use of Skinner's Horse and similar irregular horses, Mil. Records, File No. 30 A, L/MIL/5/378, IOL.

[42] L. No. 14, A. Seton, Resident in Delhi, to N.B. Edmonstone, Chief Sec. to Govt., 20 May 1809, BC, File No. 7014, extract Bengal Pol. Consult., 20 May 1809, pp. 116–17, F/4/305, IOL, Abstract Statement of one month's pay for one risala of Captain Skinner's cavalry.1 Risaldar, Rs 80; 1 Naik, Rs 50; 1 Jamadar, Rs 45; 1 Werdie Major, Rs 35; 1 Nicharchee, Rs 28; 1 Vakil, Rs 25; 5 Dafadars, Rs 20 each; 100 Sawars, Rs 28 each; 2 Bhishtis, Rs 20 each; *Total* Rs 2,433.

of this money circulated in the territory since the risaldars invested their savings there.

In the manner of Shinde, Begum Samru and George Thomas, Skinner also began to settle his troopers on land. He thereby stabilized Company rule in the region. Each soldier on his discharge was allotted 100 bighas of land.[43] On the basis of jagirs granted by Skinner groups of Jats and Gujars often started their career of upward social mobility. They began as cultivators on his farm and very often also offered to serve in his irregular cavalry. The farm acted as as a major recruitment base for Skinner. An immense amount of detail survives on some individuals because of the paintings drawn for the Company by William Fraser. For instance, Hurdut and Kohar, pictured in one of the most important of Fraser's folios, stand as representative examples of men who had come to enlist in Skinner's Horse. William Fraser, in a duplicate painting (plate 3) identified the figure on the left as 'Hurdut, by birth a Jat of Puthur village in the Paneeput district'. He was drawn in his village garb, a pitchfork of wood and a hoe for cutting thorns in his hand. His companion, with a female buffalo, identified by Fraser as Kohar, was a *gwala* or milkman. Before enlisting both these men had been working on Skinner's farm at Dhana. Apart from these men there are two paintings spaced over a period of three years, which show this transition in the status of Umee Chund, a resident of Datchour in Karnal district (plates 7 and 8).

From these contemporary paintings of Skinner's recruits one can discern the gradual process by which Skinner incorporated Mughal cultural symbols into his regiments. The introduction of these Mughal cultural norms into his regiments reinforced his credibility and created legitimacy for British rule in the region. The paintings reflect a three-stage process by which individuals achieved the prestigious position of a cavalryman. In some paintings we see Ahirs, Jats, and Gujars in their original condition as herdsmen presenting themselves to Skinner for recruitment. As we have seen, Skinner seems to have emulated the dress and deportment

[43] Extract Pol. Letter from Bengal, 21 Oct. 1820, BC, File No. 20909, p. 2, F/4/772, IOL.

of a Mughal courtier and nobleman and his troopers appear in uniforms tailored like the Mughal court dress, the angarkha. To this was added the other accessories of a nobleman's uniform: jewellery, a flowing *chadar* (long scarf), cummerbund (waist band), ornate headgear, the sword and the spear, *hookah* and jewel-bedecked horses. The angarkha was always yellow in colour. This was very similar to the saffron dress of the Rajput soldiers and it appears that this colour was deliberately chosen to keep alive the memory of the valiant Rajput tradition.[44] The close association between the status of a trooper and that of a courtier was nowhere better reflected than in the famous scroll, now in the possession of the India Office Library (plate 4), which shows a court procession of Akbar II, probably on the occasion of Id or Ramadan. In this painting Mughal courtiers and noblemen mingle freely with Skinner's recruits. This was indeed a big leap for the Jat, Gujar, and Ahir pastoral communities who had so far remained on the fringe of the Mughal political tradition. Finally, in the third stage, recruits were taught military discipline in order to enhance their indigenous fighting skills. For instance, soldiers were trained to use the matchlock while mounted on ornately decorated horses and were also issued with western-style boots while at the same time the Mughal cavalry exercise of tent-pegging was continued (plate 5).

By the amalgamation of Mughal and European military ethics Skinner, it seems, attempted to construct a new idiom of legitimacy for the Company. This new cultural idiom through and by which British authority was to be represented was based on a re-invention of the Mughal military tradition in a new form which suited the political and military interests of the Company. A group of

[44] Philip Mason, *Skinner of Skinner's Horse: a Fictional Portait* (London: Deutsch, 1979), pp. 114–15. He notes that the yellow dress, because of which the men came to be called the Yellow Boys, was modelled on the dress of mansabdars and courtiers of Jaipur state, which had supplied a large number of noblemen and courtiers to the Mughals; see also Busawan Lal, *Ameerood-daulah Muhammad Ameer Khan*, p. 316. Ameer Khan, on observing that the Rathors in the service of Man Singh of Jaipur were dressed in a uniform of yellow cloth expressed an awareness of the cultural significance this colour had in north Indian society. When the Rajputs advanced towards his army, and challenged his forces, he was reported to have commented: 'adorning of yellow dress by the Rajputs indicated their determination to fight.'

Skinner's recruits painted by Fraser illustrates the re-invented Mughal military tradition very well. The painting shows the transition to the coveted position of a Skinner trooper very vividly (plate 6). Skinner was clearly proud of the contrast between the recruits when they first arrived straight from their villages and their appearance after they had joined the regiment and were in uniform. Fraser has identified the names and villages of some of the recruits shown in plate 6.

Once again with a view to benefiting from the Mughal symbols of legitimacy, Skinner re-created the Mughal political ritual of the darbar at Hansi. But even though the spectacle of the darbar was retained, its character was changed to suit the political and military needs of the East India Company. In order to forge long-lasting ties with his troopers, Skinner, in sharp contrast to the invincible Mughal Emperors, adopted an easy and relaxed approach to his troopers. In this regard he adopted the line of the Farrukhabad nawabs, who encouraged a casual relationship with their soldiers. In his darbar he sat under a canopy with his household servants standing behind him and his soldiers squatted in long lines on either side.[45] Here, he showed a personal interest in his troopers and discussed their problems with them. His recruits took oaths on his sword which soon assumed the symbolic importance comparable to the 'colours' of the Company's peasant regiments.[46] At festivals and other important occasions Skinner made a break even from this informal norm and slipped away to serve the humblest recruit with his own hands.[47] It is here that one can discern an attempt to gradually break out of the Mughal paradigm of legitimacy by re-inventing the Mughal military–political tradition for representing British authority in India.

Skinner's popularity increased because his regiments provided income and status not only to the soldiers of the 'old military class' of Afghans, Rohillas and Pathans but also to Hindu and Muslim pastoral communities such as the Jats, Gujars and Mewatis.

[45] For a picture of Skinner's darbar see Archer, *Between Battles*.

[46] Kaye, *The Golden Calm*, p. 25.

[47.] Archer, *Between Battles*, introduction.

They could remove the stigma of their pastoral background by enlisting in his regiments and aspiring to the rank of Kshatriya and ashraf. The loosely-bonded mobile Jat, Gujar and Mewati communities of the Delhi territories had long looked for positions and status in established polities such as the Mughal Empire. Some of them had managed to fulfil their political ambitions in the eighteenth-century Indian states of Bharatpur (itself Jat), Awadh, Farrukhabad and Rohilkhand. For instance in the Farrukhabad state, the Mewatis provided protection to merchants passing on the roads by levying a small fee called *rusum*. In return for this fee they held themselves responsible for their free and undisturbed passage.[48] But in the early nineteenth century, the decline of Indian political centres, like Farrukhabad, and the Company's repugnance for mobile social groups caused them once again to look for new patrons. Skinner's re-invented Mughal military tradition was even more attractive because it was not only closer to the courtly culture in its etiquette, dress and mannerisms but also synthesized western military technology and routine.

From 1809 onwards, the political eclipse of Shinde and the increasing efforts of the Company to extinguish the power of Amir Khan further reduced employment opportunities available to Rohilla-Afghan troopers. Consequently the number of troopers free for recruitment in Skinner's regiments increased. In 1809, A. Seton, the Resident in Delhi, wrote to John Adam, Secretary

[48] L. No. 12, Collector of Etawah to Thomas Graham, President and Member Board of Revenue, FW, 16 April 1803, BRBC CCP, Consult. 2 Aug. 1803, P/90/39, IOL. In 1803, the Collector of Etawah reported to Thomas Graham, the President of the Board of Revenue, Fort William, about the claims put forward by Mewati Jamadars for the rusum they had collected on behalf of Nawab Kaim Khan of Farrukhabad, from the merchants passing through Khassgunge Secundra. They claimed that this practice of collecting rusum had existed for the last sixty years and was established by Nawab Kaim Khan. In his time rusum was charged at the following rates: 12 annas on each cart load of cayratra, 8 annas on grain and Rs 7 on each cart load of cloth. The contract for its collection had been settled with a Mewati chief, Asalat Khan, who operated between Hirduagunge and Farrukhabad. On the death of Nawab Kaim Khan, his successor Nawab Ahmad Khan was pleased to grant the villages of Srithulla, Sukan, Kagria and Jowarpur in jagir to Asalat Khan. Under the rule of the Nawab Wazir some jagirs, like Mogah and Narta, were granted to the Mewatis and their right to collect rusum was continued.

to the government in the secret department, about the popular appeal of Skinner's regiments.

The great part of the men under the service of the Pathan Chief Meer Khan, on hearing of the intention of the British government to augment Skinner's Horse, expressed their willingness to rejoin their old standards and relinquish the service in which they were employed provided they were assured that the service for which they were now required was not for the moment alone. On being encouraged by an authorized declaration to this effect considerable numbers of them joined Lt. Col. Skinner at Hansi at different intervals.[49]

He reported that the troopers brought with them many of their friends and connections from the Pathan camp. This preference for British service gave Skinner a wide field for selection. For instance, out of the large number of the Pindari leader Meer Khan's men who offered to be recruited in Skinner's regiments, only 335 of the best sawars were eventually enlisted and the remaining troopers were asked to seek employment elsewhere.[50]

Skinner's success in turning peasants into gentlemen-soldiers contributed to the establishment of the Company's political dominance and supremacy in most parts of the Ceded and Conquered Provinces and his regiments also had a very significant economic and social impact. The raising of these regiments brought both the freshly-acquired territory as well as the neighbouring polities and vital trade routes within the political, military and

---

[49] A. Seton, Resident in Delhi, to Mil. Deptt., 21 Aug. 1815, extract Sec. Letter from Bengal, 21 Aug. 1815, a copy of correspondence and proceedings on the use of Skinner's Horse and similar irregular horses, Mil. Records, File No. 30 A. L/MIL/5/378, IOL.

[50] Ibid. In this period the strength of Skinner's Corps was increased to twenty-two risalas, with approximately 3,000 men in its service. Some of the important Indian chiefs who joined Skinner's force were, from Meer Khan's camp: 5 risaldars, 1 naib risaldar, 3 jamadars, 15 dafadars, 5 nishabandar, 5 nugurche, and 335 sawars; from the Bikaner raja's territory, there were 2 risaldars, 1 jamadar, 8 dafadars, 2 nishabandar, 2 nugurche, and 300 sawars; from Mullair Cotelah, there were 2 risaldars, 6 dafadars, 2 nishabandar, 2 nugurche, and 145 sawars; from Haryana, 2 risaldars, 3 jamadars, 7 dafadars, 2 nishabandar, 2 nugurche, and 145 sawars; from Jaipur, 2 risaldars, 1 jamadar, 5 nishabandar, 2 nugurche, and 225 sawars; from Meerut, 1 risaldar, 1 naib risaldar, 6 jamadars, 8 dafadars, 1 nishabandar, 1 nugurche, and 250 sawars. The total number of sawars was 1,400, with 14 risaldars, 2 naib risaldars, 14 jamadars, 44 dafadars, 17 nishabandar and 14 nugurche.

fiscal orbit of the East India Company. The settlement of Haryana, the conciliation of the Bhatti 'tribe', the control of trade routes for horses, and the restructuring of the position of the literate service-groups were the four major cases in point.

Skinner's Men and the Settlement of Haryana

The Company's settling of Skinner's men on land created settlements of Jat and Rohilla recruits over large tracts of land in Haryana. These settlements increased considerably after the Pindari campaign of 1818 when the Company reduced Skinner's regiments and granted landholdings to the disbanded soldiers. In 1819 the Company resolved

to offer any horseman then recently discharged from the Irregular cavalry, under orders of discharge or willing to retire from the service a province of land either in the Bhuttee country or Hirrianah or any waste and unclaimed part of the territory of Delhi.[51]

Each private trooper was assigned at least 100 bighas of land with a proportionate increase according to rank.[52] This was to be held rent free for three successive generations or in the case of men without direct heirs for a term of twenty years. The salaries of all those who accepted this offer of land were stopped and the Company expected them to sell their horse and military accessories and invest their cash in land.[53] Those who refused to follow the Company's orders were discharged from service and not compensated in any other way.

In 1819, Major General David Ochterlony, the Resident in Delhi, implemented this policy with considerable success.[54] In

---

[51] Extract Pol. Letter from Bengal, 21 Oct. 1820, BC, File No. 20909, pp. 1–2, F/4/772, IOL.

[52] Ibid.

[53] Ibid.

[54] L. No. 78, G. Deedes, Sec. Sadar Board of Rev., Allahabad, to C. Macoween, Sec. to Lt. Gov. NWP, 28 June 1836, NWP, Lt. Governor's Procds. in Rev. Deptt. 20 June–26 July 1836, Procds. of Lt. Governor of NWP July 1836 No. 78, Sec. Sadar Board of Rev. 28 June 1836, P/21/48, IOL. For instance in 1836, I.C. Deedes, the Sec. to the Sadar Board of Rev. in Allahabad, recommended the case of Himmut Khan and three sawars of the disbanded Rohilla Corps to the Board of Revenue for the grant of

1809, the total strength of Skinner's Corps was reported to be approximately 3,000 men,[55] and by 1824, it had been reduced to 700.[56] This meant that approximately 2,300 troopers were settled on land in Haryana and the Bhatti country. With each trooper obtaining a minimum of 100 bighas of land at least 2,30,000 bighas of land in the region was settled by former soldiers. Not surprisingly then in 1825, much before the opening of the canal in Haryana, the revenue demand in Hansi showed an upward trend. From Rs 1,200 in 1818 it had reached Rs 1,500 in 1825.[57]

Alongside this, Skinner himself had a considerable landed estate which spanned the districts of Aligarh and Haryana. In 1809, his jagir at Aligarh yielded an annual jama of Rs 3,626 per annum.[58] The villages he possessed in the parganas of Kurrouli, which extended over approximately nineteen *mouzas*, had an annual jama of Rs 3,624. In the pargana of Khansa where he had thirteen mouzas the annual jama was Rs 2,213.[59] Moreover, Skinner possessed six mouzas which had a total jama of Rs 1,411, in the

---

fresh land to them, as in 1819, at the time their Corps was disbanded, they had not occupied the jagirs which had been granted to them. The government agreed on the condition that, 'patches of waste land could not be disposed of in a more satisfactory manner': The Sadar Board of Revenue dealt with many such petitions in a similar manner. See for example L. Nos. 115–116 and Nos. 103–104, NWP Lt. Gov. Procds. in the Rev. Deptt., 1 Oct.–3 Nov. 1836, Procds. of Lt. Gov. NWP Oct. 1836, P/217/52, IOL.

[55] A. Seton, Resident in Delhi, to Mil. Deptt., 21 Aug. 1815 extract Secret Letter from Bengal, 21 Aug. 1815, a copy of correspondence and proceedings on the use of Skinner's Horse and similar irregular horses, Mil. Records, File No. 30 A, L/MIL/5/378, IOL.

[56] File No. 38, Procds. of Mil. Deptt., Consult. 11 April 1823, NAI.

[57] Information from appendix No. 1, 1–29 Dec. 1837, NWP Procds. of Lt. Gov. NWP, Consult. 7 Dec. 1837, P/217/63, IOL.

[58] Minute of Gov.-Gen. 26 Sept. 1818, BC, File No. 20937, extract Bengal Sec. Consult. 26 Sept. 1818, pp. 15–20, F/4/775, IOL.

[59] L. No. 64, H. Newnham, Sec. to Govt. to Collectors of Aligarh, 17 Nov. 1818, BC, File No. 25807, extract Bengal Rev. Consult. 16 Dec. 1818, pp. 20–6, F/4/916, IOL. The details of the villages were as follows: Kurrouli, Karnulpur, two mouzas and jama Rs 431; in Kullali and Kylapur, three mouzas, Rs 1,001; in Shahinpur, Muzrunh, Chuarpur and Ferozpur; four mouzas, Rs 617; in Mushudpur, Noupur, Shukurpur and Khurburah; four mouzas, Rs 164.

pargana of Dunene.[60] His estate also included a collection of villages centered around Bilaspur in the district of Duncour. Some of these villages, like Dhanourie, he had purchased from his wife Ashoree Khanum and he paid an annual rent of Rs 450 for it. But some others, like Mootyna, he received as a permanent and hereditary jagir from the government.[61] Initially Skinner gave a yearly rental of Rs 428 for Mootyna but by 1821 the rental was considerably higher because Skinner's investments had improved the land.[62] Finally, Skinner also owned a big farm at Hansi and his brother, Robert Skinner, also possessed extensive tracts of land in the Aligarh district which sprawled over four mouzas in pargana Kasnah and four mouzas in pargana Dunene. Their total jama was Rs 1,950.[63]

The Settlement of the Bhattis

George Thomas' transactions with the Bhattis made the Company realize the significant role that the neighbouring territory of Bhattiana could play in the settlement of Haryana itself. In 1809, A. Seton, the Resident in Delhi, wrote to the Government:

It [Bhattee territory] is situated in the midst of a fine, rich, productive country, and if we continue on good terms with the Bhattees, it may be considered as a most convenient place for furnishing Hansi with supplies. This was one of the many considerations which induced me to open an

---

[60] Ibid. Details of villages in this pargana were as follows:

Mhohipur	1 mouza	Rs 95
Nulha	1 mouza	Rs 428
Mullourah	1 mouza	Rs 142
Ahnipur	1 mouza	Rs 137
Munghherah	1 mouza	Rs 142
Altowadah	1 mouza	Rs 52
Bilaspur	15 mouzas	Rs 427

[61] L. No. 42, Lieutenant-Colonel J. Skinner to H. Newnham Esq., Sec. to Board of Commissioners, 3 March 1821, BC, File No. 25807, extract Bengal Secret Consult. 20 April 1811, pp. 51–5, F/4/916, IOL.
[62]Ibid.
[63] L. No. 63, H. Newnham, Sec. to Board of Commissioners in Ceded & Conquered Provinces, to S. Mackenzie, in Aligarh District, 17 Nov. 1818, BC, File No. 25807, extract Bengal Rev. Consult. 16 Dec. 1818, pp. 19–27, F/4/916, IOL.

early intercourse with Khan Bahadur, the titular head of the Bhattees.[64]

The government took serious note of Seton's views, and in 1809 Skinner was sent on a political mission to the Bhatti territory. Seton was of the view that:

A person of Skinner's predicament [sic] whose character is justly held in highest esteem among the natives, who is well qualified to explain the nature of our system and who is a personal friend of Uttaoollah Khan the kinsman of Khan Bahadur ... I consider should proceed to Futtehabad to acquire some useful knowledge respecting the nature, power, and system of the Bhattees.[65]

Skinner accomplished this mission with success. In the 1820s, he resided in the Bhatti country for a considerable period of time and engaged local artists to paint the people and their lifestyle. In 1825, the knowledge of the Bhattis so acquired, was published in a section of his illuminated Persian Manuscripts—the *Tash-rih-ul-Akvam* or 'Concise Account of the People'.[66] This manuscript is of extreme significance because it is one of the early kind of district gazetteers compiled by British officers in India. It may be placed in between the late eighteenth-century Persian descriptions and topographics and the census reports and district gazetteers which were compiled in the late nineteenth century by British officers.

Moreover, after the Pindari campaigns the Bhatti lands began to be colonized by many of the disbanded soldiers of Skinner's regiments, further increasing the pool of information available to the colonial power. In 1837, Captain Thousby, the superintendent of the Bhatti territory, made it compulsory for grantees of small portions of land in the Bhatti territory to reside upon

[64] A. Seton, Resident in Delhi, to N. B. Edmonstone, Chief Sec. to Govt. Fort William, 20 March 1809, BC, File No. 7014, extract Bengal Pol. Consult., 10 April 1809, p. 257, F/4/305, IOL.

[65] L. No. 2, A. Seton, Resident in Delhi, to Gardner, 22 May 1809, BC, File No. 7015, extract Bengal Pol. Consult., 27 May 1804, pp. 185–6, F/4/305, IOL.

[66] *Tashrih ul-Akram* is an illuminated Persian manuscript in Nasta'liq acquired by the British Museum in 1865 and catalogued by Rieu in 1879. C. Rieu, *Catalogue of the Persian Manuscripts in the British Museum* (London, 1879), vol. I, p. 65; for an account of this manuscript see Cedric Dover, 'Cultural significance of Col. James Skinner', *Calcutta Review* (January 1955), pp. 18–24.

or in the vicinity of their landholdings. If these stipulations were not fulfilled their grants were resumed.[67] By 1837, when Skinner's contingent had become quite small, Bhattis themselves were recruited into a force which was largely devoted to local policing. In time many of these Bhattis were granted loans for settling in Haryana.[68]

Skinner and Mirza Azim Beg

Rural professional groups, which had served in different public capacities with the former rulers of Haryana, also found employment in Skinner's establishment. The family of a local amil of Haryana, Mirza Azim Beg, was the most important beneficiary. Azim Beg was a respectable man (ashraf) of Hansi, seventy to eighty years of age in 1809, who along with his son, llyas Beg, had been frequently employed as an administrator by the different rulers of the country. His jagir comprised the three parganas of Gwalun, Mahoalah and Keree in Hansi which yielded a total revenue of Rs 2,582.[69] In 1207 Fusli, George Thomas had granted these jagir lands, in *Istimnah*, for Rs 418, to his son llyas Beg. In 1804, after the death of Thomas, Abdus Summund Khan, the local chief of Haryana, made these grants rent free for the Beg family.[70] When the province came under Skinner's administration, Azim Beg was given a position in the military headquarters at Hansi. Here, he administered Skinner's estate and under his patronage became a powerful and wealthy zamindar.

[67] L. No. 152, S. S. Metcalfe, Commissioner Delhi, to C. Thousby, Superintendent Bhatti territory, 11 Sept. 1837; and L. No. 153, I. Thompson, officiating Sec. to Lt. Govt. NWP to S. S. Metcalfe, Commissioner Delhi, 11 Sept. 1837, NWP Lt. Gov. Procds. in the Rev. Deptt. 21 Oct.–10 Nov. 1837, Procds. of the Lt. Gov. NWP for Oct. 1837, P/217/61, IOL.

[68] L. Nos. 140–1, Sec. Sadar Board of Rev. to C. Macsuen, Sec. to the Lt. Govt. NWP and I.I. Deedes, Sec. Board of Rev. to the same, 2 Aug. 1836, NWP Procds. of Lt. Gov. NWP Aug. 1836, P/217/419, IOL.

[69] L. No. 16, E. Gardner, assistant to Resident in Delhi, to C. T. Metcalfe, Resident in Delhi, 18 Nov. 1811, BC, File No. 10012, extract Pol. letter from Bengal, 1 March 1812, p. 50, F/4/393, IOL.

[70] L. No. 15, E. Gardner, assistant Resident Delhi, to C. T. Metcalfe, Resident in Delhi, 17 Nov. 1811, ibid., pp. 44–5.

In 1809, along with the disbandment of Abdus Summund Khan's army, the Company reduced his risala as well and compensated him with a grant of Rs 17,999.14.[71] Azim Beg was soon equipped with a proper office and a staff which comprised of Devi Lal, a vakil, Kishan Lal, a munshi and Pir Buksh, a khidmatgar[72] (plate 9). By 1821, Azim Beg had expanded his landed estate by purchasing land in the village of Dhanourie in pargana Duncour. These had been purchased by his daugher, Ashoree Khanum, from a Rajput zamindar for Rs 252.8.[73] Azim Beg further consolidated his influence in the locality when Ashoree Khanum married Skinner.[74]

REVIVAL OF THE HORSE TRADE

The Company's control of the horse trade and indigenous horse-breeding zones was critical to the establishment of its political dominance in north India. Skinner's military experiment was of crucial importance in accomplishing this objective. His military contingent, in the Delhi–Haryana region, revived the horse-breeding zones,[75] markets, and trade[76] which had dried up after the decline of the royal courts of Farrukhabad, Rohilkhand, and Shinde.[77] But their dynamics were different.

In the early nineteenth century the Company's territorial expansion westward, along the river Ganges, was accompanied by an extension of its control over a large number of indigenous

---

[71] L. Nos. 98–9. A Seton, Resident in Delhi, to N. B. Edmonstone, Chief Sec. to Govt., 31 Aug. 1808, BC, File No. 7014, extract Bengal Pol. Consult, 6 Feb. 1809, pp. 114–15, F/4/305, IOL.

[72] Mildred Archer, *Company Drawings in the IOL* (London, 1972), p. 200.

[73] Deed registered by I. H. Dick, Registrar, and I. Fraser, acting Collector, R. H. Sulloh, Collector, on 9 July 1813, before zamindars Mukum Sirdhari, Zalim Singh and Kishori Ram and witnesses Kevani and Nowashi, BC, File No. 25807, extract Bengal Rev. Consult. 25 July 1822, pp. 84–90, F/4/916, IOL.

[74] Petition of Lalchund, Colonel Skinner's mukhtar, submitted to Collector, not dated, ibid., p. 93.

[75] For details of horse breeding zones see Moorcroft Report. Rs 450 in the north and Rs 2,000–3,000 in the Deccan.

[76] See Moorcroft Report.

[77] Ibid.

horse-breeding areas which were located in its newly acquired territory. There were important military and political imperatives attached to this policy. In 1809, the decision of the Court of Directors to regard the Sutlej as the western boundary of the Company's possessions was accompanied by its sanction to station Skinner's contingent permanently at Hansi. Soon the military establishment had spread its network all over the region and its demand for a ready supply of horses[78] prompted the Company to bring indigenous horse-breeding areas under its control. For similar reasons the Company began tapping new regions of supply in the Ceded and Conquered Provinces and encouraged the Kutch and Kathiawar breeding areas in Gujarat. Here, the horses were more suited for cavalry than for royal ceremonies. For this reason these regions had not been very popular with the Indian royal courts. But from 1807 the Company's army contractors began to procure their remounts for the cavalry from Kathiawar and Kutch in Gujarat, and Sindh.[79] In Sindh, the Lakhi jungle provided grass and a climate suitable for horse breeders and had been the traditional breeding area for horses. But the horses most suitable for cavalry were bred in Bhavnagar, Dolen and Cambay in Gujarat.[80] In 1807, R. T. Goodwin, Secretary to the Government, was of the opinion that there would be only one or two first-rate horses (according to the Company's definition), in a batch of

[78] Mason, *A Matter of Honour*, pp. 153 and 167. Skinner's recruits either brought their own horses or were supplied with a horse. A *bargir*, i.e. a man who was supplied with a horse, was paid less than a man who brought his own horse.

[79] T. Graham, C. Buller, Rev. Board, to J. Duncan, Governor and President in Council, Bombay, 4 Sept. 1807, BMC, Procds. 21 Dec. 1807, P/22/40, IOL.

[80] R. T. Godwin, Sec. to Govt., Some particulars of the mode of purchasing hosrses for cavalry, 21 Dec. 1807, BMC, Consult. FW, 21 Dec. 1807, P/22/40, IOL. Here, there was a species called Golewar which was of a lean and unshapely form, 'wanting in bone and strength'. The preference for lean horses had made the horses from the Junagarh area unpopular with the Company. These horses were large, full-bodied, high and handsome. Some were beautiful, and in spirit and rapidity of motion equal to any in the world. Such horses were in great demand for the court ceremonials of the Indian states. Babreawar, in the centre of the hilly district of Kathiawar, was the traditional breeding area for horses of the Gujarat Sultans. The Choathila horse, bred here, was suitable for the requirements of the Company, but the uncompromising attitude of the hill people had made it difficult for the Company to make its purchases here.

a hundred coming from Afghanistan and Sindh. But horses from Sindh were important because in Sindh the Company's officials mixed indigenously-bred horses with those brought by the Pathan merchants from Afghanistan, Kabul, Herat and Khurasan. In 1807, Goodwin expressed the Company's decisive preference for the indigenous breed of horses:

In general those [horses] bought of Hindu zamindars are the best and partake of the Marwar breed having high nose. Those bred of Musalman Grassias resemble Sindhian and Arab horses but inferior in size to the first, those in the possession of the artisans and traders are a mixture of all breeds, ill fed, ill taught, ill looking and from whom no good can be expected. The contractors bring from these countries every year from 400–600 horse.[81]

The indigenous animals were also preferred because the Chatgosheh, Turki horses available were too short for cavalry requirements.[82] Moreover, the Company, of course was less concerned with the mounted archer fighting in rough terrain than the sabre-bearing cavalryman fighting on the plains.

The expansion of the irregular cavalry regiments and Skinner's establishment during the period of war, 1816–24, made the Company seriously consider the establishment of a horse stud in the Ceded and Conquered Provinces. The idea was to have an establishment which would benefit by its location near the traditional breeding area of Sindh, take advantage of being at the mouth of the overland trade route from Afghanistan, and be close to the major demand area in Haryana. Moorcroft suggested the establishment of the Company's horse farm at Hissar, thirteen miles from Skinner's establishment at Hansi, in the Delhi Residency, and wrote to the Board of Directors explaining the reasons:

The importance of its position relatively to our purchase of horses for the remount of our Dragoons and Cavalry, camels and bullocks to replace casualties in the establishment until the Government studs shall render such no longer necessary in the two latter branches will at first sight be manifest to the Board. I calculate on bringing down the old Northern Horse by the direct roads from Multan through Bikaner to Hissar without touching

---

[81] Ibid.

[82] Ibid.

on any of the Sikh states. The exactions and dishonesty of whose chiefs have been a main cause in putting a stop to the trade in horses.[83]

He was optimistic that the immediate vicinity of Hissar to Bhatindah and the Lakhi jungle would ensure him a ready supply of its produce. In 1815, the Government sanctioned Moorcroft's plan and Major Lumsdaine became the first supervisor of the Haryana stud.[84]

It was soon evident that the military imperative which had prompted the Company to control the north Indian horse-breeding areas had provided it with significant political advantages as well. For the control of traditional breeding areas and fairs and the opening of new horse farms in the Ceded and Conquered Provinces helped to consolidate the Company's political hold in these newly-acquired territories. For instance, by the 1840s, the Company faced no major opposition on its new frontier bordering the Punjab and its success against the Sikh cavalry was made easy by its control of the horse supply areas and fairs of the region. In 1857, Surgeon General E. Balfour, the author of the *Cyclopaedia of India*, reported that under Ranjit Singh the Punjab maintained an enormous cavalry force and most of its horses came from within the country. But in 1857, Punjab was unable to meet the much reduced demands of its irregular force. Balfour noted that one of the reasons for this was that most of the broad mares had been removed from the province at the time of Punjab's annexation to the Company territory and now served the cavalry requirements of the Company.[85]

Further, the control of the horse fairs and breeding areas had important social repercussions as well. For in Hissar horse breeding and military service gradually moved the society towards sedentarization. A certain quantity of land was given to every individual

[83] Major Lumsdaine to Board of Superintendence, 11 Oct. 1815, in extract from the Proceedings of the Gov.-Gen.-in-Council in the Military Department, No. 503 dated 16 Nov. 1815, *Records of the Delhi Residency and Agency 1807–1857* (3 vols., Lahore, 1911), vol. I, p. 58.

[84] Ibid., p. 57.

[85] Surgeon Gen. Edward Balfour, *The Cyclopaedia of India and of Eastern and Southern Asia: Commercial, Industrial and Scientific Products of the Mineral, Vegetable and Animal Kingdoms, Useful Arts and Manufactures* (3 vols., London, 1885), II, p. 104.

who brought a mare for breeding. Once approved by Major Lumsdaine, the man entered into a zamindari contract with the Company. The terms of the contract laid out that when the mare died he had to provide a substitute animal at his own cost. This arrangement was known as the jagir system[86] and it attracted the mobile and nomadic semi-pastoralist trading communities of Pathans, Gujars, Jats and Bhattis who operated in the region of Rajasthan and Punjab, to settle in Haryana.[87] These communities were assured that their produce would be bought from them at a set price. In this manner villages of horse breeders were created in Hissar, Rohtas, Panipat and Sonipat districts of Haryana. In 1819, Moorcroft observed one such settlement of Jat horse breeders in Rohtas. This colony flourished on the land farmed out by the Company to Surnath, a local Jat of Rohtas, for horse breeding.[88]

TOWARDS A UNIFORM MILITARY CULTURE, 1830–40

By 1820, the military tradition developed by Skinner was fully incorporated into the Company's army even though it stood in contrast to the directly recruited peasant army of the Gangetic plains. The social and political circumstances of the Ceded and Conquered Provinces made it absolutely necessary for the Company to function through officers like Skinner who had hitherto been regarded as mavericks by its officials. Skinner's contingent consequently expanded in size and soon a large number of permanent centres controlled and co-ordinated the function of this establishment.

---

[86] This was in strong contrast to the system of rewards and incentives which worked in the Benaras–Bihar region. In these regions the Company had found communities of breeders already settled on land which did not make it necessary for it to attract new breeders to its territory. L. No. 258, W. Moorcroft, Superintendent of the Company's Stud to BBCBB, 23 April 1817, BBCBB, Consult. 23 April 1817, P/111/71, IOL.

[87] W. Moorcroft, Superintendent Company's Horse Stud to Captain G. H. Gall, Sec. to Board of Superintendence, Calcutta, 30 November 1815, *Records of the Delhi Residency*, pp. 64–6.

[88] Ibid. This area had a scanty population with a predominance of Dhangurs (who were Rajput pastoralist converts to Islam) whose meagre resources restricted them to cultivating small amounts of rice and barley.

Skinner's centre at Hansi, now recognized by the Company, controlled twelve other subordinate strong points within 250 miles of Hansi.[89] In these small centres there were bodies of cavalry and infantry organized on similar principles, while Skinner played the role of overall commander in Hansi.[90]

However, in the 1820s, when the cavalry requirements of the Empire were diminishing and the broader economic, social and political winds of change were sweeping over north India, the tension between the peasant army of the Gangetic plains and the experiment in the Ceded and Conquered Provinces surfaced again. One major reason for this was the prejudice against Eurasians which continued to simmer within the circle of Company officers. In 1822, changing its policy yet again, the Court of Directors denied a pension to Skinner and refused to recommend him for the Order of the Bath as suggested by the Military Board.[91] This seemed to suggest that the experiment of irregular forces in the Ceded and Conquered Provinces was to be abandoned in favour of the peasant tradition of the Gangetic plains. In his memoir Skinner notes that he was kindly treated by Lord Hastings

[89] Statement of Skinner's Horse showing the different commands:

	No. of men	No. of horses	Distance from headquarters (miles)
Gwalior	77	74	255
Lucknow	27	27	237
Karnal	56	56	90
Ambala	17	17	43
Hissar	104	101	18
Sudderpur	40	40	101
Delhi	50	50	90
Futtyabad	52	52	48
Ajmer	189	183	203
Meerut	13	13	126
Karnal	11	11	90
Total	636	624	

Material collected from File Nos. 38–41, Procds. of Military Department, Consult. 11 April 1823, NAI.

[90] Ibid.

[91] Fraser, *Military Memoirs of Lt. Col. James Skinner*, vol. II, p. 197. Officers of the East India Company did not want Skinner to be granted an equal status to them. On this account, despite the recommendations of the Military Department, the award of the Honour of the Bath was delayed and given to him only in 1828.

in Calcutta, but his rank was reduced to that of a risaldar of 800 horses. As he said:

My fall has been rapid....In the Maratha service from 1796-1803 I always had hope of rising. My merits were rewarded, my birth not questioned. When I entered the British service I thought I had now gained a field which will bring its fruits in perfection. No exertion on my part was left undone to bring myself forward. I thought I had now served a nation that had no prejudices against cast or colour, but alas I was mistaken...I only wanted justice which had been denied. For if they will allow me to be a native, reward me as such. Did not my exertion and fidelity for the service merit a better reward than Rs 300/months....Although my birth has been the cause of my not gaining what I deserved—that is rank—but I have proved to the world that I have served my King and country as loyally as any Briton in India.[92]

The irregular cavalry now became little more than a local police force.[93] The Company's suspicion of the trooper's loyalty and the scepticism about the political interest of the old military class was never really dispelled and in an era of retrenchment they were the first to suffer. Moreover, at the international level the military techniques and nature of warfare were also changing. Infantry regiments were becoming more important and the British Empire was facing enemies with muskets and matchlocks on its warfronts in Burma, Afghanistan and Egypt. The Indian army had to keep pace with these worldwide changes if it had to fight wars for the Empire.

Paradoxically, the expansion of the irregulars was halted but their military tradition was kept alive. Their uniforms and armour were continued and the 'era of reforms' was characterized by a kind of nostalgia for Skinner's Horse and its master. For instance, in 1829, Bentinck disbanded Skinner's regiments as part of his economy drives, but conferred the honour of the Military Order of the Bath on him.[94] The Company deliberately kept alive the

[92] *Skinner's Memoirs*, p. 128.

[93] In this period a similar role was performed by Begum Samru's contingent. In 1836, on the death of Begum Samru, the Company drew her entire force into its Saharanpur Provincial Battalion, SCPMR, 1829-31, Judicial Letters Received from Commissioners, No. 41, ARA.

[94] Fraser, *Military Memoirs of Lt. Col. James Skinner*, II, p. 201.

myth of Skinner after his death in 1841. This proved handy in attracting recruits in the region whenever the need arose. These developments were a prelude to the levelling of the variety of military traditions that constituted the Bengal Army. From the 1830s, the Company made attempts to subsume Skinner's military experience within its own peasant army tradition. The officers of the regular regiments trained the irregulars and a considerable systematization took place in their recruitment procedure. Henceforth advertisements and tenders were issued by the commanding officers for recruiting troopers.[95] Moreover, clan leaders were made to give guarantees for the loyalty of their followers.[96] The system of promotions on the pattern of the regular regiments was also introduced and, after the mutiny of 1857, attempts were made to create the impression that Skinner's military tradition was based on the ashraf Muslim class just as the peasant army experiment in the Gangetic plains relied on caste-conscious Brahmans. Skinner himself was projected as Sikander, i.e., Alexander the Great, the embodiment of military strength. *Julwatoor*, a vernacular newspaper published from Meerut in 1868, while putting forward a strong case for the guarantee of loyalty secured by confining recruitment to men of high castes, had a brilliant anecdote about the legendary Skinner:

A person was enlisted in one of his [Skinner's] regiments who gave himself out publicaly to be a Sayyid [person of respectability] though in reality he was a Bhatiyara [inn keeper]. One day Sikander Sahib saw him wipe his nose on parade using his sleeve for the purpose. He at once grew very angry and soon discovered that the man was of inferior birth. So turning to his officers he asked why the man had been employed in the regiment being by caste a Bhatiyara. Native officers replied that man was not a low caste but a Sayyid. Orders were given for strict enquiries to be made and it was soon discovered that the man was a false Sayyid. He was discharged and his property thrown away. Leaving nothing but

---

[95] Twelve such tenders were accepted in 1846 from respectable and influential individuals, most of them relatives and connections of chieftains, who arranged to bring entire contingents to join Skinner's regiment (L. No. 34, J. Skinner, Commanding 13th Cavalry to I. Currie, Sec. to Govt. of India, 16 Jan. 1846, PFD 1846, File No. 107, NAI).

[96] Ibid.

his ears and nose, he was sent to his own country which to him was but an oven.[97]

The news item itself alluded to the purpose for which it was written. This it did by noting that the moral of the story was that, 'a human being ought not even in forgetfulness to lean towards those of low caste, but always keep them at a distance. For even if they approach one ought to keep aloof from them.'[98] The Company it appears had now evolved to a stage of political maturity where it was no more willing to compromise on the traditions of high-caste peasant regiments it valued the most. The analysis of the Company's military experiment, as it evolved in the Ceded and Conquered Provinces, suggests that by the 1830s, the Company had entered a new phase of its rule over north India.

[97] Julwatoor, Meerut, 13 Jan. 1868, Govt. Tr. of Selections from the Vernacular Newspapers, Upper India, 8 Feb. 1868, Delhi, NWP Vernacular Press 1868, L/R/5/45, IOL.
[98] Ibid.

Chapter 7

The Gurkha Experiment:
1764–1857

The Company began to interfere in the affairs of Nepal at a time when the military culture of Nepal was in transition. Prithvi Narayan Shah, the Raja of Nepal (1762–74), was trying to forge a Hindu military identity amongst the heterogeneous 'tribal' groups of Nepal. His efforts to create a model Kshatriya warrior mirrored the changes taking place at the same time in Awadh, Benaras and Shinde's territories.

The Company admired the sophisticated tactics of the Gurkhas in hill warfare but in the short run it was unable to win over the personnel which constituted this military base of the Nepal kingdom. Around 1815–16, in order to meet the Nepali challenge and its own needs of policing the hills, the Company began to invent its own model of a Gurkha soldier. The 'Company Gurkha' was formed from the Kumaonis, Garhwali, and Sirmouri hill men who flocked to its service because of the Gurkha rule over their lands. This invented Gurkha tradition welded together the customs of Prithvi Narayan Shah's Gurkhas and the European practices of drill and discipline. An additional novel feature was the Company Gurkha's use of Mughal imagery which drew on the Company's tradition of exploiting Mughal symbols.

The Gurkha soldier so created continued to meet the Company's requirements in the hills. But after 1818, the Company's attention was drawn once again to the Gurkha recruits of the Nepal army.

In this period, the Company had begun to reduce its irregular cavalry regiments and was alarmed at the increasing spate of mutinies and desertions in its peasant army. The Company had also come to realize that there were difficulties in posting soldiers of Cleveland's Hill Corps in territories outside the Bihar hills. These factors shaped the Company's attitudes towards the Gurkha soldiers of Nepal.

During this period the Company might have been successful in recruiting the Gurkha soldiers of the Nepal army because the military reforms of Bhim Singh Thapa, the *pradhan mantri* (prime minister) of Nepal, 1816–39, had made the Company's army more attractive to the Gurkha soldiers. But the Company did not extend its recruitment zone into the Nepal valley despite the best efforts of British Residents, notably Brian Hodgson, who emphasized the importance of recruiting Gurkhas. This was because the strict military regulations of Bhim Singh Thapa suppressed Gurkha migration to the Company's territories. But the slow beginnings of recruitment also reflected the Company's less-than-wholehearted attitude to Gurkha recruitment in peace time.

Taking advantage of the Company's laxity, Jang Bahadur, the prime minister of Nepal (1839–56), expanded his army and strengthened the Kshatriya model. In the mid-nineteenth century, Nepal became an increasingly 'militarized' society. This proved particularly useful to the Company in the period after the mutiny-rebellion of 1857. Feeling betrayed by its peasant army, it looked to Nepal as an alternative recruitment base. The Kshatriya model of Prithvi Narayan and the Company's own model Gurkha soldier were drawn together, and Gurkha identity and religion was standardized in the years which followed the 1857 mutiny.

MILITARY IDENTITY AND THE STATE OF NEPAL, 1762–74

According to the *Vansavali,* the genealogical history of Nepal written in Parbatiya, the ruling house of the Gurkhas claimed that it was a branch of the Rana family of Chittor.[1] The family

---

[1] Daniel Wright (ed.), *History of Nepal* (London, 1877; 2nd Indian ed. Calcutta, 1958), pp. 167–73. The *Vansavali* notes that Bhupati was killed together with his son Fateh

traced its ancestry to Rishraj Bhattark, the Raja of Chittor. In 1559, Dravya Shah's conquest of the town of Gurkha marked the commencement of the phase of Gurkha expansion in the Kathmandu valley. By the late eighteenth century, the Nepal Raja, Prithvi Narayan Shah (1762–74), had consolidated Gurkha rule over the conquered lands.

Prithvi Narayan's army, recruited mainly from the hill population of Nepal and the agricultural population of the Kathmandu valley, compared very well with the predominantly Hindu peasant regiments of Cheyt Singh. An additional novel feature of. the army was the process by which a variety of 'tribal' and hill people were formed into soldiers, with specifically Gurkha identity. Prithvi Narayan gathered around him Sardars who were 'brave in the battlefield and loyal in misfortune'. Under these Sardars he collected a large army of about 4,000–5,000 men consisting predominantly of the hill 'tribes'—the Magars, the Gurangs, the Khus, and the Thakurs.[2] Prithvi Narayan encouraged the use of Hindu symbols in his regiments so as to create a Hindu military identity for these hill 'tribes'. He encouraged the Hinduization of the regiments so as to hold together his heterogeneous soldiers.

The hill Kshatriya (Hindu warrior) was created by amalgamating the practices of the hill recruits with the social customs and military practices of the Kshatriyas of the plains. The assimilation of different traditions was reflected in the names chosen for the different regiments which comprised the Gurkha army. The first two companies of infantry were composed of Gurkhas directly recruited from the Gurkha hills, and were called Sabz Bani and Brij Bani. Prithvi Narayan, after reducing Nagarkot, had raised three more companies of sipahis from the Nepal valley. These were called

---

Singh. Uday Brahma, the heir apparent, escaped and founded the town of Udaipur, while Manmath, Bhupati's yougest son, found refuge at Ujjain. Manmath had two sons, Brahmanik and Bhupal. Bhupal not being on good terms with his elder brother came and settled in the Tarai lands near Palpa. The names of his two sons Kancha and Mincha indicate that Bhupal must have married in his adopted country. Bhupal succeeded in securing Raghubansi Kshatriya brides for his sons, which helped Kancha to conquer the country of the Magars, while Mincha established himself at Nankot.

[2] MSS 10, B. H. Hodgson, 'Memoirs on the army of Nepal submitted to the Government in 1825', pp. 20–1, IOL. Hereafter Hodgson Papers.

Barakh, Old Gorakh and Ram Dal.[3] These were a mixture of names, some of which, like the Ram Dal, emphasized the Hindu overtones of the army and others, like the Gorakh Company, alluded to the local and regional character of the Gurkha ruling house. Similarly, the *Jang Nishan* or war standard had a yellow background with a figure of Hanuman embroidered on it.[4] It appears that yellow, a colour generally used by the Rajput army, was deliberately chosen to symbolically emphasize the Rajput origins of the ruling house. The figure of Hanuman further underlined the Hindu nature of the polity.[5] For similar reasons the hill Kshatriyas began to carry the sword, which was the major weapon used by the Hindu Kshatriyas of the plains, along with their traditional weapon of war, the *khukri*.[6] Interestingly enough, in this period, many of the khukris began to be decorated with small figures of the Hindu god Hanuman.[7]

The Nepal army was influenced by European and Mughal military practices as well. Prithvi Narayan emulated the European forms of drill and discipline. Each company had a pair of colours, and the soldiers were clothed in scarlet English cloth. They carried firelocks along with their swords and khukris.[8] By contrast, the soldiers were paid in a manner reminiscent of the Mughal mansabdari system. Like the Mughal Emperors, Prithvi Narayan also introduced a system of payment in jagir. Soldiers settled on these landholdings could be called for military duty any time. In peace time about sixty men per company were called from their homes and kept ready for any military eventuality. But in times of war

[3] Captain O. Cavenagh, *Rough Notes on the State of Nepal, Its Government, Army and Resources* (Calcutta, 1851), pp. 2–9.

[4] Col. W. Kirkpatrick, *An Account of the Kingdom of Nepal* (London, 1811), p. 215.

[5] Ibid.

[6] F. B. Hamilton, *An Account of the Kingdom of Nepal and of the Territories annexed to this Dominion by the House of Gorkha* (Edinburgh, 1819), p. 111; see picture of *khukri*. Kirkpatrick notes that every Nepalese wore a knife called a *khukri*, which apart from its use in war, was of great use in hacking down branches of trees that often blocked the mountain paths (*Account of Nepal*, p. 118).

[7] See for example exhibit No. 3, Gurkha *khukri c.* 1814, India Room, Sandhurst Military Academy, Sandhurst.

[8] MSS Eur. E. 68, Buchanan Hamilton, 'Nepal—Some observations,' pp. 95–6, IOL.

each company was augmented by 200–300 musketeers, and even family members of sipahis could be ordered on duty.[9] Thus Prithvi Narayan's hill Kshatriya was an amalgam, incorporating the social customs of the Kshatriyas of the plains, and the military practices of both the European as well as the Mughal army.

The military Hinduism encouraged by Prithvi Narayan Shah distanced the Hinduized Nepalese soldiers from the 'tribal' society of Nepal. For instance, in 1828, Brian H. Hodgson, the British Resident in the court of Nepal, noted that the Khus of the hill Kshatriya, who were residents of the Gorakh hills and the principal military 'tribe' of the Gurkha army, arrogated to themselves a high position in Nepalese society. All their members wore the thread and used the title of the first order of priesthood—'Opadhiah' (Upadhiyah).[10] The Khus never married, ate or communicated in any other way with hill 'tribes' who did not wear the high-caste thread.[11] The Magar 'tribe', originally followers of Buddhism, also acquired hill Kshatriya status in Prithvi Narayan's army.[12] They received the titles of Opadhiah and followed dietary habits similar to the Khus.[13] Similarly, the Gurang 'tribals', even though placed very low in the social hierarchy of the Himalayan 'tribes', preserved the same scruples of diet that had been adopted by the Hinduized Khus and the Magars. It was an accepted belief in Nepal that those Gurangs who had not joined the army and had continued to live in their native haunts, along the Himalayan

[9] Ibid.

[10] Hodgson Papers, p. 20.

[11] Ibid., p. 12. All the Khus 'tribe' who called themselves Brahmin Pandits were descended from members of the 'sacred order' who had married women of the Khus caste. Of these there were many in the Gurkha army and they inherited their father's title though they were in fact Khus or hill Kshatriyas or Khutree. Another group of mixed parentage were the offspring of the Khus father and any Magar, Gurang or Newar 'tribal' women, who called themselves Khus, and were recruited into the army. But they could not marry or eat with a Khus, not even with their own father. In the Gurkha army this category of Khus were generally employed as camp menials and tent pitchers.

[12] T. Smith, *Narrative of 5 Years Residence at Nepal* (2 vols., London, 1852) I, pp. 132–3, 135. The original seat of the Magars was the central and lower part of the mountains, between the Bhere and Massyande rivers. In the social hierarchy of Nepali society their status was considered lower than the Khus and they were not entitled to the thread.

[13] Ibid., pp. 132–3.

tract, 'wallow in all the filth of Buddhism, receive the religious ministry of the vile Lamas and eat anything and everything.'[14] In the Nepal valley, the Gurkhas often reproached those Gurangs and Magars who had not associated with the military institutions of the ruling house and had remained attached to Buddhism or Lamaism.[15] In the 1820s, Hodgson commented on the creation of this new Hindu Kshatriya identity in the 'tribes' of the Nepal valley:

As none but an ostensibly Brahmanical Hindoo can enter the Gurkha army and hence all the Muggurs and Goorungs who have taken service have brahmins for priests and subject their diet to the canon of purity and impurity....And if you would anger a soldier of either of these castes you need only call him that he is a Muggur and a Goorung.[16]

But this specific form of hill Hinduism also made the hill Kshatriyas appear very distinct from the high castes of Hindustan. For instance, in their diet and habits, the hill Kshatriyas observed the Brahmanical rules of purity and impurity, but they incorporated certain additional features in what was commonly accepted as an average high-caste diet. For instance, the hill Kshatriyas did not eat fowl or fowl's eggs, but had no objection to eating duck and its eggs. Similarly fish and all sorts of game were licit food to them.

It is then not surprising that this military Hinduism of Nepal made the Gurkha sipahis very different from the high-caste Hindu sipahis in the Company's service. As we have already seen, their dietary habits were different from the predominantly vegetarian Brahman and Rajput sipahis of the Bengal Army. Interestingly, this specifically Himalayan military Hinduism was best reflected in the Gurkhas' use of mounted guns which were worked by hand and not dragged by bullock train.[17] The hill Kshatriyas' belief with respect to the sacred cow apparently prevented their using bullocks for draught purposes. Ironically, this was a Hindu high-caste notion prevalent exclusively in the Gurkha regiments

---

[14] Hodgson Papers, notes, paragraph 11.

[15] Ibid. The Gurangs or Magars not associated with the army belonged geographicaly to the Himalayan or Bhotiyan region, and followed the Buddhist religion which was practised in the region.

[16] Ibid.

[17] Cavenagh, *The State of Nepal*, p. 13.

of Nepal. The Company's predominantly Hindu sipahis, from Hindustan, had no objection to the use of the bullock as a draught animal at least in regard to military service.[18] Again, European travellers to Nepal noted that the Gurkha sipahis did not participate in the large-scale rituals of Hindu festivals like Dussehra. In 1767, Captain George Kinloch who travelled extensively in Nepal, commented on the distinctive character of Gurkha Hinduism:

That although the Gurkhas profess the Hindu religion but, I believe, know little of any other deity but Bum Singh (Gurkha military governor of Kumaon).[19]

As in the case of the Bhumihar sipahis of the plains, this invented Gurkha tradition very often came into conflict with the Brahmanical figures of religious authority who questioned the sanctity of the hill Kshatriyas created by Prithvi Narayan Shah. This became particularly acute when the expansion of the Gurkha state into the Nepal valley and into Kumaon and Garhwal brought it into direct contact with the Pande and Joshi Kumaonis and Garhwali Brahmans. The conflict between the Kshatriyas and the Brahmans was to some extent resolved by the creation of a special figure of religious authority—the Rajguru—who appears to have mediated between the interests of Kshatriyas and Brahmans.[20] He was a wealthy and influential person in the state and had a large income from government lands, and also from the fines inflicted on the people for violation of caste rules. The position of the Rajguru was hereditary in nature and the soldiers as well as the King had to carry out his religious behests. Besides these measures, the Gurkhas gave the Brahmans certain social and legal concessions, while the administrative power was entirely vested in the hands of the Kshatriyas.[21] Many other local priests, gurus and purohits

---

[18] Ibid. Horses were very expensive and therefore were seldom used. However, some years later, elephants were used for transporting men and military goods.

[19] MSS Eur. F/128/140, No. 2, 'Journal of Captain George Kinloch on the Expedition to Nepal begun 26 August 1767', 2 vols., I, pages not marked, IOL.

[20] Wright, *History of Nepal*, p. 26.

[21] H. A. Oldfield, *Sketches from Nepal—Historical and Descriptive* (2 vols., London, 1880), I, p. 303. Brahmins were exempt from capital punishment. The punishment prescribed for them for violation of the endogamous marriage system was also much less severe

were also patronized by the rulers. Lands were assigned to them and rich temples were endowed in their favour.[22] In all these different ways the Brahman priesthood was kept satisfied and it continued to provide legitimacy to the Gurkha state.

GURKHA EXPANSION, 1774–1814

Important political, social, and economic developments took place in the territories which the Gurkhas had subordinated to their rule in the period 1774–1814. These were the areas located in and around the hill kingdoms of Kumaon, Garhwal and Sirmour which a year later (1814–15), became the Company's major recruiting grounds for enlisting Gurkha soldiers into its army.

At the time of Prithvi Narayan Shah's death the Gurkha state had expanded into the Nepal valley. In the period 1774–90, the Gurkha state extended to the neighbouring hill kingdoms of the Chaubisi rajas (1787), Sikkim (1787), Kumaon (1790), Garhwal (1803), and Sirmour (1805). By 1805, under the aegis of Prithvi Narayan's son Bahadur Shah and later during the prime ministership of Bhim Singh Thapa, the Gurkha kingdom had expanded as far as the banks of the Sutlej.

In each of these regions, the extension of Gurkha rule eroded the existing structures of power and replaced them by the Gurkha army and figures of Gurkha religious authority, notably the Rajguru. At the same time the revenue of the newly-conquered territory was used to sustain and strengthen the Gurkha army and polity. For instance, in Kumaon, the local rajas had derived authority from their patronage of the Brahman Joshi priesthood. Their power was dependent on the support of the zamindars and peasantry, who supplied them with soldiers.[23] The Gurkhas eroded both these structures of power and authority. The Gurkha soldiers in Kumaon were granted jagirs for military service. In order to derive the maximum revenue from these jagirs they exploited the zamindars

---

than it was for the rest of the citizens.

[22] Ibid.

[23] J. B. Fraser, *Journal of a Tour through Part of the Snowy Range of the Himalaya Mountains* (London, 1820), p. 537; see also Home Misc. No. 644, 645, IOL.

to the utmost. This eroded the rural base of the Kumaon raja[24] and resulted in the emigration of a large number of zamindars and peasants from the region.[25] Moreover, the Gurkhas seized the zamindar's crops for the purpose of supplying food to their military contingents. This left little for the zamindar with which he could pay tribute to the rulers. As a penalty for not paying tribute, the Gurkha sipahi forced the zamindar to give up one member of his family, who then became a bonded serf in the ruling house.[26] This often prompted the local peasants and zamindars to enlist in large numbers in the local levies the Gurkhas recruited in the region. In this way they escaped being forced into labour by the Gurkha ruling house. For instance, in 1814, there were approximately 800 Kumaonis reported to be serving the Gurkhas.[27] These Kumaoni levies were kept distinct from the regular troops of Nepal.[28]

[24] 'Statistical Sketch of Kumaon', Parts I and II by G. W. Traill, Commissioner of Kumaon, 16 April 1823, BC, File No. 21951, F/4/828, IOL. Traill reported that the Gurkha army was further expanded after the conquest of Kumaon. To pay the large number of soldiers, the Gurkha ruling house parcelled out all the villages which had been hitherto reserved for the support of the Gurkha court and their attendants.

[25] Ibid.; also see L. No. 63, A. Seton, Commissioner Bareli, to W. B. Edmonstone, Sec. to Govt., Sec. and Pol. Deptt., Ceded Provinces, 25 Jan. 1806, BC, File No. 63, extract Bengal Sec. Consult., 13 Feb. 1806, pp. 7–10, F/4/204, IOL. Seton reported that he had received information of over 1,200 Kumaoni peasants fleeing to Rohilkhand so as to escape the atrocities of the Gurkhas. They were said to have migrated with their cattle, their agricultural implements, and all the belongings they could carry. Seton wanted to settle them on the wastelands in the northern woods of Rohilkhand. Often violence broke out between these migrating groups—at times they fought with the Nepalese troops. In one such instance Seton reported that the Kumaoni peasantry attacked and killed a Gurkha soldier because the latter had plundered their property.

[26] Fraser, Journal, p. 219; see also Captain H. Y. Hearsey to John Adam, Sec. to Govt., 24 Aug. 1814, cited in B. P. Saksena (ed.), UP State Records Series, selections from English records No. 3 historical papers relating to Kumaon 1809–1842 (Lucknow, 1956), pp. 1–9. The revenue drawn by the Gurkhas from the province of Kumaon amounted to about 250,000 rupees. They had taken all the rent-free lands from the Brahmins and this increased the revenue to 325,000 rupees. There were about 400 troops in Kumaon, stationed in different garrisons.

[27] L. No. 267, Captain H. Hearsey to John Adam, Sec. to Govt., undated, Home Misc./646, IOL.

[28] Fraser, Journal, appendix No. 8, pp. 537–8. Fraser noted that each soldier on his return from service or when he was discharged obtained a small subsistence allowance, generally

In 1805, G. W. Traill, the Commissioner of Kumaon, noted a similar pattern in the Gurkha conquest of Garhwal. The Gurkha soldiers exploited, to the utmost, the revenue resources of their jagirs. This weakened the zamindars and the peasantry, and weakened the rural base of the Garhwal raja. Here, the peasantry was forced to surrender grain and cloth to the value of three lakhs of rupees, in tribute to the Gurkha ruling house.[29] Under the strain of taxation, a large number of dispossessed Garhwali peasants enlisted in the locally-recruited Gurkha levies.[30] Whenever peasant recruits were lacking, the Gurkhas resorted to 'slave plundering'. This was a form of recruitment in which sons of local zamindars were kidnapped and then trained in military skills so as to serve in the Gurkha army.[31]

Soon after the conquest of Garhwal, Sirmour was occupied.[32] The state had never been very formidable and it relied on temporary levies raised for occasional service. The hill chieftaincies over which Sirmour claimed tributary authority—Jubul, Utruck, Ruter,

---

in the form of a landholding. They were armed in much the same way as the regular troops, but were far inferior in strength, activity and gallantry to the Gurkha troops recruited in Nepal. None but those on military duty were permitted to go armed, and a severe penalty was inflicted on those who, when not on duty, were found carrying offensive weapons.

[29] Captain H. Y. Hearsey to John Adam, Sec. to Govt., 24 Aug. 1814, cited in Saksena, *Historical Papers relating to Kumaon 1809–1842*, pp. 1–9.

[30] Fraser, *Journal*, appendix No. 3, pp. 517–18.

[31] Ibid., p. 218; also see Captain H. Hearsey to John Adam, Sec. to Govt., 24 Aug. 1814, cited in Saksena, *Historical Papers relating to Kumaon 1809–1842*, pp. 1–9. He reported that upwards of 30,000 males and females were sold, and carried away for slavery. Nearly 80,000 men and women emigrated in 1811–12, and the country was nearly depopulated. The villages had gone to ruin and a jungle had emerged in a place where, in 1809, he had seen cultivation thriving; see also Captain H. Hearsey, 'Memorandum relating to the late family and government of the Rajas of Srinagar and Garhwal', Home Misc./646, IOL. He notes the oppressed state of zamindars under the Gurkha rule.

[32] Fraser, *Journal*, p. 74. Sirmour state was divided into 27 parganas, of which the valley called Kearda-Dhoon was the only one capable of being fully and richly cultivated. The revenue from this valley was never very large, and the depopulation and ruin during the Gurkha occupation reduced it further. In fact the total amount of revenue which the Nepalese Government drew from it never exceeded Rs 85,000, excluding the revenue obtained from the petty states dependent on it which were separately assessed.

Bulsum, Raeen, Seeli and Sari—supplied levies to the Sirmour raja. Most of these levies were armed with bows, arrows and axes. Select troops carried swords or were supplied with matchlocks.[33] The Gurkhas banished or dispersed these chiefs and created new officers to fill the different posts of trust in the kingdom. The chief zamindars were very often carried away from their farms and families as hostages and the general population of Sirmour was disarmed.[34] By 1818, Sirmour had been politically extinguished.

Captain Hearsey, posted in Kumaon in 1814, reported that the total strength of the army under Amar Singh Thapa, the Gurkha Commandant, consisted of approximately 6,000 fighting men. The women who followed the army camp increased the number to 12,000. This army consisted of about 1,800 or 2,000 Gurkhas from Nepal, and the remainder were people from Palpah, Kumaon and Garhwal. He reported that necessity had compelled the Kumaonis and Garhwalis to join the army, and on six rupees per month they would willingly enlist in the Company's army.[35]

The state of Nepal was in this state of development when the Gurkha war brought it in direct confrontation with the East India Company. In 1815, Nepal's defeat in this war deprived it of its possessions in Kumaon, Garhwal and Sirmour. The people it had recruited from these lands now became one of the major pools of recruits available to the Company for its army. It was here that the Company began creating its 'new' Gurkha sipahi.

THE CREATION OF A GURKHA IDENTITY

The military preparation for the Gurkha war was accompanied by a series of political arrangements calculated to 'engage in the Company's cause the expelled chiefs of the ancient hill principalities reduced by the Gurkhas, and thus to draw to the Company's side their former subjects.'[36] The Governor-General did not

---

[33] Fraser, *Journal*, p. 74.

[34] See Home Miscellaneous/652, No. 12002, IOL.

[35] Captain H. Hearsey to J. Adam, Sec. to Govt., 24 Aug. 1814, cited in Saksena, *Historical Papers relating to Kumaon 1809–42*, p. 8.

[36] B. D. Sanyal, *Nepal and the East India Company* (London, 1965), pp. 146–7.

want territorial acquisition between the Sutlej and the Jamuna. The hill chiefs were expected to allow free passage for the merchants of the East India Company and to provide military service to the Company at short notice. They were also expected to assist in the supply and accommodation of British troops during the military operations.[37]

This military strategy was accompanied by the enlistment of a large number of troops from the kingdoms of Kumaon, Garhwal and Sirmour into the Company army. The Company's service was a welcome refuge to those Kumaonis, Garhwalis and Sirmouris who had been dispossessed of their high political and military status by the Gurkhas. William Fraser, the Political Agent in Nepal during the war and later posted as the Commissioner of Delhi, was entrusted with the task of recruiting these hill levies. He never experienced any problem in recruiting. In 1814, nearly 1,000 men from Sirmour had enlisted into the irregular corps.[38] In Garhwal, many landholders supplied their levies to the Company,[39] and many Kumaonis willingly flocked to the Company's service. In 1814, Major General Wood recruited a large contingent, called the Pahariah Regiment, from Bootwal. The recruits joined the service because Wood claimed that he would soon settle them on landholdings.[40] The total strength of the irregular levies assembled during 1814–15 amounted to 7,000 men. Apart from the highlanders, this figure also included a sprinkling of Sikhs, Pathans, Mewatis and others.[41] Out of these irregulars there were only 200 Gurkha recruits. They included the soldiers of the Gurkha garrison of Chupal. They had capitulated on the condition that they would be recruited into the Company's army. There were about 100 of them and their number swelled to 200 after some

[37] See for restoration of chiefs in Garhwal and Kumaon, Home Misc./646, No. 267, IOL; for the restoration of the Sirmour Raja see BC, File No. 21944, F/4/827, IOL.

[38] Fraser, *Journal*, p. 76.

[39] Ibid., p. 80.

[40] Petition of a Subahdar of this regiment asking for pension, 24 May 1823, GCRR PM, Basta No. 7, vol. no. 64, File No. 78, ARA; see also Fraser, *Journal*, pp. 100–1. Fraser recruited a large number of professionally trained Rohillas, 100 Pathans and 600 Mewatis from Rohilkhand, Saharanpur, Bareli and parts of Kumaon.

[41] Ibid., p. 80.

troops deserted from the Gurkha garrison at Jytuk.[42] The Company admired the Gurkhas' proficiency in hill warfare and made efforts to win over more Nepalese sipahis from the Nepal kingdom. For instance, Edward Gardner, the Commissioner of Kumaon, negotiated with Amar Singh Thapa (the Gurkha Commander) and Bum Sah (the Gurkha Governor of Kumaon) to desert to the Company service, but none of these offers prompted any major desertions.[43]

The Nepal war of 1815 increased the Company's admiration for the Gurkhas. But for a variety of reasons it was unable to attract the Gurkhas to its service. First, the Nepalese government, even after the peace treaty which had put an end to the Gurkha war, continued with its unco-operative attitude towards the Company. Nepal did not allow the British Resident in Kathmandu to interfere in its affairs, and the Company could not get permission to send its recruiting parties to Nepal.[44] Finally, the Nepal government imposed rigid restrictions on the movement of Gurkhas outside the Nepal territory. This made it difficult for the Gurkha soldiers to desert to the Company's army.[45] Interestingly enough, the Company too had its reservations about switching its recruiting base to the Nepal valley. In 1816, the Company was preoccupied with organizing its irregular cavalry to combat the mounted warriors—the Pindaris, the Marathas and the Afghans. The Gurkha sipahis, being good infantrymen, were not suited for such warfare. Moreover, the Company's less-than-wholehearted efforts towards Gurkha recruitment was also because it did not possess any detailed knowledge of the Gurkhas. Significantly, in this period the Company's attitude towards the Gurkhas was determined by the views of military commandants and civil servants posted in Nepal. William Fraser, the Company's political agent in Nepal, had

---

[42] Ibid., p. 101.

[43] J. Adam, Sec. to Govt., to C. T. Metcalf, Resident at Delhi, Secret Deptt., Camp Newalgunj, 23 Oct. 1814, cited in Saksena, *Historical Papers related to Kumaon 1809–42*, pp. 16–23.

[44] I. A. Nicol, Adjtt. Gen., to Sec. to Govt., Pol. Deptt., 8 Jan. 1825, Home Misc./665, IOL.

[45] Hodgson Papers, p. 41.

recruited Gurkhas for the purpose of policing and used them as foraging parties during the war. The Company was influenced by his idea that the Gurkhas 'could be used only for such purposes'.[46]

In this period of doubt and uncertainty, unable to successfully attract the core of the Nepali army, the Company began instead to invent its own model of a Gurkha soldier. The Company created a Gurkha sepoy figure which was moulded out of the Kumaoni, Garhwali and Sirmouri recruits Fraser had assembled in the region. These irregular levies of Fraser, had of course, a sprinkling of Gurkhas from Nepal as well. This invented Gurkha tradition welded together the customs of Prithvi Narayan Shah's Gurkhas and the Western practices of drill and discipline. The Company also allowed Mughal imagery and deportment to persist as they had done in the plains. For instance, in one of the pictures of military recruits, apparently drawn by Fraser and included in Skinner's album, the dress of the Gurkhas displays a considerable variety as it is not yet standardized. Only the man on the extreme left called Himmut, and described as a Khutree, is dressed in a manner typical of later Gurkha soldiers. Otherwise their dress seems to be typical of what might be called the 'Mughal fringe' (plate 10).[47]

After the Gurkha war, Fraser's 7,000-strong irregular levy was reorganized into four Gurkha battalions.[48] These battalions performed police duties for the Company.[49] One of these battalions

[46] Fraser, *Journal*, pp. 94, 128–9. According to Fraser the Gurkha foraging parties successfully coerced people to sell their grain to the army.

[47] Uniformity in dress, deportment and religious observations developed much later with the continuous association of the Gurkhas with the Bengal Army.

[48] The first two were called the 1st and 2nd Battalions of the Nassara Regiment which derived its name from the Nassiri hills from where most of its recruits came. The Sirmour Battalion, which had Sirmouri and Garhwali recruits, and the Kumaon Levy, which was stationed at Almora, formed the remaining 2 irregular corps. The Nassara regiment is now known as the 1st Gurkha Rifles, the Sirmour Battalion is called the 2nd Gurkha Rifles, and the Kumaon Levy is known as the 3rd Gurkha Rifles.

[49] S. Young, Pol. Agent at Dehra Dun, to Commissioner, 18 May 1838, DDPMR, judicial letters issued May 1838–May 1840, DRA. He reported that there were no police Thanahs or establishments in the Dun valley, but the services of the Gurkha Guards, stationed at Lakerghat and Kansraw, were available till June, when they too

called the Sirmour Battalion or the 2nd King Edwards Own Gurkha Rifles has a written regimental history.[50] In this work it is possible to trace the Company's invention of a new Gurkha identity within this regiment. In 1815, it consisted of 1,223 recruits, chiefly Hindus from the Sirmour state which the Gurkhas had conquered in 1805. It also had Garhwalis, Kumaonis and some Gurkhas from Nepal. The regiment was initially based at Nahan, the capital of Sirmour state, and the men wore their own mountaineer's dress. However, from 1816, the Company began to amalgamate the Sirmouri military practices with the 'tribal' customs of the Gurkhas of Nepal. To these were added European military uniforms and ethics. The Company armed the recruits with weapons it associated with the Gurkhas.[51] These consisted of the old Brown Bess, a long bayonet, and the traditional khukri which these hill men had not previously used. The Company also introduced a uniform for this corps consisting of a mixture of European and Gurkha garments and the Sirmouris' native headgear. It was a dark green coatee with tails looped up, black facings and high shoulder wings. They wore white drill trousers and Gurkha shoes. The sipahis were allowed to wear their own tightly bound black headdress as neither the Gurkha puggaree or heavy European headdress was viewed with pleasure by them. However, they later received a green shako and in the fashion of the Company's soldiers they were provided with a leather belt with a pouch attached to it.[52] After the 1824–6 siege of Bharatpur their uniform was modified and the leather shako was introduced.[53]

---

moved out of the region due to the unhealthiness of the season. Also see Pre-Mutiny Records, office of the Commissioner of Kumaon, vol. 8. These contain several cases of complaints against men of the Kumaon Provincial Battalion who were stationed for the performance of civilian duties on the frontier of Kumaon. The men were within the jurisdiction of the local Magistrate and were tried by the civil and criminal courts of the region.

[50] Col. L. W. Shakespear, *History of the 2nd King Edward's Own Goorkha Rifles* (Aldershot, 1912).

[51] Ibid., p. 29.

[52] Ibid.

[53] Ibid. Blue drill trousers were now worn by officers and men. The piping on the breast was changed to red, and buglers wore scarlet coatees with green facing.

The Company soon began to encourage the celebration of Hindu festivals like Dussehra in the Sirmour Regiment. Dussehra was seldom celebrated in the Gurkha regiments of Nepal. However, it became a popular public ritual in the Sirmour Regiment because most of the troops, being Hindus from Sirmour and Garhwal, showed an enthusiasm for its celebration. However, in the Sirmour Regiment the Dussehra celebrations were woven into the military practices adopted from the Gurkha and the European armies, and a distinctively non-Brahman form of 'tribal' Dussehra celebration was standardized in the regiment. Here, Dussehra was characterized by the sacrifice of a number of goats and buffaloes, and the decapitation was done by the 'national weapon' of the sipahi—the khukri.[54] In the 1840s, Captain T. Smith, the Assistant Political Resident in Nepal from 1841 till 1845, reported that these sacrifices were made at the rural shrine erected for the purpose and the slaughter took place amidst firing of cannon and fusils. Generally, the most expert swordsman was chosen for the buffalo sacrifice and he performed the act after various incantations.[55] The sacrifice of buffaloes suggests the distinct incorporation of 'tribal' Nepalese rituals into the Sirmour Regiment.

But if Dussehra celebrations, characteristic of the Company's peasant army, were encouraged, certain practices of the Nepalese army were introduced as well. For instance, the Company allowed the sipahis to live with their wives and families in the sipahi lines. This was a practice of the Nepal army, but was unheard of in the Company's regiments stationed in the plains. Similarly, the Company allowed local hill customs and practices, such as sorcery or 'back magic', to continue in its Sirmour Regiment.[56] The Company's newly-created Gurkha sipahi regiments were

[54] Ibid.

[55] Smith, *Narrative II*, pp. 257–8.

[56] I. H. Batten, Assistant Commissioner in charge of Garhwal, to Government, 28 June 1837, Pre Mutiny Records Pauri Garhwal Judicial Letters issued, March 1837–March 1840, vol. 2 DRA. Until as late as 1837, the Company had no law or uniform practice to deal with cases of black magic or witchcraft. Cases which were brought to its notice in Kumaon were referred to the court in Almora. Most often both the accuser and accused were compelled to sign a penal bond that they would not 'molest' each other in future. This applied to both civilian as well as military men who were referred to the court.

used mainly for policing duties although they were fully armed for major conflicts on the war front. This was a result of Fraser's assessment of the Gurkhas as best suited for such duties. Consequently, for the well-armed Gurkha, sipahi parades were few, drills mostly under native officers, and there were no field days. The period of peace which followed the siege of Bharatpur (1818) was accompanied by the increased use of the Sirmour Regiment for policing duties and other civilian jobs. These included a variety of tasks from guarding the Haridwar highway to the suppression of internal riots and disturbances.[57] It was only in 1849, at the time of the Sikh war, that this Corps was made into a General Service Corps, and placed under the direct authority of the Commander-in-Chief.[58]

In the 1840s, T. Smith noted that the sons and other relatives of former soldiers were recruited into the Company's Sirmour Regiment. Its regimental lines, in Dehra Dun, acted as a military colony of such Gurkhas. The sons of old soldiers grew up in the lines and their fathers trained them in military skills. Even as children they identified with the Corps and aspired for the honour of carrying fusils in its regiments. In his account of the Sirmour Regiment Smith noted that:

Indeed the principal amusement of the little broad-faced urchins who crowd the Lines is 'playing the soldier' and aping their seniors in the performance of the 'manual and platoon' and light infantry manoeuvres. Little fellows of 3-4 years of age draw up to the side of the road when an officer passes and salute him with dignity and solemnity perfectly edifying.[59]

These evolving regimental traditions made the Gurkha sipahis in the Company's service not only distinct from the purabia sipahis of the plains, but also very different from the Gurkha sipahis of the Nepal state. In 1857, the distinctiveness of the Company's

---

[57] Shakespear, *History of the 2nd King Edward's Own Goorkha Rifles*, pp. 25–6, p. 30. The sepoys of this Corps participated in the siege of Bharatpur. Besides performing this duty they worked on the construction of the canal which Captain Young had inaugurated in the region. In 1842-8 they were sent to suppress the Muharram riots in Bareli, and in 1843 they were sent to defuse the tension in Kaithal.

[58] Ibid., p. 39.

[59] Smith, *Narrative*, II, pp. 259–60.

Gurkha sipahi was best reflected in the comments the Gurkhas of the Sirmour Regiment, training at the musketry school at Ambala, made on the purabia sipahis. In those days the handling of the new, greased cartridges, the end of which had to be bitten off before loading, was much resented by the majority of the troops. But the Company's Gurkhas who had become aware of the native corps' mutinous and insubordinate feelings in regard to these cartridges, requested permission to pitch their tents with those of the British soldiers. They had no desire to be mixed with the '*kala logue*' (dark people) as they called the native soldiery in their disaffected mood.[60] They also wanted these cartridges to be distributed to them in order to show the purabias that they had no fellow feeling with them on this question. Colonel Greathed, Commandant of the School, at once acceded to their request and 'expressed his great satisfaction at their conduct'. On 6 April 1857, having completed their course, the party marched back to Dehra Dun. Here, they were thought none the less of by their comrades for having used the greased cartridges.[61]

The second phase of the Company's relations with the Gurkhas occurred between 1820 and 1839. This was the period when the Company showed a keen interest in the Gurkha recruits of the Nepal army. The timing of this need for recruiting Gurkha soldiers was significant. It may be attributed to a variety of factors. First, it had to do with the general problem of discipline and control within the Company army. The peasant army was becoming increasingly unreliable and after the Pindari campaign of 1818 the Company had started distancing itself from its irregular cavalry regiments. Secondly, military and political developments within Nepal, particularly in the latter period of Bhim Singh Thapa's rule, made the Company's service more attractive to the Gurkhas of Nepal. Finally, in the 1820s with the arrival of Brian H. Hodgson as the British Resident in Nepal, an exhaustive study of the Gurkha

[60] Shakespear, *History of the 2nd King Edward's Own Goorkha Rifles*, p. 42.
[61] Ibid.

military–political organization, ethnography, and language commenced. Hodgson's study increased the Company's knowledge and information about the Gurkhas. These developments led to discussions on the possibility of switching the recruitment base to the Nepal valley. But the Company's lukewarm approach to Gurkha recruitment in peacetime decided the issue against the Gurkhas. This gave the Gurkha state ample opportunity to continue with its experiments in the formation of a Hindu military identity.

The Problems of Military Discipline and Control

From the mid–1820s Gurkhas became the centre of discussion as prospective recruits for the Company's army. This was related to the general problem of control and discipline the Company experienced within its peasant army. As chapter 2 has already shown, the 1820s was a decade of mutinies,[62] and the Company had begun to doubt the reliance it could place on its Hindustani soldiers. Interestingly, as it attempted to grapple with the problems within the peasant regiments, its military experts repeatedly suggested that it provide some counterpoise to the pampered sipahis of the Gangetic valley. They urged the recruitment of Gurkhas and argued that these soldiers would constitute the new element of strength and reliability in the army. In 1824, a proposal was made to the Commander-in-Chief to establish a recruiting depot at Lohouaghat, in the province of Kumaon, to enlist Gurkhas. In the same year Lieutenant Lawrence, Adjutant of the 2nd Nusseree Battalion, reported the existence of about 1,500–2,000 Gurkha Dakhili troops in the province of Dhoti (in Nepal), near Lohouaghat. He reported that they were eager to enter the Company's service which the Lohouaghat establishment would encourage.[63] But the project was shelved because the Commander-in-Chief expressed his doubts about the ability of the Gurkha soldiers to serve on the plains. Moreover, the government did

---

[62] The Barrackpur mutiny in 1824–5 alarmed the Company the most.

[63] President Fort William to Sec. to Govt. Pol. Deptt. and extract from a letter from Lt. Lawrence, Adjt. 2nd Nusseree Battalion, 8 Dec. 1824, Home Misc./665, IOL.

not sanction the project because of the adverse effects it might have on political relations with Nepal.[64]

The Restructuring of the Nepal Army

The politics of Nepal from 1816 till 1839 was dominated by Bhim Singh Thapa, the Kshatriya prime minister of the minor King Vikram Singh. As was characteristic of the Gurkha military–political tradition, the prime minister represented the royalty and derived his power from the military establishment of the Gurkhas. Hemmed in on all sides by the East India Company, with which it was bound by treaty obligations, this was a period of peace for the Nepal kingdom. But a nation which was created through the formation of an army, and one in which national identity was linked to military identity became shaky when the long period of peace (1816–42) provided no outlet for the military careers and aspirations of its people. To avert a military and political upheaval, Bhim Singh Thapa began to expand the army and intensified military discipline. He increased the peacetime strength of the army from 6,000 fighting men[65] to 10,000 men.[66] The war establishment of the army was increased to 20,000 men. To provide military experience to the maximum number of aspirants, the government continued to rotate its soldiers annually. All enlistment was done for only one year; after which, a periodical dismissal of soldiers took place, and these temporarily dismissed soldiers were called Dakhili troops.[67]

Bhim Singh Thapa further emphasized the importance of European military skills and discipline. Hodgson noted that during

[64] Ibid.

[65] Captain H. Y. Hearsey to John Adam, Sec. to Govt., 24 Aug. 1814, cited in Saksena, *Historical Papers relating to Kumaon 1809–42*, pp. 1–9. Hearsey, while reporting on the strength of the Nepal army, writes that in 1814 this was the peace establishment of the army, of which only 1,800 or 2,000 were real Gurkhas, the rest being Kumaoni and Garhwali troops.

[66] Hodgson Papers, pp. 36–8.

[67] Ibid., p. 38. When out of service, they wandered in the jungles in pursuit of game, or amused themselves at home practising archery, or lived in sheer idleness. Since it was only on rare occasions that they condescended to practise agriculture, when they were restored to the ranks they appeared with 'no rustic gait or unsoldier-like awkwardness'.

Thapa's rule the structure of the Gurkha army had become very similar to that of the East India Company's army:

The Nepalese give in general a preference to our light Infantry exercise. In all the evolutions of which they are perfect, as well as in the bugle calls to which those evolutions are performed, the men are daily and sometimes twice a day on parade and the fruits of this perseverance are that they go through their evolution with a precision and despatch worthy of our regulars. Their muskets are excellent, their accoutrements respectable and are subjected to all the vigour of our system without one title of abatement.[68]

Apart from the emulation of Western modes of drill and parade, the Gurkha troops, like the soldiers of the Company army, were also constrained to live in barracks. In 1823, the first pakka cantonment was established for the Gurkha troops.[69]

However, Bhim Singh Thapa's military reorganization created problems for the Nepal state. First, there was a major incompatibility between the cantoning of sipahis in barracks and the system of paying them in land jagirs. For the soldier could not manage his jagir if he was permanently cantoned in barracks. Many of the Gurkha sipahis complained about this practice to Hodgson:

They are obliged, they said (rightly), to look after their *khets* (fields) if they would reap due profit from them and yet the power of doing so is hardly compatible with appearing daily on parade and answering a roll call night and morning in the cantonments. They must run (they said) to and from parade to their homes with hardly the privilege of a few hours' stay there, or they will inevitably be too late for the roll call.[70]

When these troops were told that the English sepoys always lived in barracks, they answered, 'pay us as the English sepoys and we will gladly do so likewise.'[71] Secondly, the army reforms created a problem of unemployment in Nepal. The state trained more men as professional soldiers than it could employ. The surplus

---

[68] Ibid., p. 8.

[69] Ibid. The Campoo were regarded as the best battalions of the state, and their strength, together with the Palpa Brigade which had about 1,500 men, was approximately 4,000. Next to them, and somewhat inferior, was the Sri Mihur Paltan. This had 500 men and was stationed at Kathmandu.

[70] Ibid., pp. 36–8.

[71] Ibid.

soldiery caused disaffection in the army and made the Gurkhas look towards the Company army for employment. Moreover, the expanded peacetime establishment of the army aggravated the problem of the Dakhili troops in Nepal. These were the professionally trained Gurkha soldiers who had been temporarily dismissed from Gurkha service under the system of annual rotation. But finding no employment for long periods of time within Nepal, they became a threat to the Gurkha state. For they could be easily lured by the Punjab state in the west, the East India Company in the east and south, and the Chinese in the north. Hodgson reported that many of the Gurkha sipahis who happened to meet the Company's sipahis, on the border of Nepal and India, expressed a desire to be employed in the Company's service. They were reported to have told the Company sipahis:

Hey Tewaree!! you are a lucky fellow—never made dakhareeah (off the roll by rotation), always in receipt of 8 Siccas while we poor fellows every year are left to shift for ourselves to make a mere subsistence by carrying loads like a cooly for we have no land of our own. We are soldiers, arms are our trade and vocation and gladly would we serve anywhere if we could get regular pay.[72]

In their conversation with the Company sipahis the Gurkha soldiers reflected an awareness of the Company being a better employer. But they also revealed the restrictions their government had imposed on their moving out of the country. This had made it impossible for them to join the Company army. They were only allowed to leave the country for performing pilgrimage in Hindustan. But that too was allowed only once in several years. While in Hindustan, as pilgrims, a few Gurkha sipahis did manage to get into the Company's service. But the others felt deprived and returned home. The Gurkhas also revealed their inability to desert and escape on the quiet because of the fear that their families, left back home in their villages, would be harassed by the Nepal government.[73]

From 1839, the new Prime Minister Pande's military reforms further increased the Company's popularity amongst the Gurkha

[72] Ibid., pp. 39–40.
[73] Ibid., p. 41.

soldiers. One of the first moves of the new prime minister was to expand and remodel the military on which Bhim Singh had rested his power.[74] Pande continued with the system of drills and parades which had been introduced by Prithvi Narayan. He introduced the English chako, or the red coat of the Company's sepoys, as the uniform for his soldiers when they were on drill, but when on ordinary duty they wore their traditional dress. This consisted of a cotton turban, dyed black or blue, with the badge of the regiment, in gold or silver, tied in front with a silver chain. Along with this, they wore a loose red, blue or black cotton jacket which came down over the hips. Their uniform also included loose woollen or cotton trousers, a cummerbund, and shoes without gaiters and stockings.[75]

Pande resumed all rent-free grants so as to meet the expense of his expanded military establishment. The chiefs were subjected to a system of contributions. Approximately 30,000 pounds sterling was demanded from each of them and soldiers were deputed all over the country to enforce these exactions.[76] In 1838, the army was most disaffected when Pande introduced a system of money payment. This commutation into money payments, on a uniform scale for all persons of the same rank, was accompanied by a great reduction in the pay of all ranks of people.[77] The discontent soon resulted in Pande's removal by the King and the measure was revoked. But in general the army reforms of this period created disaffection and unemployment amongst the soldiers and increasingly attracted them towards the Company's army.

---

[74] Ibid., pp. 36–8. Masses of troops hitherto concentrated in the capital were dispersed throughout the country. Large numbers were sent to strengthen the frontier garrisons. Artillery and 3,000 infantry were marched off to stations in the interior.

[75] Hodgson MSS, 9, Ethnography, Army, Omras prior to the Tellingas or Regular troops, pp. 107–43, IOL.

[76] Hodgson Papers, p. 40.

[77] Hodgson MSS, 9, Ethnography, Army, Omras prior to the Tellingas or Regular troops, p. 120, IOL. In Bhim Singh Thapa's ministry it was usual to give different rates of pay to the individuals of the same rank serving in the same Company. Rates were often settled on the recommendation of the minister and other commanders.

Hodgson's Nepal Residency, 1823–39

The Company's attention was also drawn to the Gurkha soldiers by Brian H. Hodgson, British Resident in Nepal, who had worked as G. W. Traill's assistant in the Commissionary of Kumaon. Traill, was known as the King of Kumaon for his assertiveness and independence in policy matters. This training proved handy to Hodgson. The British Resident in Kathmandu had been given full discretionary powers to decide upon the plan of action in Nepal. Since 1816, as assistant to Edward Gardner, the first British Resident in Nepal, Hodgson had managed the politics of Nepal amicably. Indeed, the period of peace which followed his posting in Nepal was utilized by him to pursue his academic interests. He perfected his knowledge of the Gurkhali language and made an exhaustive study of the ethnography, language, politics and army of Nepal. Until the mid-1840s, Hodgson's exhaustive reports on the Gurkhas, their organization, and ethnography remained the only source of information about the region and its people. Hodgson's views and stereotypes about the martial qualities of the Gurkhas continued to influence the Company's attitudes towards the Gurkhas throughout the late nineteenth century.

From 1820 to 1843, Hodgson remained attached to the Residency of Nepal in varying capacities (1825–33 as the Assistant Resident to E. Gardner and 1833–43 as the Resident in Kathmandu). In Bentinck and Lord Auckland, Hodgson found Governor Generals who allowed him independence in policy matters and sufficient discretionary powers of interference in the court politics of Nepal. But even though his academic worth was recognized by these Governor-Generals, the large-scale military retrenchment and fiscal cuts which they initiated did not allow for any of Hodgson's suggestions to be implemented.

Hodgson was very vociferous in putting forward a strong case for recruiting Gurkhas into the Company's army. He considered this the only alternative to the worsening military discipline and control in the Bengal Army. In 1832, he summed up his report on the Gurkhas to the government:

These Highland soldiers who despatch their meal in half an hour, and satisfy their ceremonial law by merely washing their hands and face and taking off their turbans before cooking, laugh at the pharisaical rigour of our Sepoys who must bathe from head to foot and make Puja ere they begin to dress their dinner, must eat nearly naked in the coldest weather and cannot be in marching trim again in less than three hours—the best part of the day. In war, the former (i.e., Gurkhas) carry several days' provision on their backs. The latter (the Company's old Sepoys) would deem such an act intolerably degrading. The former see in foreign service nothing but the prospect of gain and glory. The latter can discover in it nothing but pollution and peril from unclean men and terrible wizards and goblins and evil spirits.[78]

Hodgson calculated that there were at that time in Nepal no less than 30,000 Dakhilis, or soldiers off the roll by rotation, and these belonged to the Khus, Magar, and Gurang tribes. He was of the view that the Company should utilize the services of these men:

Such are their energy of character, love of enterprise, and freedom from the shackles of caste, that I am well assured their services, if obtained, would soon come to be most highly prized. In my humble opinion they are by far the best soldiers in India. If they are not made participators of our renown in arms, I conceive that their gallant spirit and unadulterated military habits might be relied on for fidelity; establishment would serve to counterpoise the influence of nationality.[79]

Hodgson considered that if the Gurkha soldiers were not incorporated into the Company army they would very soon pose a serious military threat to the Company. In 1837, Hodgson drew attention to the danger the Company had run into by allowing the Nepal state to continue with its military expansion. In a letter to J. R. Colvin, Secretary to government, he wrote:

We now see the fruits of our mistakes....In the 20 years that we have been here we have seen nothing but drills and parades, heard nothing but the roar of cannon and the clink of hammer...soldiers have been and are heads of the law and finance at Kathmandu and administrators of the interior....They are everything and they are and have been headed by a plenary viceroy (Bhim Singh) which must support its habitual aggression

---

[78] Hodgson's Report dated Oct. 1832, taken from *Selections from the Records of the Government of Bengal* (No. XXVII, Calcutta, 1857), cited in W. W. Hunter, *Life of B. H. Hodgson, British Resident at the Court of Nepal* (London, 1896), p. 108.

[79] Ibid.

at home and pandering to the soldiery and teaching them to look to aggression abroad.[80]

While the academic worth of Hodgson's report was noted the government failed to follow up his suggestions. This was because they happened to arrive in the midst of the twelve years' peace between the fall of Bharatpur, in 1827, and the Afghan war in 1839. It was only at the time of the Afghan War of 1839 that the Company realized, for the first time, the danger which the Gurkhas could pose on the border while the military contingents of the Company were involved on the western frontier. But Auckland was too preoccupied with the Afghan problem to give serious consideration to the Gurkhas. He merely posted an army of 20,000 men on the frontier with Nepal. The Resident in Kathmandu was instructed to preserve a stern attitude towards the Darbar but not to precipitate a war.

The Militarized Nepal Kingdom, 1839–56

The arrival of Lord Ellenborough as the next Governor-General initiated a policy of 'non-interference' with the internal politics of the native states. This change in the East India Company policy changed the nature of the Nepal Residency. The Resident's power of independent discretionary action in handling the situation in Nepal was eroded. Hodgson vehemently resisted this erosion of his power. Consequently, the relations between him and Lord Ellenborough became very strained. In 1843, Lord Ellenborough terminated his Residency and appointed Sir Henry Lawrence as the new Resident in Kathmandu. Lawrence was directed by the Governor-General to carry out the Company's dictates of non-interference in the internal affairs of Nepal. The policy at this stage towards Nepal was that the Company was not interested in annexing Nepal provided she kept her turbulent nobles and soldiers away from the Company's territories. In such circumstances the Resident had to be a watchman on military and diplomatic duty with little concern for the internal intrigues of the Darbar.

[80] B. H. Hodgson to J. R. Colvin, Private Sec. to Gov. Gen., 24 June 1837, ibid., pp. 154–5.

He was to serve as the Company's agent at Kathmandu to look exclusively after the affairs of trade and external relations of this mountain principality.

Accordingly the policy of recruiting Gurkhas was shelved. Taking advantage of the Company's policy of non-interference, Jang Bahadur expanded the military–political tradition of the Gurkhas. The strength of the army was increased to 26,000 men of which nearly two-thirds were attached to the regular battalions and the remainder composed of local or irregular troops.[81]

Jang Bahadur's fascination with and keenness for the adoption of western skills and discipline intensified the westernization of the Gurkha military–political tradition that had been initiated by Prithvi Narayan. Most of the battalions, in keeping with the Hindu Gurkha military-political traditions of Prithvi Narayan Shah, were designated by the names of Hindu divinities. Often, like the practice prevalent in the Bengal army, they were also named after their distinguished officers.[82] Jang Bahadur even toyed with the idea of paying his troops at certain fixed rates, in cash, according to their ranks as was the practice in the Company's army.[83]

Apart from these changes in the organizational structure of the army, Jang Bahadur continued with the practice of casting cannon and manufacturing firearms. The foundry at Kathmandu flourished, as did the large manufactory of firearms at Reutana. Bayonets, rifles and muskets were also manufactured in these manufactories.[84] There were three principal magazines situated in Kathmandu, Bhatgaon, and Reutana, and the Kathmandu magazine contained 25,100 stand of arms.[85] Jang Bahadur also continued with the system of 'rotation of troops' which provided the experience of military service and a Kshatriya identity to

[81] Cavenagh, *Rough Notes on the State of Nepal*, pp. 2–9.

[82] Ibid. Some of the names were Ram Dal, Gunner Dal, Rifle Regiment, Sri Nath, Indra Dal, Ram Prithvi Dal, Singh Nath, etc.

[83] Ibid. The grades for non-commissioned officers were: Captain, Rs 3,000–4,000; Lieutenant, Rs 1,500–3,000; Subahdar, Rs 1,000–1,500; Jamadar, Rs 400–1,000; Havaldar and Naik, Rs 200–600; and Sepoys, Rs 100–300. Part of this salary was paid in cash and the rest in the form of a jagir.

[84] Ibid.

[85] Ibid., pp. 15–16.

In 1857, such disillusioned Company troopers looked to Indian patrons to restore them to the military status which Company officers, like Skinner, had made popular in the region. But while Skinner had recreated the Mughal military–political tradition, these rebel leaders claimed to restore the Mughal Emperor and the eighteenth-century Muslim ruling houses directly. It was for these reasons that Delhi remained the focus of activity for the regular and the irregular rebel regiments stationed in the Ceded and Conquered Provinces.[16] At Delhi, noted Company subahdars, like Bakht Khan, furthered their military ambitions by their claims to restore the Mughal Emperor to the throne of Delhi, thereby becoming popular leaders of the Company's disgruntled cavalrymen. In 1857, Bakht Khan was reported to be in possession of about 400 sawars, who were chiefly men of the Company's 8th Irregulars, 1,500 sipahis, four guns, thirty elephants and about seventy-five stud colts from the Company's horse stud at Hapur.[17] A similar pattern was followed in the Rohilkhand, Shahjahanpur and Bulandshahr region where local rulers restored their polities using the support of the Company troopers who sought stable political structures to restore their lost status.[18]

The deep intermeshing of military power with politics that characterized the first hundred years of Company rule in north India, was once again evident in the way the Company managed to crush the 1857 disturbances and restore its political dominance. The loyal support for the Company came from the Gurkha forces which it had built up as a military form distinct from the peasant

---

(Asian Studies Centre, South Asian Series occasional paper no. 17, Michigan State University), appendix III, p. 156.

[16] Lt.-Col. G. H. D. Gimlette, *A Postscript to the Records of the Indian Mutiny: An attempt to trace the subsequent careers and fate of the rebel Bengal regiments, 1857–8* (London, 1927), pp. 192–206.

[17] See L. No. 21 of 1850. G. P. Money, Magistrate and Collector of Shahjehanpur, to R. Alexander, Commissioner of Rohilkhand, 9 Sept. 1858: *Narrative of Events Attending the Outbreak of Disturbances and the Restoration of Authority in the District of Shahjehanpur, in 1857–8*, vol. 3, UP Archive No. 465, UPSA.

[18] E. T. Stokes, 'Nawab Walidad Khan and the 1857 struggle in the Bulandshahr district', in E. T. Stokes (ed.), *The Peasant and the Raj: Studies in Agrarian Society and Peasant Rebellion in Colonial India* (Cambridge, 1978), pp. 140–84.

army and the cavalry regiments of the plains. The incomplete and tentative military experiment with the Gurkhas (chapter 7) appears to have finally paid off. In the manner of the peasant sipahis the Company's Gurkha sipahis had also gone through a phase of Hinduization and modernization. However, the different historical contexts in which the two traditions were shaped produced very different results. In 1815, the Gurkha regiments were hurriedly assembled to fight the Gurkha war. They were recruited from a variety of hill people and were consequently organized on a military principle and ideology very different from that which promised a high-caste status to the peasant sipahis of the plains. Unlike the peasant sipahis, the 'Company Gurkha' was formed out of a variety of Mughal, hill and plain traditions in the specific context of the Gurkha war of 1815. The variety of cultural influences which moulded the Company's Gurkhas pre-empted the standardization of a high-caste Gurkha identity. In 1843, T. Smith, the Assistant Political Resident in Nepal, noted the cordiality between the sipahis and their officers in the Sirmour Regiment of Gurkhas which he implicitly compared with the caste-conscious sipahi regiments he had observed on the plains:

A 6'2" Grenadier would offer a cheroot to the 'little Gorkee' as he styled him. The latter would take it from him with a grin. When this tall and patronising comrade stooped down with a lighted cigar in his mouth the little mountaineer never hesitated a moment puffing away at it with the one just received. No qualms of conscience although generally high caste Hindus.[19]

In 1857, the notion of 'hill Hinduism' which the Company had encouraged in its Gurkha regiments proved very handy in using the Gurkhas against the rebellious caste-conscious Rajput-Brahman sipahis of the plains. For instance, the rebellious Sappers and Miners, against whom the Sirmour Battalion of Gurkhas was dispatched, were reported to have attempted to lure the Gurkhas to their cause by selling to them the 'religion in danger' idea which had become popular among the rebels. They tried to dissuade the Gurkhas from going to Meerut where they said, 'the atta (flour for making bread) was nothing but ground-up bullock bones'.

[19] Smith, *Narrative of 5 Years Residence at Nepal*, II, p. 247.

To this the Gurkhas were reported to have replied that, 'the Regiment was going wherever ordered, and they obeyed the bugle call'.[20] Colonel L. W. Shakespear, the compiler of the regimental history of the Sirmour Battalion, praised the loyalty the Gurkhas displayed to the Company when they set fire to the Hindu village of Bhola near Bulandshahr and fired at Brahman offenders who were captured there and in the neighbouring village of Chandpur.[21] These acts of loyalty prompted the Company to take its Gurkha military tradition more seriously. The vast resources of manpower, especially of trained soldiers, which the Company had hitherto allowed to develop in Nepal was to become the focus of its attention in the period which followed the 1857 mutiny.

Paradoxically, in 1857, the military traditions which the Company had hitherto placed on the fringes of its army, were drawn into the forefront of imperial expansion. The Gurkhas were one such case. The other was the Company's regular cavalry regiments and its long-time ally, the Rampur state cavalry. But like the Gurkha regiments, the loyalty of the Rampur cavalry regiments also generated considerable tension both within the ranks of the rebel regiments, and amongst the civilian population once the mutiny had assumed the nature of a general insurrection. Indeed it was often made a target of mob fury and attack. The famous Kaddu Khani incident was a case in point.[22] An employee of the Rampur cavalry was buying a *kaddu* (pumpkin) in a bazar when he picked up a quarrel with one Usman Khan of Moradabad. Usman Khan was badly mauled by the Rampur soldiers and had to return home wounded. The people of Moradabad went on a rampage and about ten to twelve people eventually killed the sipahi. Hakim Sadat Ali Khan tried to pacify things and sent the kotwal to bring Usman Khan to the kotwali for medical treatment. But while he was on his way some soldiers of the Rampur army pounced on him and killed him. This escalated

---

[20] Shakespear, *History of the 2nd King Edward's Own Goorkha Rifles*, p. 44.

[21] Ibid., p. 45.

[22] Najmul Ghani, *Akhbar-us-Sanadid* (*A History of the Eminent Persons of North India*), (2 vols., Lucknow, 1918), vol. I, p. 66.

the violence in the town and angry mobs attacked and ravaged the Rampur army's station and army posts. But throughout these disturbances the Company supported the Rampur army and commended it for its loyal support in crushing the unrest.[23]

The events of 1857 left permanent scars on the region which had once been the major supplier of the Company's soldiers. However, the colonial state emerged undeterred, now deploying plans for tapping alternative recruiting zones which its earlier military policies in Nepal and Punjab had prepared for it. As the Company's frontier had now rolled into the Punjab and it had made political headway in Nepal, it extended the recruiting ground available. In the post-1857 period the Company's 'rebellious' purabia sipahis and Rohilla troopers were soon to be ousted from the position of dominance which they had enjoyed in the Indian army. Their place was to be filled by the hill recruits from Nepal who had proved their loyalty in 1857 and fresh peasant sipahis from Punjab to which the Company now had easy access.

Thus the significance of the Company's military culture, as it evolved between 1770 and 1830, was reflected in the political vicissitudes of its rule in north India. In 1857, the Company was under threat from elements of the military tradition that had hitherto been in the forefront of imperial expansion. But that very military culture was also able to provide a new support on which the British could reconstruct their political and military dominance.

[23] Ibid.

Bibliography

PRIMARY SOURCES

LONDON

British Library

George Thomas Papers, Abstract, part I on the North West parts of India. Add. 13579

Hastings Papers, Copies of essays etc. Add. 29234

Wellesley Papers 1798–1805. Add. 13856

Public Records Office

Cornwallis Papers, PRO/30/11/184

India Office Library

Boards Collection.

Hamilton, Buchanan. Nepal—some observations. MSS Eur. E.68.

Hodgson, B.H. Memorandum relative to the Gurkha army 1825, MSS 10.

——Ethnography, army, omras prior to Tellingas or Regular troops. MSS 9. Home Miscellaneous Series.

Documents omitted from correspondence of Bentinck. Typescript copies by C. H. Philips, MSS Eur. E. 424.

C. Nesbitt Thompson Papers, MSS Eur. D. 1083. Letters from A. Cleveland 1782–3.

Journal of Captain George Kinloch on the expedition to Nepal begun 26 August 1767, No. 2. MSS Eur. F/28/140/1.

Moorcroft, William, Journal number 1, from Srinagar to Nahr, February 4–23, MSS Eur. D236 A(I).

North-Western Provinces Revenue Records, 1836–46.

Bengal Board of Commissioners, Bihar and Benares, 1803–5.

Bengal Board of Revenue, Lower Provinces, 1816–22.

Bengal Criminal Judicial, 1801–16.

303

Bengal Criminal Judicial Lower Provinces, 1816–34.
Bengal Criminal Judicial Western Provinces, 1816–34.
Bengal Military Consultations, 1770–1830.
Bengal Revenue Consultations, 1774–90.
Bengal Revenue Board of Commissioners, Ceded & Conquered Provinces, 1803–05.
Bengal Political Consultations, 1818–30, and 1828–38.
Bengal Secret Consultations, 1772–78.
Bengal Secret Military Consultations, 1757–93.
Bengal Sadar Board of Revenue North Western Provinces, 1829–40.
Strachey, Richard, Correspondence as Resident in Lucknow, 30 November 1815–24 January 1817, MSS Eur. D. 514/3.

NEW DELHI
National Archives
NAI Calender of Acquired Documents III.
Proceedings of the Foreign Department Political, 1756–80.
Proceedings of the Foreign Department Secret, 1830–9 and 1840–9.
Proceedings of the Foreign Department Secret Political, 1830–9 and 1840-49.
Proceedings of the Military Department, 1786–1830.

LUCKNOW
Uttar Pradesh State Archives
Mutiny Narratives, 1857–8.
Proceedings of the Board of Commissioners, Bihar and Benares, 1816–21.
Proceedings of the Board of Commissioners, Ceded and Conquered Provinces, 1807–22.
Proceedings of the Board of Revenue Fort William, 1803–7.
Proceedings of the Board of Revenue Western Provinces, 1822–9.
Pre-mutiny Kumaon Division Records, 1830–57.
Pre-mutiny Revenue Records-Revenue Correspondence, 1812–29.

ALLAHABAD
Allahabad Regional Archives
Agra Commissionary Pre-mutiny Records.
Allahabad Pre-mutiny Judicial Miscellaneous Records.
Benares Residents Proceedings.
Gorakhpur Commissionary Pre-mutiny Records.
Meerut Collectorate Pre-mutiny Records.
Mirzapur Commissionary Pre-mutiny Records.
Saharanpur Collectorate Pre-mutiny Records.
Dehra Dun Regional Archives, Dehra Dun.
Dehra Dun Commissionary Pre-mutiny Records.
Paurhi Garhwal Commissionary Pre-mutiny Records, 1814–57.

PATNA
Bihar State Archives
Bhagalpur Revenue Records, 1770–1830.
Monghyr District Records, 1812–30.
Muzaffarpur Collectorate Records, 1782–1830.
Muzaffarpur District Records, 1782–1830.
Purnia District Records, 1775–1830.

CALCUTTA
West Bengal State Archives
Board of Revenue Miscellaneous Proceedings, 1788–1853.
Proceedings of the Board of Revenue Invalids, 1803–05.

Theses

Brodkin, E.I. 'Rohilcund from conquest to revolt: 1774–1858'. University of Cambridge, Ph.D thesis, 1968.
Gommans, J. 'Legitimacy and conquest in late Mughal India. Afghan state formation in Farrukhabad and Rohilkhand: 1707-1774'. University of Leiden, MA thesis, 1987.
Khan, I. G. 'Revenue, agriculture and warfare: technology, knowledge and the post-Mughal elites in Northern India, from the mid-eighteenth to the early nineteenth century'. SOAS, Ph.D thesis, 1990.
Pratap, A. 'Paharia ethnography and the archaeology of the Rajmahal Hills'. University of Cambridge, Ph.D thesis, 1987.
Prior, K. H. 'The British administration of Hinduism in North India 1780-1900'. University of Cambridge, Ph.D thesis, 1990.
Skaria, A. 'A Forest polity in Western India; the Dangs 1800–1920'. University of Cambridge, Ph.D thesis, 1992.
Singha, R. ' "A despotism of law": British criminal justice and public authority in North India, 1772–1837'. University of Cambridge, Ph.D thesis, 1990.
Waltraud, E. 'Treatment of European Lunatics in India'. SOAS, Ph.D thesis, 1987.

Published Sources

Urdu

Ali, S. Altaf. *Hayat-i-Hafiz Rahmat Khan* (Badaun, 1933).
Ghani, N. *Tarikh-i-Awadh* (4 vols., Lucknow, 1919).
Akhbar-us-Sanadid (2 vols., Lucknow, 1918).
Inayatullah, Maulana Abdul. *Tazkira-i-Ulema-i-Firangi Mahal* (Lucknow, 1349 AH).

Kanhyalal, Pandit. *Tarikh-i-baghawati-i-hind*, 1857 (Matba Newal Kishore, Kanpur, 6th ed., December 1916).
Rahman, Syed Sabahuddin Abdul. *Hindustan-ke ahde waste ka fauji nizam* (Azamgarh, 2nd ed., 1981).
Sadruddin Maulvi. *Tarikh-i-Shahjehanpur* (Lucknow, 1919).

Hindi

Jain, J. *Begum Sumroo* (Surat, 1917).
Nagar, Amritlal. *Ankhon dekha gadar* (Delhi, 1986).
Saraswati, S. *Bhumihar Brahmin parichai* (Benares, 1917).
Saran, R. *Kanyakubjaon ka itihas* (Benares, 1919).
Banerji, Durga Das. *Amar jiban katha* (Calcutta, 1857).

Translations into English

Baksh, M. Faiz. *Tarikh-i-Farahbaksh*. Tr. W. Hoey as *Memoirs of Delhi and Faizabad* (2 vols., Allahabad, 1889).
Bahadur, Mustajab Khan. *Gulistan-i-Rahmat*. Tr. C. Elliott (London, 1889).
Hamilton, C. *An Historical Relation of the Origin, Progress and Final Dissolution of the Government of Rohilla Afghans in the Northern Province of Hindustan* (London, 1787).
Hussein, G. *The Seir Mutaqherin or Review of Modern Times, being an History of India from year 118th 1194 of the Hedirah* (3 vols., reprint Lahore, 1975).
Khan, Fakir Khair-ud-din. *Tuhfa-i-Taza*. Tr. C.F. Curwen as *Balwantnamah* (Allahabad, 1857).
Khan, Sir Sayyid Ahmad. *Asbab-i-Baghawat-i-Hind*. Tr. Major-General G. F. I. Graham and Sir Aucklan Colvin as *History of Bijnor Rebellion*. Tr. Hafeez Malik and Morris Bembo (Asian Studies Centre, South Asian Series, occasional paper No. 17, Michigan State University).
Sharar, Abdul Halim. *Guzashta mashriqi tamaddum ka akhri namunah*. Tr. and ed. F. S. Harcourt and Fakhir Hussain as *Lucknow: the Last Phase of an Oriental Culture* (reprint, New Delhi, 1993).
Sitaram, *From Sepoy to Subedar: being the life and adventures of Subedar Sita Ram, a native officer of the Bengal army, written and related by himself*. Tr. Lt. Col. Norgate and ed. J. Lunt (reprint Hongkong, 1970).

English

Astruc, J. *A Treatise of the Venereal Disease* (2 vols., reprint London, 1985).
Bayly, W. H. *Venereal Disease, its Prevention, Symptoms and Treatment* (2 vols., London, 1850)
Broughton, T.D. *Letters Written in a Maratha Camp during the Year 1809—description of the costume, character, manners, domestic habits and religious ceremonies of the Marathas (London, 1813).*

Butter, D. *Outlines of the Topography and Statistics of the Southern Districts of Oudh* (Calcutta, 1839).

Colebrooke, J. E. *Digest of Regulations and Laws Enacted by the Governor General in Council under the Presidency of Bengal* (Calcutta, 1807).

Compton, H. *A Particular Account of the European Adventurers in India, 1784–1803* (London, 1892).

Crooke, W. *The Tribes and Castes of the North West Province and Oudh* (2 vols., Calcutta, 1896).

Datta, K. K. *Selections from the Judicial Records of the Bhagalpur District Office 1792–1805* (Calcutta, 1909).

——*Biography of Kunwar Singh and Amar Singh* (Patna, 1957).

——*History of the Freedom Movement in Bihar* (Patna, 1957).

Deanes, A. *A Tour through the Upper Provinces of Hindustan Comprising a Period between 1804–1814* (London, 1823).

Deloche, J. (ed.) *Les Memoires de Wendel Sur Les Jats, Pathans et les Sikhs* (Paris, 1979).

Fraser, J. B. *Military Memoirs of Lt. Col. James Skinner* (2 vols., 1955).

——*Journal of a Tour through Part of the Snowy Range of the Himalaya Mountains* (London, 1820).

Firminger, K. W. *The Fifth Report from the Select Committee of the House of Commons on the Affairs of the East India Company 28th July 1812* (Calcutta, 1917).

Francklin, W. *The History of the Reign of Shah Aulum, the Present Emperor of Hindustan* (London, 1798).

——*Military Memoirs of George Thomas* (Calcutta, 1803).

Freemantle, S. H. *Report on the Second Settlement of Rae Bareli district, Oudh 1897* (Allahabad, 1898).

Gimlette, Lt. Col. G. H. D. *A Postscript to the Records of the Indian Mutiny. An attempt to trace the subsequent careers and fate of the rebel Bengal regiments 1857–8* (London, 1927).

Hamilton, Buchanan. *Journal of Buchanan Hamilton, kept during the survey of the district of Bhagalpur in 1810–11* (ed.) C. E. A. W. Oldham (Patna, 1930).

——*An Account of the Kingdom of Nepal and of the Territories Annexed to This Dominion by the House of Gorkha* (Edinburgh, 1819).

Hamilton, W. *A Geographical, Statistical and Historical Description of Hindustan and the Adjacent Countries* (London, 1820).

Hastings, W. *A Narrative of the Insurrection which Happened in the Zamindary of Benares in the Month of August 1781 and of the Governor General in that District, with an Appendix of Authentic Papers and Affidavits* (Calcutta, 1853).

Heber, B. (ed.) M. A. Laird. *Bishop Heber in Northern India. Selections from Heber's Journal* (ed.) (London, 1971).

Hodges, W. *Travels in India: 1780–83* (London, 1793).

Kirkpatrick, W. *An Account of the Kingdom of Nepal* (London, 1811).

Lal, Busawan. *Memoirs of the Pathan Soldier of Fortune, the Nawab Ameerood-doulah Muhammad Ameer Khan* (Calcutta, 1832).

Leupolt, C. B. *Recollections of an Indian Missionary* (London, 1856).

Martin, M. *The History, Antiquities, Topography and Statistics of Eastern India* (2 vols., reprint Delhi, 1976).

————*The Despatches, Minutes and Correspondence of the Marquis of Wellesley during the Administration of India* (3 vols., 1828).

Mcpherson, H. *Final Report on the Survey and Settlement Operations in the District of Santal Parganas 1898–1907* (Calcutta, 1909).

Moreland, W. H. *Final Report on the Settlement of Land Revenue in the Unao District, Oudh* (Allahabad, 1896).

Nevill, H. R. *Meerut: A Gazetteer, volume 4 of the district gazetteers of the United Provinces of Agra and Oudh* (Allahabad, 1904).

Oldfield, H. A. *Sketches from Nepal—historical and descriptive* (2 vols., London, 1880).

Oldham, W. *Historical and Statistical Memoir of the Ghazipore District* (2 vols., Allahabad, 1876).

O' Malley, L. S. S. *Bihar and Orissa District Gazetteers, Shahabad* (rev. ed. Patna, 1924).

————*Bihar and Orissa District Gazetteers, Monghyr* (rev. ed. Patna, 1926).

————*Bihar and Orissa District Gazetteers, Champaran* (rev. ed. Patna, 1938).

————*Bihar and Orissa District Gazetteers, Saran* (rev. ed. Patna, 1930).

Park, F. *Wanderings of a Pilgrim in Search of the Picturesque* (2 vols., London, 1850).

Parliamentary Papers, Accounts and Papers, East India–China Session, 1857–58, vol. XLIII.

Pennant, T. *A View of Hindustan* (2 vols., London, 1798).

Rankine, R. *Notes on the Medical Topography of the District of Saran* (Calcutta, 1839).

Records of the Delhi Residency and Agency 1807–57 (Lahore, 1911).

Saksena, B. P. *UP State Records Series, Selections from English Records Number 3, Historical Papers relating to Kumaon, 1809–42* (Lucknow, 1956).

Sanders, J. F. *Final Settlement Report of the Pratapgarh District, Oudh* (Allahabad, 1896).

Sarkar, J. (ed.) *Daulat Rao Sindhia and Northern Indian Affairs, 1810–18, English Records of Maratha History: Poona Residency Correspondence* (14 vols., Bombay, 1951).

Shakespear, L. W. *History of the 2nd King Edwards Own Goorkha Rifles* (Aldershot, 1912).

Sherring, M. A. *Hindu Tribes and Castes as Represented in Benares* (London, 1872).

Shore, J. *Memoirs of the Life and Correspondence of John, Lord Teignmouth, by his Son J. Shore* (London, MDCCCXLIII).

Sleeman, W. *A Journey through the Kingdom of Oudh in 1849–50* (2 vols., London, 1858).

————*Rambles and Recollections of an Indian Official* (reprint, Karachi, 1973).

Smith, T. *Narrative of Five Years Residence at Nepal* (2 vols., London, 1852).
Tennant, W. *Indian Recreations* (2nd ed. London, 1802).
Tour, N. M. de la. *History of Ayder Ali Khan, Nabab Behadur* (London, 1784).
Twining, T. *Travels in India a Hundred Years Ago* (London, 1893).
Oldham, W. *Historical and Statistical Memoirs of the Ghazipore District* (Allahabad, 1876).

SECONDARY SOURCES

Alam, M. *Crisis of Empire in Mughal North India, Awadh and Punjab: 1707–48* (Delhi, 1986).
Ali, A. *The Mughal Nobility under Aurangzeb* (Bombay, 1966).
Archer, M. *Company Drawings in the India Office Library* (London, 1972).
———*Between Battles: The Album of Colonel James Skinner* (London, 1982).
———and T. Falk. *India Revealed: the arts and adventures of James and William Fraser 1801–35* (London, 1989).
Barnett, R. *North India between Empires: Awadh, the Mughals and the British, 1720–1801* (Berkeley, 1980).
Bayly, C. A. 'The age of hiatus: The North Indian economy and society, 1830–50', in C. H. Phillip and M. D. Wainwright (ed.), *Indian Society and the Beginning of Modernization* (London, 1976), pp. 83–105.
———*Rulers, Townsmen and Bazaars: North Indian society in the age of British expansion 1770–1870* (Cambridge, 1983).
———'The origins of Swadeshi (home industry): cloth and Indian society, 1700–1939', in A. Appadorai (ed.), *The Social Life of Things: commodities in cultural perspective* (Princeton, 1986), pp. 285–322.
———'Two Colonial Revolts: The Java War 1825–30 and the Indian Mutiny of 1857–59', in Kolff, D. and C. A. Bayly (ed.), *Two Colonial Empires* (Netherlands, 1986), 111–37.
———'India and West Asia 1700–1830', *Asian Affairs* (XIX, OS. Vol. 7, part 1, February 1988).
———*Imperial Meridien: the British Empire and the world 1780–1830* (London, 1989).
———*The Illustrated History of Modern India* (New Delhi, 1991).
Balfour, G. E. *The Cyclopedia of India and of Eastern and Southern Asia: commercial, industrial, scientific products of the mineral, vegetable and animal kingdoms, useful arts and manufactures* (3 vols., London, 1885).
Barat, A. *The Bengal Native Infantry: its organization and discipline 1796–1852* (Calcutta, 1962).
Ballhatchet, K. *Race, Sex and Class under the Raj: imperial attitudes and policies and their critics 1793–1905* (London, 1980).
Banerji, B. *Begum Samru* (Calcutta, 1925).

Brodkin, E. I. 'British India and the abuses of power: Rohilcund under early Company rule', *IESHR* (vol. X, No. 2, June 1973), pp. 129–56.

Butler, W. *An Autobiography* (London, 1911).

Chinnian, P.C. *The Vellore Mutiny, 1806* (Madras, 1982).

Cohn, B. S. *An Anthropologist among the Historians and Other Essays* (New Delhi, 1987).

Crawford, D. G. *A History of the Indian Medical Service 1600–1913* (2 vols., London, 1914).

Dover, C. 'Cultural significance of Col. James Skinner', *Calcutta Review* (January 1955), pp. 17–24.

Feiling, K. *Warren Hastings* (London, reprint 1966).

Fisher, M. H. *A Clash of Cultures: Awadh, British and the Mughals* (New Delhi, 1987).

Freitag, S. 'State and community: symbolic popular protest in Benaras public arenas' in S. Freitag (ed.), *Culture and Power in Banaras: community, performance and environment 1800–1980* (Berkeley, 1989), pp. 203–28.

Frykenberg, R. E. *Guntur District 1788–1848: a history of social influence and central authority in south India* (London, 1965).

Hamid, Maj. Gen. S. Shahid. *So They Rode and Fought* (Kent, U.K., 1983).

Hasan, S. N. 'The position of zamindars in the Mughal Empire', *IESHR*, vol. I, No. 4 (1964), pp. 106–19.

Hennessy, M. *The Rajah of Tipperary* (London, 1971).

Hobsbawm, E. and Ranger, T. *The Invention of Tradition* (Cambridge, 1983).

Hodson, Lt. C.V.P. *Historical Records of the Governor General's Bodyguard* (Calcutta, 1910).

Hutchinson, L. *European Freebooters in Mughal India* (London, 1964).

Irvine, W. 'The Bangash Nawabs of Farrukhabad: A chronicle, 1713–1857', *JASB*, vols. I and II, numbers 47 and 48 (1878 and 1879), pp. 93–383 and 49–169.

Kaye, M. M. *The Golden Calm—an English lady's life in Mughal Delhi—reminiscences by Emily, Lady Clive Bayley and by her father Sir Thomas Metcalfe* (Delhi, 1980).

Khan, A. R. *Chieftains in the Mughal Empire during the Reign of Akbar* (Simla, 1977).

Kokan, M. Y. *Arabic and Persian in Carnatic 1710–1960* (Madras, 1974).

Kolff, D. *Naukar, Rajput and Sepoy: The ethnohistory of the military labour market in Hindustan, 1450–1850* (Cambridge, 1990).

Kopf, D. *British Orientalism and the Bengal Renaissance: the dynamic of Indian modernization 1773–1835* (Princeton, 1969).

Lambrick, H.T. *Sir Charles Napier and Sind* (Oxford, 1952).

Llewellyn-Jones, R. *A Fatal Friendship: the nawabs, the British and the city of Lucknow* (Delhi, 1985).

Lutgendorf, P. 'Ram's story in Shiva's city: public arenas and private patronage', in S. Freitag (ed.), *Culture and Power in Banaras: community, performance and environment 1800–1980* (Berkeley, 1989), pp. 34–61.

Mann, M. 'The corps of invalids', *JSAHR*, vol. LXVI, No. 265, Spring 1988, pp. 5–23.

Marshall, P. J. *Bengal: the British bridgehead of eastern India 1740–1828. The New Cambridge History of India* (Cambridge, 1987).

——— 'British economic and political expansion: The case of Oudh', *MAS*, vol. 9, No. 4 (October 1975), pp. 465–82.

———'Western arms in maritime Asia in the early phases of expansion', *MAS*, vol. 14, No. 1 (February 1980).

Marshall, P. J. and G. William, *The Great Map of Mankind: British perceptions of the world in the age of enlightenment* (London, 1982).

Mason, P. *A Matter of Honour: an account of the Indian army, its officers and men* (London, 1974).

———*Skinner of Skinner's Horse: a fictional portrait* (London: Deutsch, 1979).

Metcalf, T. R. *Land, Landlords and the British Raj* (Berkeley, 1979).

Moosvi, S. *The Economy of the Mughal Empire c. 1595* (Delhi, 1987).

Morrell, W. P. *British Colonial Policy in the Age of Peel and Russell* (Oxford, 1930).

Mukherjee, R. 'Trade and empire in Awadh 1765–1804', *Past and Present*, no. 94 (February 1982), pp. 85–102.

———' "Satan let loose upon earth": the Kanpur massacres in India in the revolt of 1857', *Past and Present*, No. 128 (August 1990).

Naqvi, H. K. *Mughal Hindustan* (Karachi, 1972).

Norris, J. B.*The First Afghan War, 1838–42* (Cambridge, 1967).

Orme, R. *Historical Fragments of the Mogul Empire, of the Morattoes and of the English Concern in Indostan from the Year MDCLIX* (ed.) J. P. Guha (London, 1974).

Pemble, J. *The Invasion of Nepal: John Company at war* (Oxford, 1971).

———'Resources and techniques in the second Maratha war', *Historical Journal*, vol. xix (1976), pp. 374–404.

Porter, R. *Mind-forg'd Manacles: a history of madness in England from the Restoration to the Regency* (London, 1987).

———'Medicine and the enlightenment in 18th century England', *The Society for the Social History of Medicine* (Bulletin 25, Dec. 1979), pp. 27–41.

Prebble, J. *Mutiny: Highland regiments in revolt, 1743–1804* (Harmondsworth, 1977).

Rana, R. P. 'Agrarian revolt in north India during the late 17th century and early 18th century', *IESHR*, Nos. 3 and 4 (July–December 1981), pp. 287–326.

Ravindran, T. K. 'The Kurichiya rebellion of 1812', *Journal of Kerala Studies*, vol. III, part I (March 1976), pp. 532–44.

Redlich, F. *The German Military Entrepreneur and His Workforce—a study in European economic and social history* (Wiesbaden, 1964–5).

Sanyal, B. D. *Nepal and the East India Company* (London, 1965).

Sen, S. *The Military System of the Marathas* (Calcutta, 1958).

Sidney, L. *Dictionary of National Biography* (London, 1894).

Sinha, B. K., *The Pindaris 1778–1818* (Calcutta, 1971).

Sinha, D. P. *British Relations with Awadh, 1801–56: a case study* (Delhi, 1983).

Sinha, N. K. *Ranjit Singh* (Calcutta, 1933).

Shaw, Lt. T. 'On the inhabitants of the hills near Rajmahal', *Journal of Asiatic Research*, vol. IV, pp. 45–107.

Sherwill, W. S. 'Notes upon a tour through the Rajmahal hills', *Journal of the Asiatic Society of Bengal* (1851), pp. 450–603.

Stein, B. 'State formation and economy reconsidered', *MAS*, vol. 19, part 3, (July 1985), pp. 387–413.

Stokes, E. *The Peasant and the Raj: studies in agrarian, social and peasant rebellion in colonial India* (Cambridge, 1978).

————*The English Utilitarians and India* (Oxford, 1959).

————'British expansion in India in the 18th century', *Past and Present*, No. 58 (February 1973).

————*The Peasant Armed: the Indian revolt of 1857* (ed.) C.A. Bayly (Oxford, 1986).

Strachan, H. *Wellington's Legacy: the reform of the British army 1830–54* (Manchester, 1984).

Wainwright, M. D. and Phillips, C. H. (ed.), *Indian Society and the Beginning of Modernization, c. 1830–50* (SOAS, 1976).

William, J. *An Historical Account of the Rise and Progress of the Bengal Infantry from its Formation in 1757 to 1796* (London, 1817).

Wilkinson, H. *Two Monsoons: the life and death of Europeans in India* (London, 1987).

Yang, A. *The Limited Raj: agrarian relations in colonial India, Saran district 1793–1920* (Berkeley, 1989).

Index